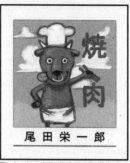

尾田栄一郎

The kanji reads "grilled meat." --Editor

I heard that the world's population grows by 200,000 people every day. The world has more than five billion people. Sometimes, I think it's kind of weird how today we eat meat, tomorrow we eat meat, and every day, all over the world, most people eat animals, and yet animals never disappear. To all the animals, I'd really like to say *thanks for the meal.*

Let's begin volume 44!!!

-Eiichiro Oda, 2006

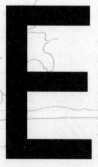

E iichiro Oda began his manga career at the age of 17, when his one-shot cowboy manga **Wanted!** won second place in the coveted Tezuka manga awards. Oda went on to work as an assistant to some of the biggest manga artists in the industry, including Nobuhiro Watsuki, before winning the Hop Step Award for new artists. His pirate adventure **One Piece**, which debuted in **Weekly Shonen Jump** in 1997, quickly became one of the most popular manga in Japan.

ONE PIECE VOL. 44
WATER SEVEN PART 13

SHONEN JUMP Manga Edition

STORY AND ART BY EIICHIRO ODA

English Adaptation/Jake Forbes
Translation/John Werry
Touch-up Art & Lettering/John Hunt
Design/Fawn Lau
Supervising Editor/Alexis Kirsch
Editor/Yuki Takagaki

ONE PIECE © 1997 by Eiichiro Oda. All rights reserved.
First published in Japan in 1997 by SHUEISHA Inc., Tokyo.
English translation rights arranged by SHUEISHA Inc.

The stories, characters and incidents mentioned in this publication are
entirely fictional.

Printed in the U.S.A.

Published by VIZ Media, LLC
P.O. Box 77010
San Francisco, CA 94107

10 9 8 7
First printing, May 2010
Seventh printing, December 2015

www.viz.com

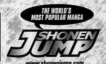
THE WORLD'S MOST POPULAR MANGA
SHONEN JUMP
www.shonenjump.com

SHONEN JUMP MANGA

ONE PIECE

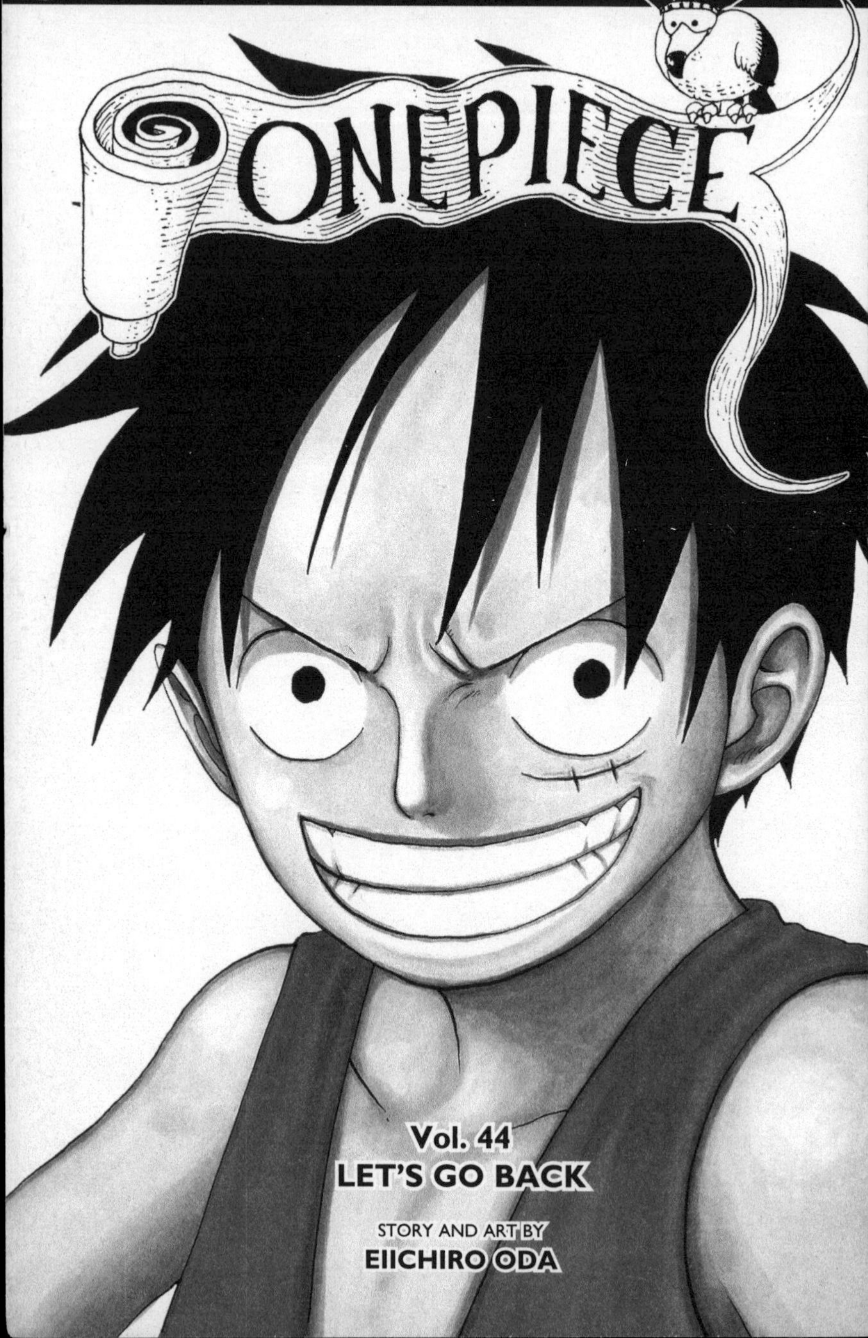

Vol. 44
LET'S GO BACK

STORY AND ART BY
EIICHIRO ODA

Cipher Pol No. 9

An undercover intelligence agency under the direct supervision of the World Government. They have been granted the right to kill uncooperative citizens.

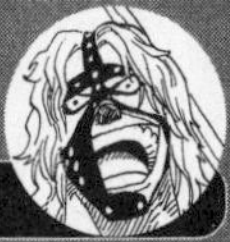

Director

Spandam

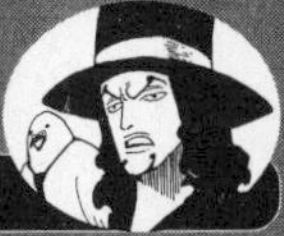

Rob Lucci & Hattori

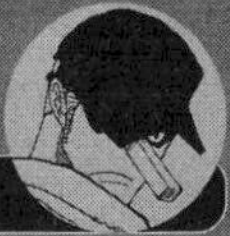

Kaku

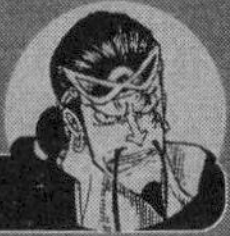

Jabra

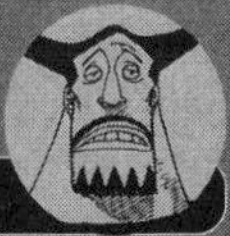

Blueno

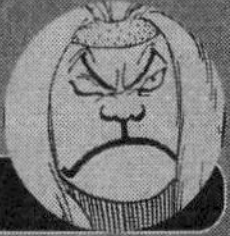

Kumadori

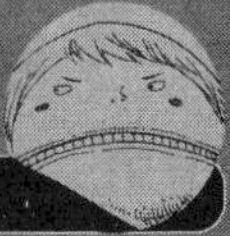

Fukurô

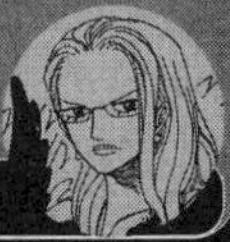

Kalifa

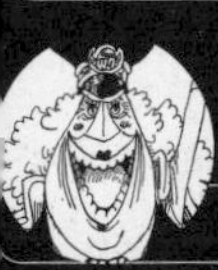

Formerly the beautiful secretary of Tom's Workers. Now stationmaster of Shift Station.

Kokoro

The Straw Hats

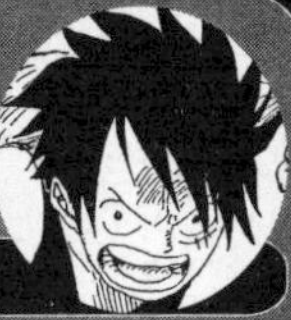

Boundlessly optimistic and able to stretch like rubber, he is determined to become King of the Pirates.

Monkey D. Luffy

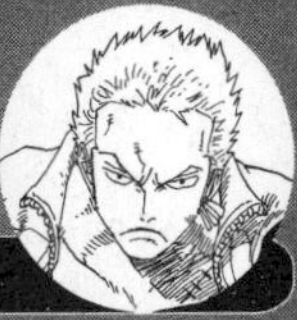

A former bounty hunter and master of the "three-sword" style. He aspires to be the world's greatest swordsman.

Roronoa Zolo

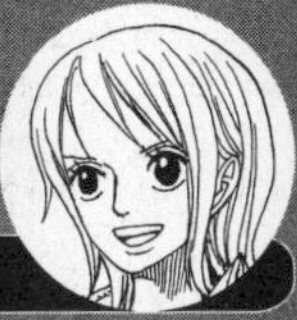

A thief who specializes in robbing pirates. Nami hates pirates, but Luffy convinced her to be his navigator.

Nami

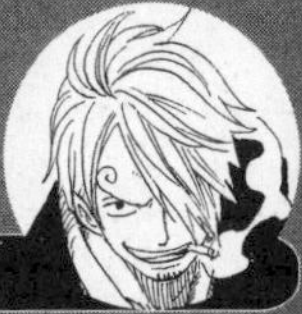

The bighearted cook (and ladies' man) whose dream is to find the legendary sea, the "All Blue."

Sanji

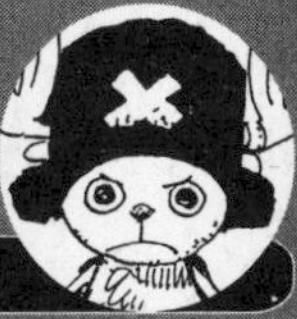

A blue-nosed man-reindeer and the ship's doctor.

Tony Tony Chopper

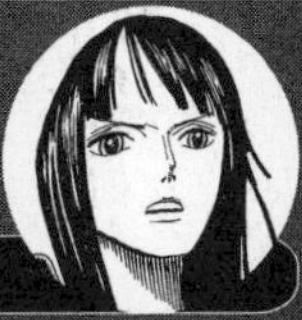

A mysterious woman in search of the Ponegliff on which true history is recorded.

Nico Robin

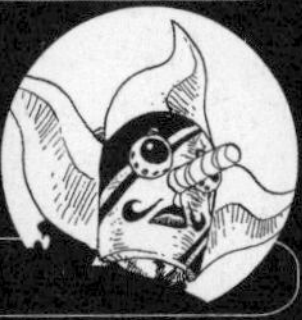

Usopp's "good friend", a superhero who's come to save Luffy and company... or at least that's what he says.

Sniper King

THE STORY OF ONE PIECE

Volume 44

Monkey D. Luffy started out as just a kid with a dream—to become the greatest pirate in history! Stirred by the tales of pirate "Red-Haired" Shanks, Luffy vowed to become a pirate himself. That was before the enchanted Devil Fruit gave Luffy the power to stretch like rubber, at the cost of being unable to swim—a serious handicap for an aspiring sea dog. Undeterred, Luffy set out to sea and recruited some crewmates—master swordsman Zolo; treasure-hunting thief Nami; lying sharpshooter Usopp; the high-kicking chef Sanji; Chopper, the walkin' talkin' reindeer doctor; and the mysterious archaeologist Robin.

After many adventures have left their ship, the *Merry Go*, in less than seaworthy condition, the Straw Hats crew set sail for the city of Water Seven in the hopes of finding a shipwright to join their crew. There they learn that the ship is beyond repair, and so Luffy reluctantly decides to find a new ship. Usopp, however, is fiercely opposed to this decision and leaves the crew.

The covert government agency Cipher Pol No. 9 has also come to Water Seven, looking for the blueprints for the ancient weapon the Pluton. They capture Robin and the hot-headed ship dismantler Franky, both of whom are key to unlocking the Pluton's secrets. CP9's leader, Spandam, leads Robin to the Gates of Justice, where he accidentally presses the button for a Buster Call. This summons the Navy to annihilate Enies Lobby and everyone on it! Meanwhile, Zolo and the others vanquish their CP9 opponents and finally catch up with Robin. Only Rob Lucci remains, but Luffy is having the fight of his life against his opponent's incredible strength!

The Franky Family

Professional ship dismantlers, they moonlight as bounty hunters.

The master builder and an apprentice of Tom, the legendary shipwright.

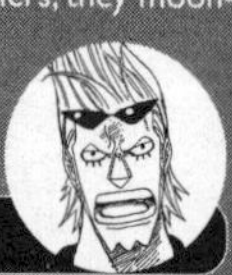

Franky (Cutty Flam)

The Square Sisters

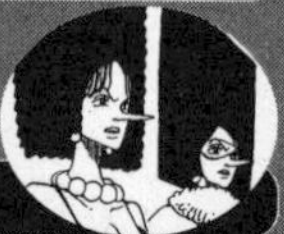

Kiwi & Mozu

Galley-La Company

A top shipbuilding company. They are purveyors to the World Government.

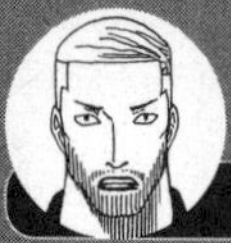

Mayor of Water Seven and president of Galley-La Company. Also one of Tom's apprentices.

Iceberg

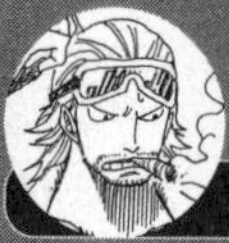

Rigging and Mast Foreman

Paulie

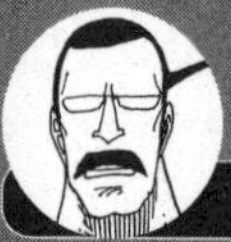

Pitch, Blacksmithing and Block-and-Tackle Foreman

Peepley Lulu

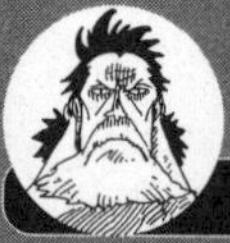

Cabinetry, Caulking and Flag-Making Foreman

Tilestone

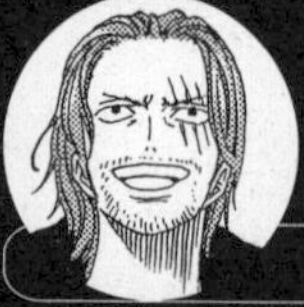

A pirate that Luffy idolizes. Shanks gave Luffy his trademark straw hat.

"Red-Haired" Shanks

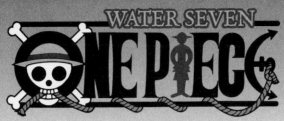

Vol. 44
Let's Go Back

CONTENTS

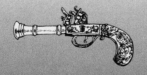

Chapter 420:
BUSTER CALL

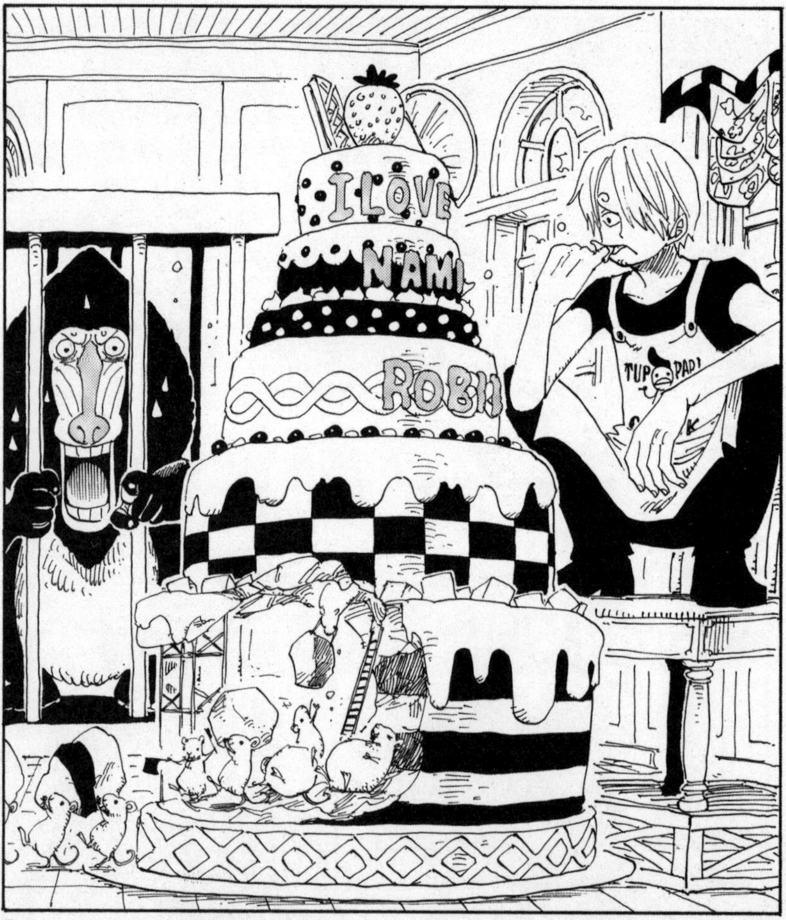
I LOVE
NAMI
ROBIN
TUP PAPI

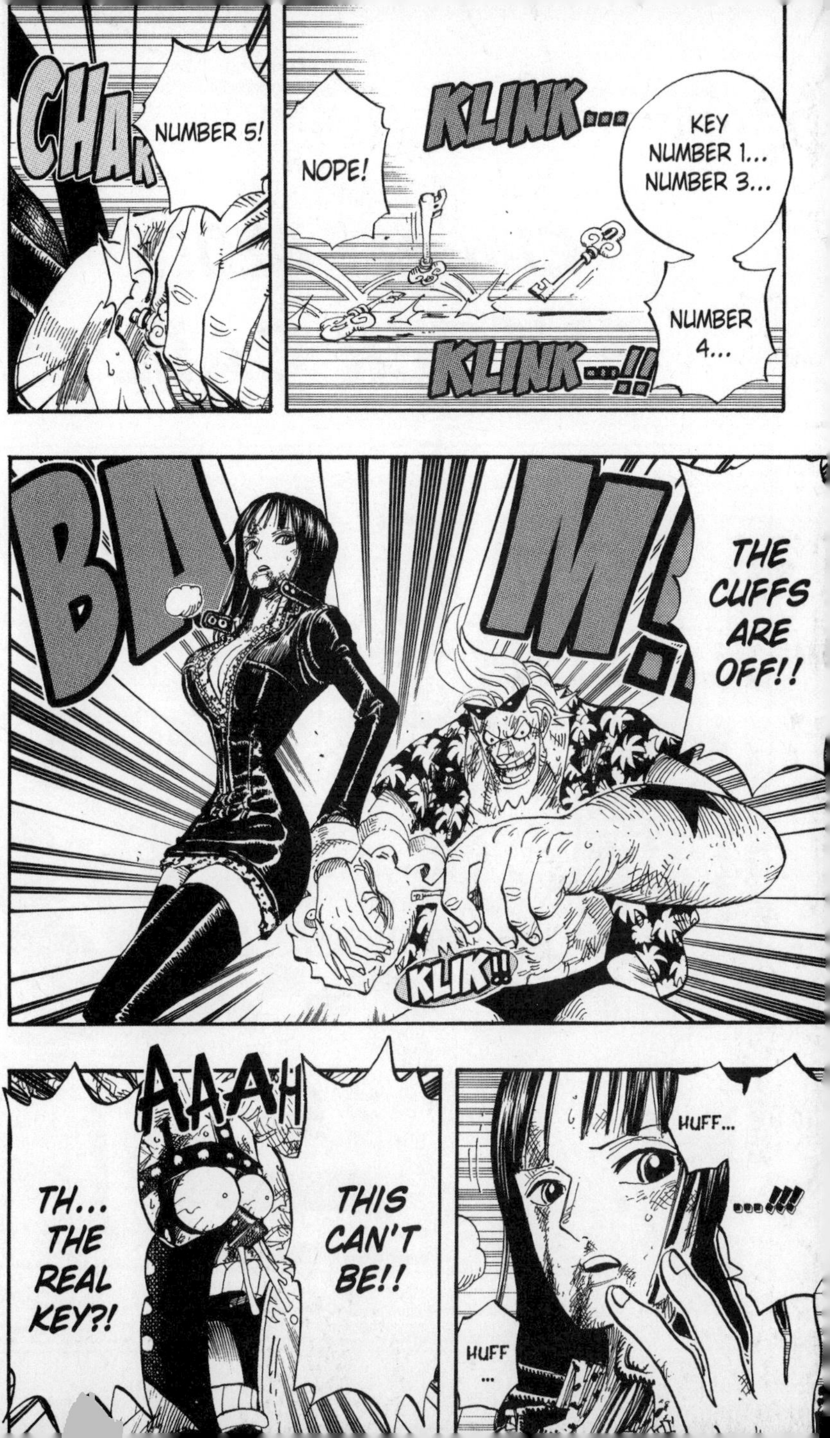

KEY NUMBER 1... NUMBER 3...
KLINK...
NOPE!
NUMBER 4...
KLINK...!!
CHA
NUMBER 5!
THE CUFFS ARE OFF!!
BAM!
KLIK!!
HUFF...
...!!!
HUFF ...
AAAH
THIS CAN'T BE!!
TH... THE REAL KEY?!

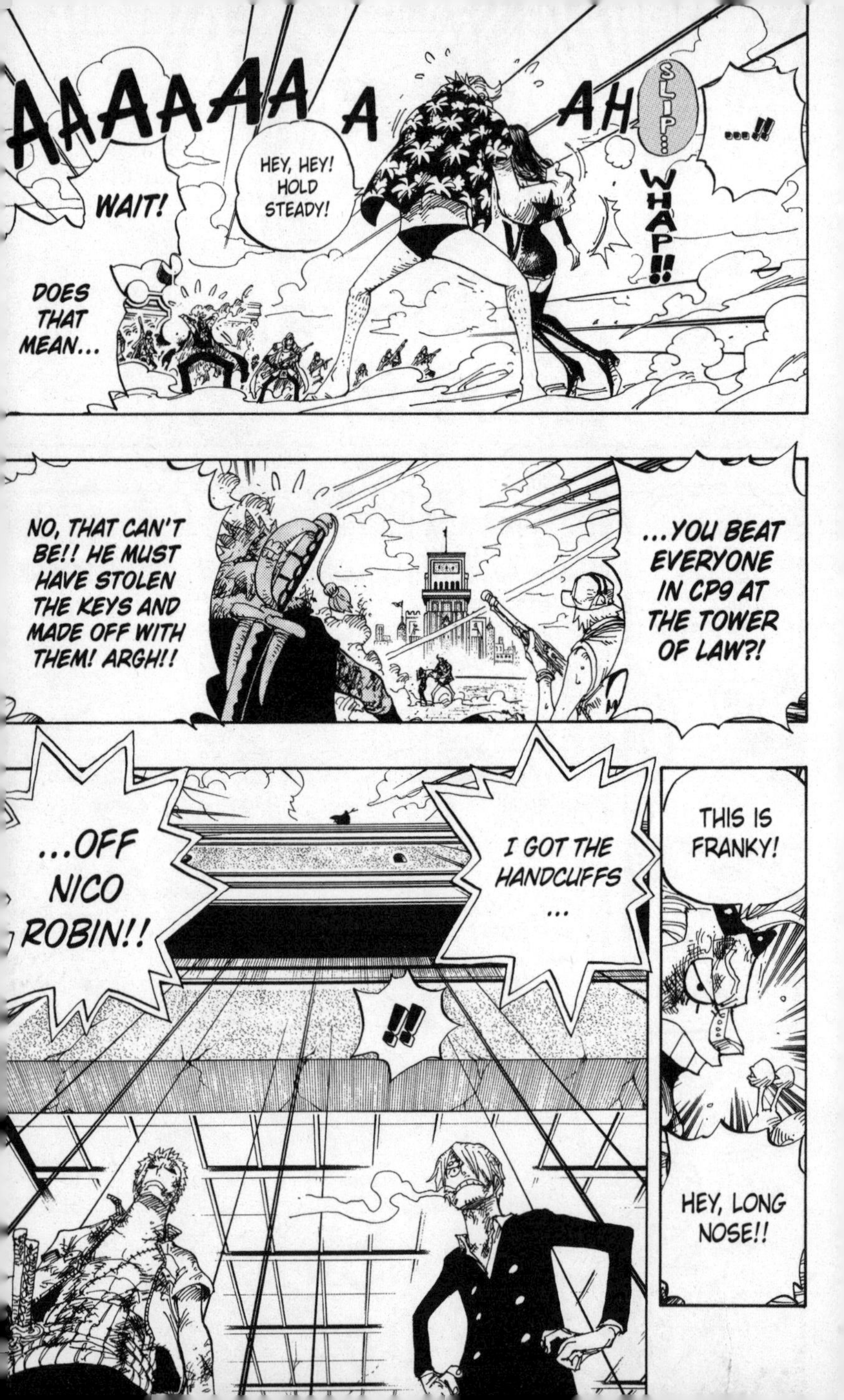
...!!
SLIP...
WHAP!!
AAAAAAA A AH
HEY, HEY! HOLD STEADY!
WAIT!
DOES THAT MEAN...
...YOU BEAT EVERYONE IN CP9 AT THE TOWER OF LAW?!
NO, THAT CAN'T BE!! HE MUST HAVE STOLEN THE KEYS AND MADE OFF WITH THEM! ARGH!!
THIS IS FRANKY!
HEY, LONG NOSE!!
I GOT THE HANDCUFFS ...
...OFF NICO ROBIN!!
!!

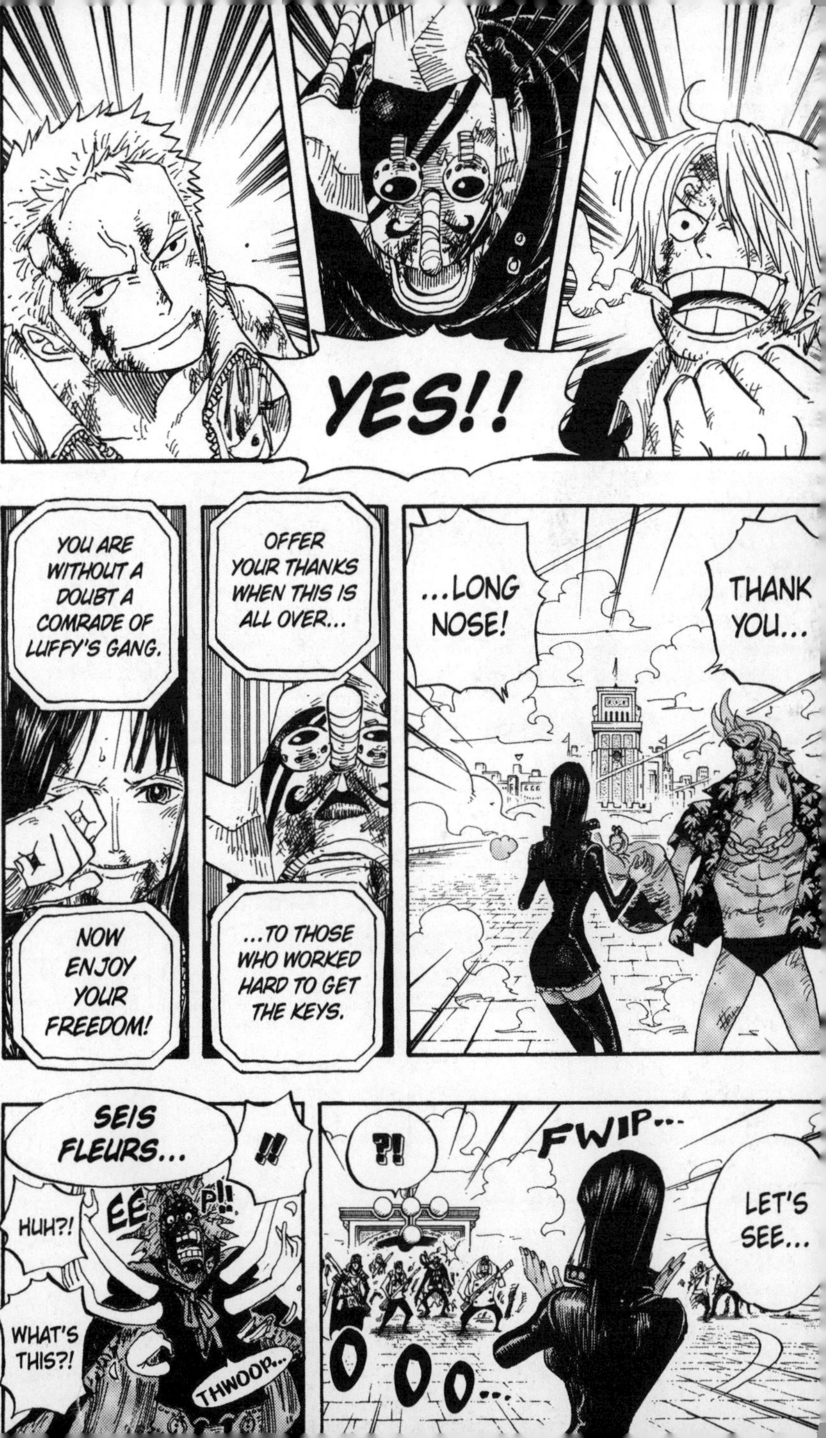
YES!!
THANK YOU...
...LONG NOSE!
OFFER YOUR THANKS WHEN THIS IS ALL OVER...
...TO THOSE WHO WORKED HARD TO GET THE KEYS.
YOU ARE WITHOUT A DOUBT A COMRADE OF LUFFY'S GANG.
NOW ENJOY YOUR FREEDOM!
LET'S SEE...
FWIP...
?!
OOO...
SEIS FLEURS...
!!
EEP!!
HUH?!
WHAT'S THIS?!
THWOOP...

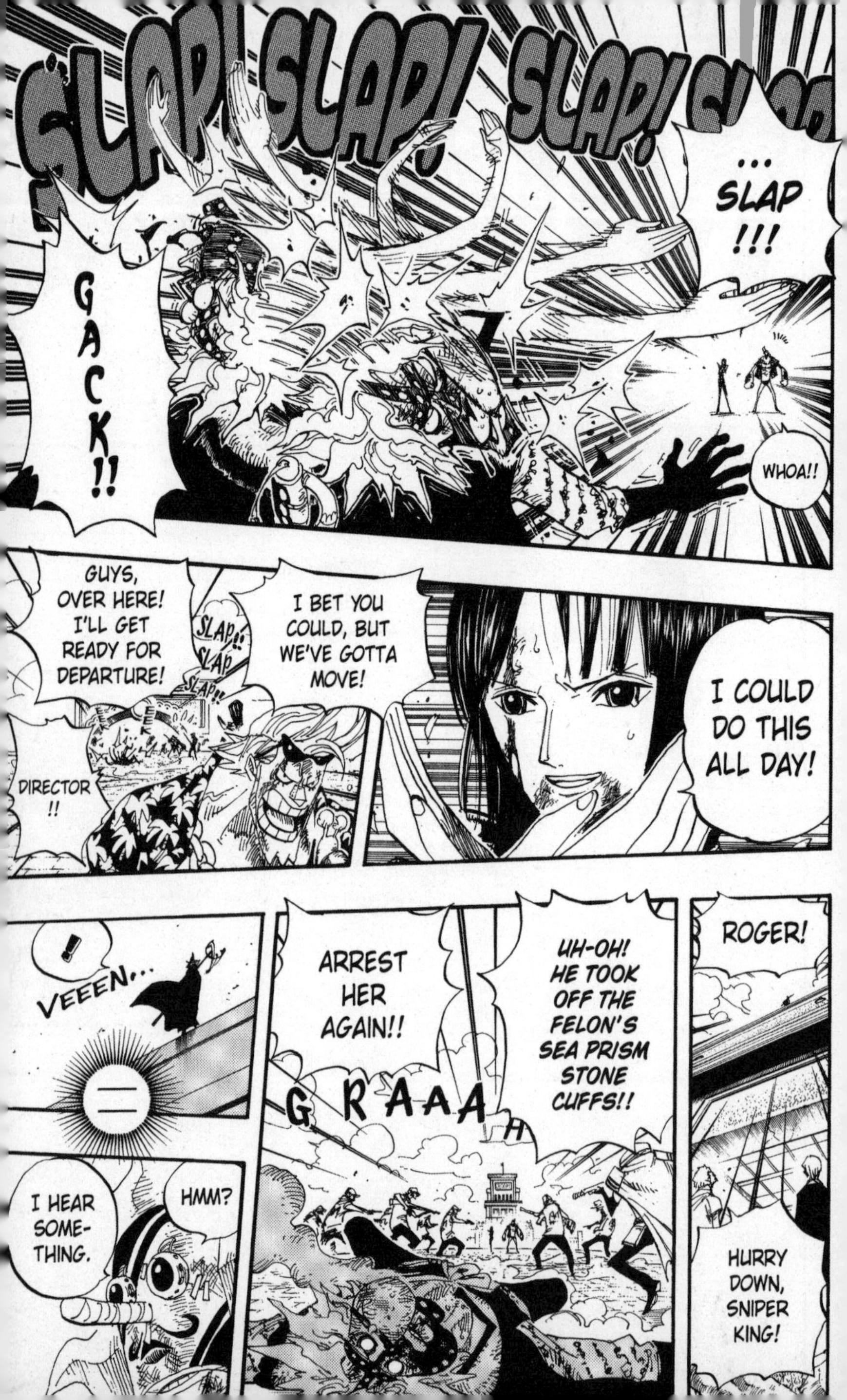
SLAP! SLAP! SLAP!
... SLAP!!!
GACK!!
WHOA!!
I COULD DO THIS ALL DAY!
I BET YOU COULD, BUT WE'VE GOTTA MOVE!
SLAP!! SLAP SLAP!!
GUYS, OVER HERE! I'LL GET READY FOR DEPARTURE!
DIRECTOR!!
ROGER!
HURRY DOWN, SNIPER KING!
UH-OH! HE TOOK OFF THE FELON'S SEA PRISM STONE CUFFS!!
ARREST HER AGAIN!!
GRAAAAH
!
VEEEN...
HMM?
I HEAR SOME-THING.

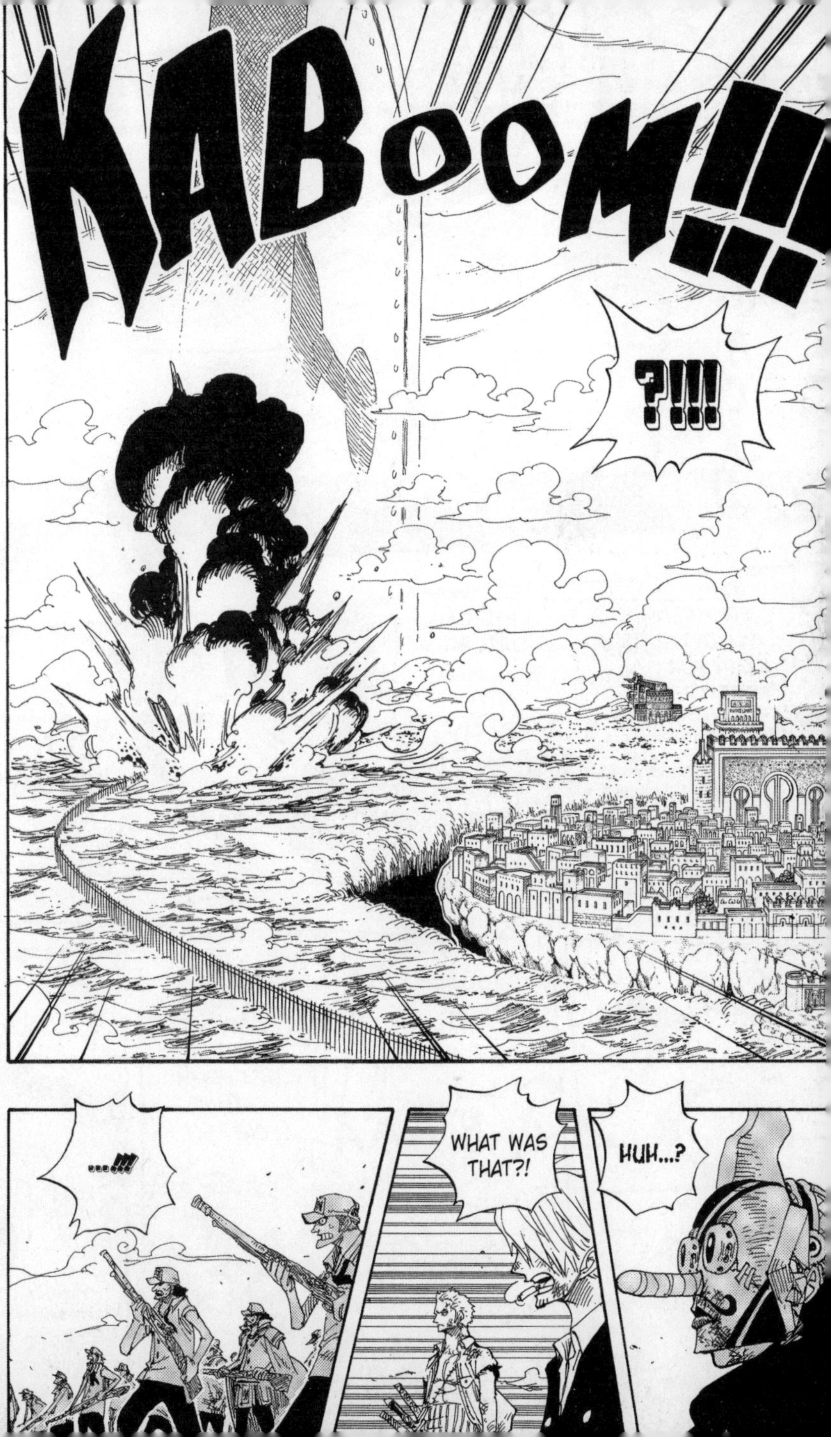
KABOOM!!!
?!!!
HUH...?
WHAT WAS THAT?!
...!!!

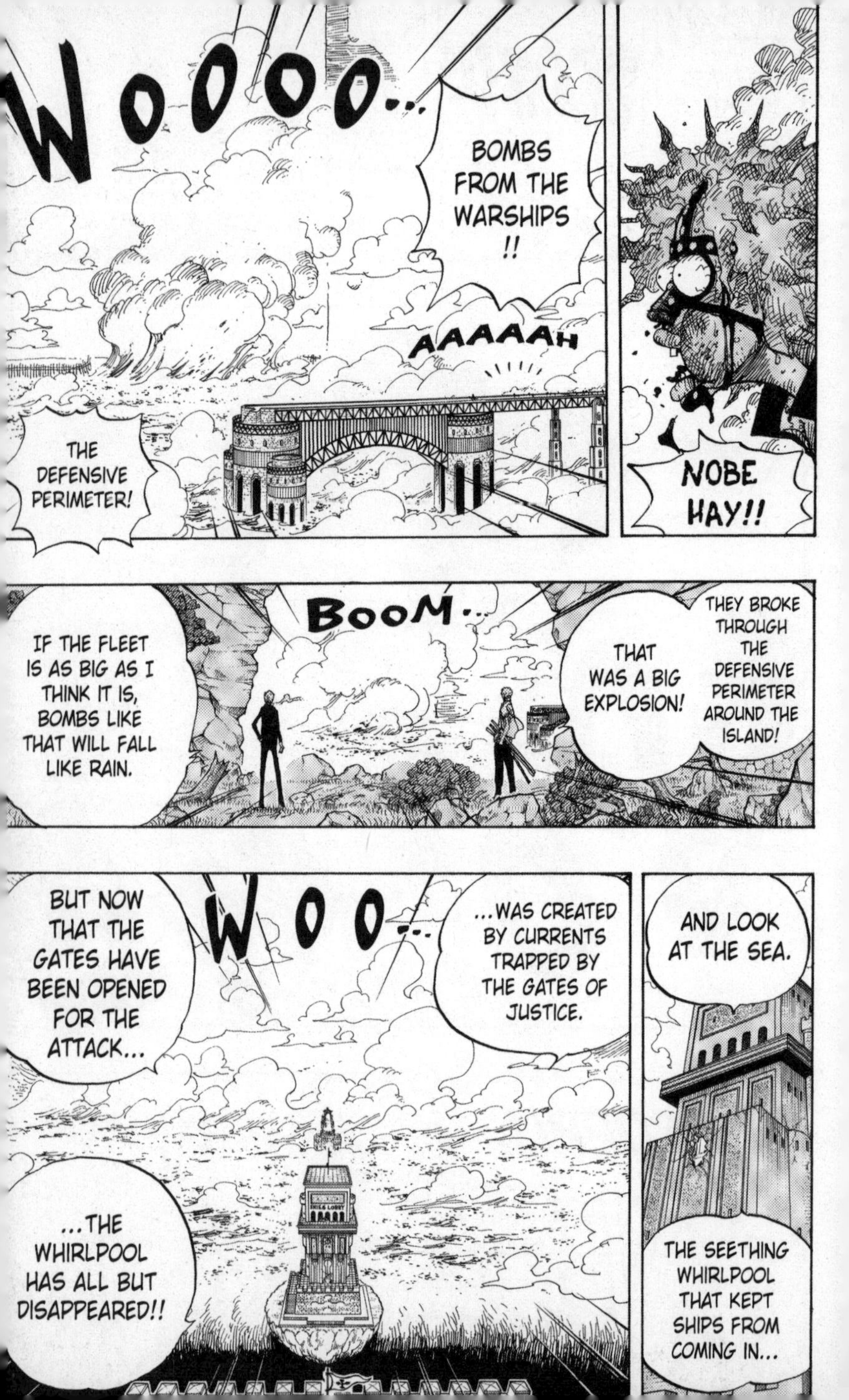
NOBE HAY!!
BOMBS FROM THE WARSHIPS !!
WOOOO...
AAAAAH
THE DEFENSIVE PERIMETER!
THEY BROKE THROUGH THE DEFENSIVE PERIMETER AROUND THE ISLAND!
THAT WAS A BIG EXPLOSION!
BOOM...
IF THE FLEET IS AS BIG AS I THINK IT IS, BOMBS LIKE THAT WILL FALL LIKE RAIN.
AND LOOK AT THE SEA.
THE SEETHING WHIRLPOOL THAT KEPT SHIPS FROM COMING IN...
...WAS CREATED BY CURRENTS TRAPPED BY THE GATES OF JUSTICE.
WOO...
BUT NOW THAT THE GATES HAVE BEEN OPENED FOR THE ATTACK...
...THE WHIRLPOOL HAS ALL BUT DISAPPEARED!!

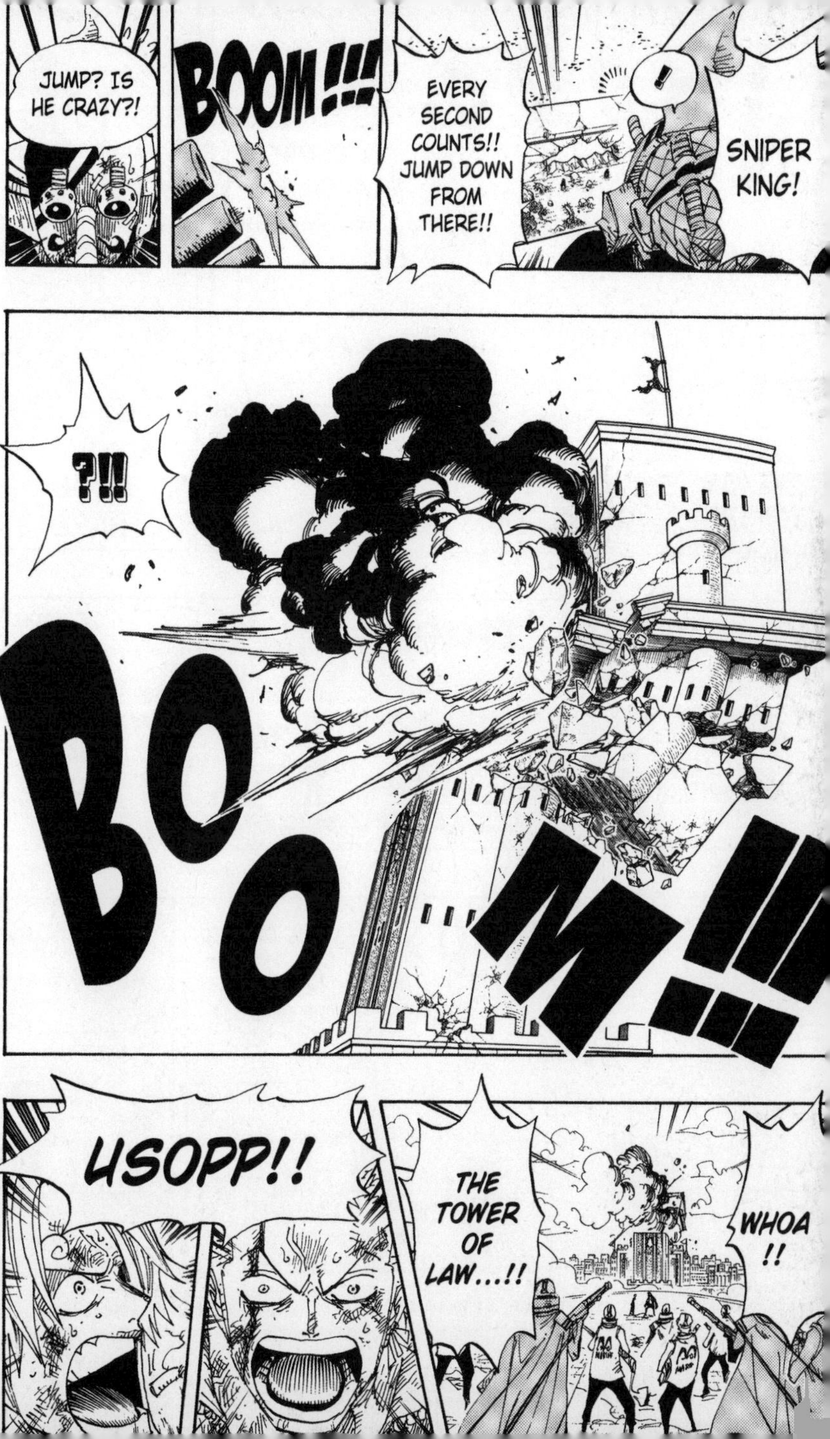
SNIPER KING!
EVERY SECOND COUNTS!! JUMP DOWN FROM THERE!!
BOOM!!!!
JUMP? IS HE CRAZY?!
?!!
BOOM!!!!
WHOA!!
THE TOWER OF LAW...!!
USOPP!!

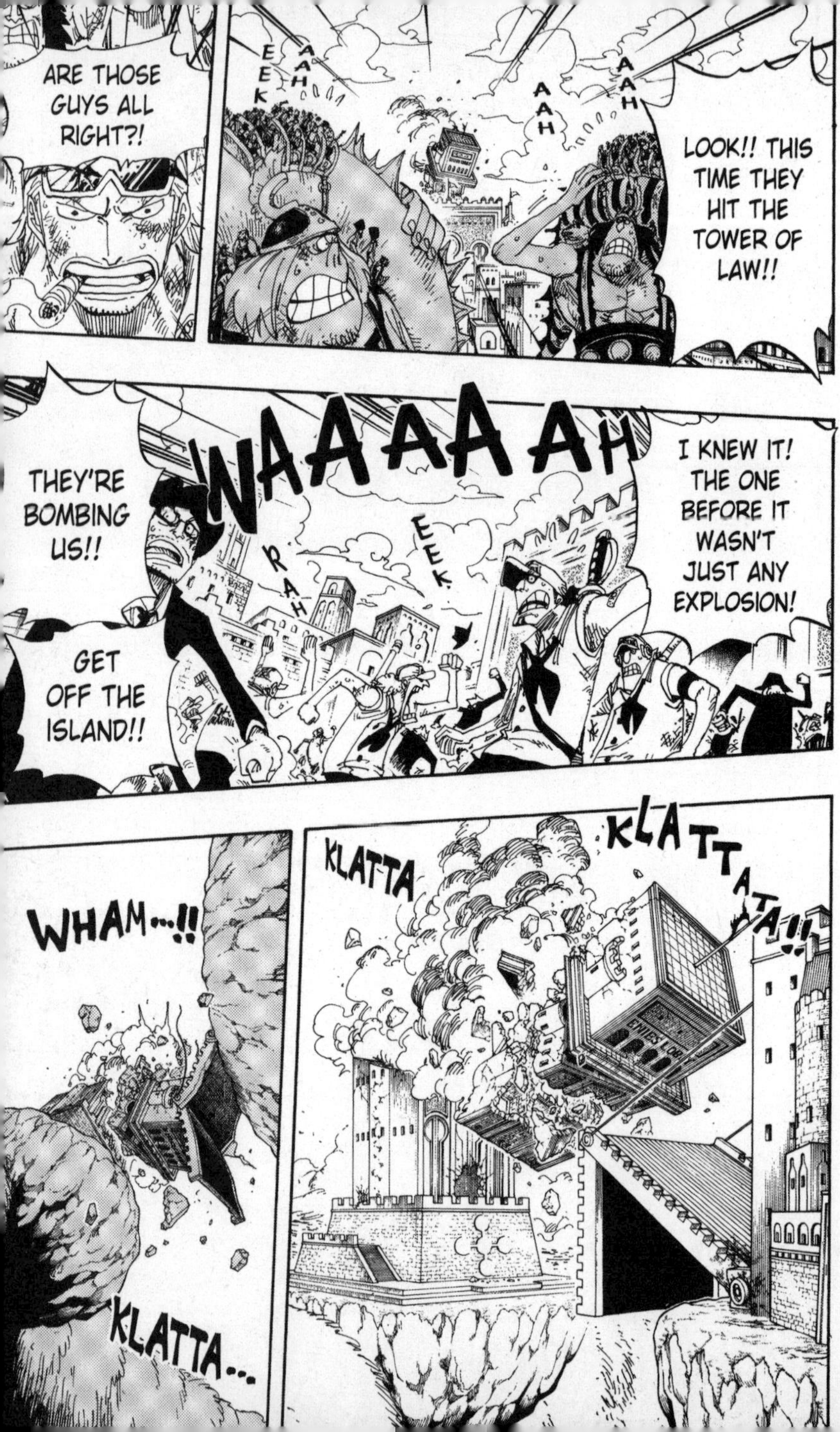
AAH
AAH
LOOK!! THIS TIME THEY HIT THE TOWER OF LAW!!
AAH
EEK
ARE THOSE GUYS ALL RIGHT?!
WAAAAAH
I KNEW IT! THE ONE BEFORE IT WASN'T JUST ANY EXPLOSION!
EEK
RAH
THEY'RE BOMBING US!!
GET OFF THE ISLAND!!
KLATTATA!!
KLATTA
WHAM...!!
KLATTA...

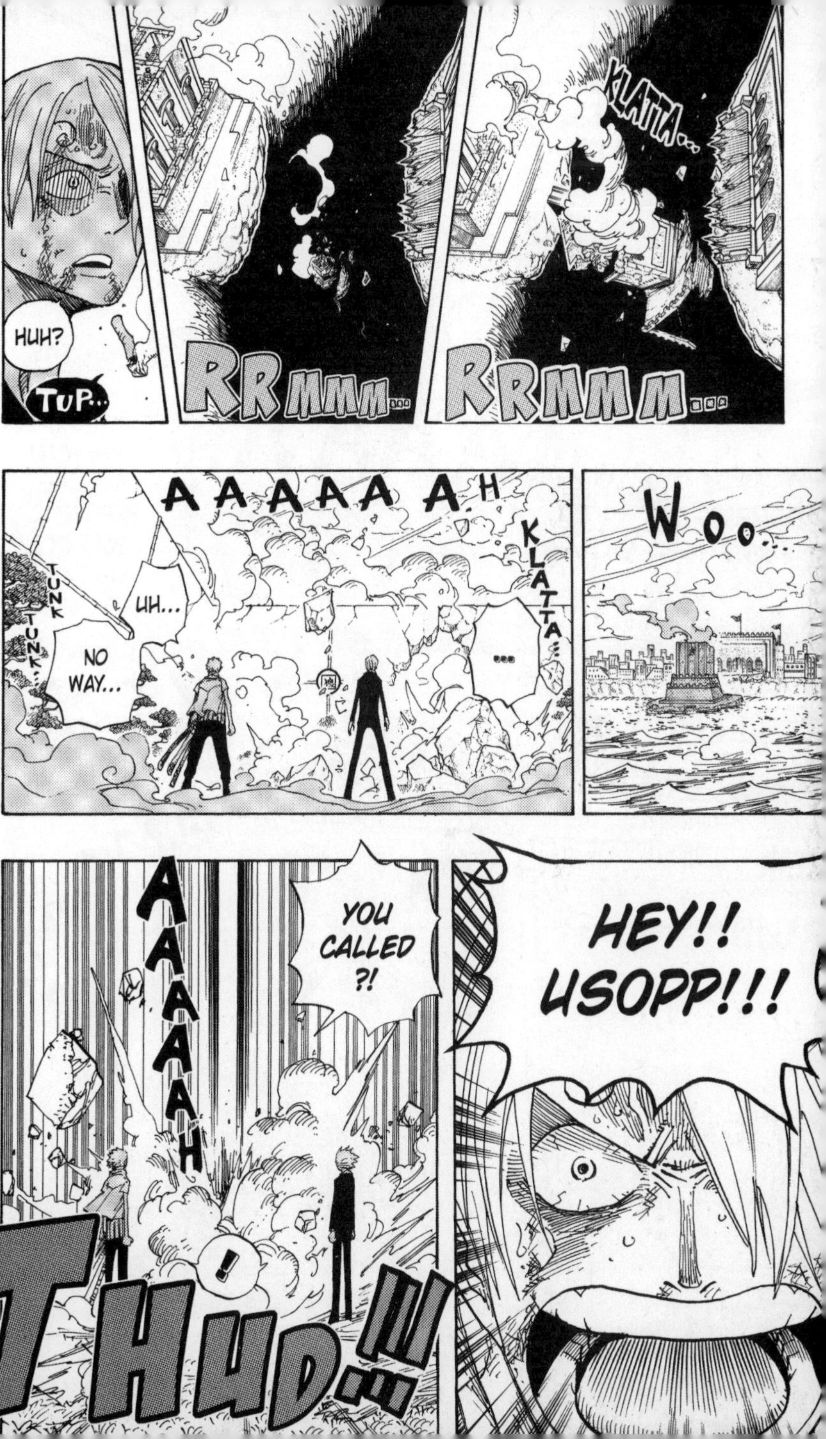
KLATTA...
RRMMMM...
RRMMMM...
HUH?
TUP...
WOO...
AAAAAAH
KLATTA...
...
UH...
NO WAY...
TUNK TUNK...
HEY!! USOPP!!!
YOU CALLED ?!
AAAAAAH
!
THUD!!!

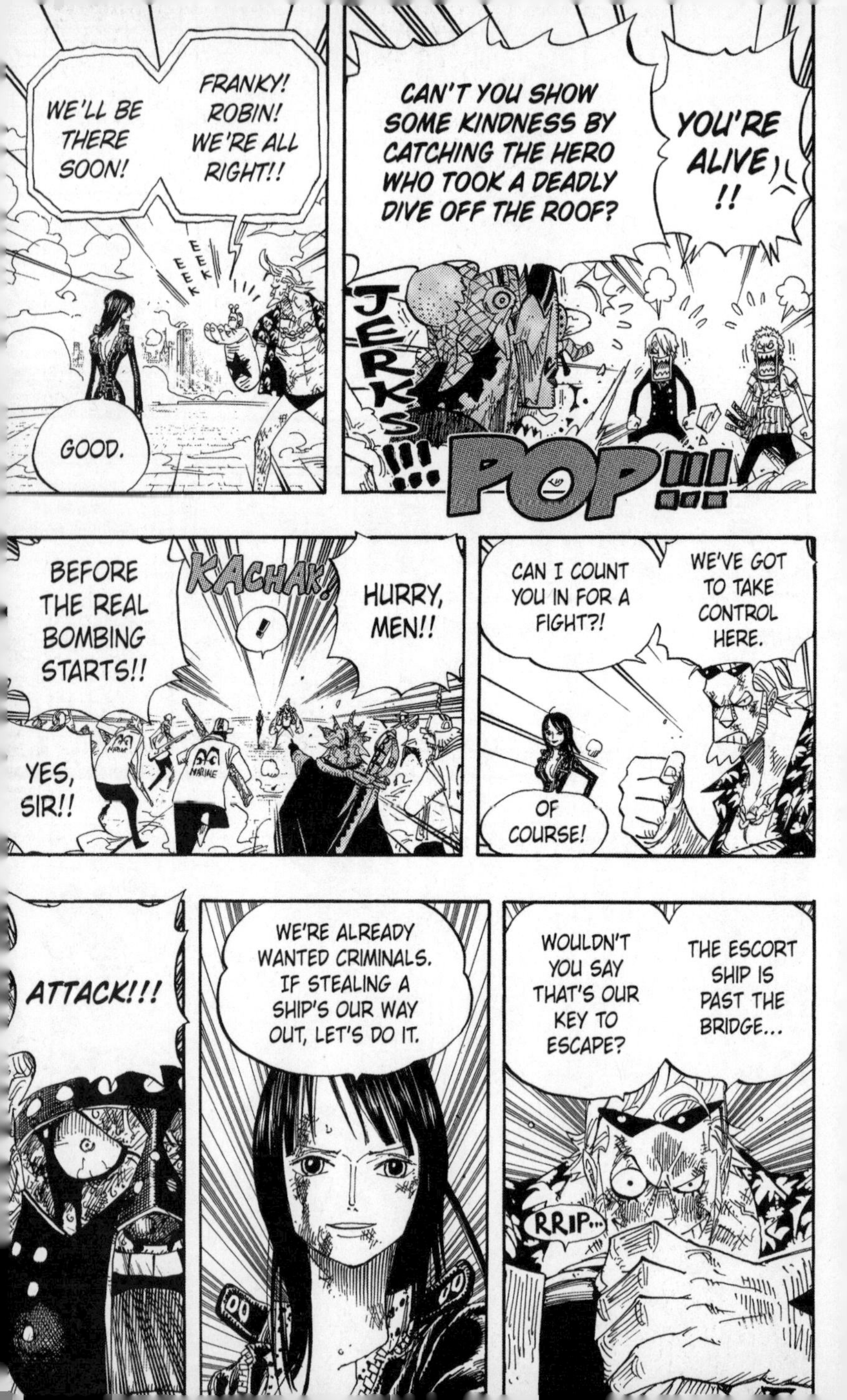
YOU'RE ALIVE!!
CAN'T YOU SHOW SOME KINDNESS BY CATCHING THE HERO WHO TOOK A DEADLY DIVE OFF THE ROOF?
JERKS!!!
POP!!!!
FRANKY! ROBIN! WE'RE ALL RIGHT!!
WE'LL BE THERE SOON!
EEK EEK
GOOD.
WE'VE GOT TO TAKE CONTROL HERE.
CAN I COUNT YOU IN FOR A FIGHT?!
OF COURSE!
HURRY, MEN!!
KACHAK!
!
BEFORE THE REAL BOMBING STARTS!!
YES, SIR!!
THE ESCORT SHIP IS PAST THE BRIDGE...
WOULDN'T YOU SAY THAT'S OUR KEY TO ESCAPE?
RRIP...
WE'RE ALREADY WANTED CRIMINALS. IF STEALING A SHIP'S OUR WAY OUT, LET'S DO IT.
ATTACK!!!

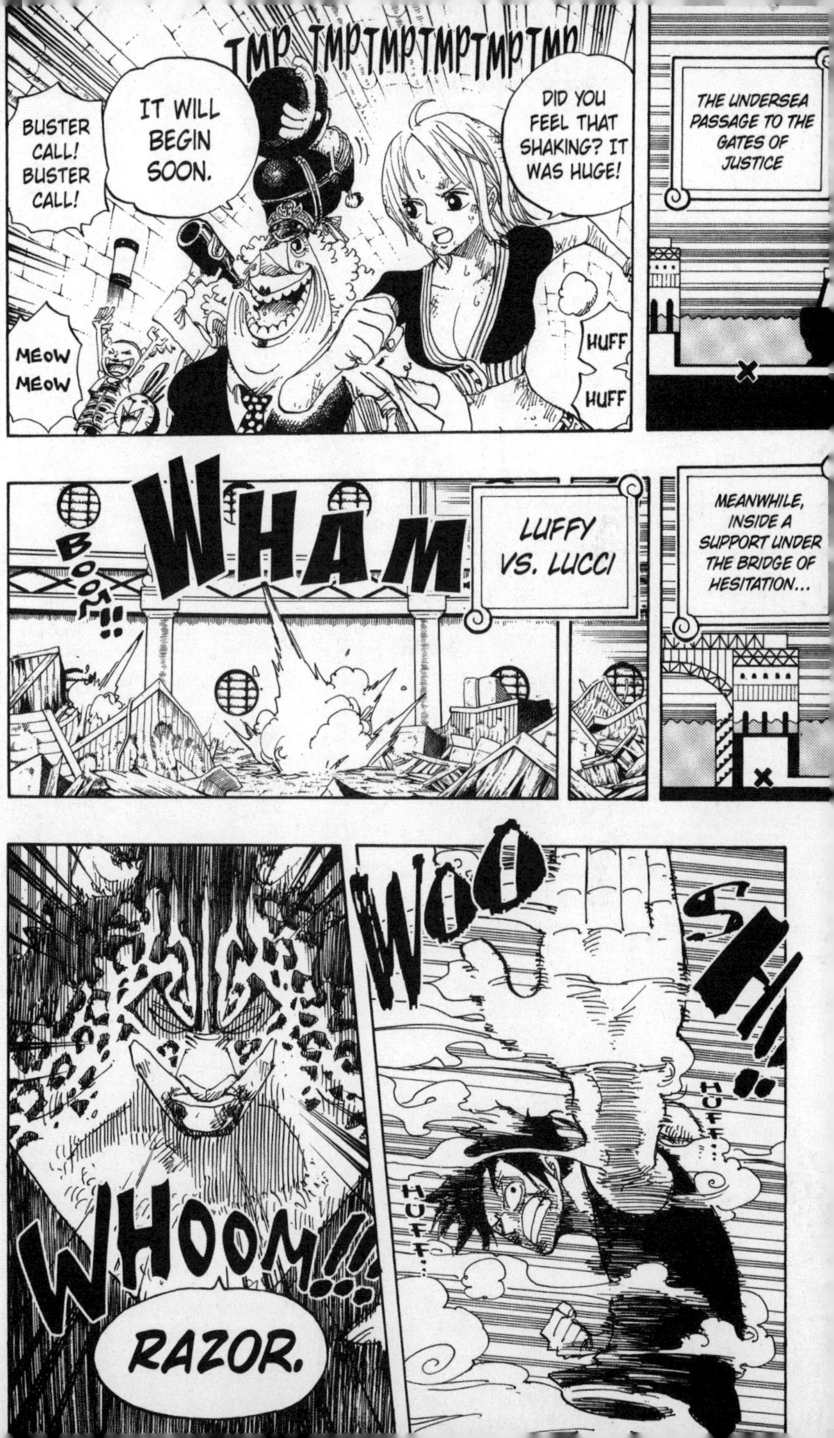
THE UNDERSEA PASSAGE TO THE GATES OF JUSTICE
TMP TMPTMPTMPTMPTMP
DID YOU FEEL THAT SHAKING? IT WAS HUGE!
HUFF
HUFF
IT WILL BEGIN SOON.
BUSTER CALL! BUSTER CALL!
MEOW MEOW
MEANWHILE, INSIDE A SUPPORT UNDER THE BRIDGE OF HESITATION...
LUFFY VS. LUCCI
WHAM
BOOM!!
WOOSH!!
HUFF...
HUFF...
WHOOM!!!
RAZOR.

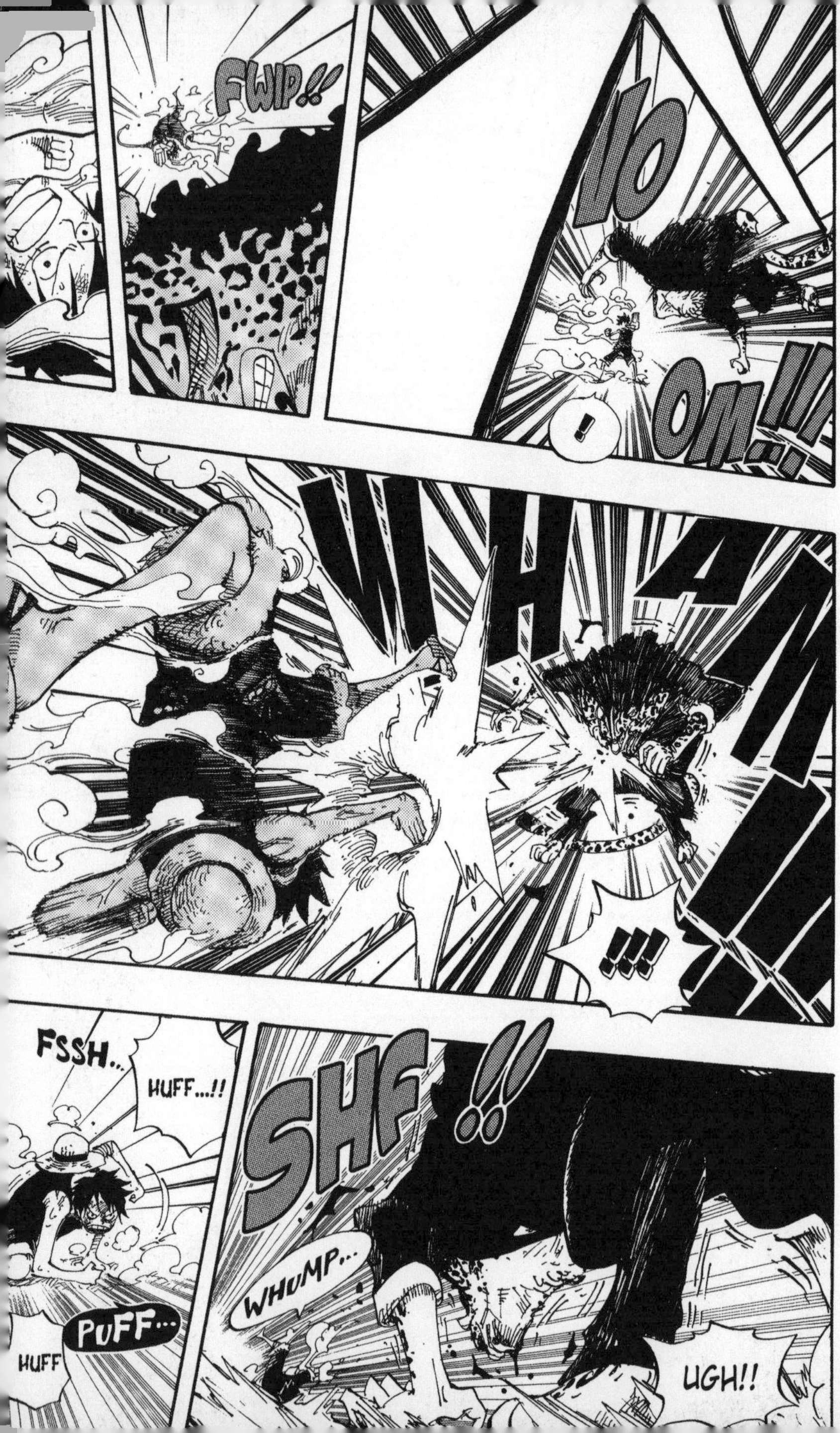
OM..!!!
!
FWIP!!
WHAM
!!!
SHF!!
WHUMP...
UGH!!
FSSH...
HUFF...!!
PUFF...
HUFF

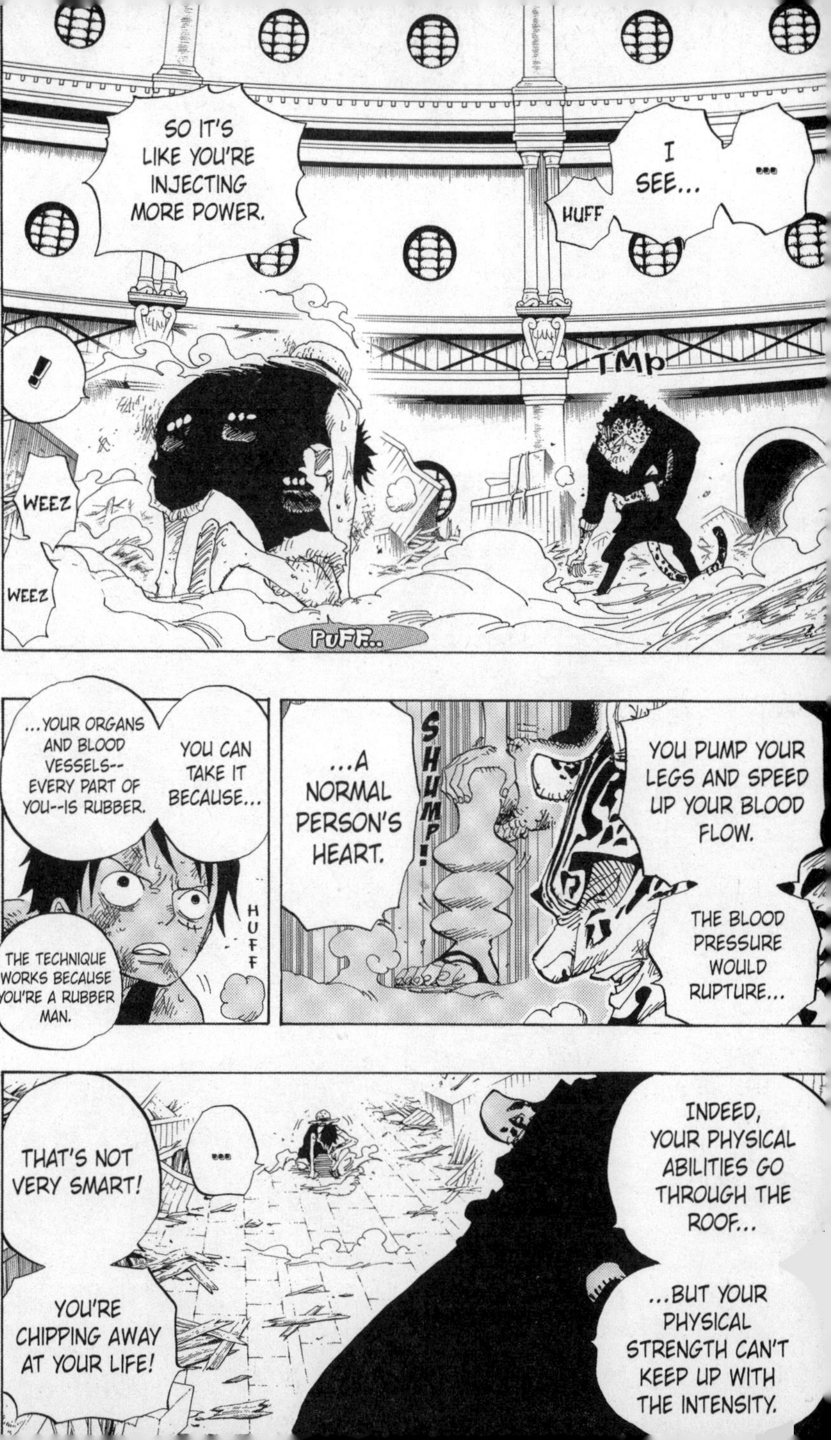
I SEE...
...
HUFF
SO IT'S LIKE YOU'RE INJECTING MORE POWER.
TMP
!
WEEZ
WEEZ
PUFF...
YOU PUMP YOUR LEGS AND SPEED UP YOUR BLOOD FLOW.
THE BLOOD PRESSURE WOULD RUPTURE...
...A NORMAL PERSON'S HEART.
SHUMP!!
YOU CAN TAKE IT BECAUSE...
...YOUR ORGANS AND BLOOD VESSELS--EVERY PART OF YOU--IS RUBBER.
HUFF
THE TECHNIQUE WORKS BECAUSE YOU'RE A RUBBER MAN.
INDEED, YOUR PHYSICAL ABILITIES GO THROUGH THE ROOF...
...BUT YOUR PHYSICAL STRENGTH CAN'T KEEP UP WITH THE INTENSITY.
...
THAT'S NOT VERY SMART!
YOU'RE CHIPPING AWAY AT YOUR LIFE!

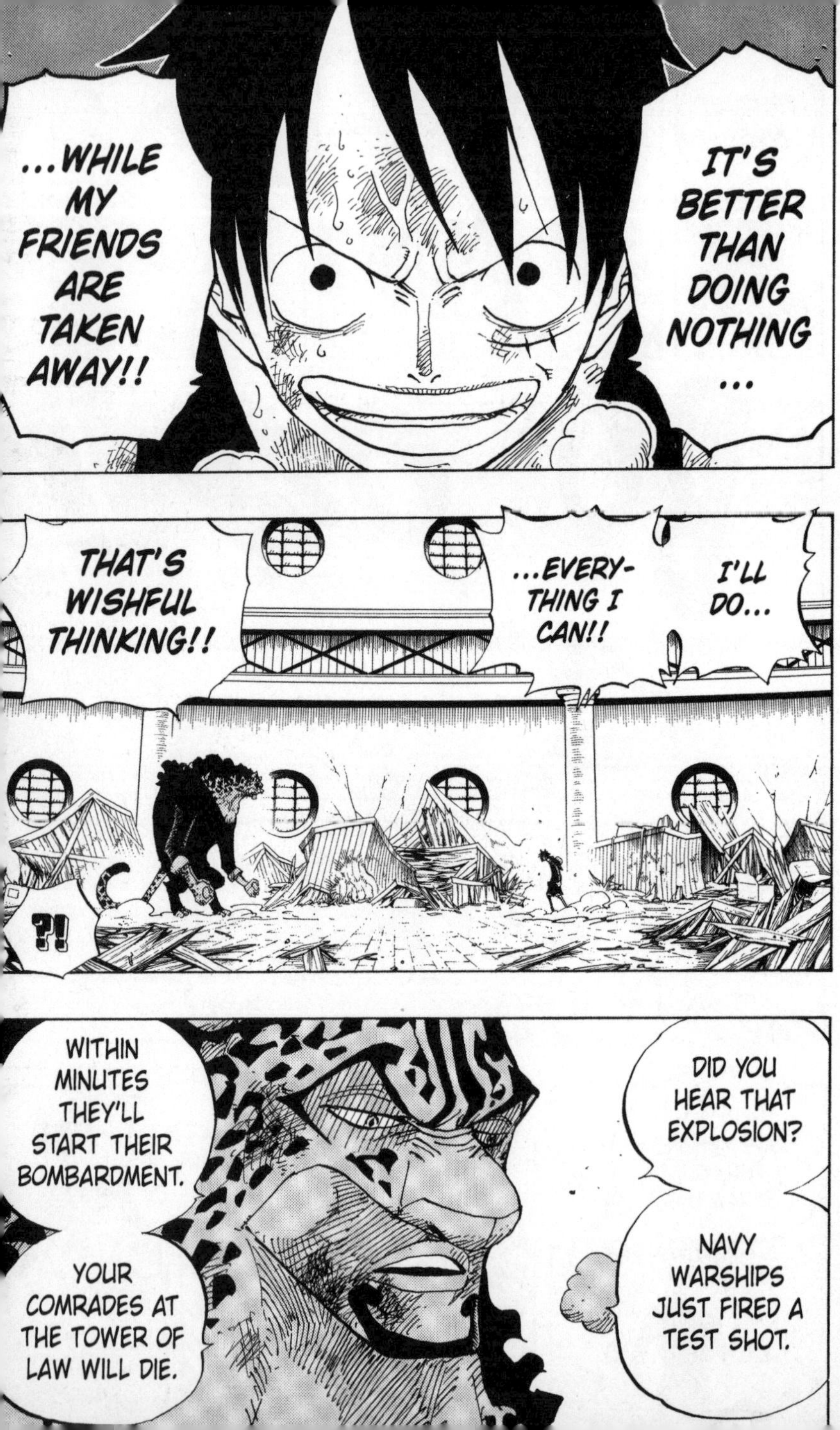
IT'S BETTER THAN DOING NOTHING...
...WHILE MY FRIENDS ARE TAKEN AWAY!!
I'LL DO...
...EVERY-THING I CAN!!
THAT'S WISHFUL THINKING!!
?!
DID YOU HEAR THAT EXPLOSION?
NAVY WARSHIPS JUST FIRED A TEST SHOT.
WITHIN MINUTES THEY'LL START THEIR BOMBARDMENT.
YOUR COMRADES AT THE TOWER OF LAW WILL DIE.

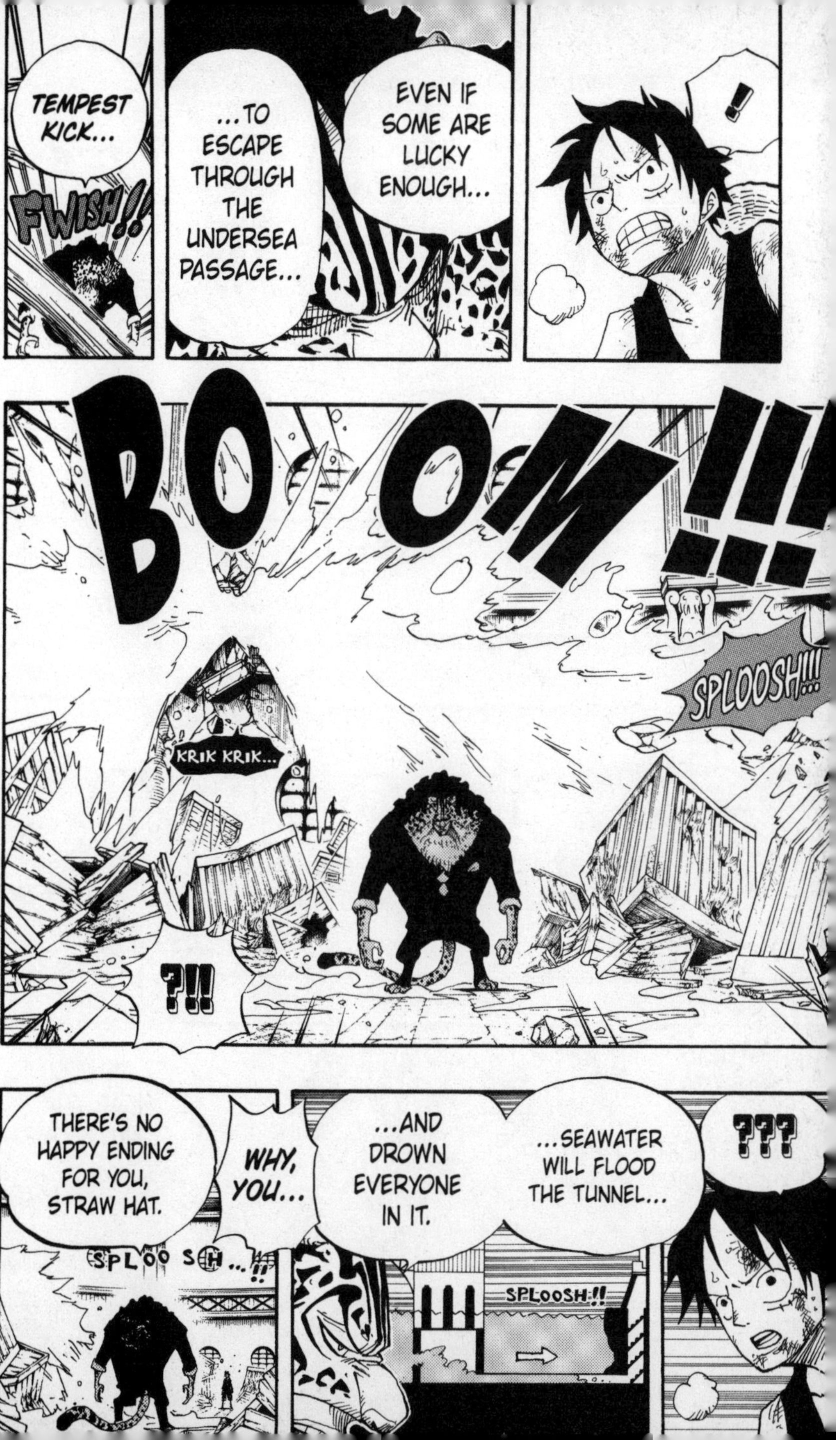
!
EVEN IF SOME ARE LUCKY ENOUGH...
...TO ESCAPE THROUGH THE UNDERSEA PASSAGE...
TEMPEST KICK...
FWISH!!
BOOM!!!
SPLOOSH!!!
KRIK KRIK...
?!!
???
...SEAWATER WILL FLOOD THE TUNNEL...
...AND DROWN EVERYONE IN IT.
SPLOOSH!!
WHY, YOU...
THERE'S NO HAPPY ENDING FOR YOU, STRAW HAT.
SPLOOSH...!!

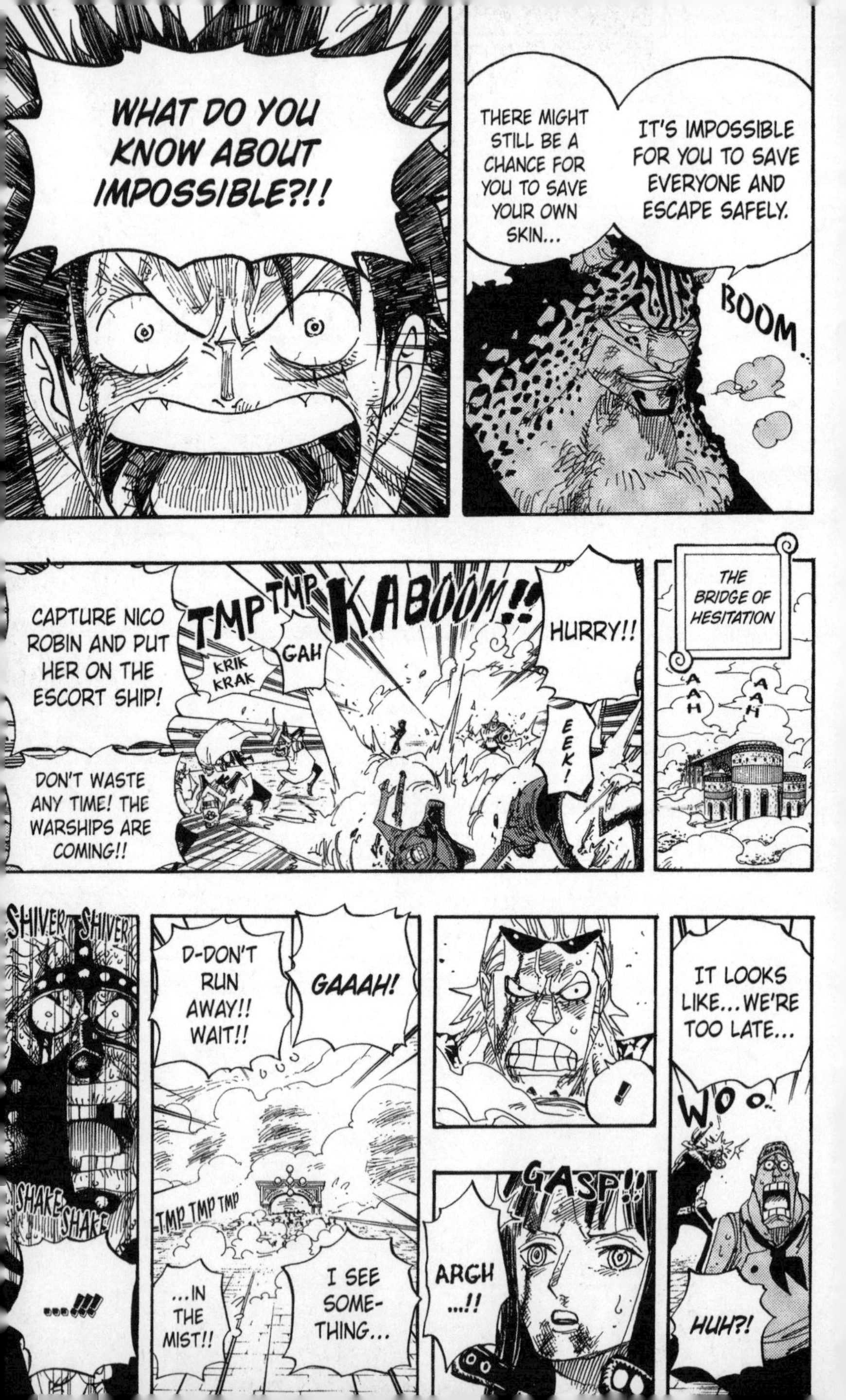
IT'S IMPOSSIBLE FOR YOU TO SAVE EVERYONE AND ESCAPE SAFELY.
THERE MIGHT STILL BE A CHANCE FOR YOU TO SAVE YOUR OWN SKIN...
BOOM..
WHAT DO YOU KNOW ABOUT IMPOSSIBLE?!!
THE BRIDGE OF HESITATION
AAH
AAH
HURRY!!
KABOOM!!
TMP TMP
GAH
KRIK KRAK
EEK!
CAPTURE NICO ROBIN AND PUT HER ON THE ESCORT SHIP!
DON'T WASTE ANY TIME! THE WARSHIPS ARE COMING!!
IT LOOKS LIKE...WE'RE TOO LATE...
WOO..
HUH?!
!
GASP!!
ARGH ...!!
GAAAH!
D-DON'T RUN AWAY!! WAIT!!
I SEE SOME-THING...
...IN THE MIST!!
TMP TMP TMP
SHIVER SHIVER
SHAKE SHAKE
...!!!

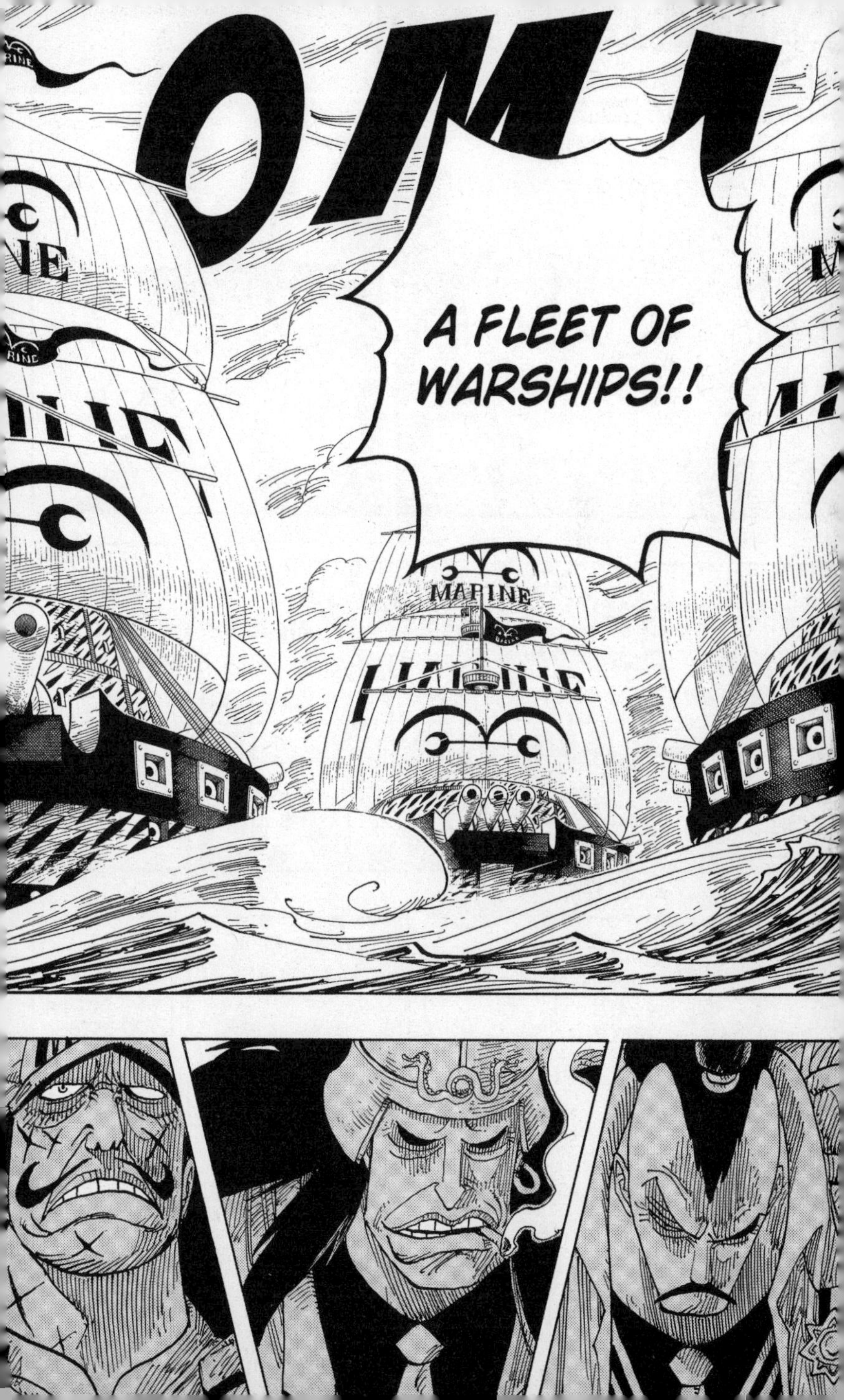
A FLEET OF WARSHIPS!!
MARINE

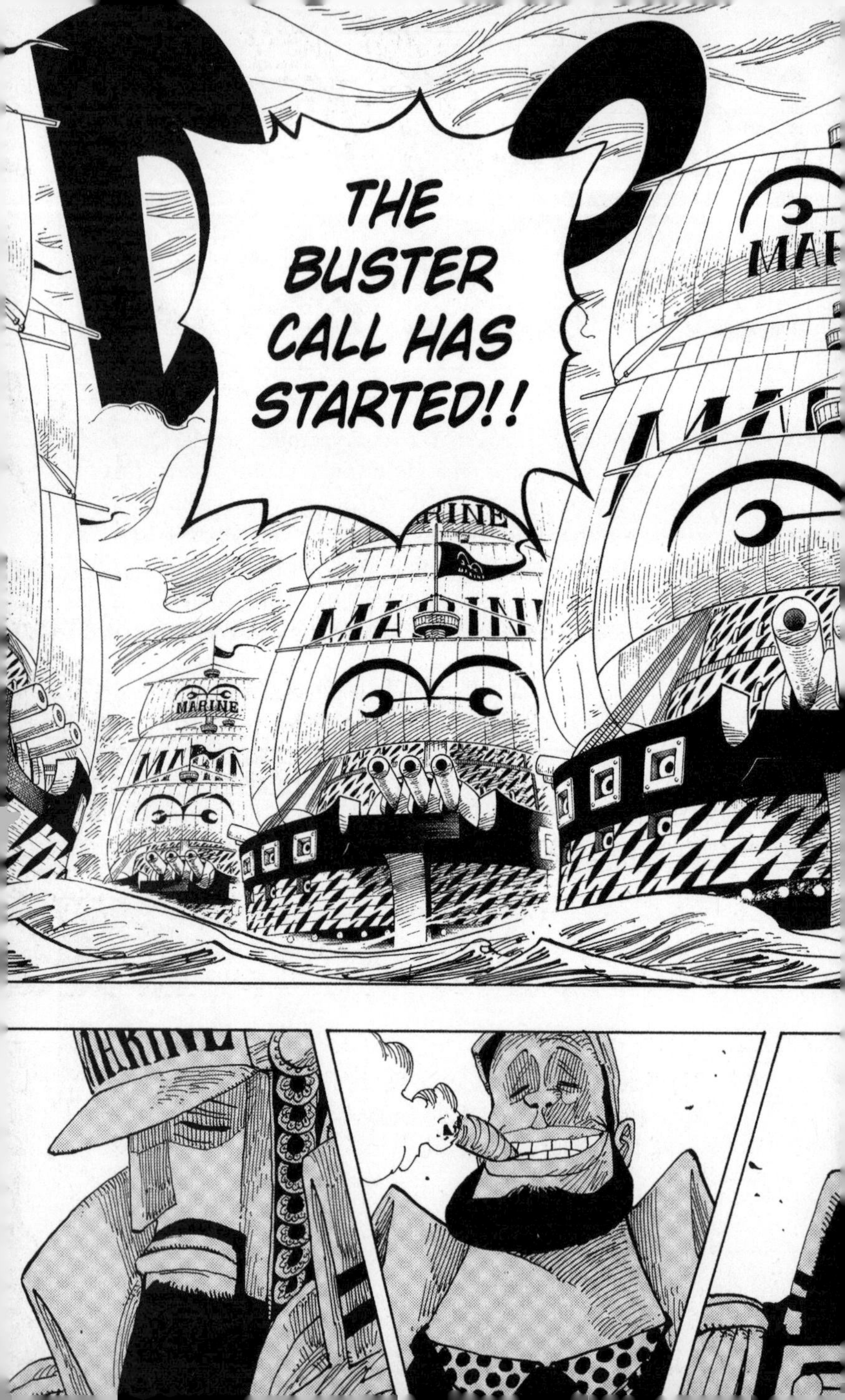
THE BUSTER CALL HAS STARTED!!

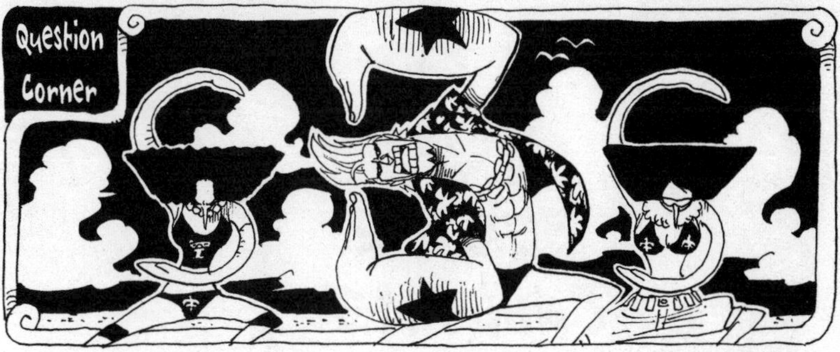
Question Corner

Reader (Q): Hello, Oda Sensei! You can never introduce the Question Corner because others beat you to it! Sorry, but... I'm one of them. (DOOM) So let's decide with rock-paper-scissors! That'll make it fair! All right, let's start! ♪ One...two...three!! ♪ Oh, I lost. ☆ Oh well! Let's begin the Question Corner!!

--Kayu

Oda (A): You said it!! Heeeey!! Can't you wait?! Don't you think there's something wrong with that?! Argh!! Now I'm ticked! This time I'm going to include more Question Corners! Darn it!

Q: Good morning, Oda Sensei! I've got a question! The CP9 outfits sure can stretch! How many Gum-Gums can they stretch?

--Ashi

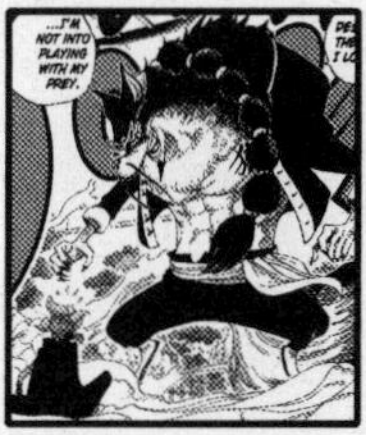
...I'M NOT INTO PLAYING WITH MY PREY.

A: They do stretch indeed. Pretty funny, huh? About 50 Gum-Gums, wouldn't you say?!

Chapter 421:
GEAR THREE

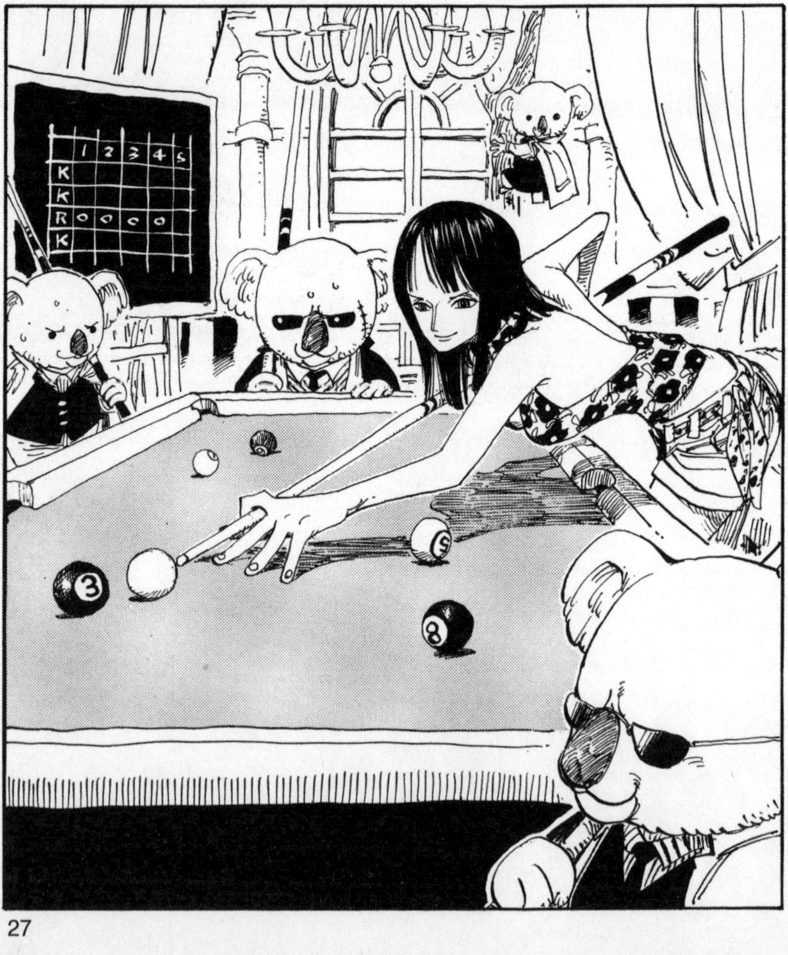
1 2 3 4 5
K
K
R
K

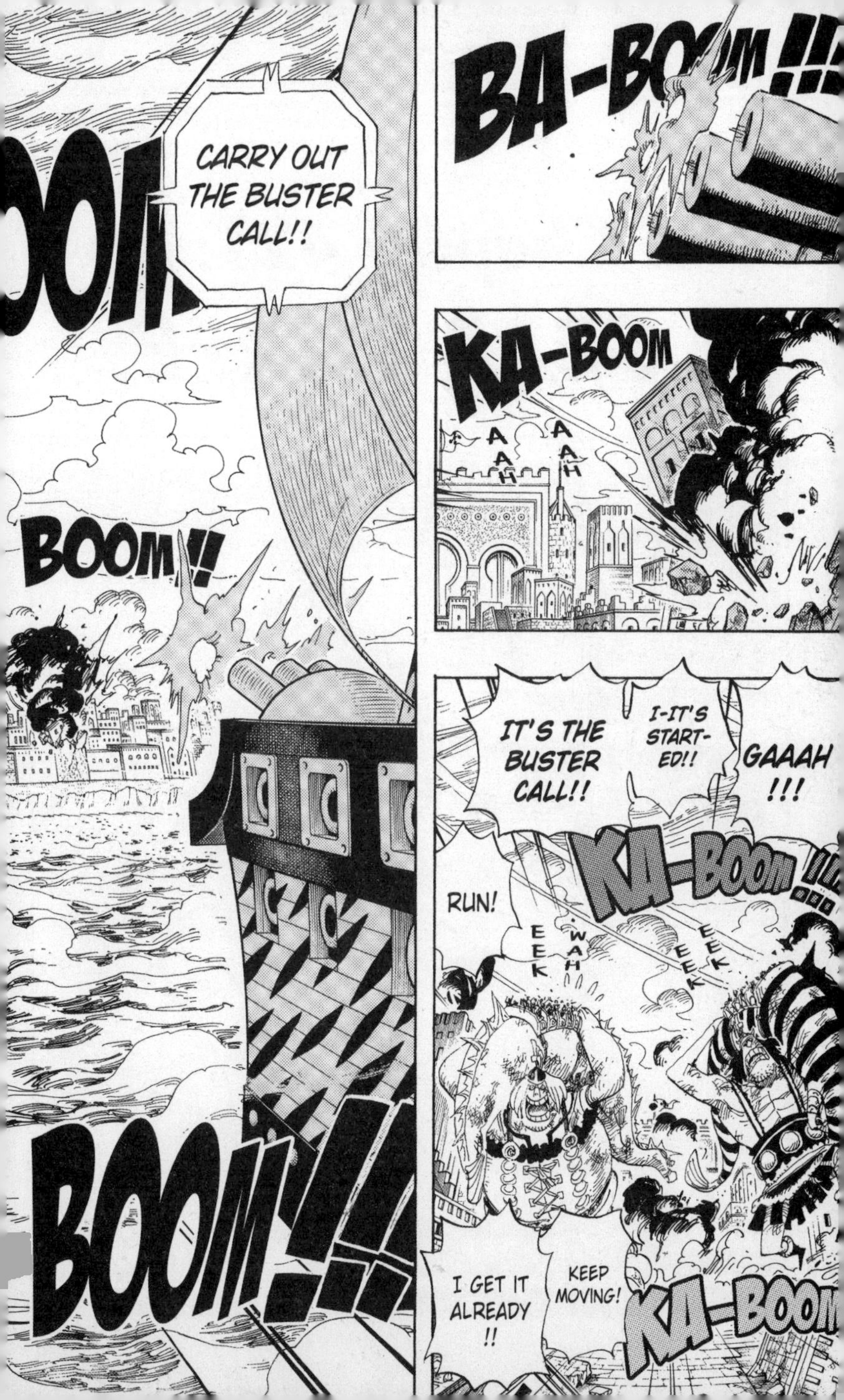
BA-BOOM!!!
KA-BOOM
AAAH
AAAH
GAAAH!!!
I-IT'S STARTED!!
IT'S THE BUSTER CALL!!
KA-BOOM!!!
EEK
EEK
WAH
EEK
RUN!
KEEP MOVING!
I GET IT ALREADY!!
KA-BOOM
CARRY OUT THE BUSTER CALL!!
BOOM!!
BOOM!!!

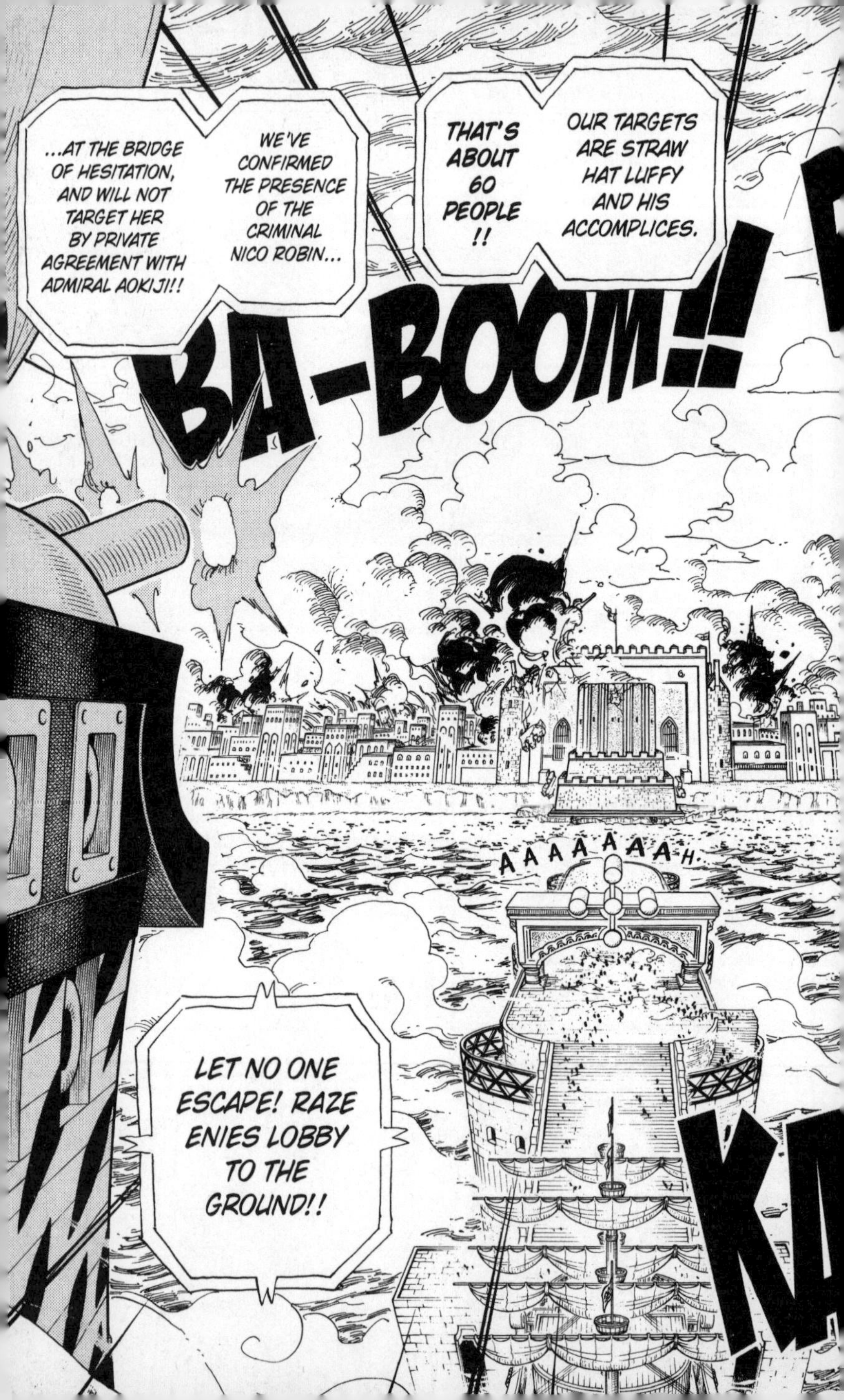
OUR TARGETS ARE STRAW HAT LUFFY AND HIS ACCOMPLICES.
THAT'S ABOUT 60 PEOPLE!!
WE'VE CONFIRMED THE PRESENCE OF THE CRIMINAL NICO ROBIN...
...AT THE BRIDGE OF HESITATION, AND WILL NOT TARGET HER BY PRIVATE AGREEMENT WITH ADMIRAL AOKIJI!!
BA-BOOM!!
AAAAAAAAH
LET NO ONE ESCAPE! RAZE ENIES LOBBY TO THE GROUND!!

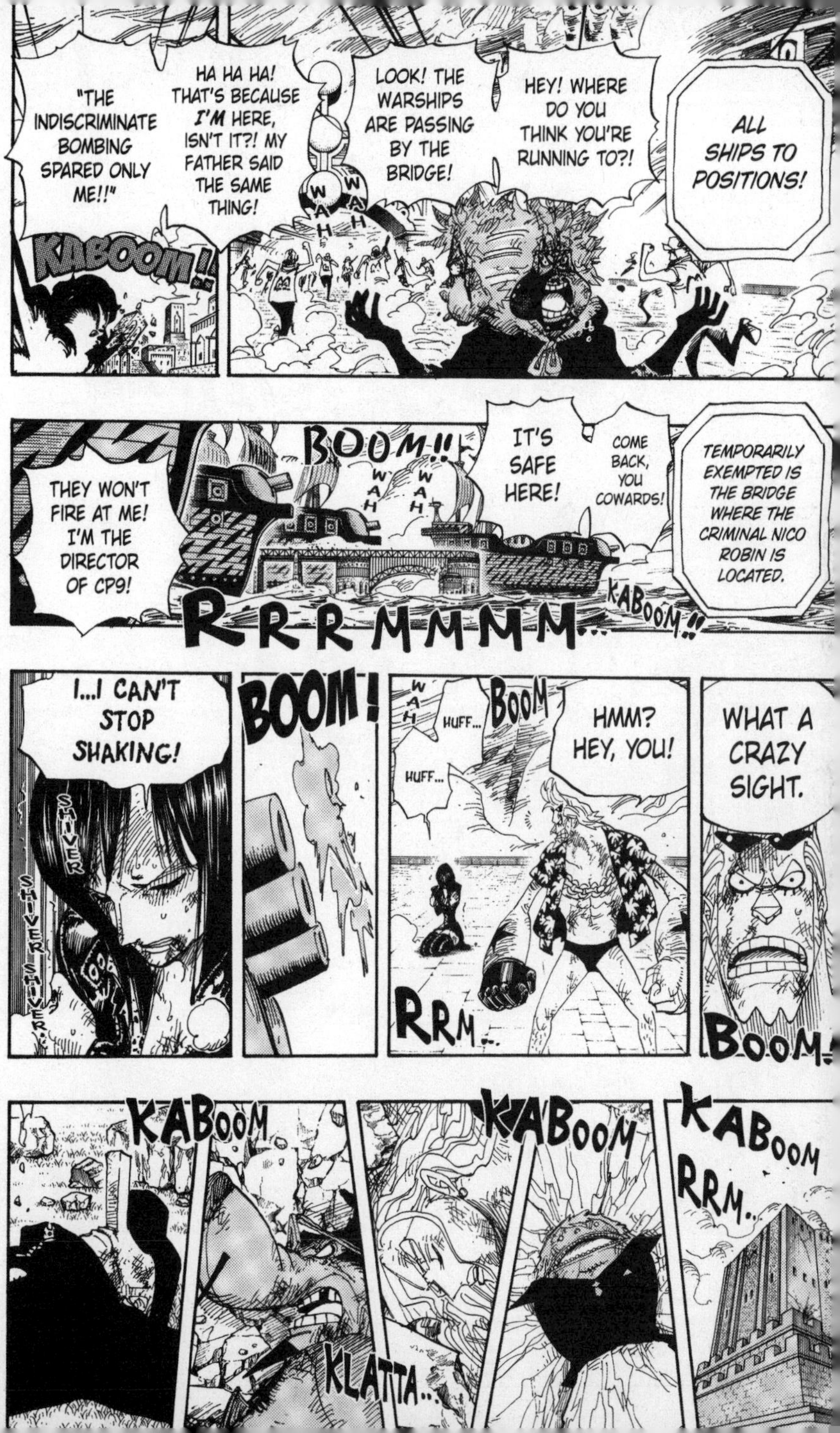
ALL SHIPS TO POSITIONS!
HEY! WHERE DO YOU THINK YOU'RE RUNNING TO?!
LOOK! THE WARSHIPS ARE PASSING BY THE BRIDGE!
WAH
WAH
HA HA HA! THAT'S BECAUSE I'M HERE, ISN'T IT?! MY FATHER SAID THE SAME THING!
"THE INDISCRIMINATE BOMBING SPARED ONLY ME!!"
KABOOM!!
TEMPORARILY EXEMPTED IS THE BRIDGE WHERE THE CRIMINAL NICO ROBIN IS LOCATED.
COME BACK, YOU COWARDS!
IT'S SAFE HERE!
WAH
WAH
BOOM!!
THEY WON'T FIRE AT ME! I'M THE DIRECTOR OF CP9!
KABOOM!!
RRRMMMM...
WHAT A CRAZY SIGHT.
BOOM!
HMM? HEY, YOU!
BOOM
HUFF...
HUFF...
WAH
RRM...
BOOM!
I...I CAN'T STOP SHAKING!
SHIVER
SHIVER SHIVER...
KABOOM
RRM...
KABOOM
KLATTA...
KABOOM

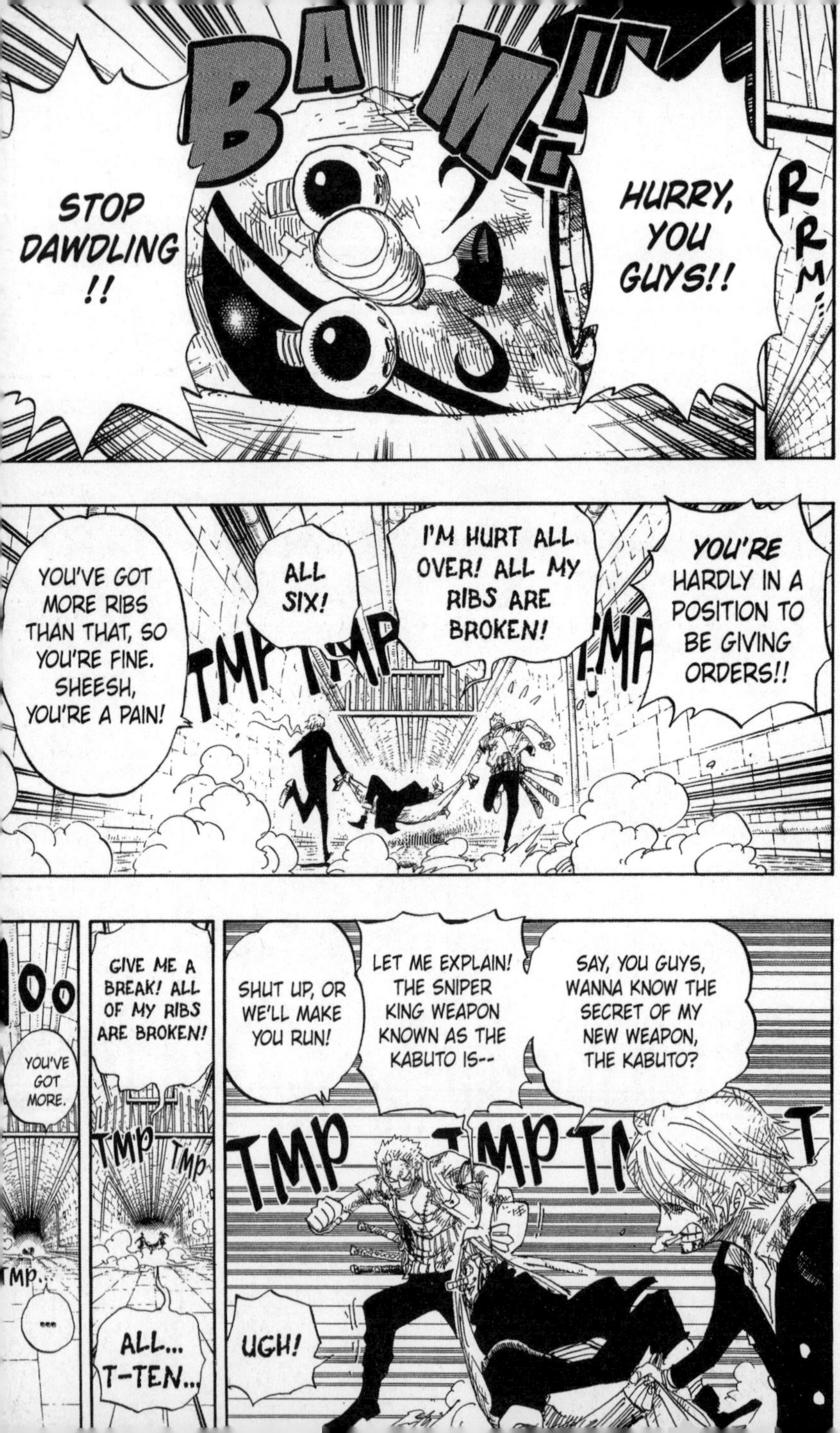

RRM...
HURRY, YOU GUYS!!
BAM!!
STOP DAWDLING!!
YOU'RE HARDLY IN A POSITION TO BE GIVING ORDERS!!
I'M HURT ALL OVER! ALL MY RIBS ARE BROKEN!
ALL SIX!
TMP TMP TMP
YOU'VE GOT MORE RIBS THAN THAT, SO YOU'RE FINE. SHEESH, YOU'RE A PAIN!
SAY, YOU GUYS, WANNA KNOW THE SECRET OF MY NEW WEAPON, THE KABUTO?
LET ME EXPLAIN! THE SNIPER KING WEAPON KNOWN AS THE KABUTO IS--
SHUT UP, OR WE'LL MAKE YOU RUN!
TMP TMP TMP
UGH!
GIVE ME A BREAK! ALL OF MY RIBS ARE BROKEN!
TMP TMP
ALL... T-TEN...
YOU'VE GOT MORE.
TMP...
...

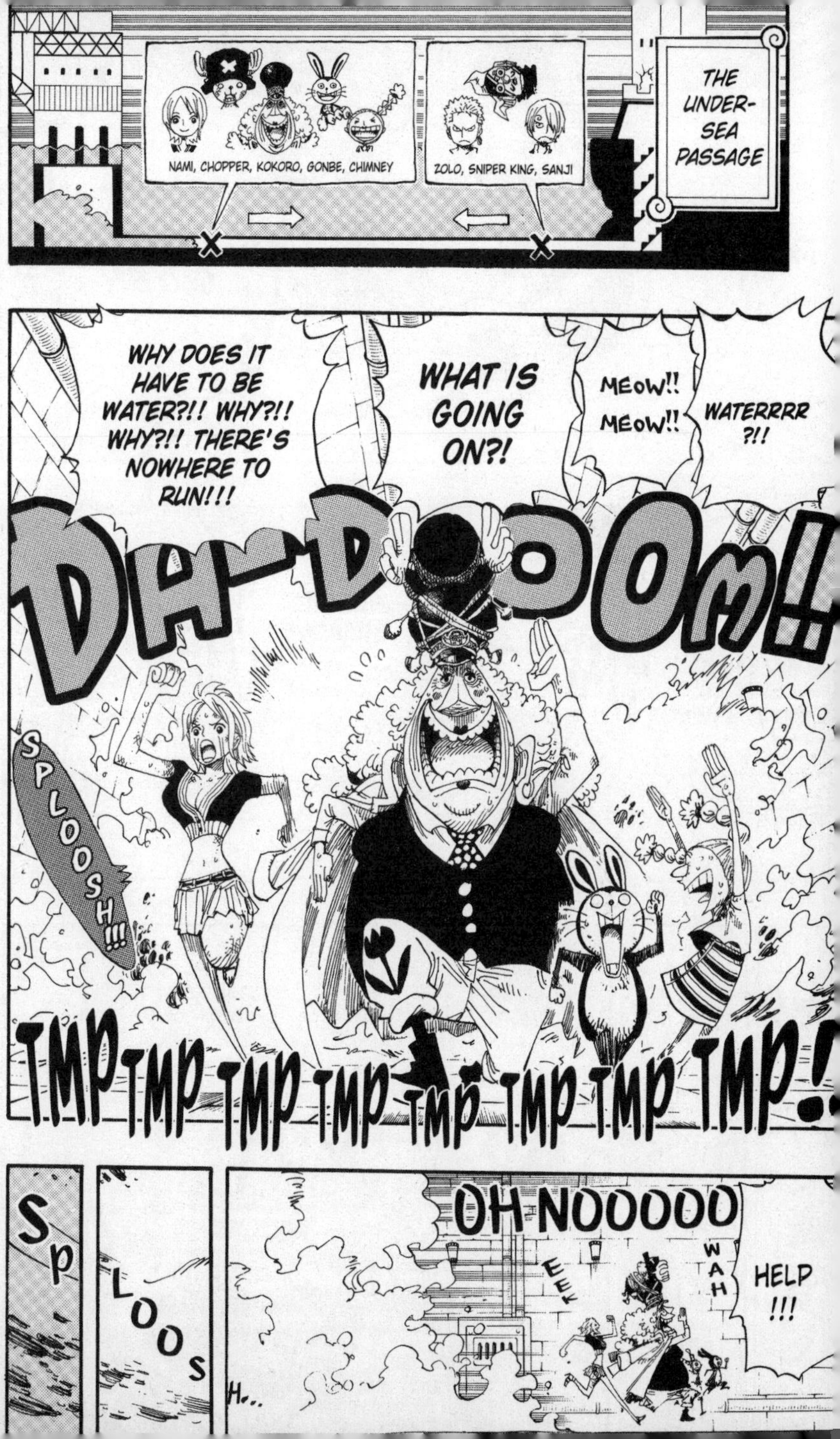
THE UNDER-SEA PASSAGE
ZOLO, SNIPER KING, SANJI
NAMI, CHOPPER, KOKORO, GONBE, CHIMNEY
WATERRRR ?!!
MEOW!! MEOW!!
WHAT IS GOING ON?!
WHY DOES IT HAVE TO BE WATER?!! WHY?!! WHY?!! THERE'S NOWHERE TO RUN!!!
DA-DOOOM!!
SPLOOSH!!!
TMP TMP TMP TMP TMP TMP TMP TMP!!
HELP !!!
WAH
OH NOOOOO
EEK
SPLOOSH...
Sp

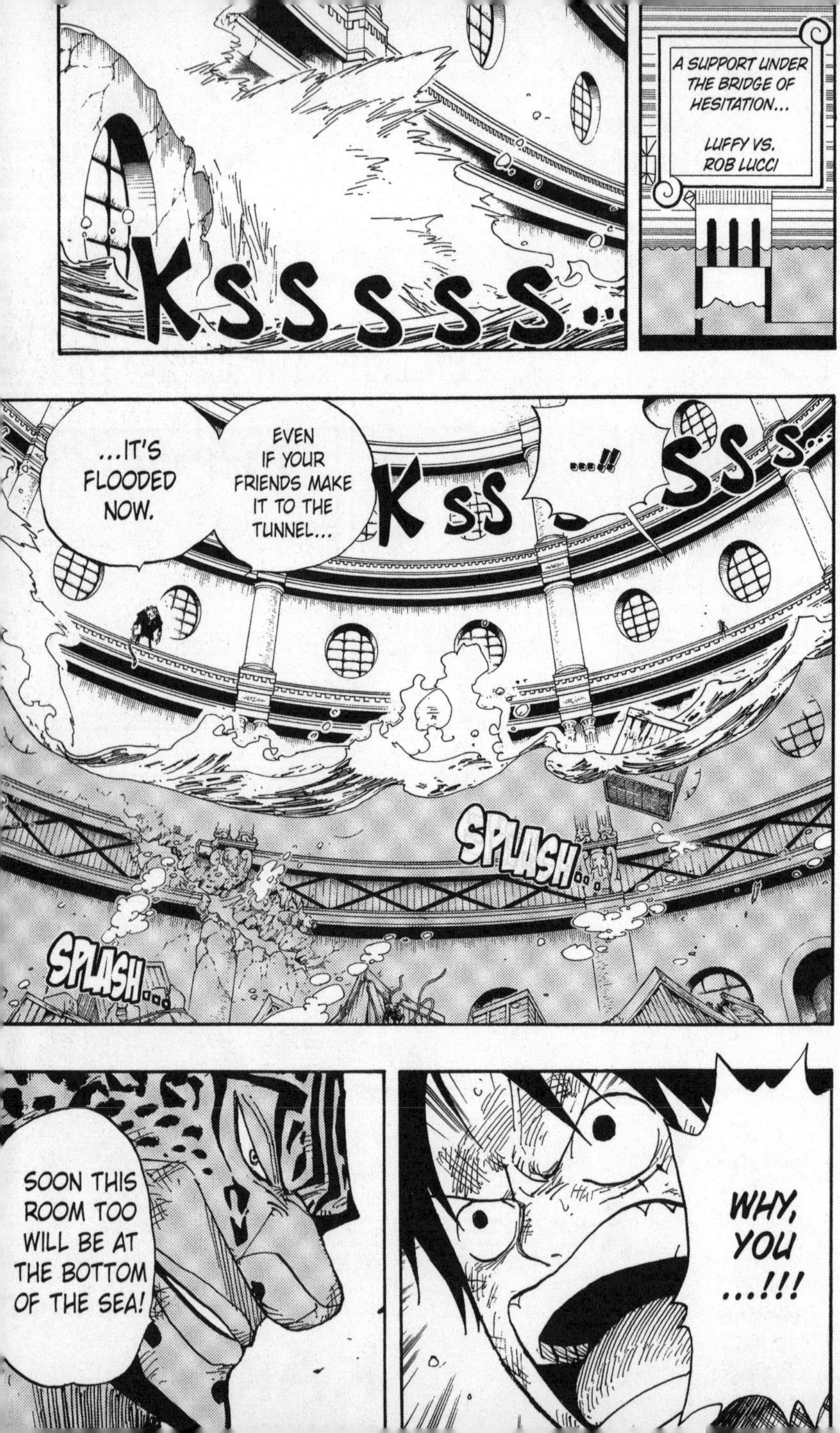
A SUPPORT UNDER THE BRIDGE OF HESITATION...
LUFFY VS. ROB LUCCI
KSSSSS...
SSS...
KSS...!!
EVEN IF YOUR FRIENDS MAKE IT TO THE TUNNEL...
...IT'S FLOODED NOW.
SPLASH...
SPLASH...
WHY, YOU ...!!!
SOON THIS ROOM TOO WILL BE AT THE BOTTOM OF THE SEA!

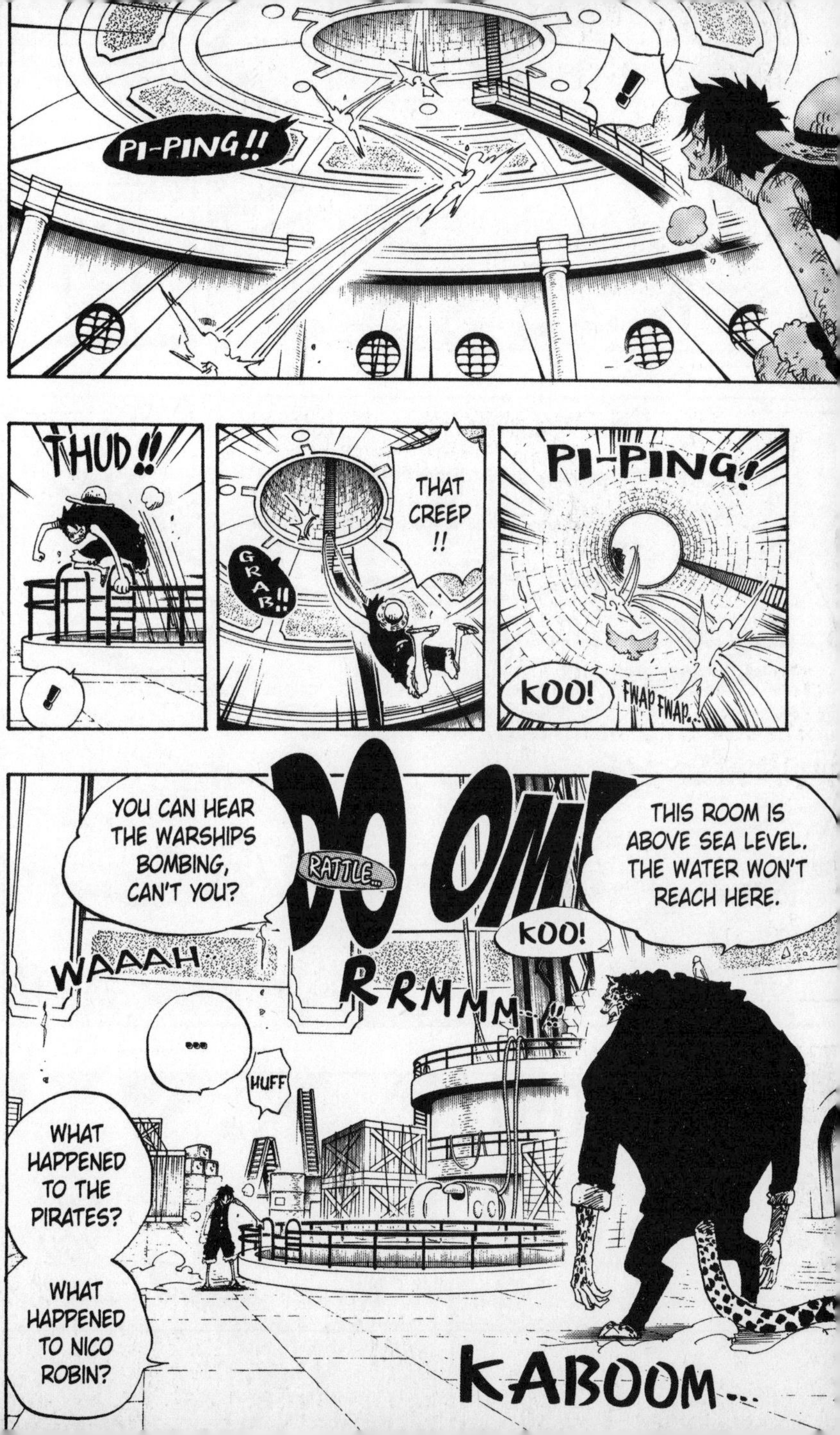
!
PI-PING!!
PI-PING!
KOO!
FWAP FWAP...
THAT CREEP!!
GRAB!!
THUD!!
!
DOOM
THIS ROOM IS ABOVE SEA LEVEL. THE WATER WON'T REACH HERE.
KOO!
RATTLE...
YOU CAN HEAR THE WARSHIPS BOMBING, CAN'T YOU?
WAAAH...
RRMMM...
...
HUFF
WHAT HAPPENED TO THE PIRATES?
WHAT HAPPENED TO NICO ROBIN?
KABOOM...

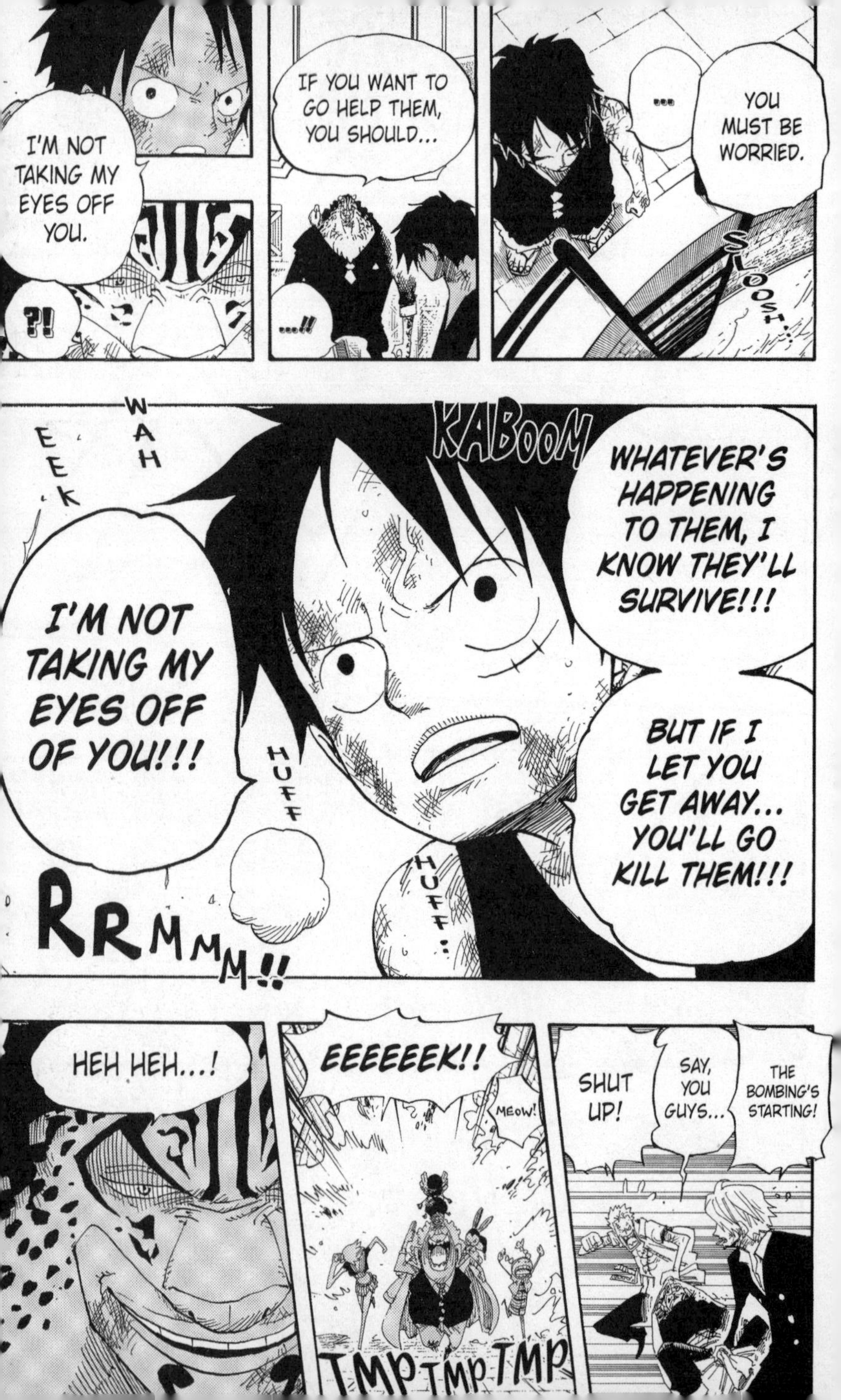
YOU MUST BE WORRIED.
...
SLOOSH...!
IF YOU WANT TO GO HELP THEM, YOU SHOULD...
...!!
I'M NOT TAKING MY EYES OFF YOU.
?!
KABOOM
WHATEVER'S HAPPENING TO THEM, I KNOW THEY'LL SURVIVE!!!
BUT IF I LET YOU GET AWAY... YOU'LL GO KILL THEM!!!
WAH
EEK
I'M NOT TAKING MY EYES OFF OF YOU!!!
HUFF
HUFF
RRMMM!!
THE BOMBING'S STARTING!
SAY, YOU GUYS...
SHUT UP!
EEEEEEK!!
MEOW!
TMP TMP TMP
HEH HEH...!

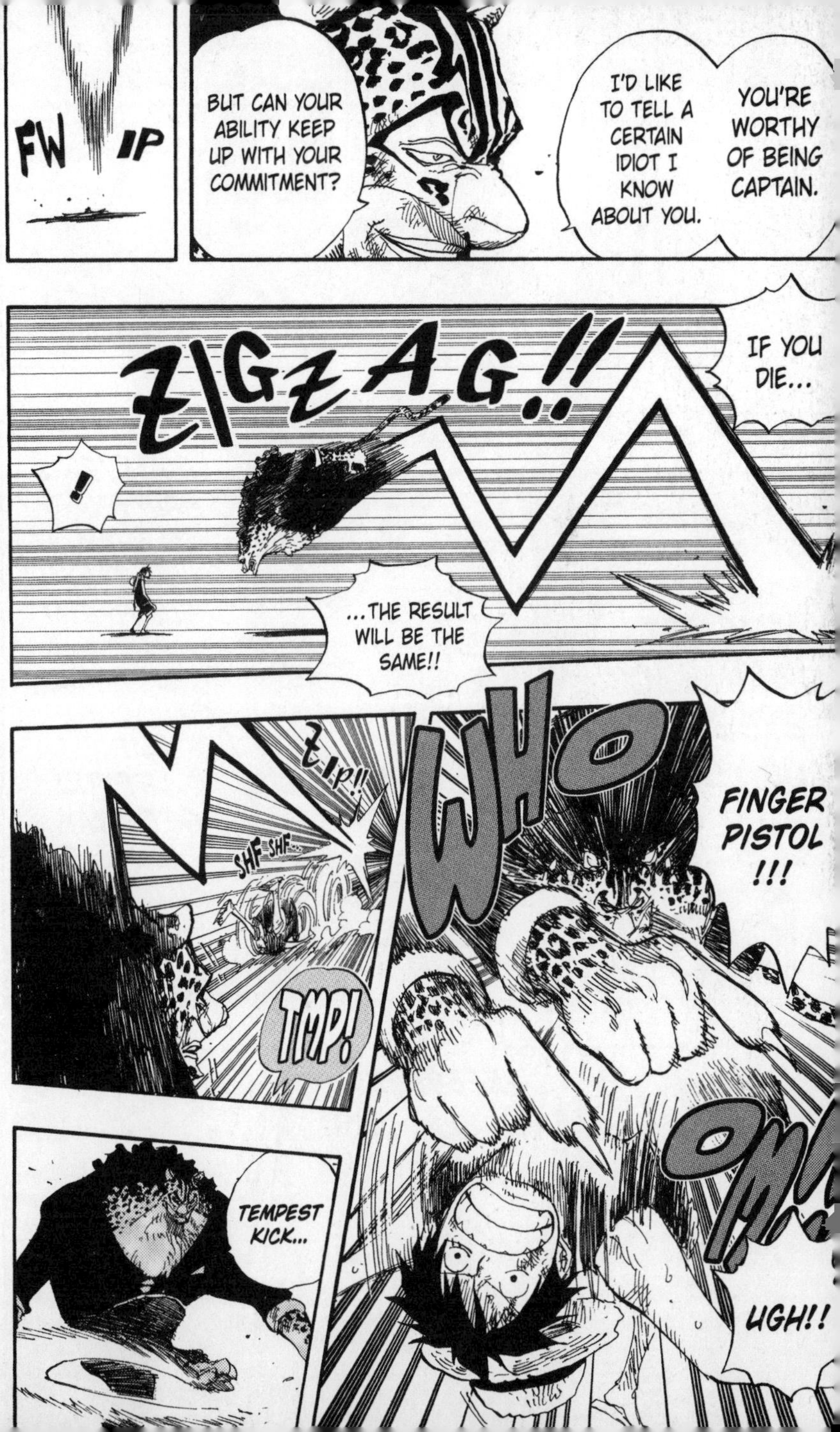
I'D LIKE TO TELL A CERTAIN IDIOT I KNOW ABOUT YOU.
YOU'RE WORTHY OF BEING CAPTAIN.
BUT CAN YOUR ABILITY KEEP UP WITH YOUR COMMITMENT?
FWIP
IF YOU DIE...
ZIGZAG!!
!
...THE RESULT WILL BE THE SAME!!
WHO
OM
FINGER PISTOL!!!
UGH!!
tip!!
SHF SHF...
TMP!
TEMPEST KICK...

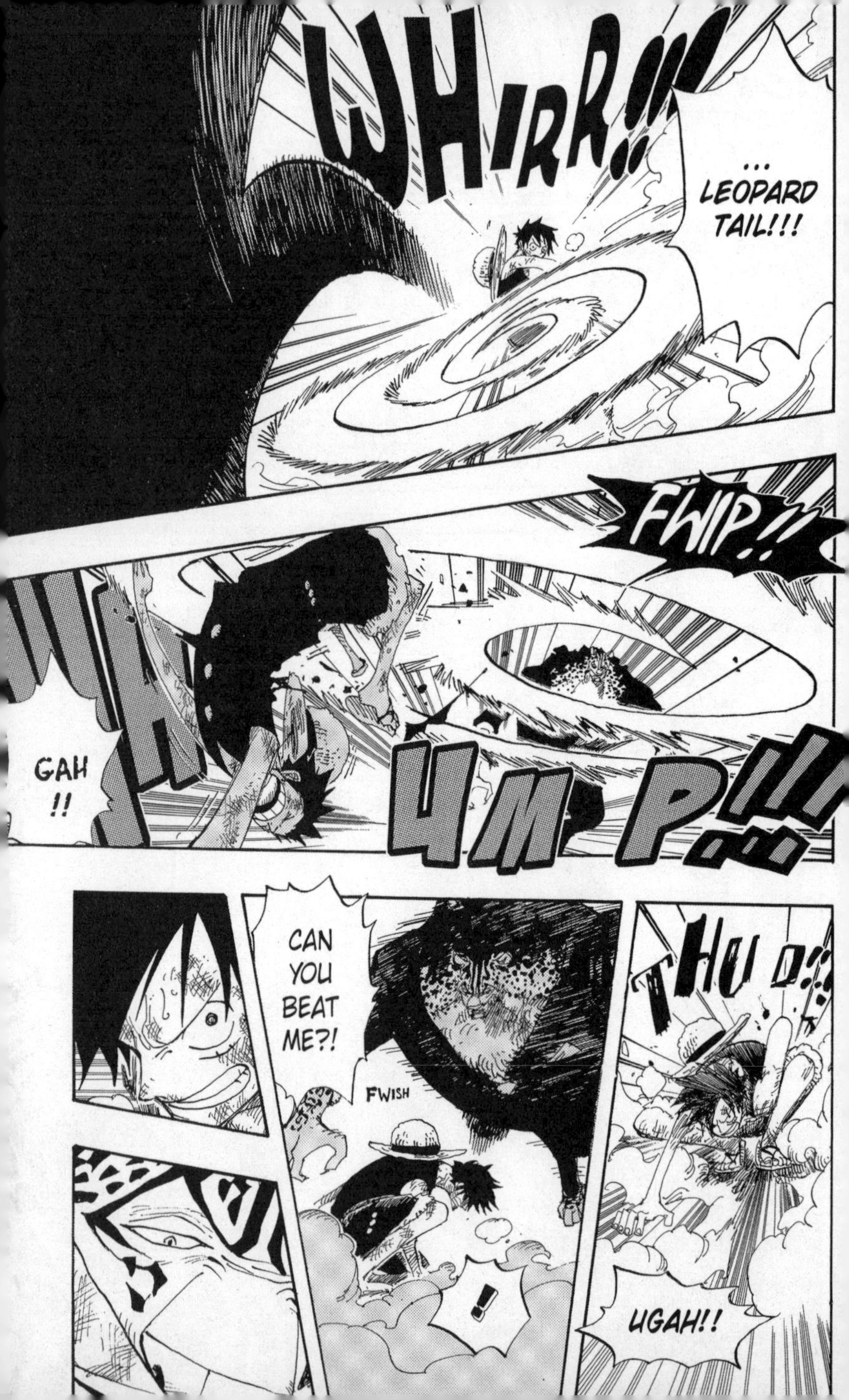
WHIRR!!!
... LEOPARD TAIL!!!
FWIP!!
GAH !!
THUD!!
UGAH!!
CAN YOU BEAT ME?!
FWISH
!

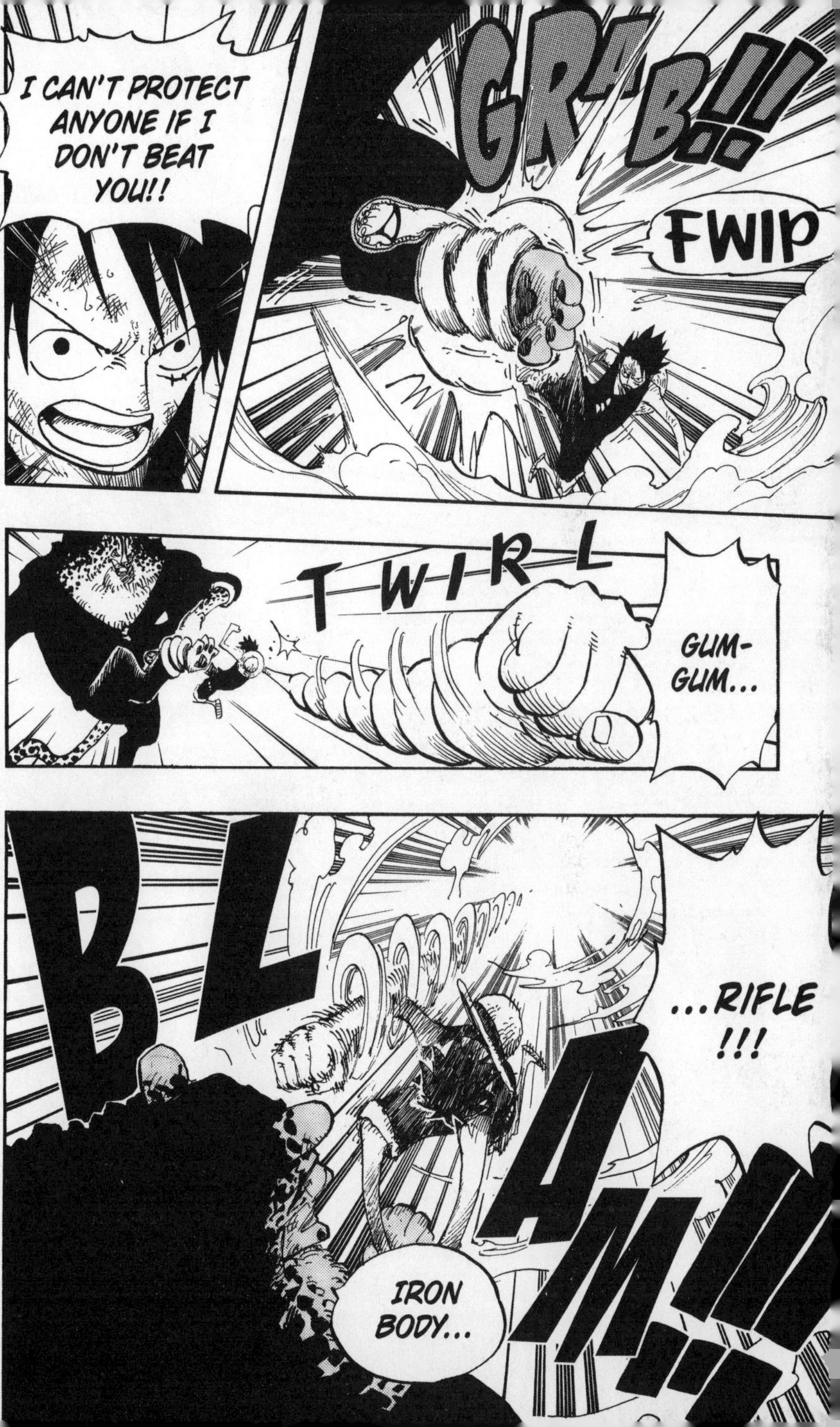
GRAB!!!
FWIP
I CAN'T PROTECT ANYONE IF I DON'T BEAT YOU!!
TWIRL
GUM-GUM...
...RIFLE !!!
IRON BODY...
BLAM!!!

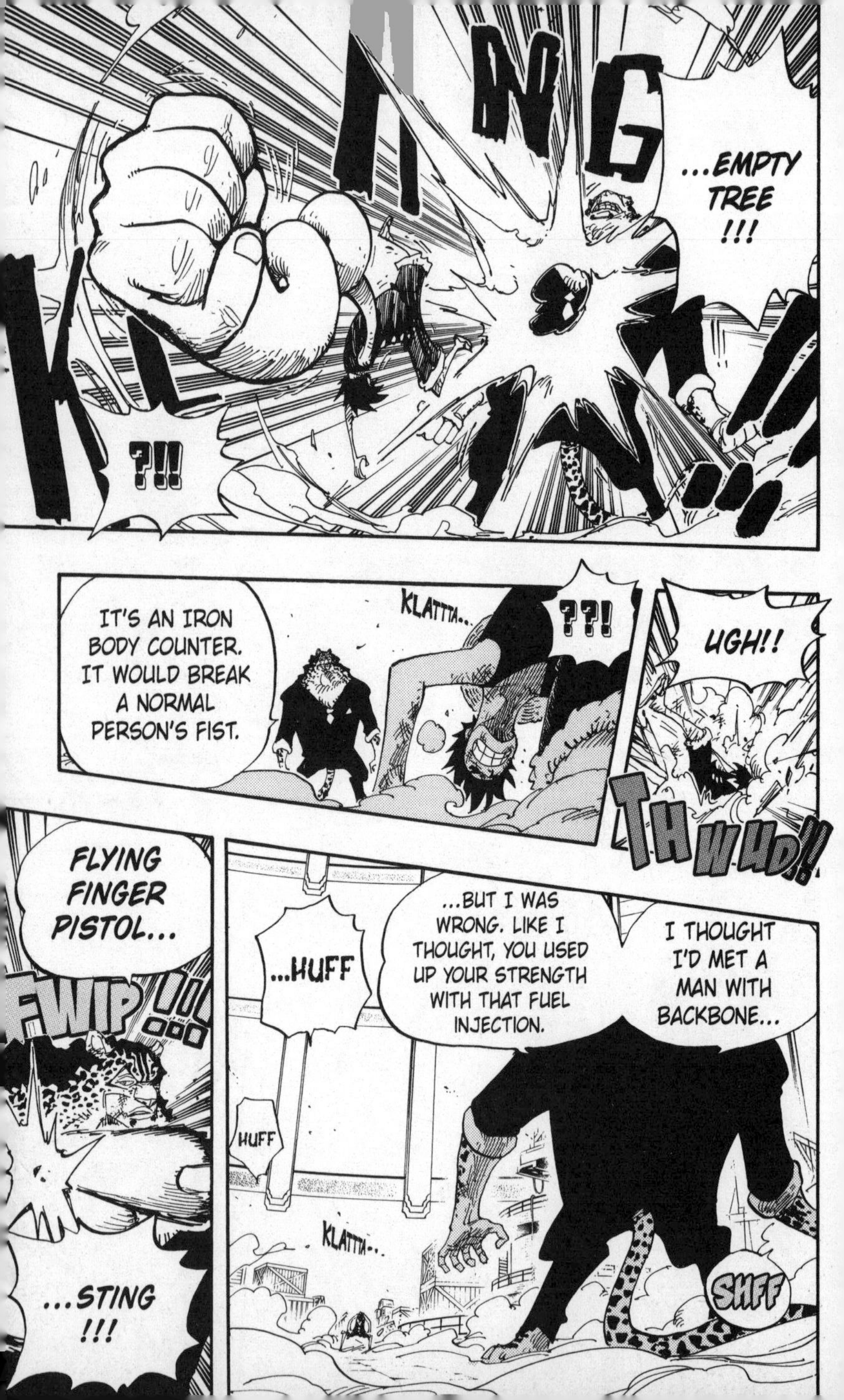
...EMPTY TREE !!!
?!!
UGH!!
THWUD!!
??!
KLATTTA...
IT'S AN IRON BODY COUNTER. IT WOULD BREAK A NORMAL PERSON'S FIST.
I THOUGHT I'D MET A MAN WITH BACKBONE...
...BUT I WAS WRONG. LIKE I THOUGHT, YOU USED UP YOUR STRENGTH WITH THAT FUEL INJECTION.
...HUFF
HUFF
KLATTTA...
SHFF
FLYING FINGER PISTOL...
FWIP!!!
...STING !!!

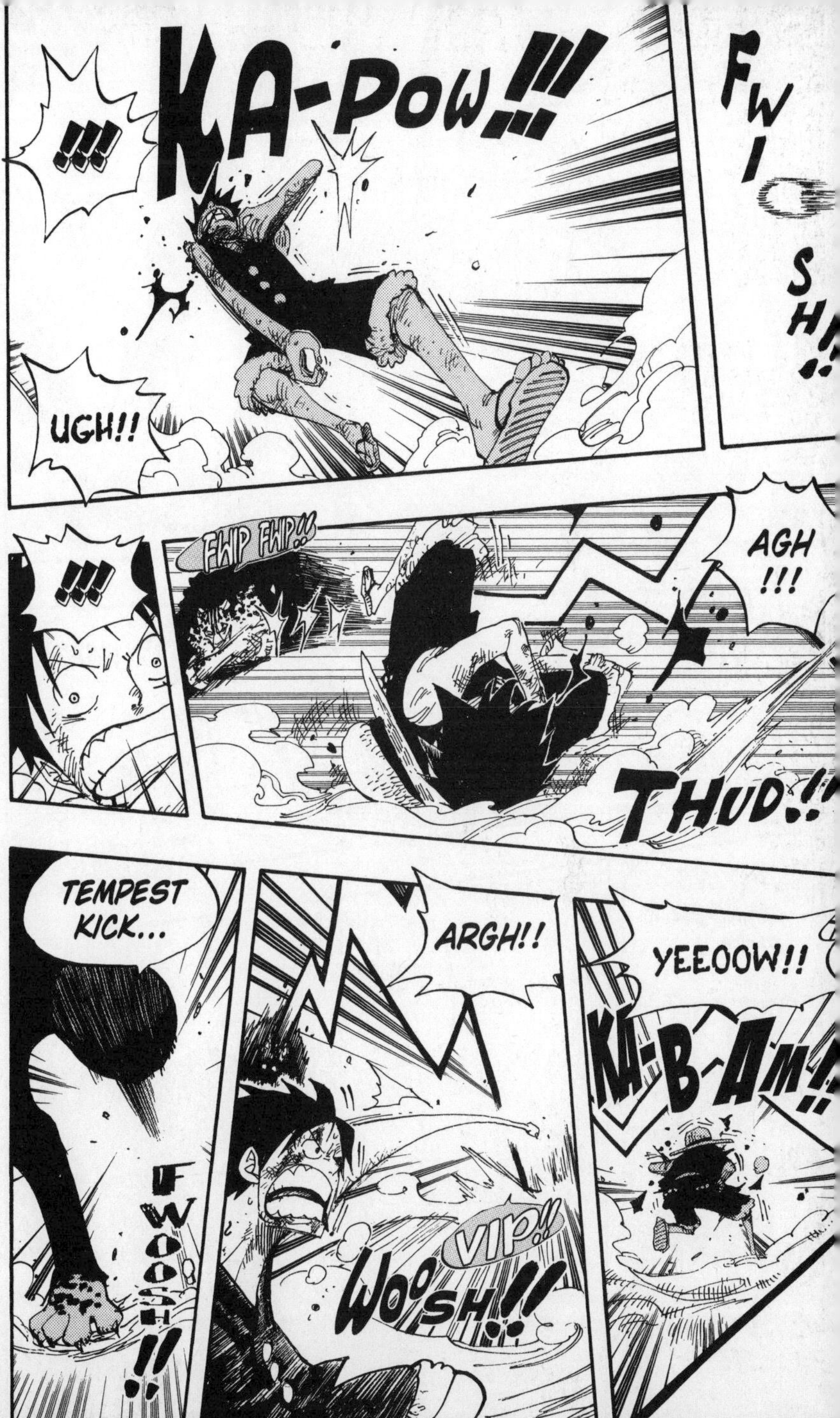
FWISH!!
KA-POW!!!
!!!
UGH!!
AGH !!!
FWIP FWIP!!
THUD!!
!!!
YEEOOW!!
KA-B-AM!!
ARGH!!
VIP!!
WOOSH!!
TEMPEST KICK...
FWOOSH!!

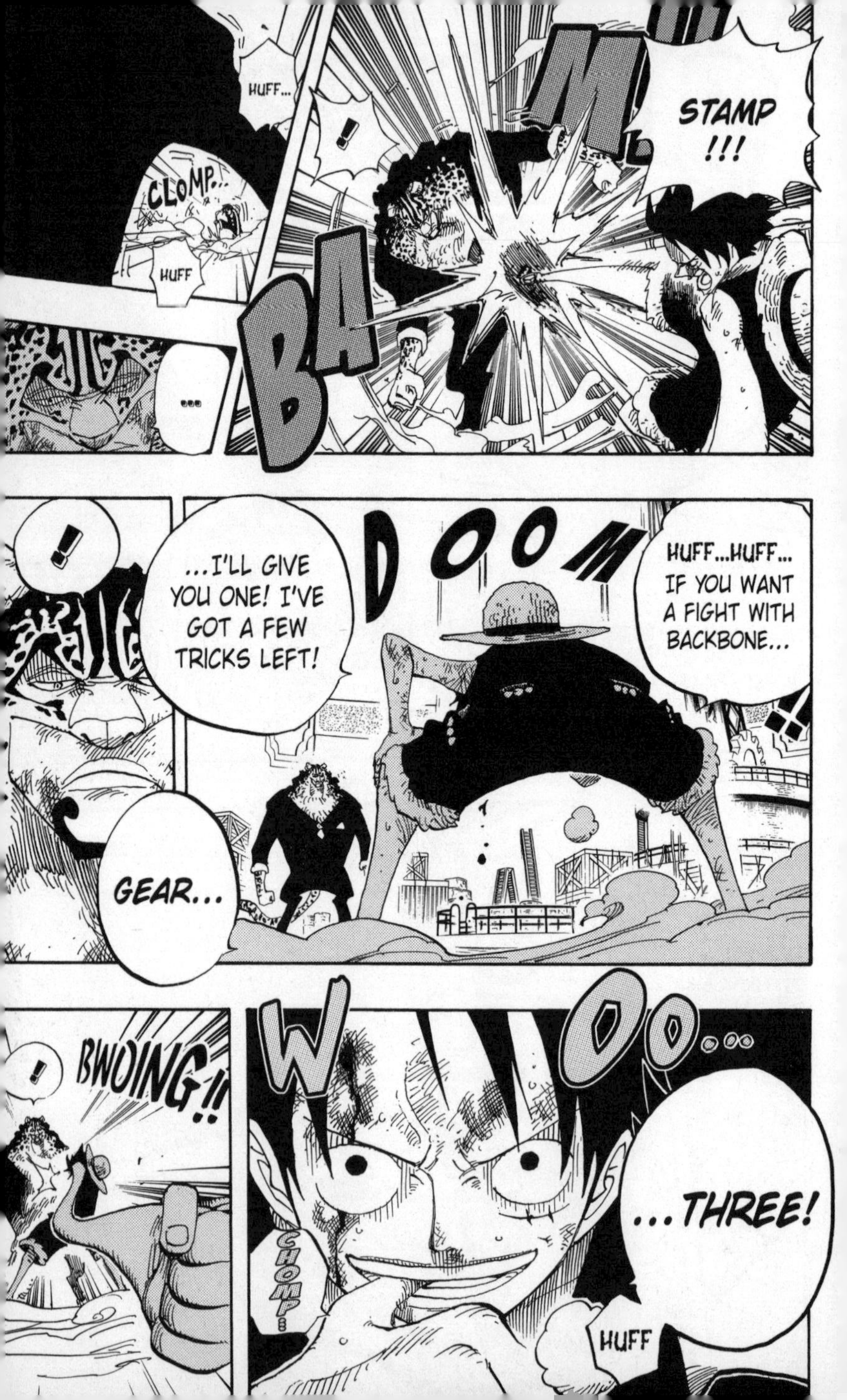
STAMP !!!
BAM
!
HUFF...
CLOMP...
HUFF
...
HUFF...HUFF... IF YOU WANT A FIGHT WITH BACKBONE...
DOOM
...I'LL GIVE YOU ONE! I'VE GOT A FEW TRICKS LEFT!
!
GEAR...
WOO...
...THREE!
CHOMP!!
HUFF
BWOING!!
!

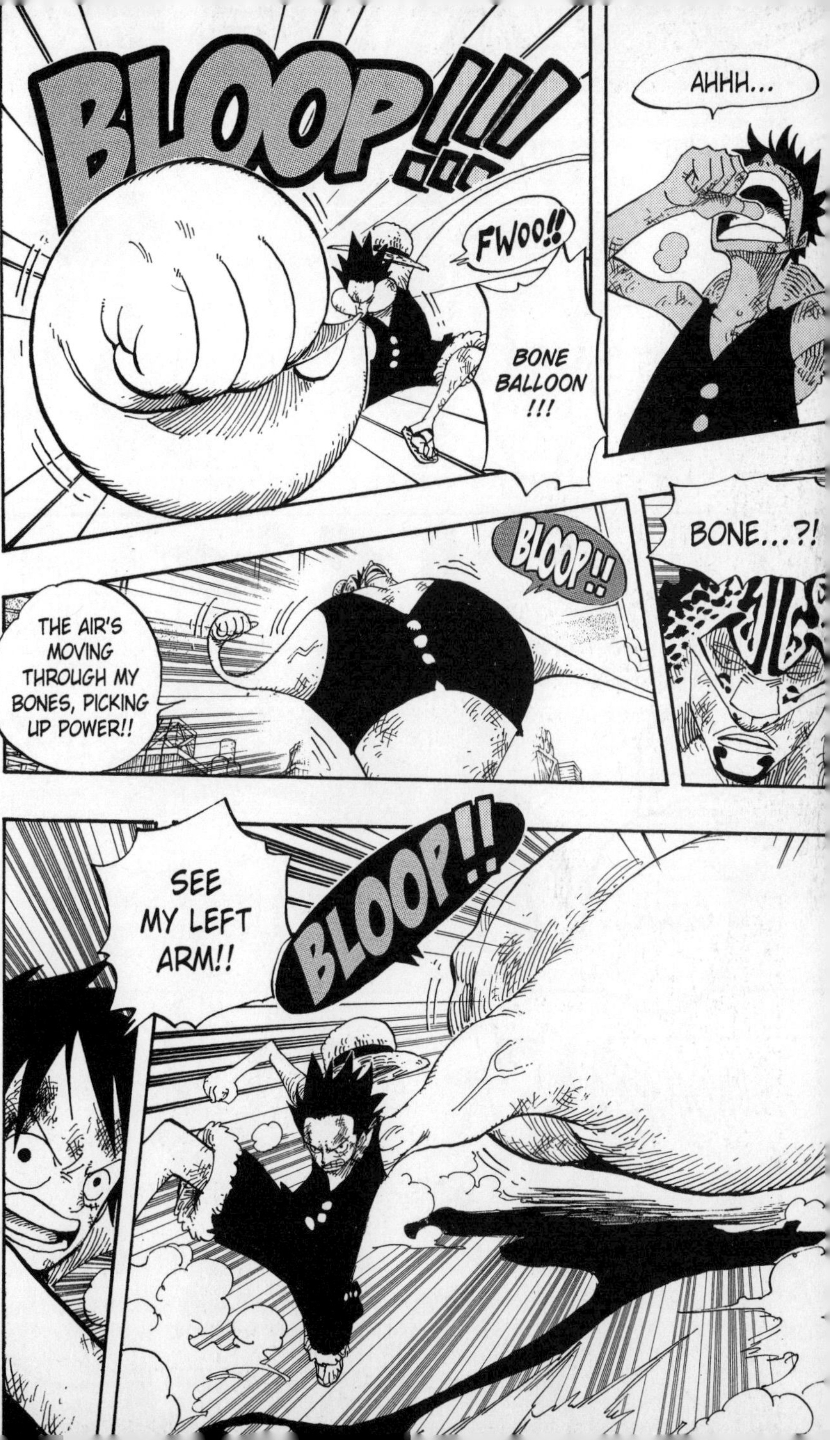
AHHH...
BLOOP!!!
FWOO!!
BONE BALLOON !!!
BONE...?!
BLOOP!!
THE AIR'S MOVING THROUGH MY BONES, PICKING UP POWER!!
BLOOP!!
SEE MY LEFT ARM!!

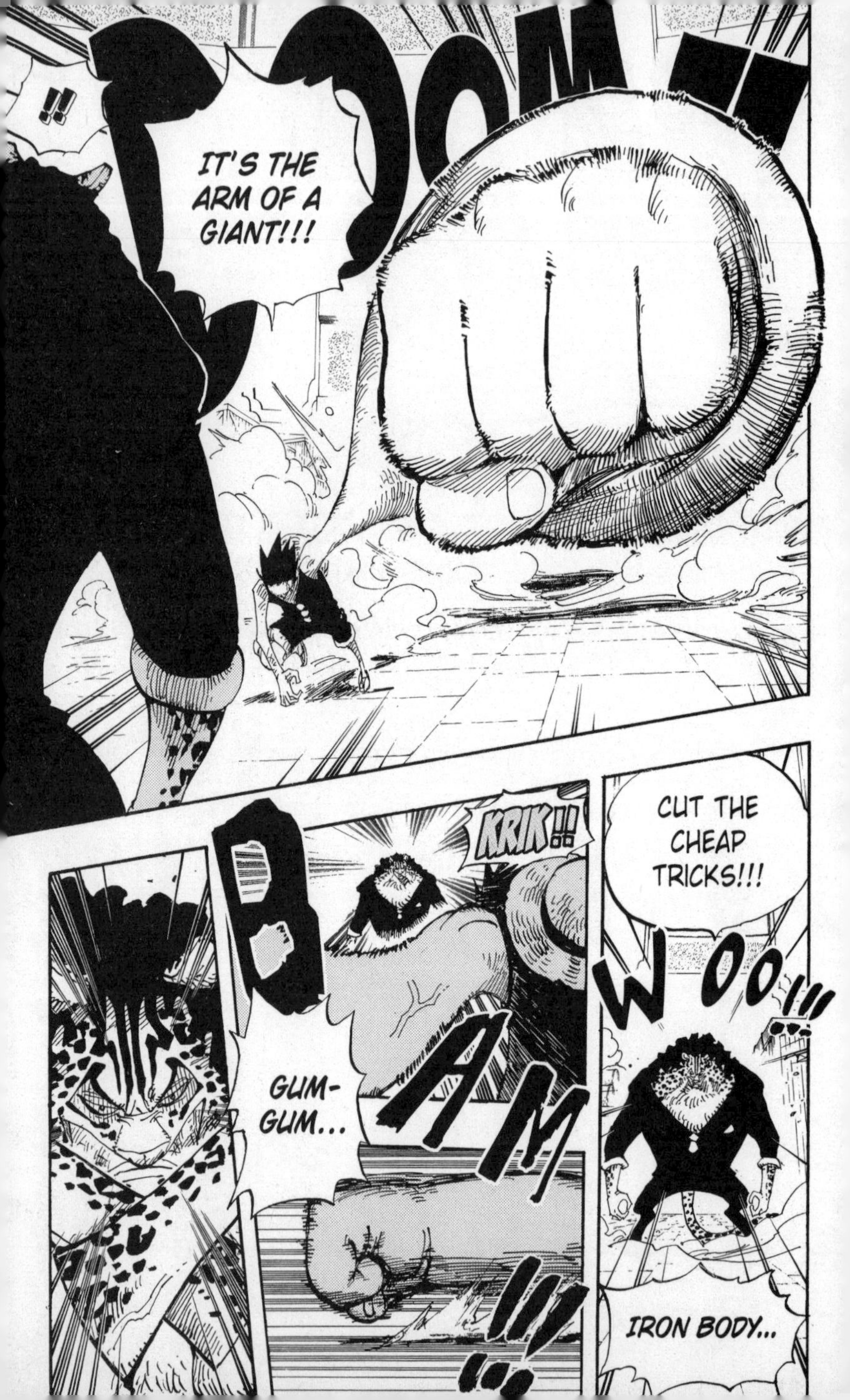
!!
IT'S THE ARM OF A GIANT!!!
CUT THE CHEAP TRICKS!!!
IRON BODY...
KRIK!!
GUM-GUM...

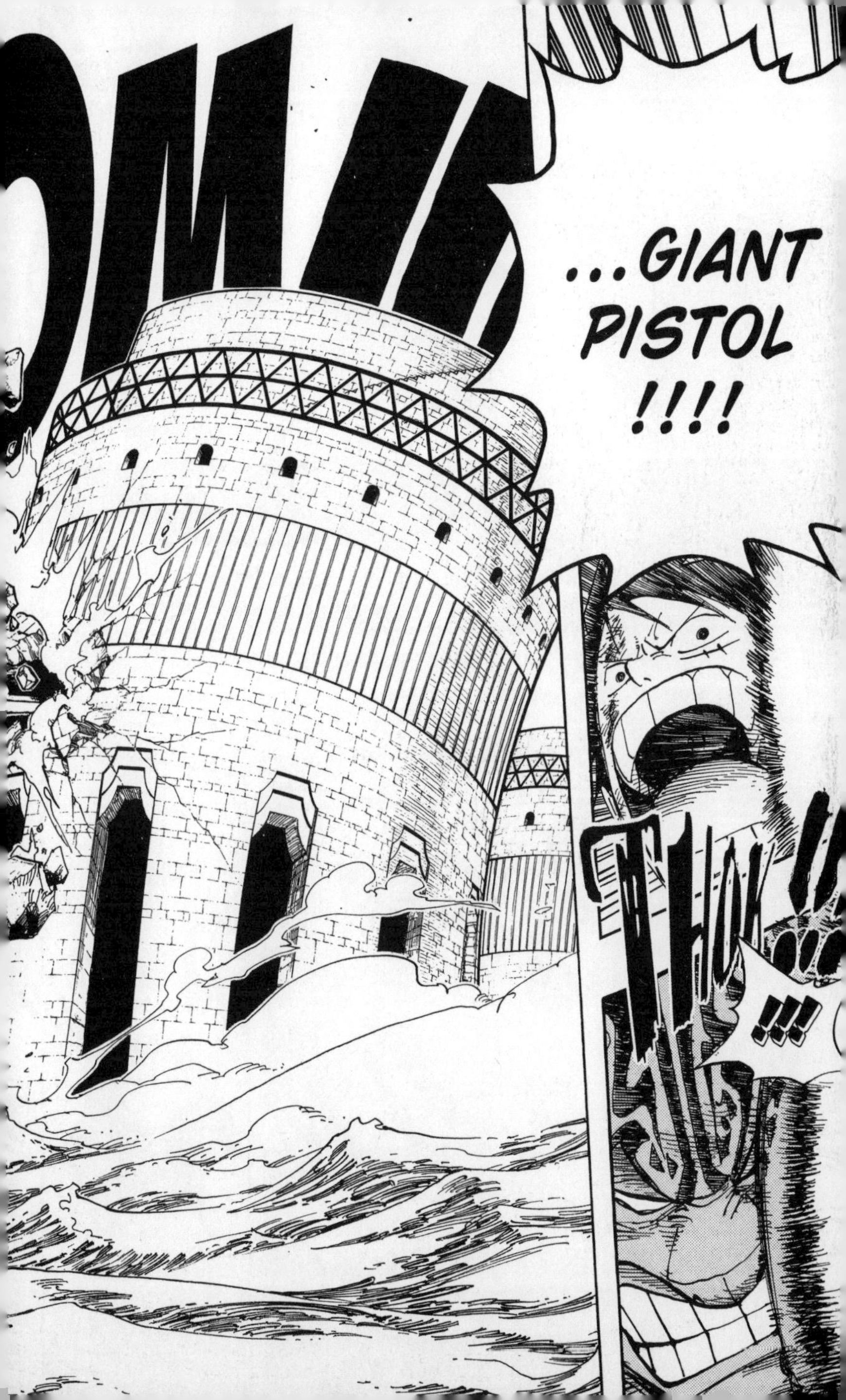
...GIANT PISTOL !!!!
THOK!!

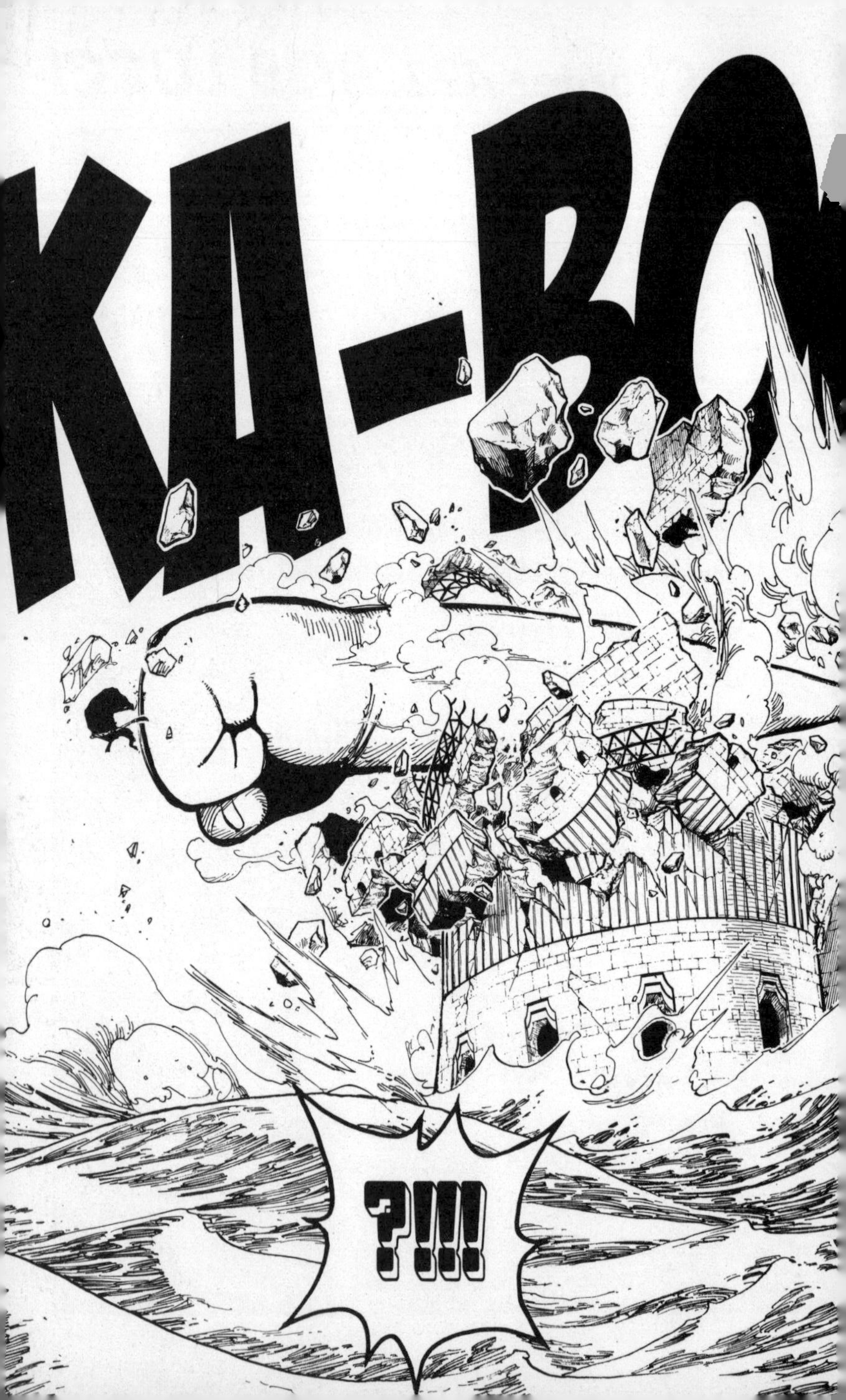
KA-BO
?!!!

Chapter 422: ROB LUCCI

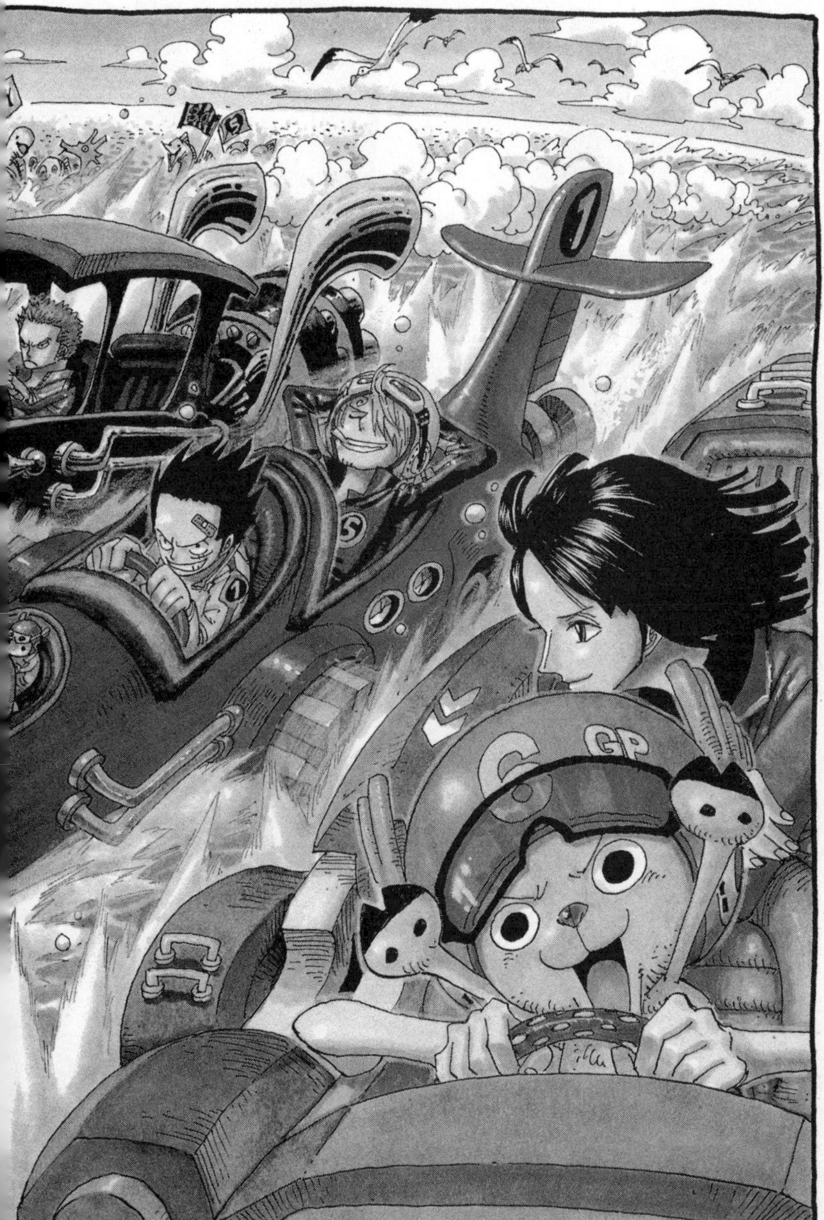

GP

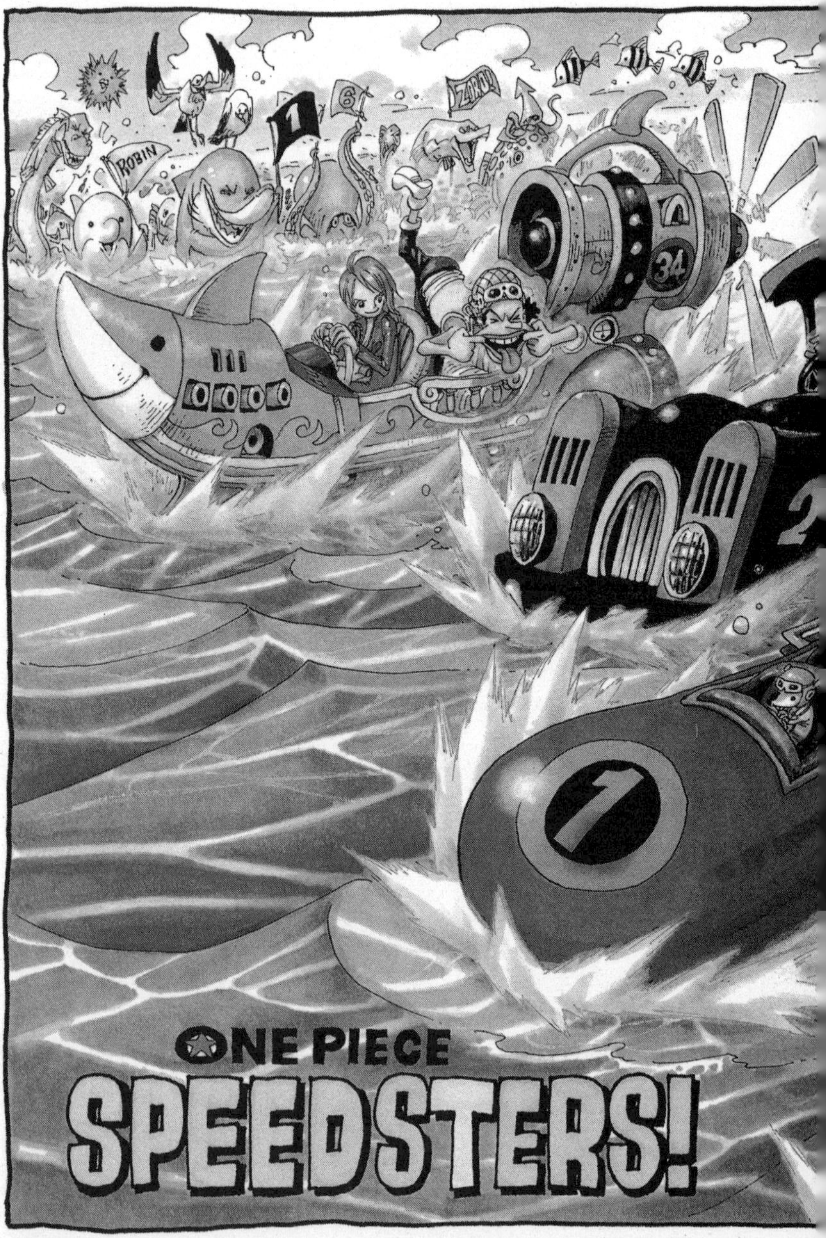
ROBIN
ONE PIECE
SPEEDSTERS!

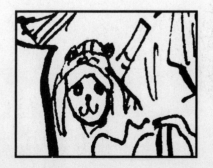

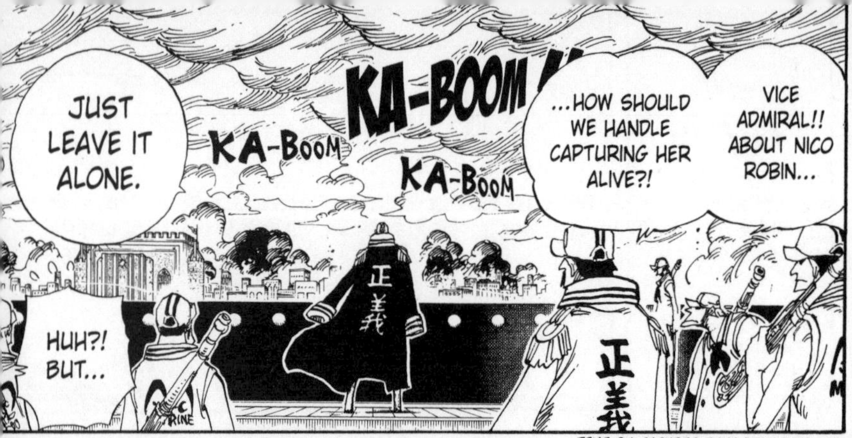
VICE ADMIRAL!! ABOUT NICO ROBIN...
...HOW SHOULD WE HANDLE CAPTURING HER ALIVE?!
KA-BOOM!!
KA-BOOM
KA-BOOM
JUST LEAVE IT ALONE.
HUH?! BUT...

TEXT ON JACKETS SAYS "JUSTICE"--ED.

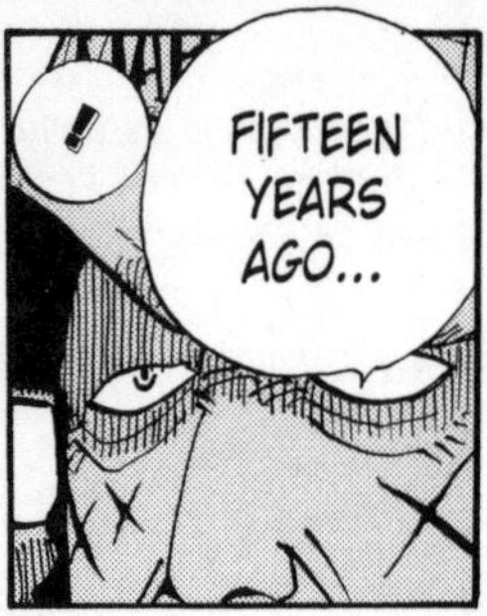
!
FIFTEEN YEARS AGO...

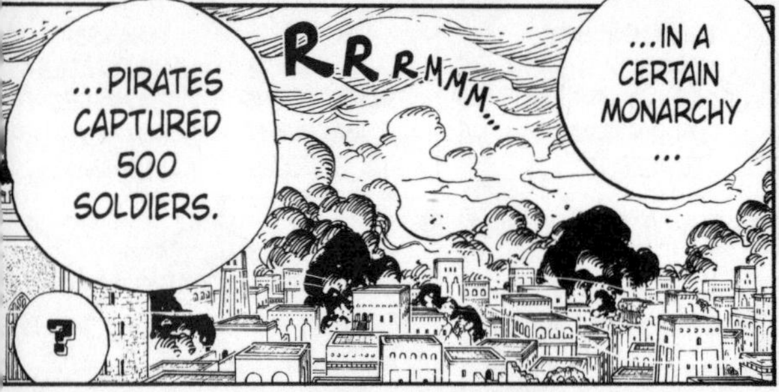
...IN A CERTAIN MONARCHY ...
RRRMMMM...
...PIRATES CAPTURED 500 SOLDIERS.
?

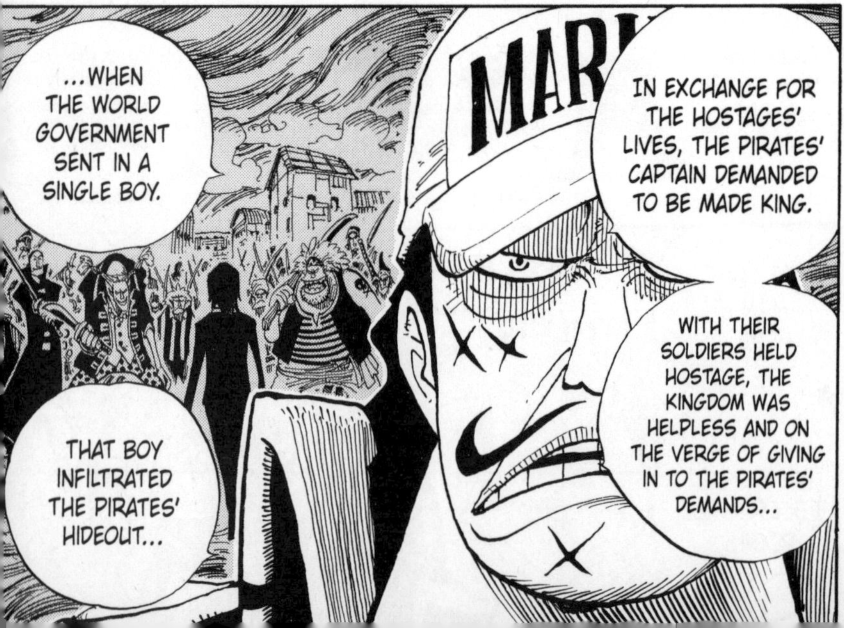
IN EXCHANGE FOR THE HOSTAGES' LIVES, THE PIRATES' CAPTAIN DEMANDED TO BE MADE KING.
WITH THEIR SOLDIERS HELD HOSTAGE, THE KINGDOM WAS HELPLESS AND ON THE VERGE OF GIVING IN TO THE PIRATES' DEMANDS...
...WHEN THE WORLD GOVERNMENT SENT IN A SINGLE BOY.
THAT BOY INFILTRATED THE PIRATES' HIDEOUT...

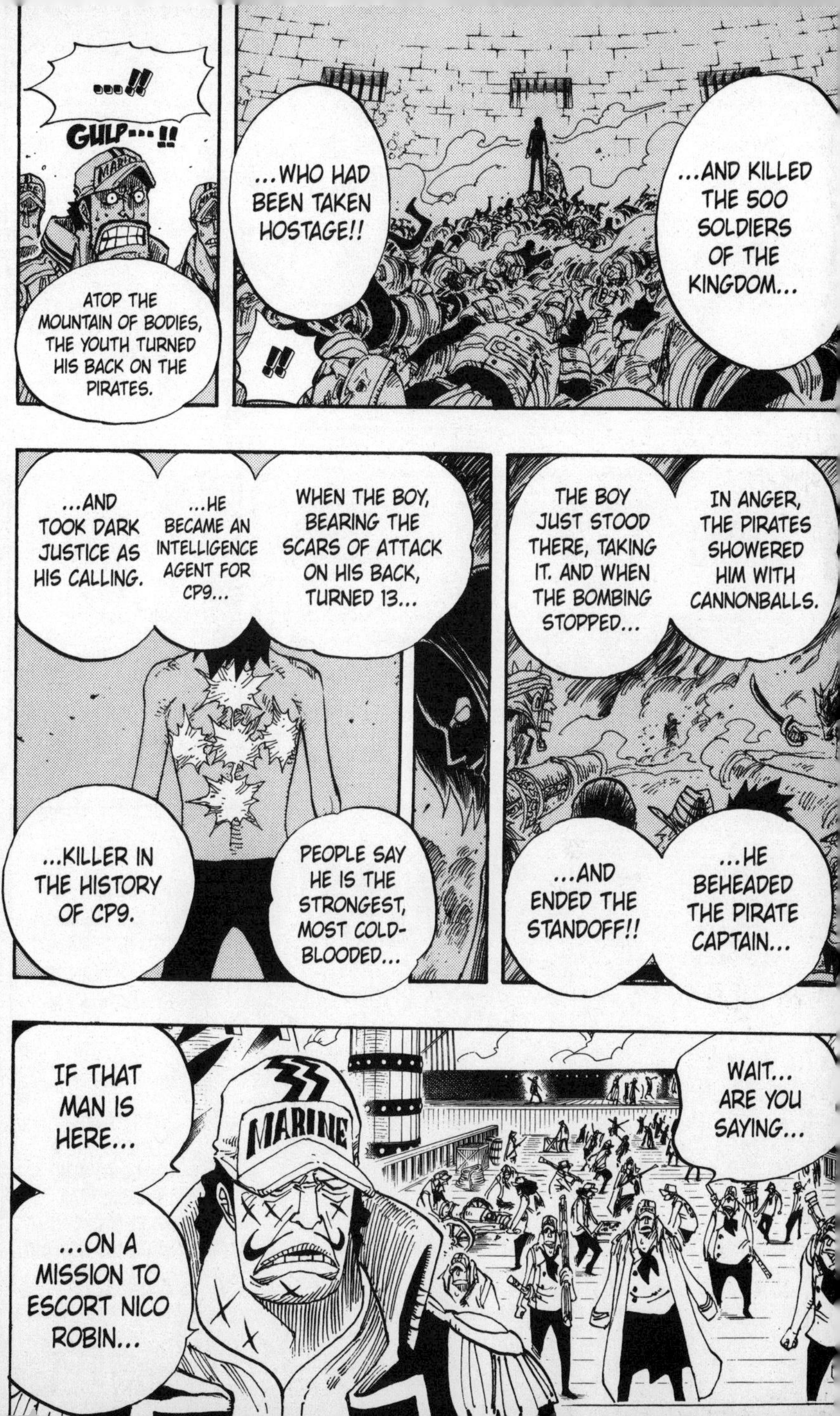
...AND KILLED THE 500 SOLDIERS OF THE KINGDOM...
...WHO HAD BEEN TAKEN HOSTAGE!!
!!
...!!
GULP...!!
ATOP THE MOUNTAIN OF BODIES, THE YOUTH TURNED HIS BACK ON THE PIRATES.
IN ANGER, THE PIRATES SHOWERED HIM WITH CANNONBALLS.
THE BOY JUST STOOD THERE, TAKING IT. AND WHEN THE BOMBING STOPPED...
...HE BEHEADED THE PIRATE CAPTAIN...
...AND ENDED THE STANDOFF!!
WHEN THE BOY, BEARING THE SCARS OF ATTACK ON HIS BACK, TURNED 13...
...HE BECAME AN INTELLIGENCE AGENT FOR CP9...
...AND TOOK DARK JUSTICE AS HIS CALLING.
PEOPLE SAY HE IS THE STRONGEST, MOST COLD-BLOODED...
...KILLER IN THE HISTORY OF CP9.
MARINE
WAIT... ARE YOU SAYING...
IF THAT MAN IS HERE...
...ON A MISSION TO ESCORT NICO ROBIN...

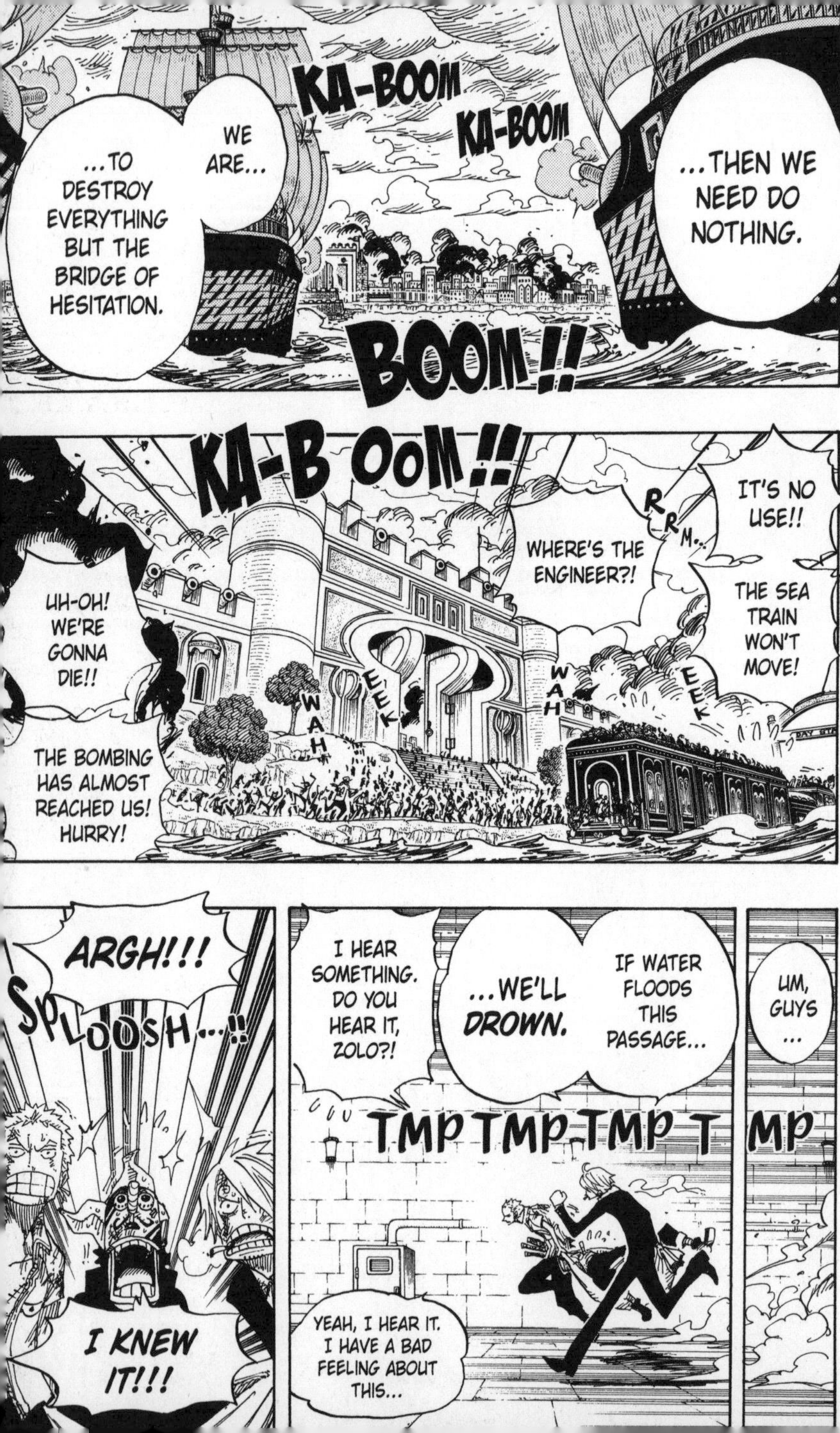
...THEN WE NEED DO NOTHING.
KA-BOOM
KA-BOOM
WE ARE...
...TO DESTROY EVERYTHING BUT THE BRIDGE OF HESITATION.
BOOM!!
KA-BOOM!!
IT'S NO USE!!
THE SEA TRAIN WON'T MOVE!
RRRM..
WHERE'S THE ENGINEER?!
EEEK
WAH
EEEK
WAH
UH-OH! WE'RE GONNA DIE!!
THE BOMBING HAS ALMOST REACHED US! HURRY!
UM, GUYS ...
IF WATER FLOODS THIS PASSAGE...
...WE'LL DROWN.
I HEAR SOMETHING. DO YOU HEAR IT, ZOLO?!
TMP TMP TMP TMP
YEAH, I HEAR IT. I HAVE A BAD FEELING ABOUT THIS...
ARGH!!!
SPLOOSH...!!
I KNEW IT!!!

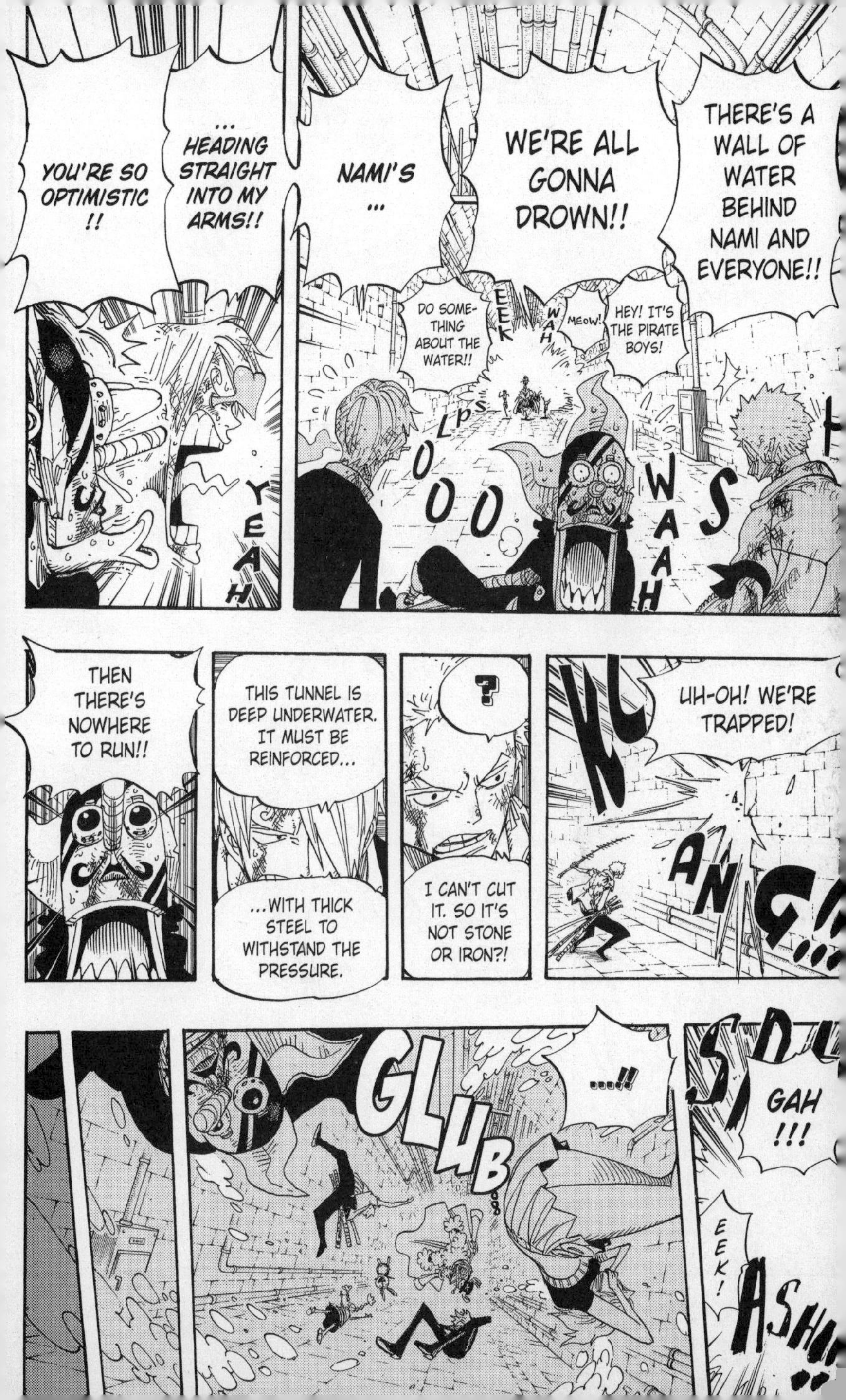
THERE'S A WALL OF WATER BEHIND NAMI AND EVERYONE!!
WE'RE ALL GONNA DROWN!!
NAMI'S ...
HEY! IT'S THE PIRATE BOYS!
MEOW!
WAH
EEK
DO SOMETHING ABOUT THE WATER!!
WAAAH
... HEADING STRAIGHT INTO MY ARMS!!
YOU'RE SO OPTIMISTIC !!
YEAH
UH-OH! WE'RE TRAPPED!
?
I CAN'T CUT IT. SO IT'S NOT STONE OR IRON?!
THIS TUNNEL IS DEEP UNDERWATER. IT MUST BE REINFORCED...
...WITH THICK STEEL TO WITHSTAND THE PRESSURE.
THEN THERE'S NOWHERE TO RUN!!
GAH !!!
EEK!
...!!
GLUB

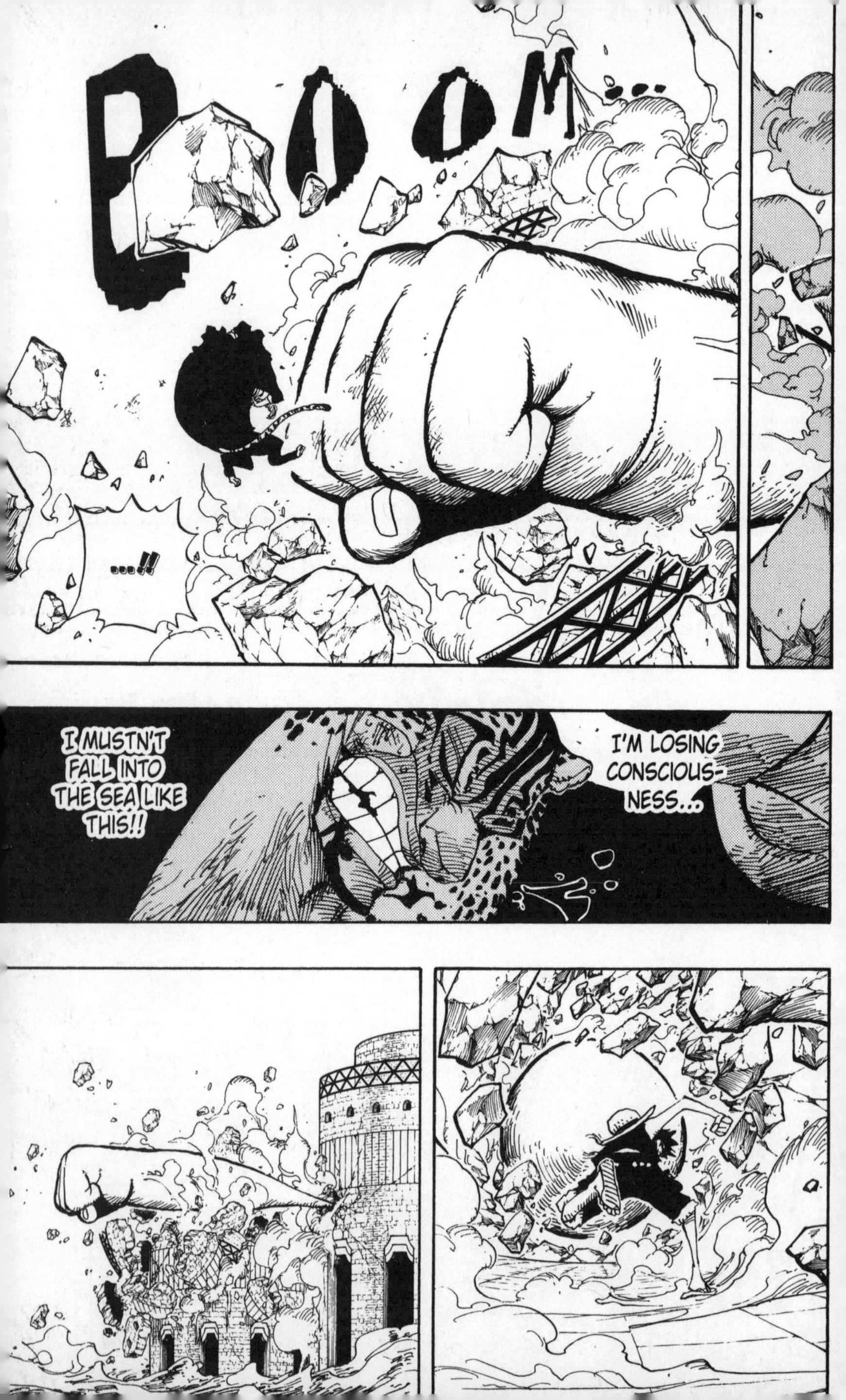
BOOM...
...!!
I'M LOSING CONSCIOUS-NESS...
I MUSTN'T FALL INTO THE SEA LIKE THIS!!

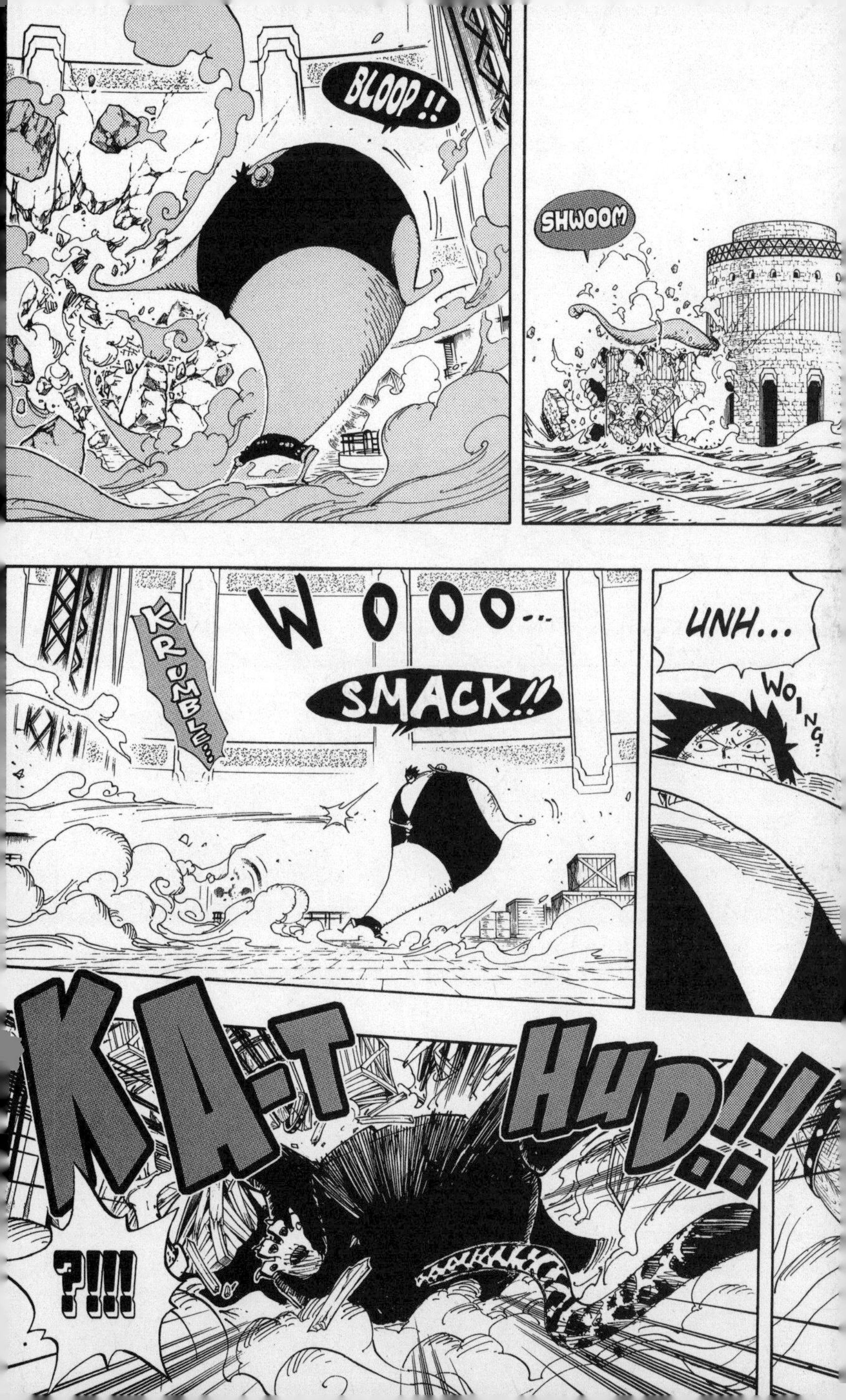
SHWOOM
BLOOP!!
UNH...
WOING!!
WOOO...
SMACK!!
KRUMBLE...
KA-THUD!!
?!!!

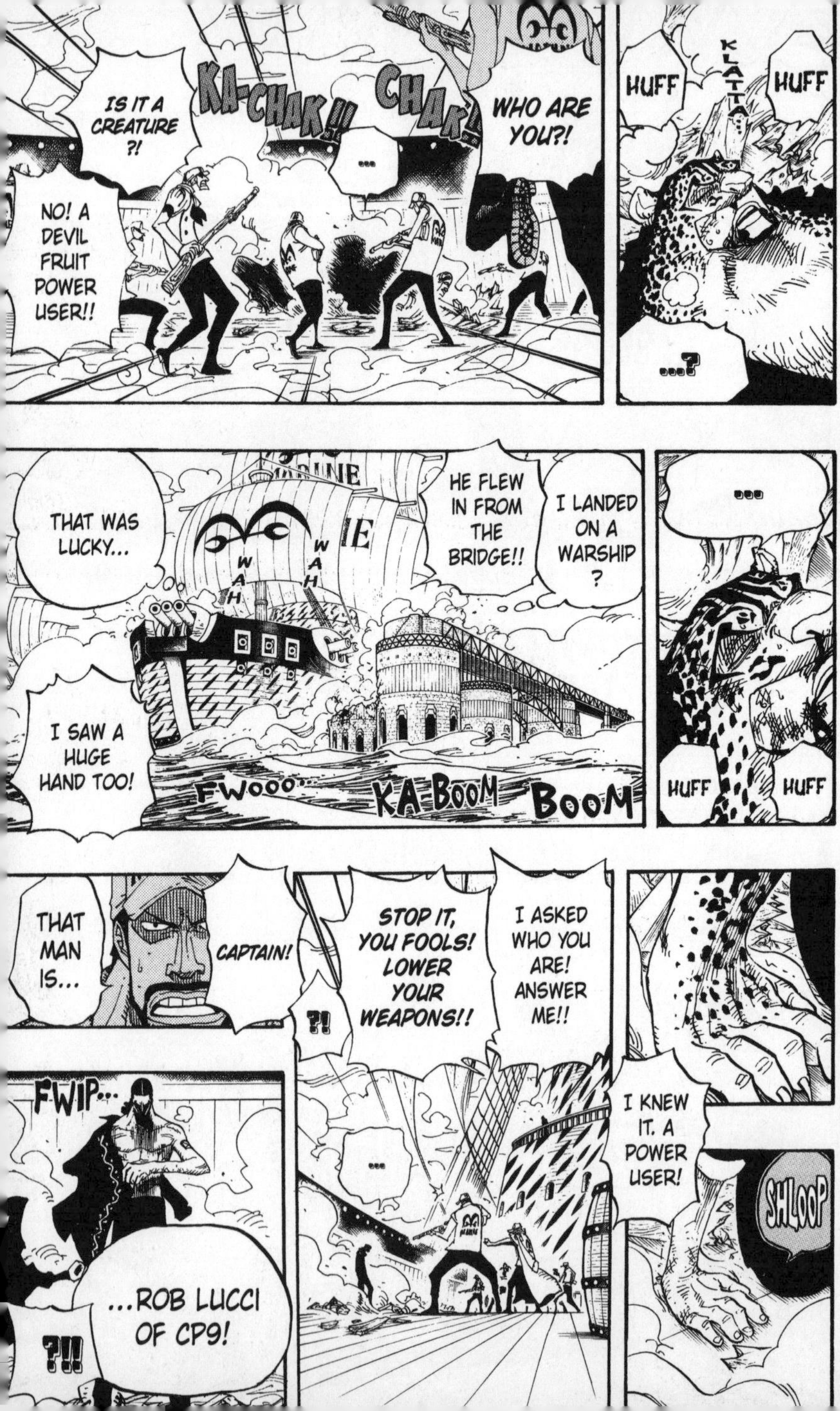
HUFF
KLATTA
HUFF
...?
WHO ARE YOU?!
CHAK!!
...
KA-CHAK!!
IS IT A CREATURE ?!
NO! A DEVIL FRUIT POWER USER!!
...
HUFF
HUFF
I LANDED ON A WARSHIP ?
HE FLEW IN FROM THE BRIDGE!!
WAH
WAH
THAT WAS LUCKY...
I SAW A HUGE HAND TOO!
BOOM
KA-BOOM
FWOOO...
I KNEW IT. A POWER USER!
SHLOOP
I ASKED WHO YOU ARE! ANSWER ME!!
STOP IT, YOU FOOLS! LOWER YOUR WEAPONS!!
?!
...
CAPTAIN!
THAT MAN IS...
FWIP...
...ROB LUCCI OF CP9!
?!!

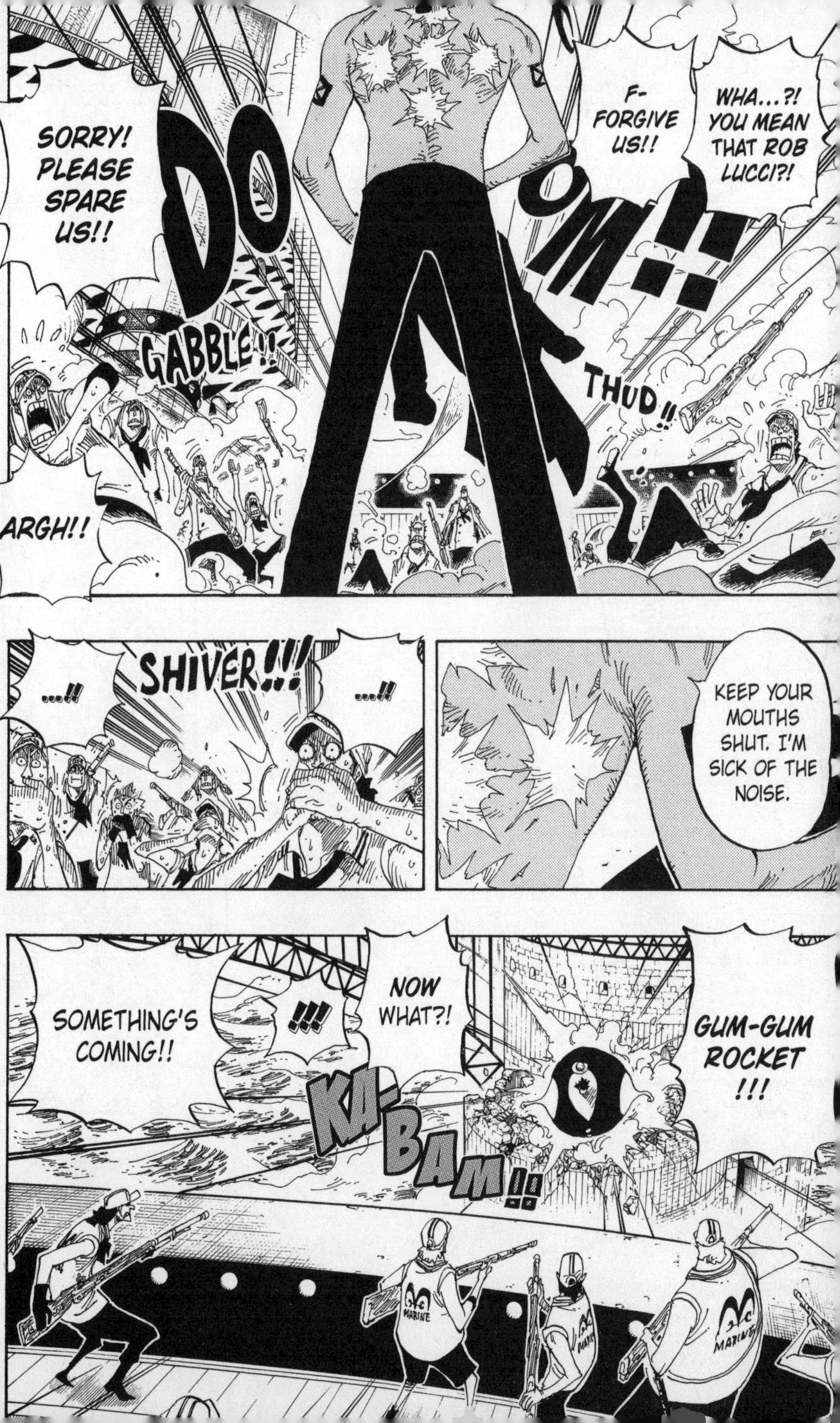
WHA...?! YOU MEAN THAT ROB LUCCI?!
F-FORGIVE US!!
DOOM!!
SORRY! PLEASE SPARE US!!
THUD!!
GABBLE!!
ARGH!!
KEEP YOUR MOUTHS SHUT. I'M SICK OF THE NOISE.
...!!
SHIVER!!!
...!!
GUM-GUM ROCKET!!!
NOW WHAT?!
!!!
SOMETHING'S COMING!!
KA-BAM!!

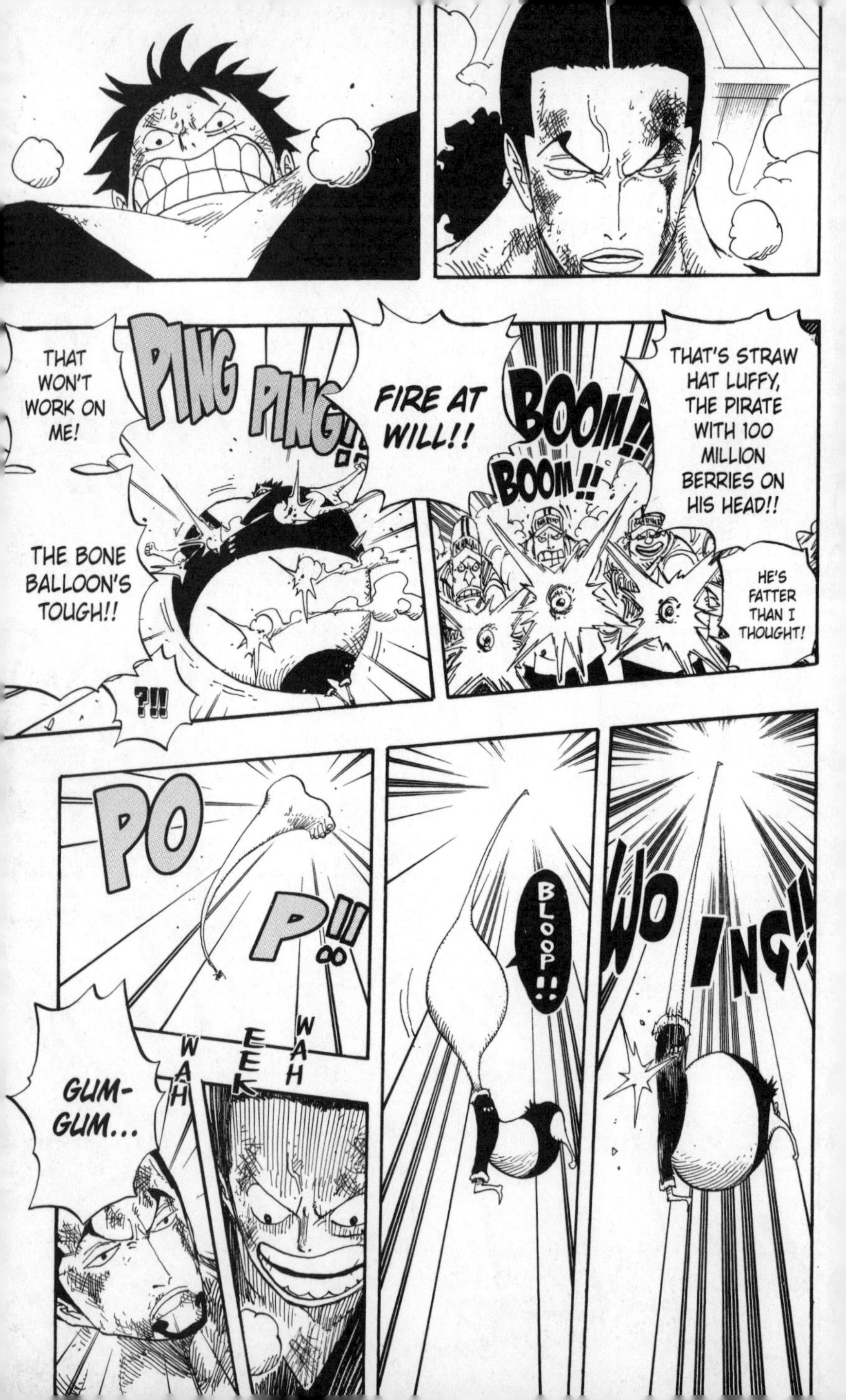
FIRE AT WILL!!
THAT'S STRAW HAT LUFFY, THE PIRATE WITH 100 MILLION BERRIES ON HIS HEAD!!
BOOM!!
BOOM!!
HE'S FATTER THAN I THOUGHT!
PING PING!!
THAT WON'T WORK ON ME!
THE BONE BALLOON'S TOUGH!!
?!!
WO ING!!
BLOOP!!
POP!!
WAH
EEK
WAH
GUM-GUM...

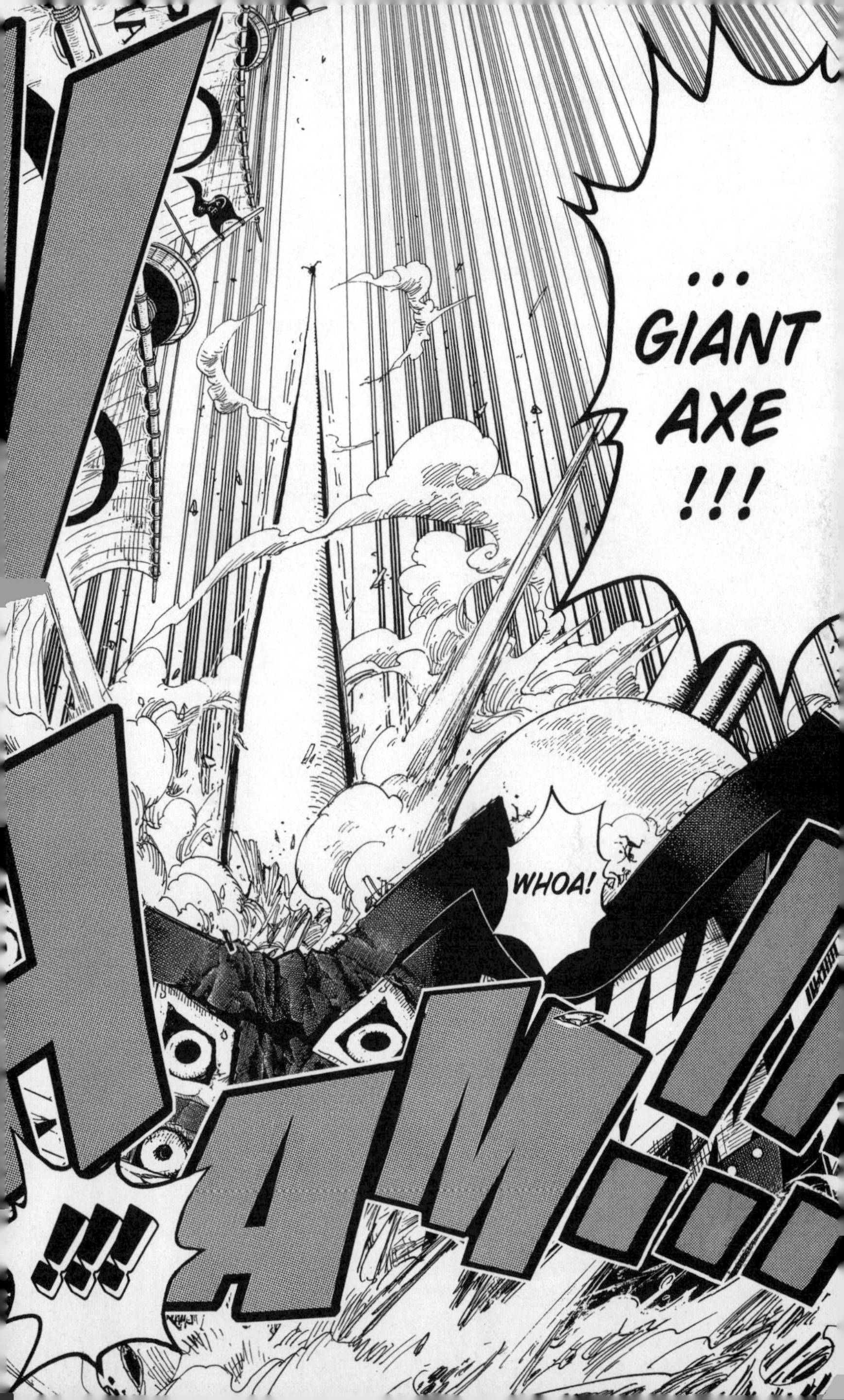
... GIANT AXE !!!
WHOA!

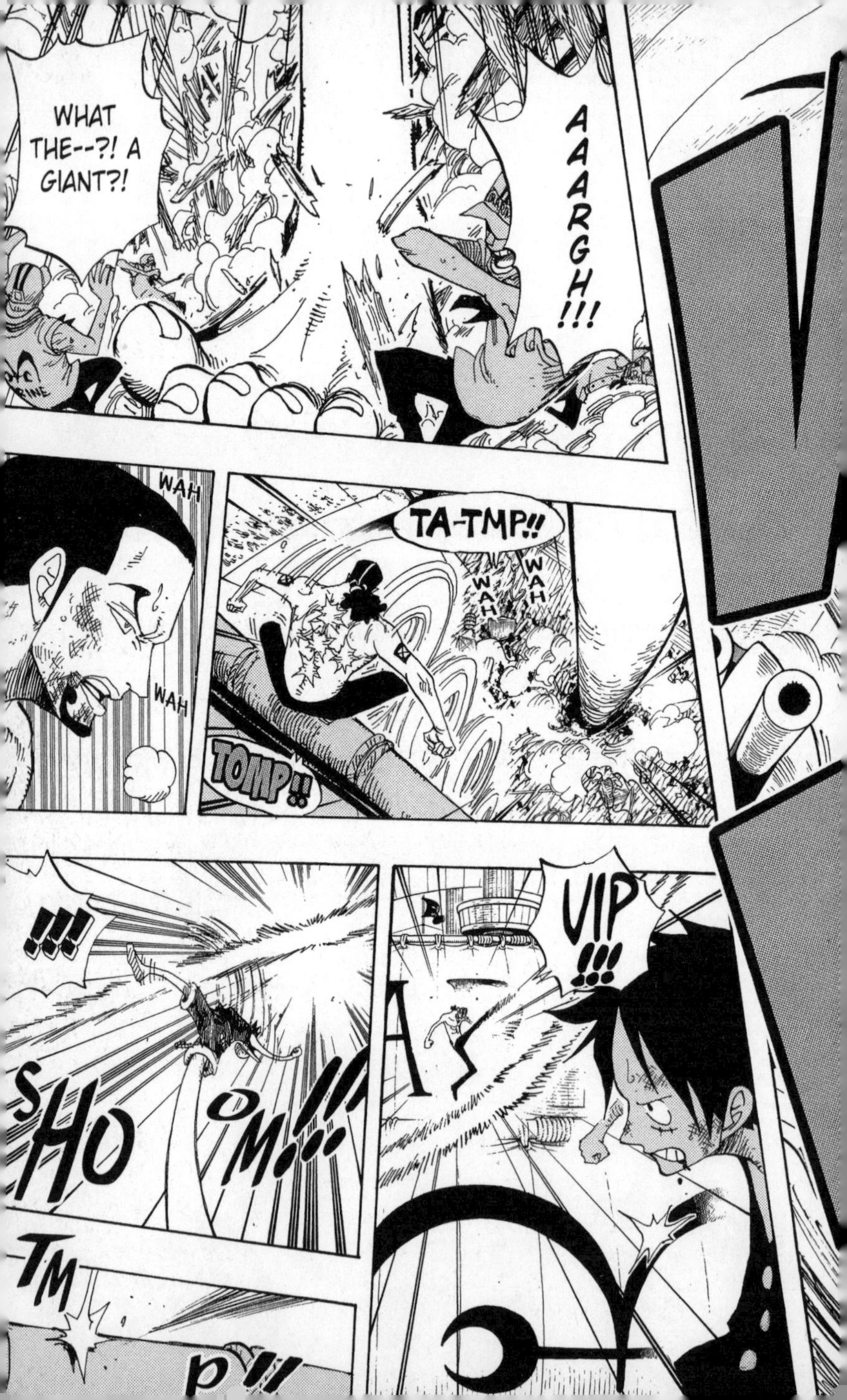
AAAARGH!!!
WHAT THE--?! A GIANT?!
TA-TMP!!
WAH
WAH
TOMP!!
WAH
WAH
VIP!!!
SHOOM!!!
!!!
TMP!!

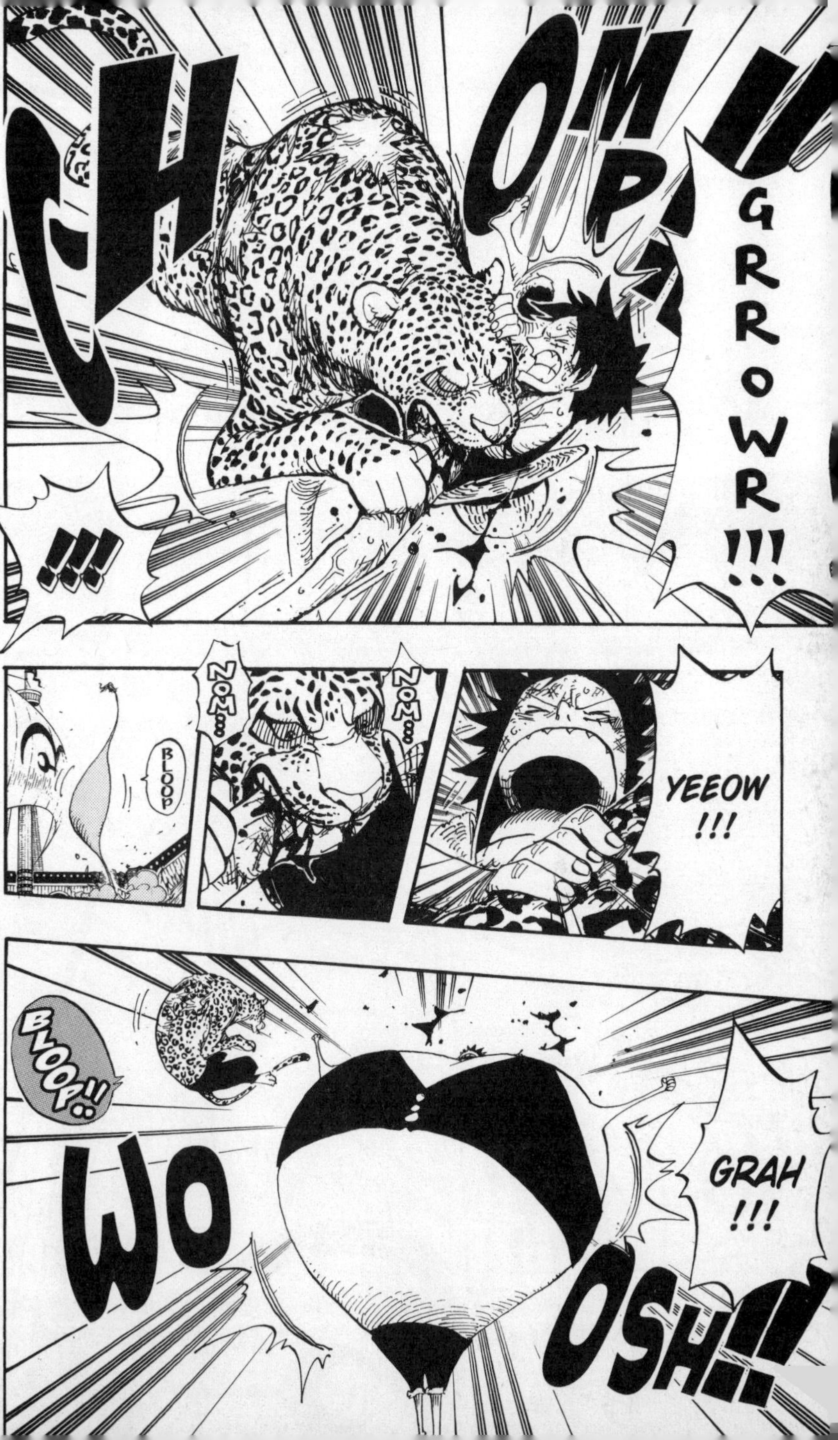

GRRROWR!!!
CHOMP
!!!
YEEOW !!!
NOM!!
NOM!!
BLOOP
GRAH !!!
WOOSH!!
BLOOP!!

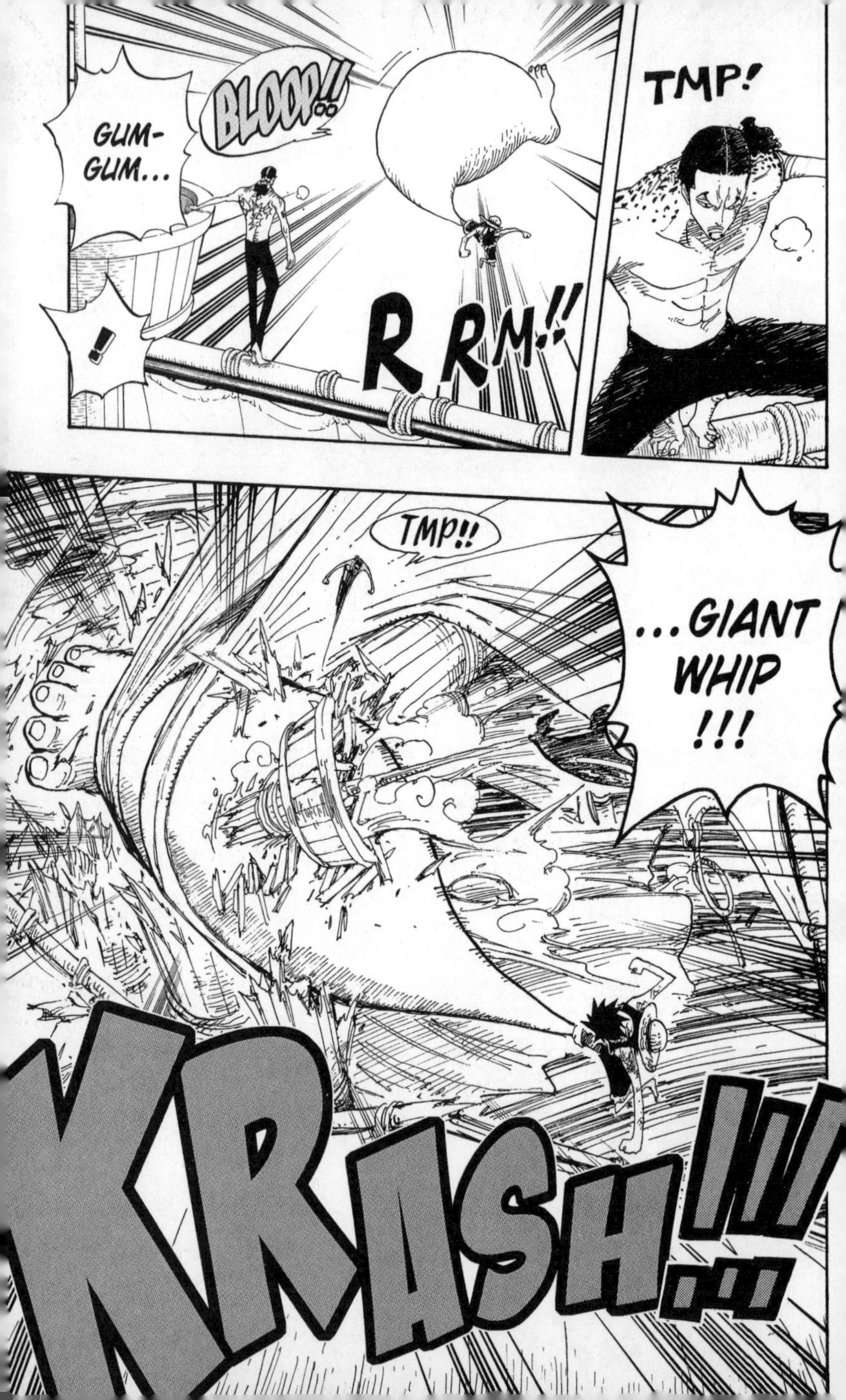
TMP!
BLOOP!!
GUM-GUM...
RRM!!
!
...GIANT WHIP!!!
TMP!!
KRASH!!!

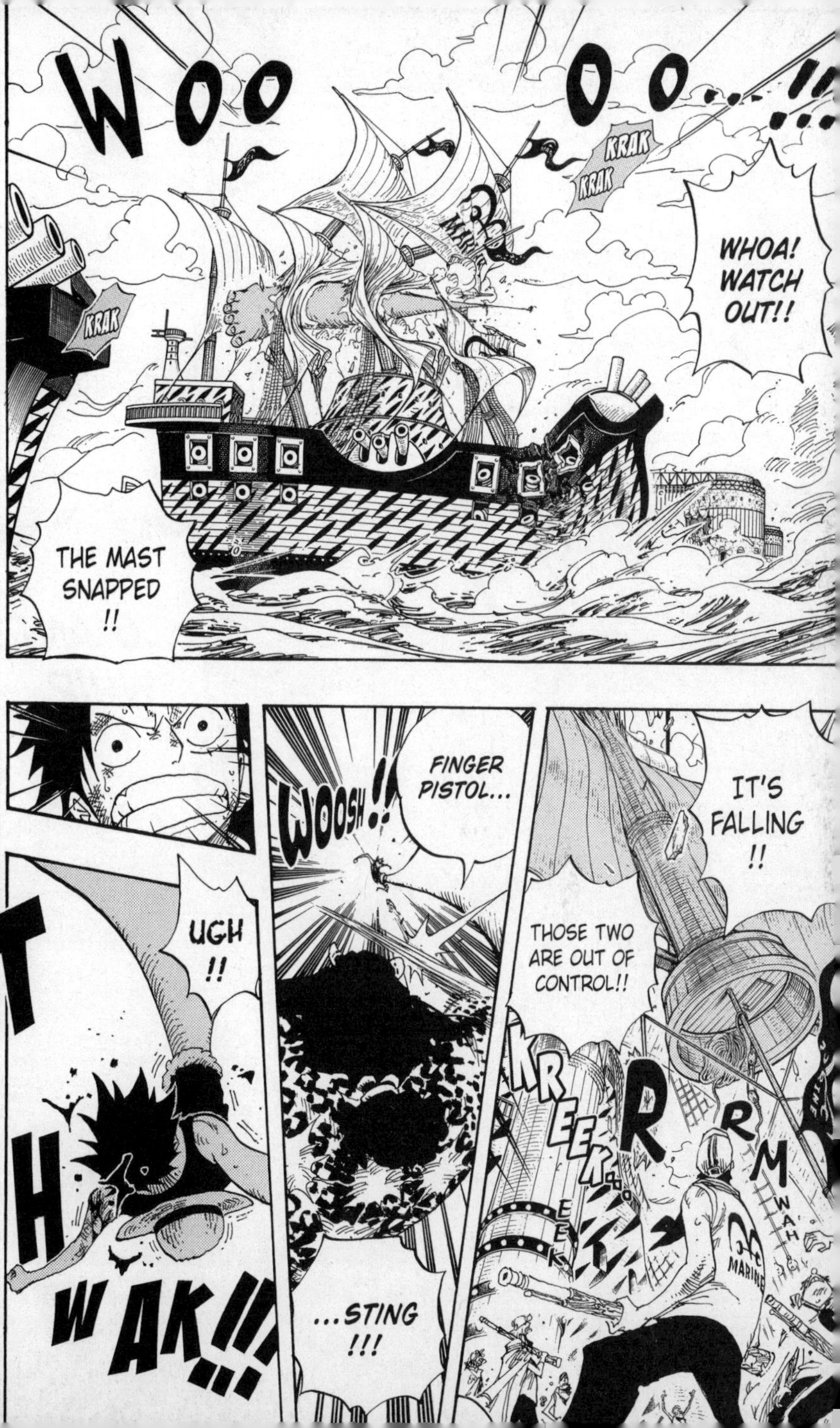
WOO OO...!!
KRAK
KRAK
KRAK
WHOA! WATCH OUT!!
THE MAST SNAPPED !!
IT'S FALLING !!
THOSE TWO ARE OUT OF CONTROL!!
KREEK...
EEEK
RRRM
WAH
MARINE
FINGER PISTOL...
WOOSH!!
...STING !!!
UGH !!
THWAK!!!

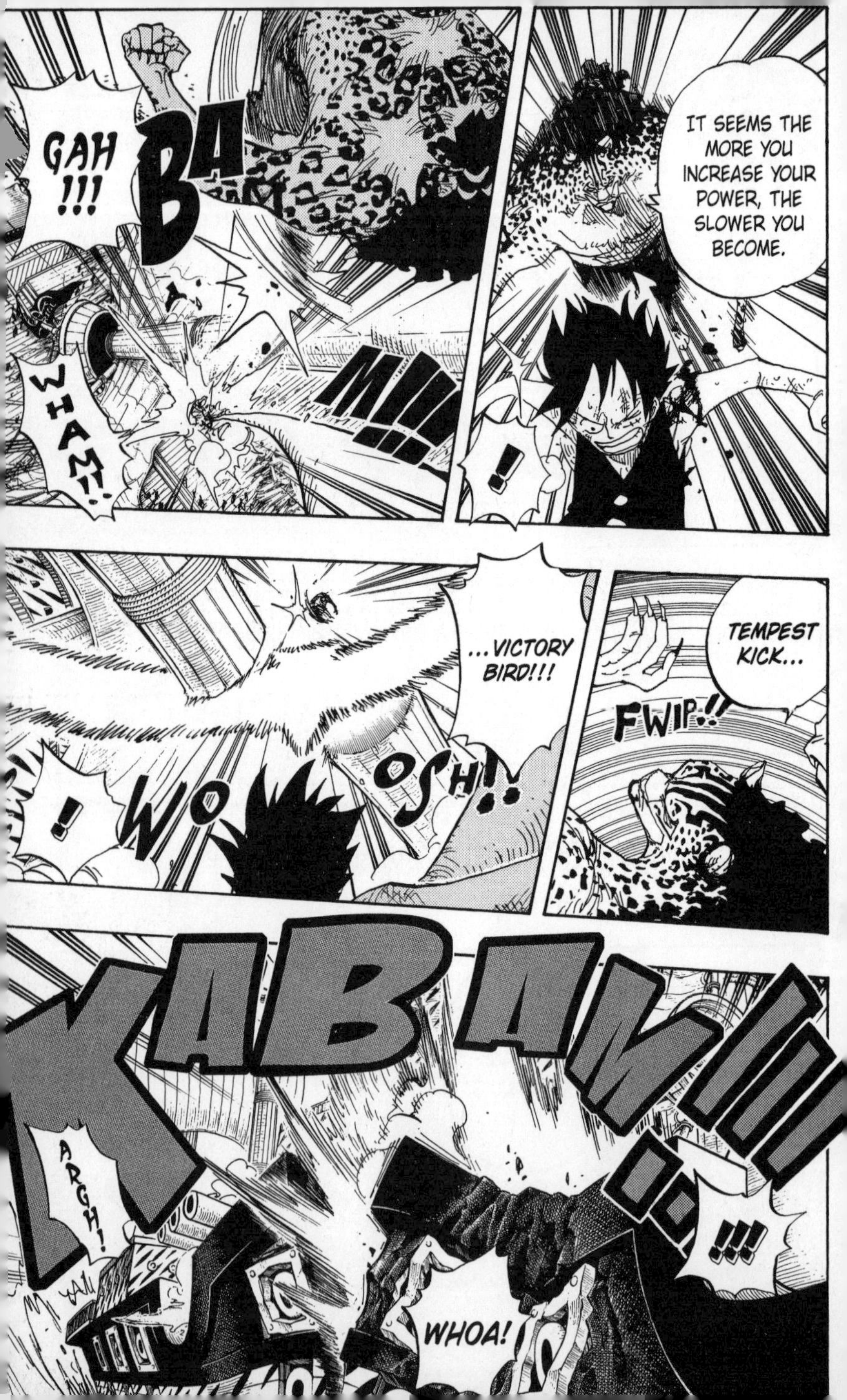
IT SEEMS THE MORE YOU INCREASE YOUR POWER, THE SLOWER YOU BECOME.
!
GAH !!!
BAM!!
WHAM!!
TEMPEST KICK...
FWIP!!
...VICTORY BIRD!!!
WOOSH!!
!
KABAM!!
!!!
ARGH!
WHOA!

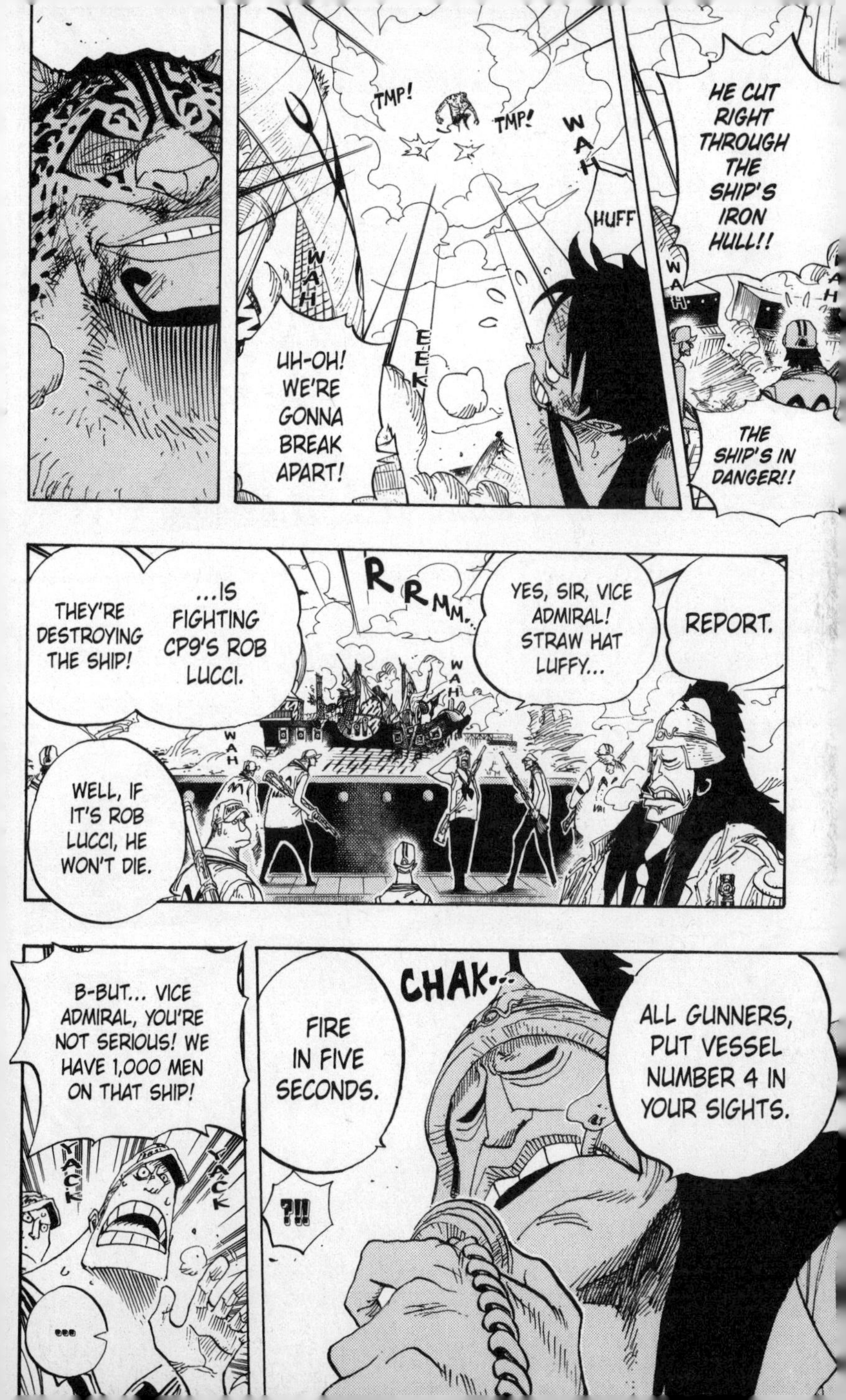
HE CUT RIGHT THROUGH THE SHIP'S IRON HULL!!
WAH
THE SHIP'S IN DANGER!!
TMP!
TMP!
WAH
HUFF
WAH
EEK
UH-OH! WE'RE GONNA BREAK APART!
REPORT.
YES, SIR, VICE ADMIRAL! STRAW HAT LUFFY...
RRMM..
...IS FIGHTING CP9'S ROB LUCCI.
THEY'RE DESTROYING THE SHIP!
WAH
WAH
WELL, IF IT'S ROB LUCCI, HE WON'T DIE.
CHAK...
ALL GUNNERS, PUT VESSEL NUMBER 4 IN YOUR SIGHTS.
FIRE IN FIVE SECONDS.
?!!
B-BUT... VICE ADMIRAL, YOU'RE NOT SERIOUS! WE HAVE 1,000 MEN ON THAT SHIP!
YACK
YACK
...

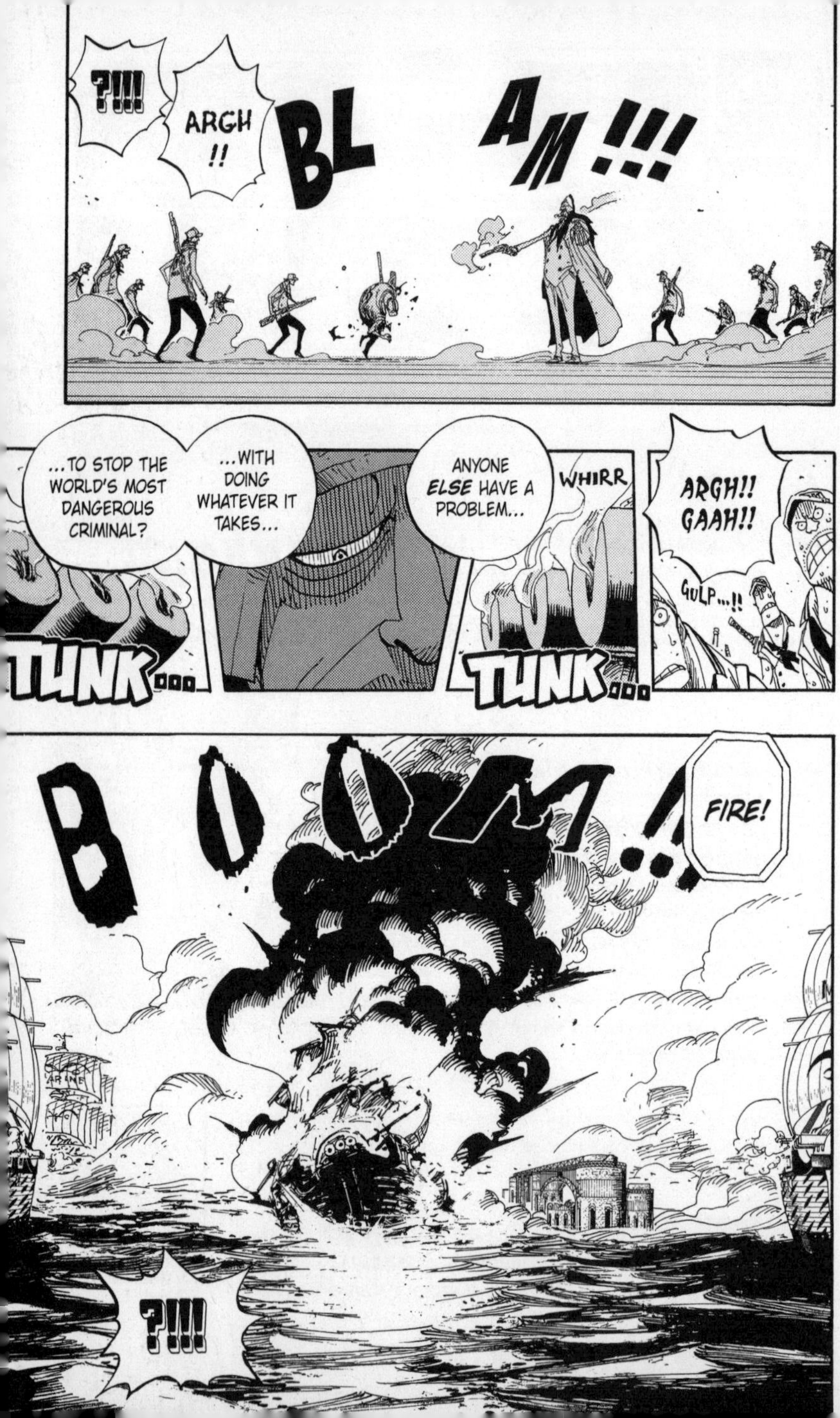
BLAM!!!
ARGH !!
?!!!
ARGH!! GAAH!!
GULP...!!
WHIRR
ANYONE ELSE HAVE A PROBLEM...
TUNK...
...WITH DOING WHATEVER IT TAKES...
...TO STOP THE WORLD'S MOST DANGEROUS CRIMINAL?
TUNK...
FIRE!
BOOM..!!
?!!!

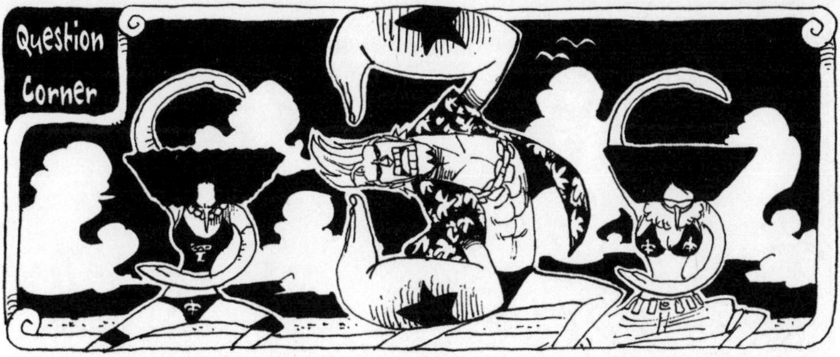
Question Corner

Q: Sensei… do you ever think about wearing women's clothes?

--Wishes to Remain Anonymous

A: No!!!

Q: Oda Sensei, I have a question. In chapter 405: Power, in volume 42, Franky had "BF36" written on his shoulders, when he did his Tracking Franky Destroy Cannon attack. That stands for Battle Franky 36, doesn't it? How about it?

--Sniper Q

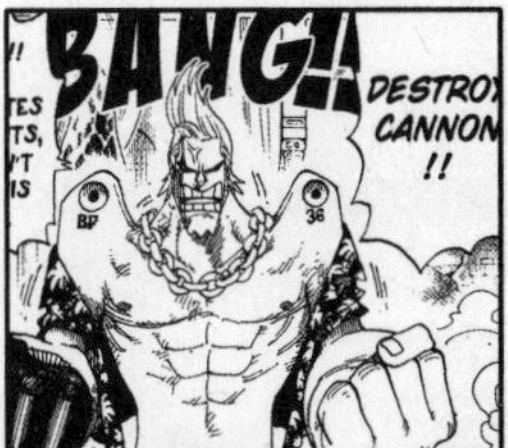
BANG!!
BF
36

A: Yes!! You're right. That's what it stands for. As you can tell from reading Franky's flashbacks, he made warships called Battleship Franky and numbered them up through 35. Later, he got hurt when the ships he had built hurt his loved ones, and so he used the same technological skill to revive himself, carved "BF36" on his body, and stopped making warships. He became a dismantler of ships after that.

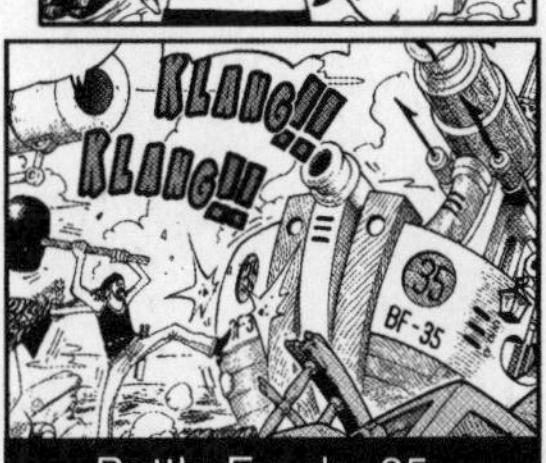
KLANG!!
KLANG!!
35
BF-35
Battle Franky 35

Q: I've been wondering for some time now what kind of person Kumadori's mother was.

--Yasuhiko-kun

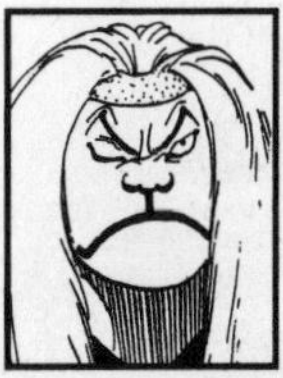

A: 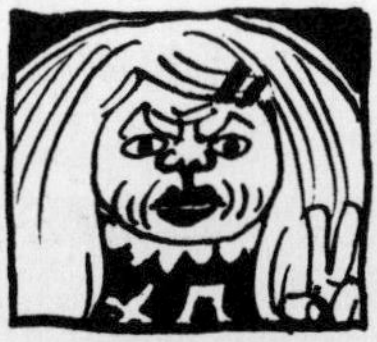

Okay. She's actually still alive.
Occupation: Assassin
Name: Kumadori Yamanbako

Chapter 423:
MERMAID LEGEND

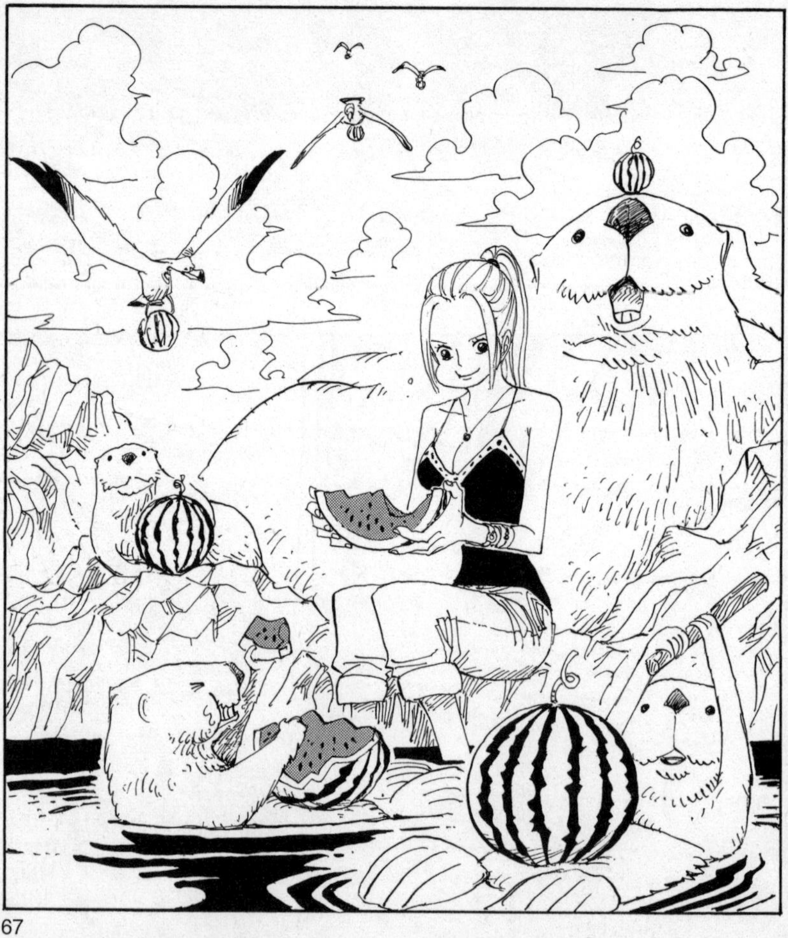

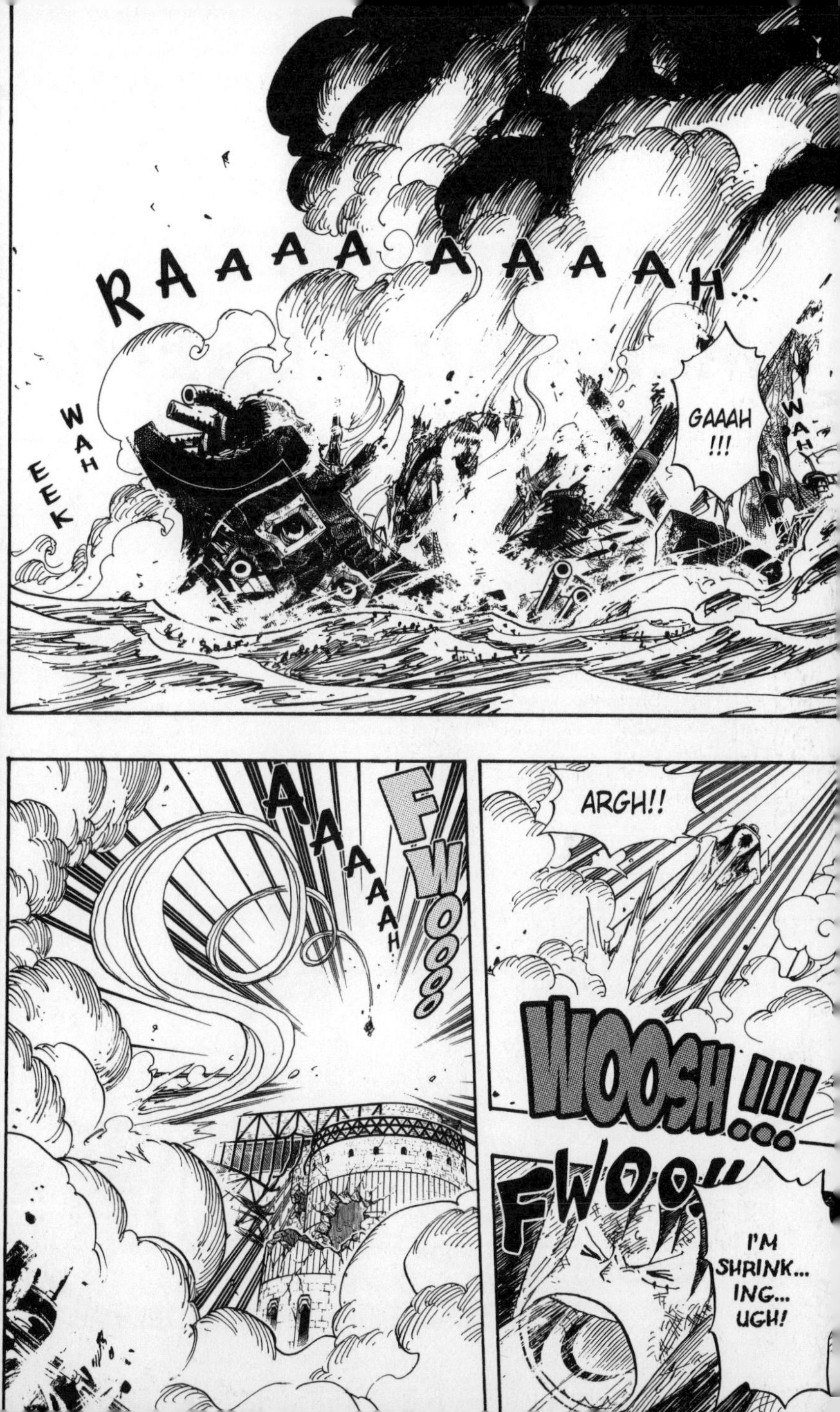
RAAAAAAAAAH...
WAH
GAAAH!!!
WAH
EEK
ARGH!!
WOOSH!!!!...
FWOO..
I'M SHRINK... ING... UGH!
AAAAAAH
FWOOOO

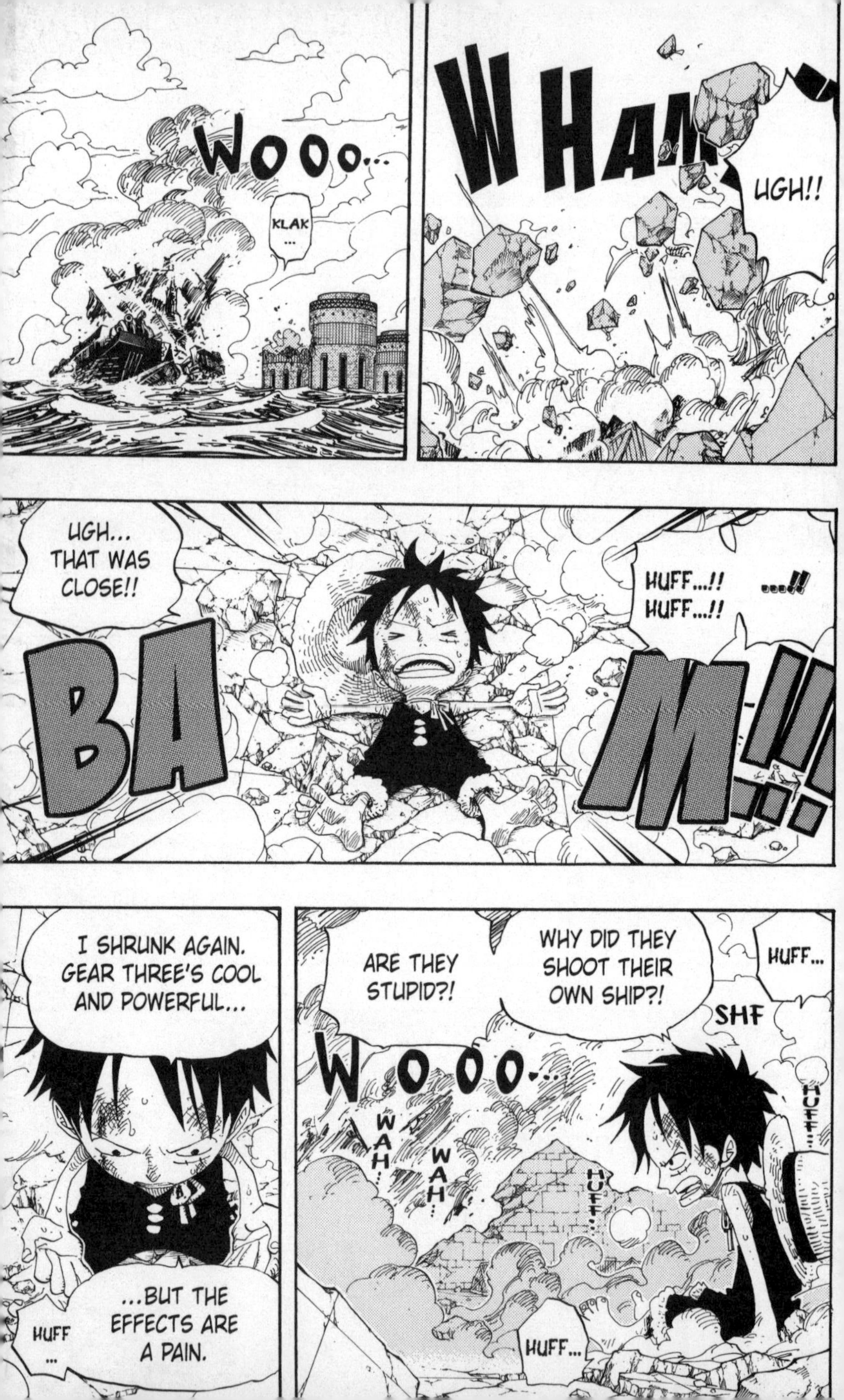
WHAM
UGH!!
WOOO...
KLAK...
...!!
HUFF...!! HUFF...!!
BAM!!
UGH... THAT WAS CLOSE!!
HUFF...
SHF
WHY DID THEY SHOOT THEIR OWN SHIP?!
ARE THEY STUPID?!
HUFF...
WOOO...
WAH...
WAH...
HUFF...
HUFF...
I SHRUNK AGAIN. GEAR THREE'S COOL AND POWERFUL...
...BUT THE EFFECTS ARE A PAIN.
HUFF...

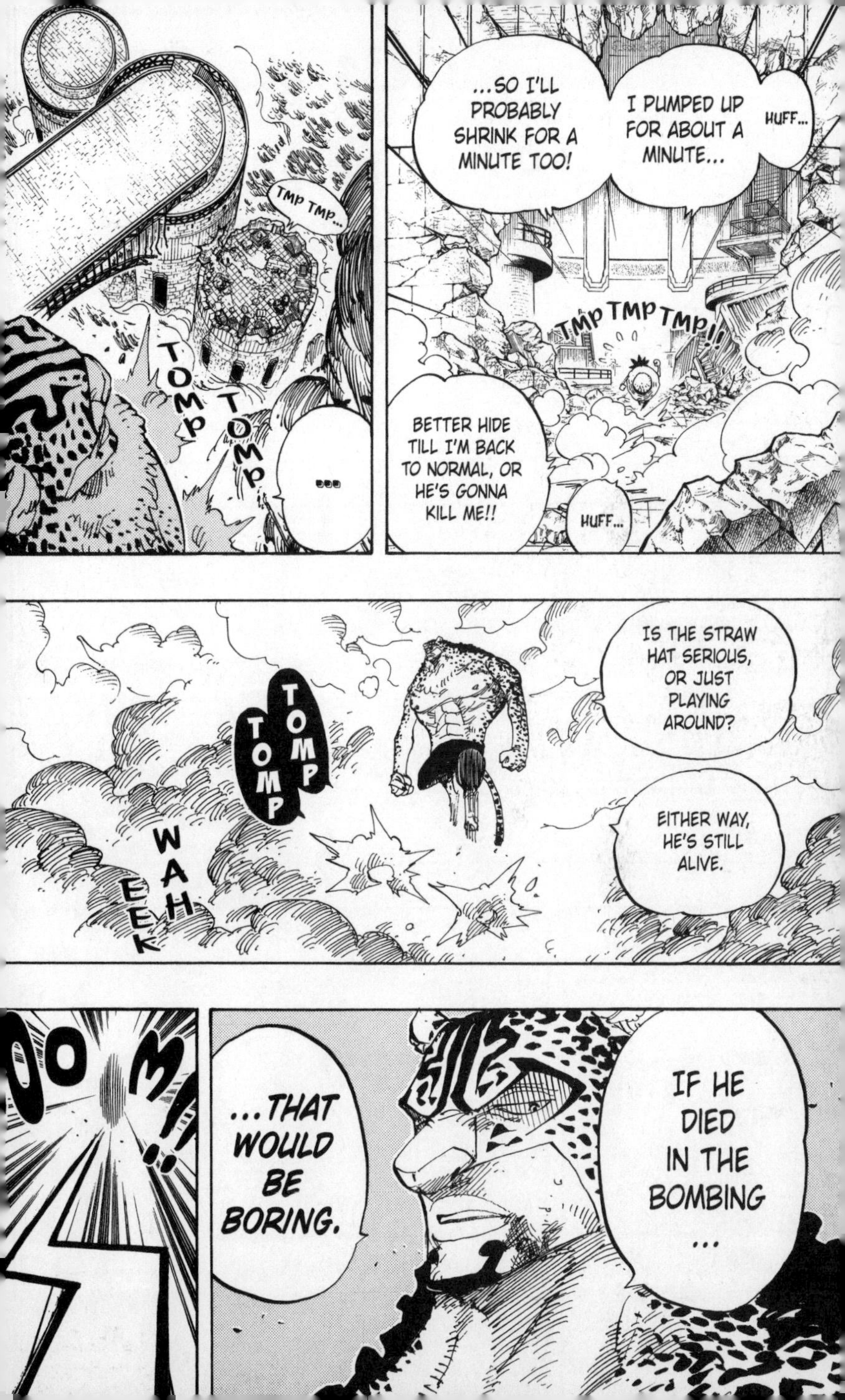
I PUMPED UP FOR ABOUT A MINUTE...
HUFF...
...SO I'LL PROBABLY SHRINK FOR A MINUTE TOO!
TMP TMP TMP!!
BETTER HIDE TILL I'M BACK TO NORMAL, OR HE'S GONNA KILL ME!!
HUFF...
TMP TMP...
TOMP
TOMP
...
IS THE STRAW HAT SERIOUS, OR JUST PLAYING AROUND?
EITHER WAY, HE'S STILL ALIVE.
TOMP TOMP
WAH
EEK
IF HE DIED IN THE BOMBING ...
...THAT WOULD BE BORING.
OOM!!

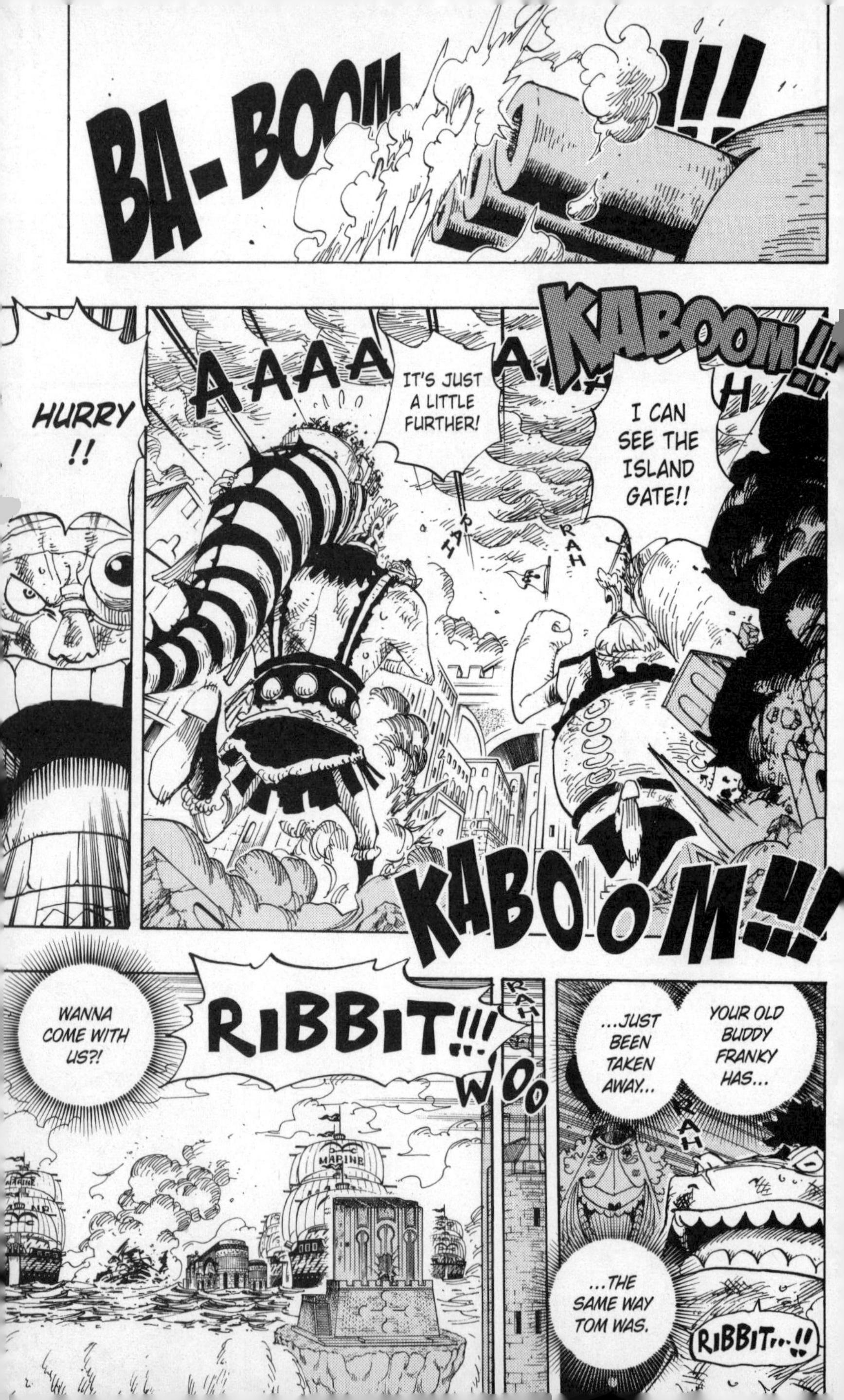
BA-BOOM!!!
KABOOM!!
H
I CAN SEE THE ISLAND GATE!!
RAH
IT'S JUST A LITTLE FURTHER!
AAAAA
RAH
KABOOM!!!
HURRY!!
YOUR OLD BUDDY FRANKY HAS...
...JUST BEEN TAKEN AWAY...
RAH
...THE SAME WAY TOM WAS.
RIBBIT...!!
RAH
WOO
RIBBIT!!!
WANNA COME WITH US?!

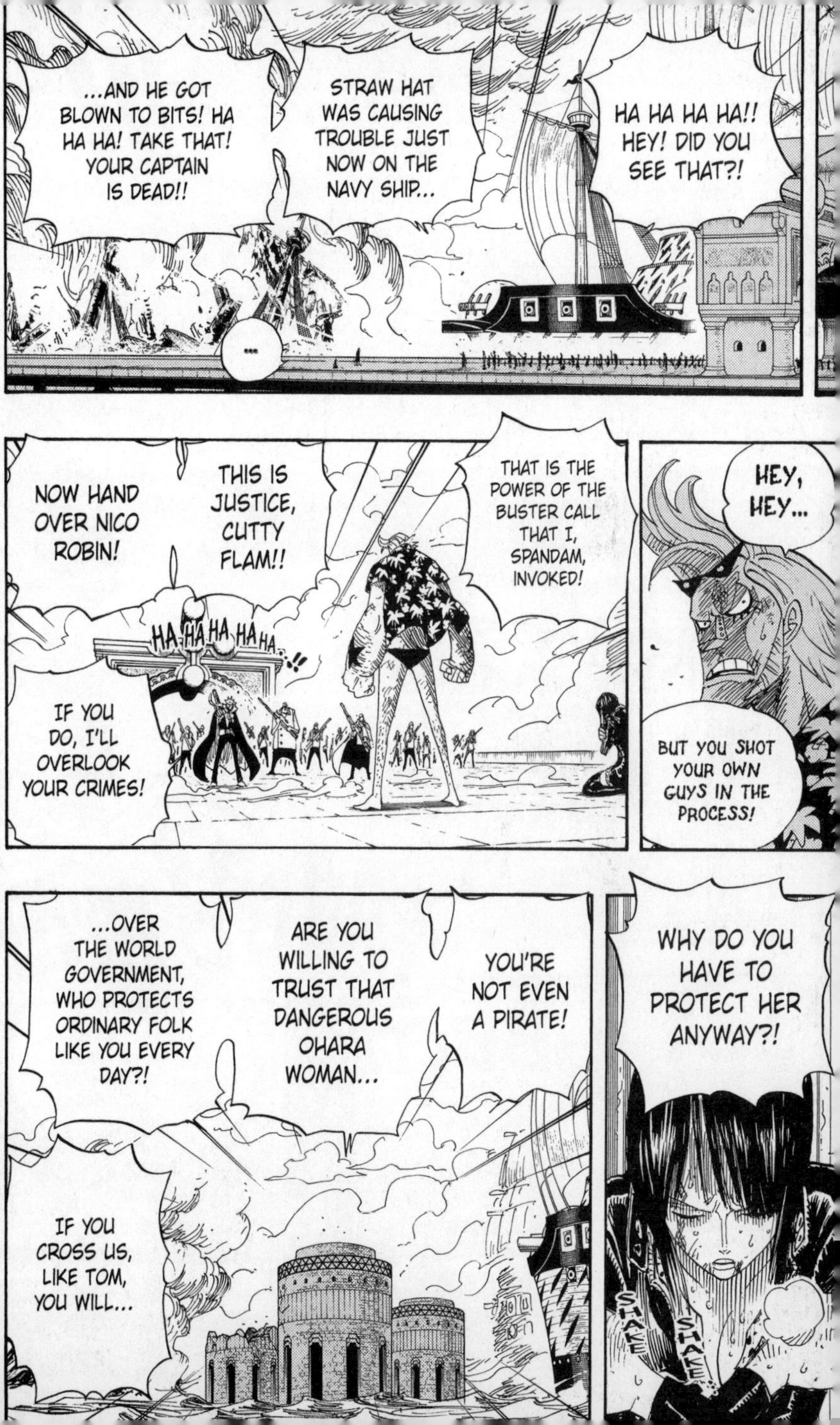
HA HA HA HA!! HEY! DID YOU SEE THAT?!
STRAW HAT WAS CAUSING TROUBLE JUST NOW ON THE NAVY SHIP...
...AND HE GOT BLOWN TO BITS! HA HA HA! TAKE THAT! YOUR CAPTAIN IS DEAD!!
...
HEY, HEY...
BUT YOU SHOT YOUR OWN GUYS IN THE PROCESS!
THAT IS THE POWER OF THE BUSTER CALL THAT I, SPANDAM, INVOKED!
THIS IS JUSTICE, CUTTY FLAM!!
NOW HAND OVER NICO ROBIN!
HA HA HA HA HA...!!
IF YOU DO, I'LL OVERLOOK YOUR CRIMES!
WHY DO YOU HAVE TO PROTECT HER ANYWAY?!
SHAKE
SHAKE
YOU'RE NOT EVEN A PIRATE!
ARE YOU WILLING TO TRUST THAT DANGEROUS OHARA WOMAN...
...OVER THE WORLD GOVERNMENT, WHO PROTECTS ORDINARY FOLK LIKE YOU EVERY DAY?!
IF YOU CROSS US, LIKE TOM, YOU WILL...

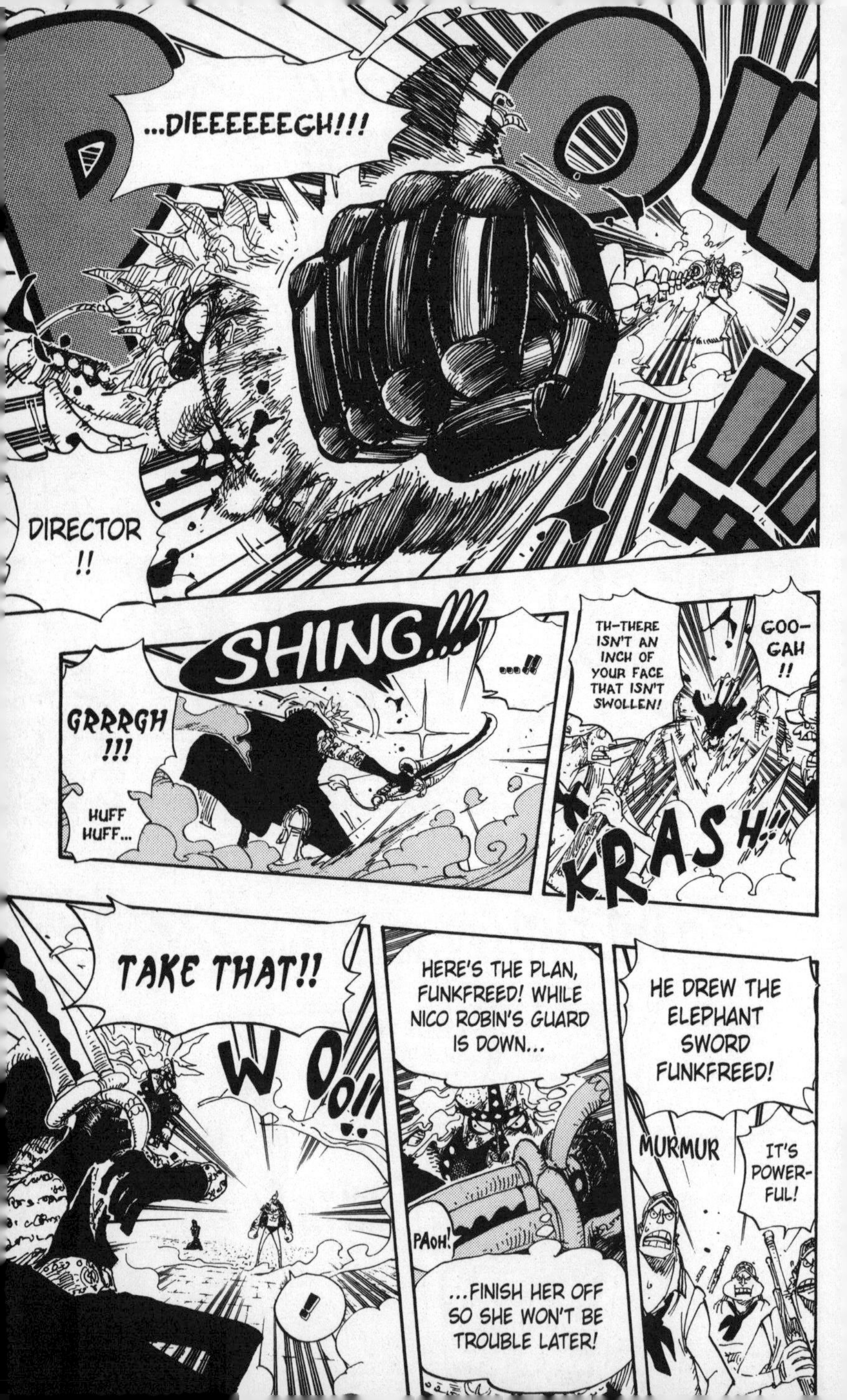
...DIEEEEEEGH!!!
DIRECTOR !!
TH-THERE ISN'T AN INCH OF YOUR FACE THAT ISN'T SWOLLEN!
GOO-GAH !!
KRASH!!
SHING!!!
...!!
GRRRGH !!!
HUFF HUFF...
HE DREW THE ELEPHANT SWORD FUNKFREED!
IT'S POWER-FUL!
MURMUR
HERE'S THE PLAN, FUNKFREED! WHILE NICO ROBIN'S GUARD IS DOWN...
PAOH!
...FINISH HER OFF SO SHE WON'T BE TROUBLE LATER!
TAKE THAT!!
WOO!!
!

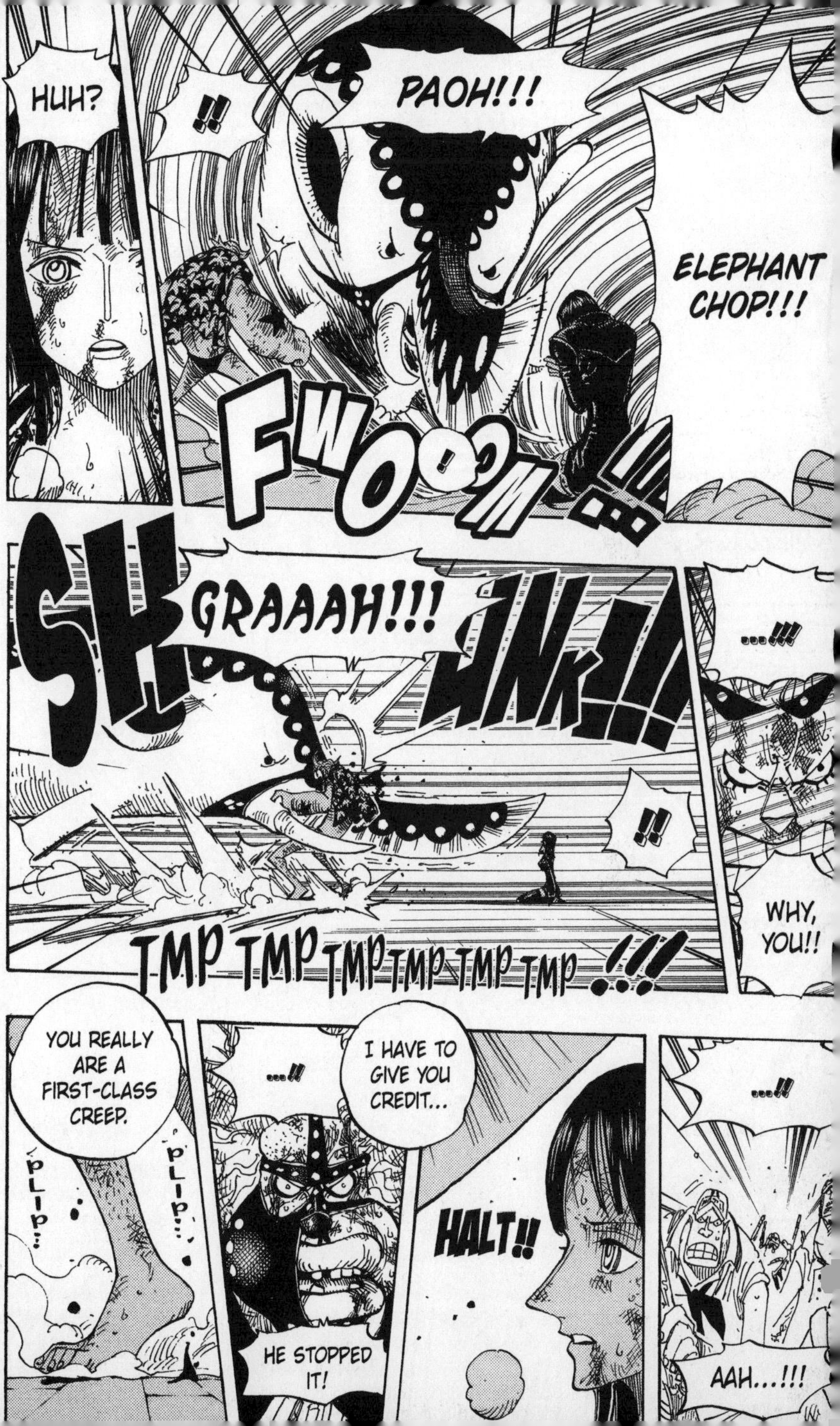
PAOH!!!
!!
ELEPHANT CHOP!!!
FWOOOM!!!
HUH?
...!!!
WHY, YOU!!
SHUNK!!!
GRAAAH!!!
!!
TMP TMP TMP TMP TMP TMP!!!
...!!
AAH...!!!
HALT!!
I HAVE TO GIVE YOU CREDIT...
...!!
HE STOPPED IT!
YOU REALLY ARE A FIRST-CLASS CREEP.
PLIP...
PLIP...

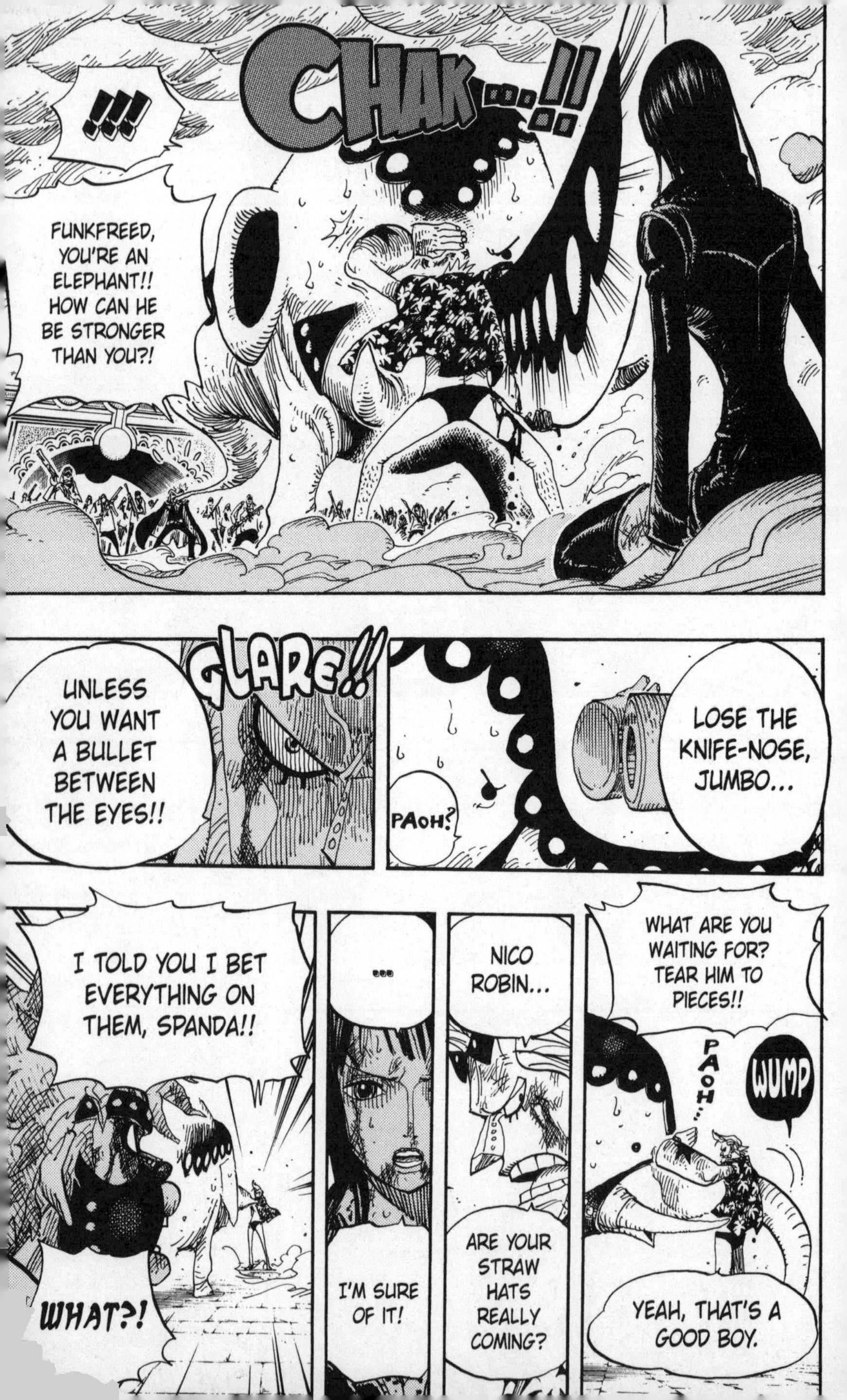
CHAK...!!
!!!!
FUNKFREED, YOU'RE AN ELEPHANT!! HOW CAN HE BE STRONGER THAN YOU?!
LOSE THE KNIFE-NOSE, JUMBO...
PAOH?
GLARE!!
UNLESS YOU WANT A BULLET BETWEEN THE EYES!!
WHAT ARE YOU WAITING FOR? TEAR HIM TO PIECES!!
WUMP
PAOH...
YEAH, THAT'S A GOOD BOY.
NICO ROBIN...
ARE YOUR STRAW HATS REALLY COMING?
...
I'M SURE OF IT!
I TOLD YOU I BET EVERYTHING ON THEM, SPANDA!!
WHAT?!

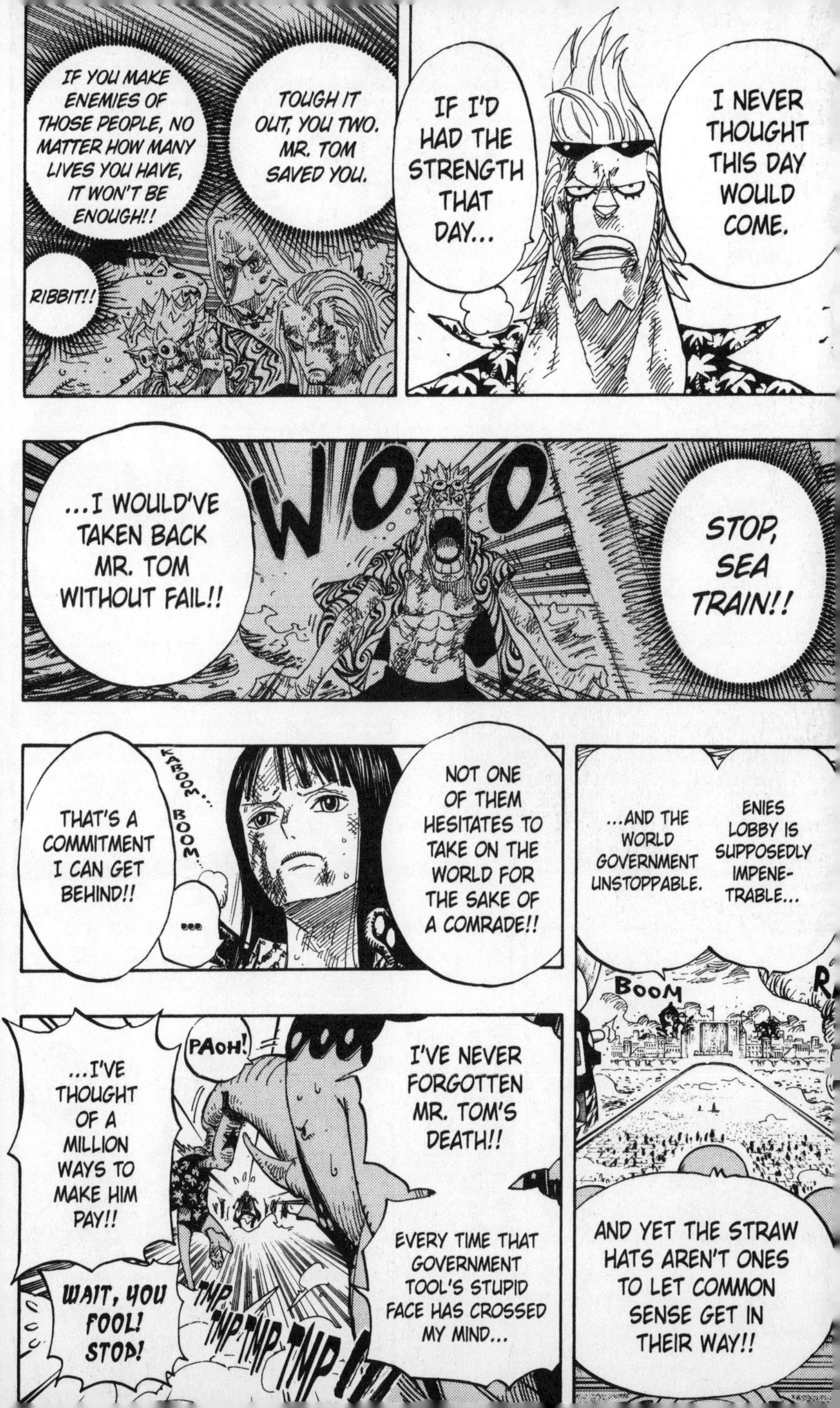
I NEVER THOUGHT THIS DAY WOULD COME.
IF I'D HAD THE STRENGTH THAT DAY...
TOUGH IT OUT, YOU TWO. MR. TOM SAVED YOU.
IF YOU MAKE ENEMIES OF THOSE PEOPLE, NO MATTER HOW MANY LIVES YOU HAVE, IT WON'T BE ENOUGH!!
RIBBIT!!
STOP, SEA TRAIN!!
WOO
...I WOULD'VE TAKEN BACK MR. TOM WITHOUT FAIL!!
ENIES LOBBY IS SUPPOSEDLY IMPENE-TRABLE...
...AND THE WORLD GOVERNMENT UNSTOPPABLE.
BOOM
AND YET THE STRAW HATS AREN'T ONES TO LET COMMON SENSE GET IN THEIR WAY!!
NOT ONE OF THEM HESITATES TO TAKE ON THE WORLD FOR THE SAKE OF A COMRADE!!
KABOOM... BOOM...
THAT'S A COMMITMENT I CAN GET BEHIND!!
...
I'VE NEVER FORGOTTEN MR. TOM'S DEATH!!
EVERY TIME THAT GOVERNMENT TOOL'S STUPID FACE HAS CROSSED MY MIND...
PAOH!
...I'VE THOUGHT OF A MILLION WAYS TO MAKE HIM PAY!!
WAIT, YOU FOOL! STOP!
TMP TMP TMP TMP

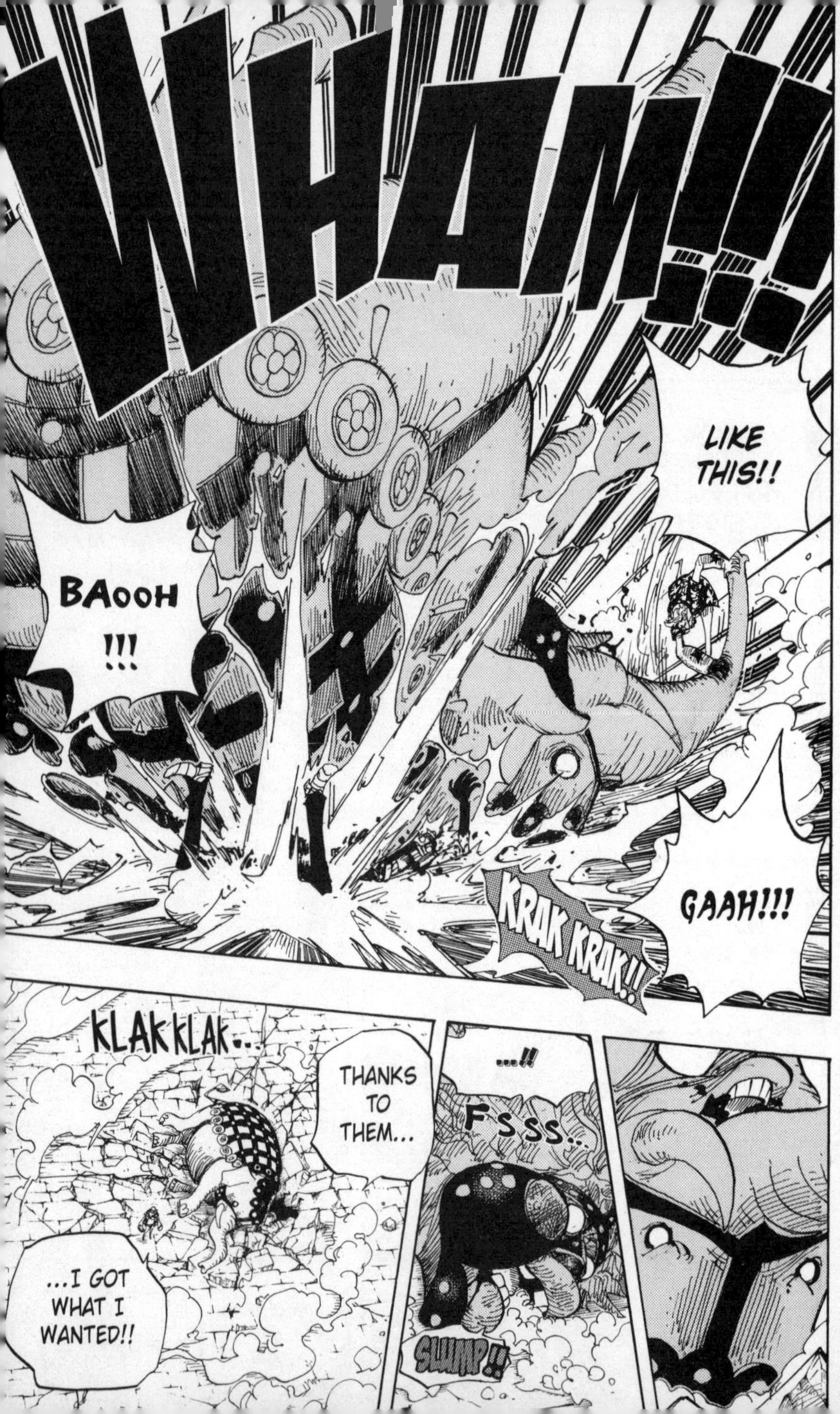
WHAM!!!
LIKE THIS!!
BAOOH !!!
GAAH!!!
KRAK KRAK!!
...!!
FSSS..
SLUMP!!
KLAK KLAK..
THANKS TO THEM...
...I GOT WHAT I WANTED!!

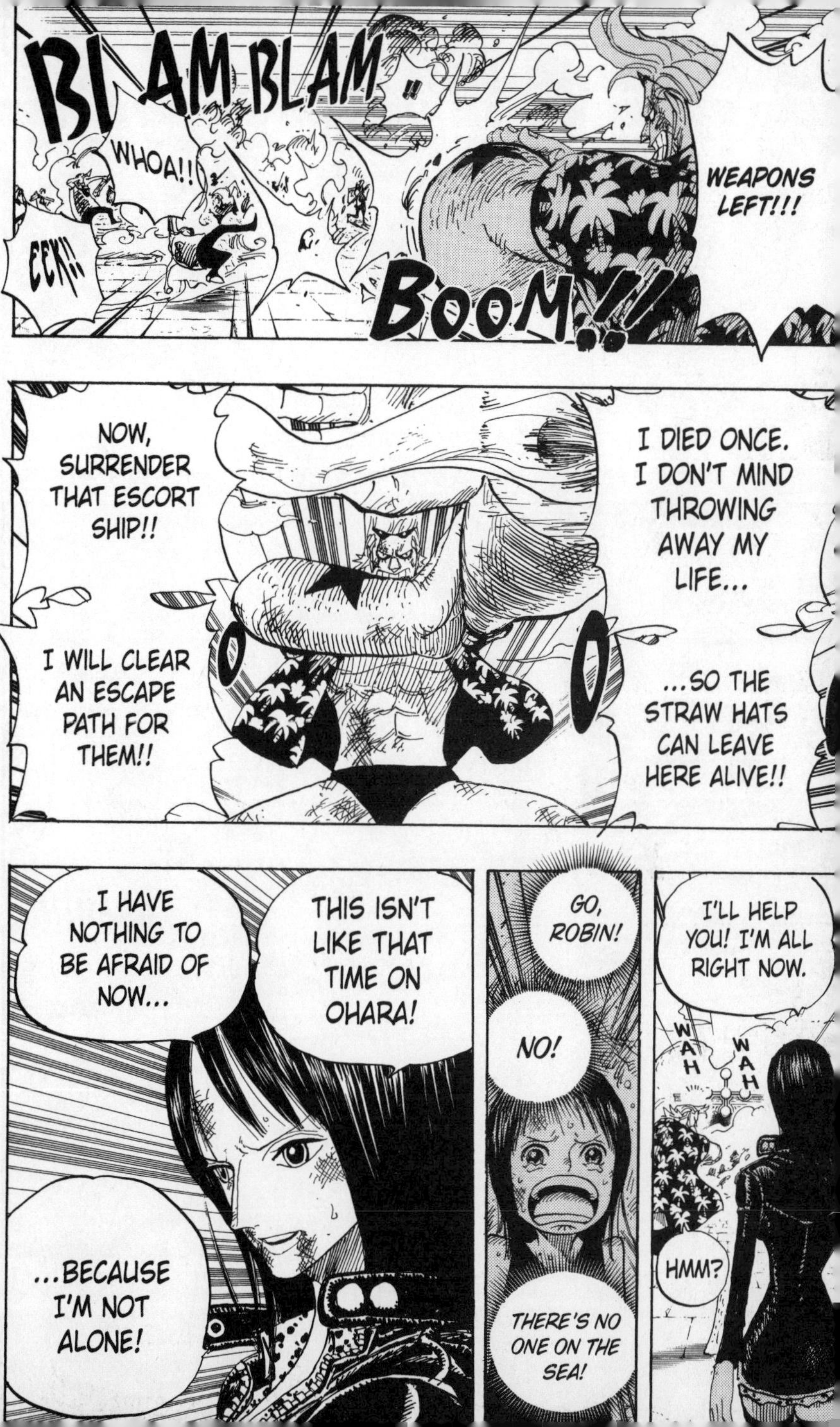
WEAPONS LEFT!!!
BLAM BLAM
WHOA!!
EEK!!
BOOM!!
I DIED ONCE. I DON'T MIND THROWING AWAY MY LIFE...
...SO THE STRAW HATS CAN LEAVE HERE ALIVE!!
NOW, SURRENDER THAT ESCORT SHIP!!
I WILL CLEAR AN ESCAPE PATH FOR THEM!!
I'LL HELP YOU! I'M ALL RIGHT NOW.
WAH
WAH
HMM?
GO, ROBIN!
NO!
THERE'S NO ONE ON THE SEA!
THIS ISN'T LIKE THAT TIME ON OHARA!
I HAVE NOTHING TO BE AFRAID OF NOW...
...BECAUSE I'M NOT ALONE!

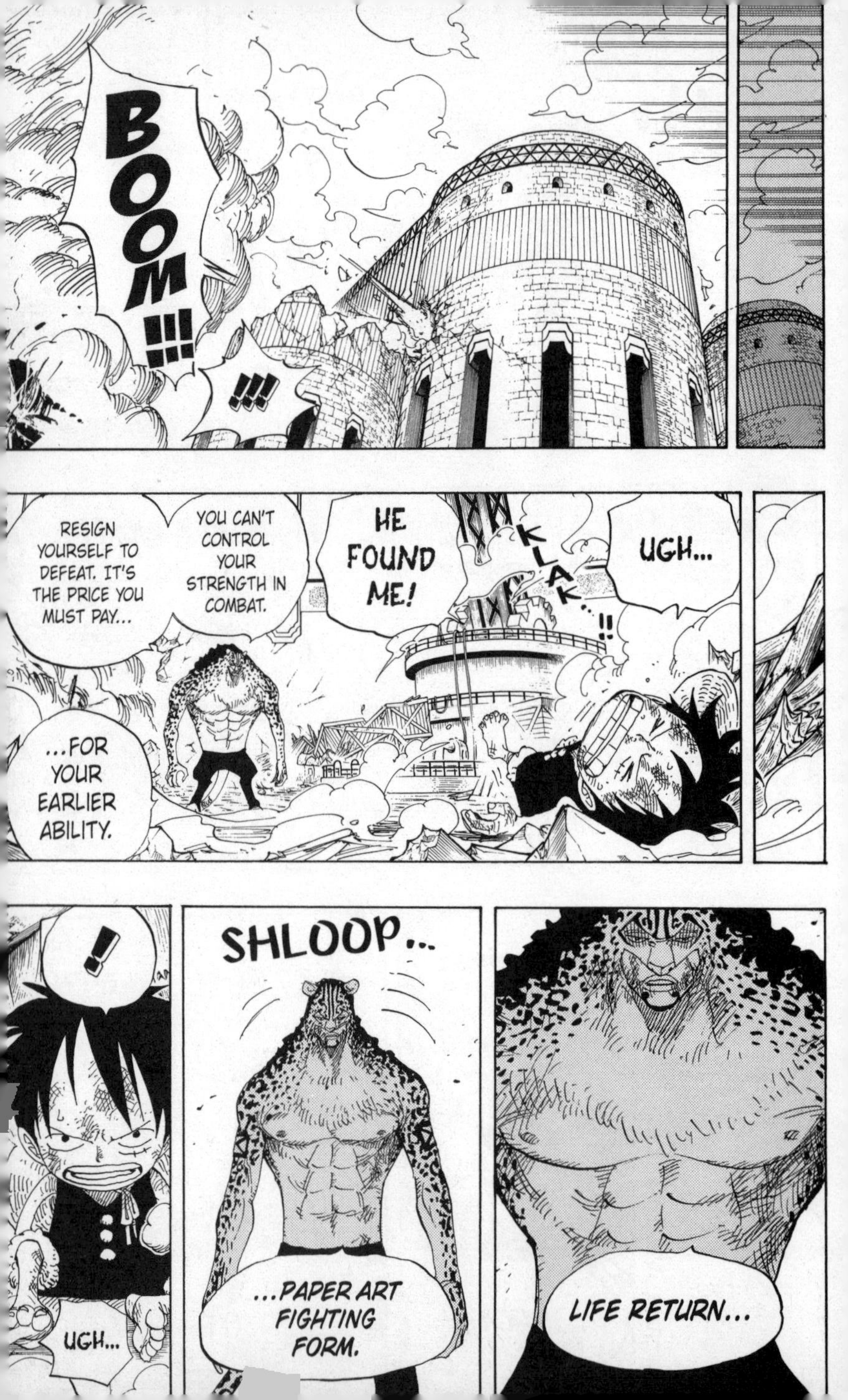
BOOM!!!
!!!
UGH...
KLAK...!!
HE FOUND ME!
YOU CAN'T CONTROL YOUR STRENGTH IN COMBAT.
RESIGN YOURSELF TO DEFEAT. IT'S THE PRICE YOU MUST PAY...
...FOR YOUR EARLIER ABILITY.
LIFE RETURN...
SHLOOP...
...PAPER ART FIGHTING FORM.
!
UGH...

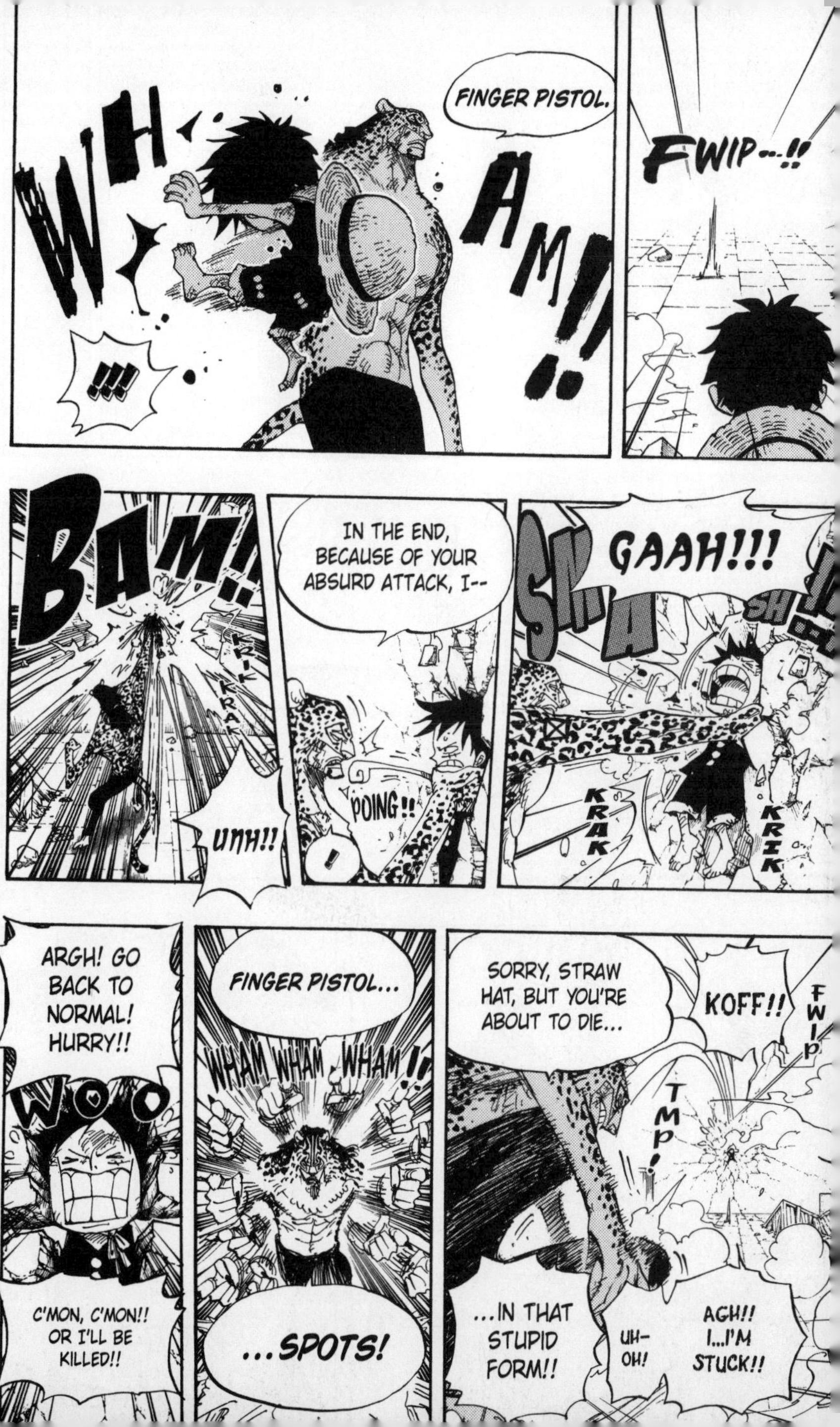
FWIP--!!
FINGER PISTOL.
WHAM!!
!!!
GAAH!!!
SMASH!!
KRAK
KRIK
IN THE END, BECAUSE OF YOUR ABSURD ATTACK, I--
POING!!
!
BAM!!
KRIK KRAK
UNH!!
FWIP
KOFF!!
SORRY, STRAW HAT, BUT YOU'RE ABOUT TO DIE...
TMP!
AGH!! I...I'M STUCK!!
UH-OH!
...IN THAT STUPID FORM!!
FINGER PISTOL...
WHAM WHAM WHAM!!
...SPOTS!
ARGH! GO BACK TO NORMAL! HURRY!!
WOO
C'MON, C'MON!! OR I'LL BE KILLED!!

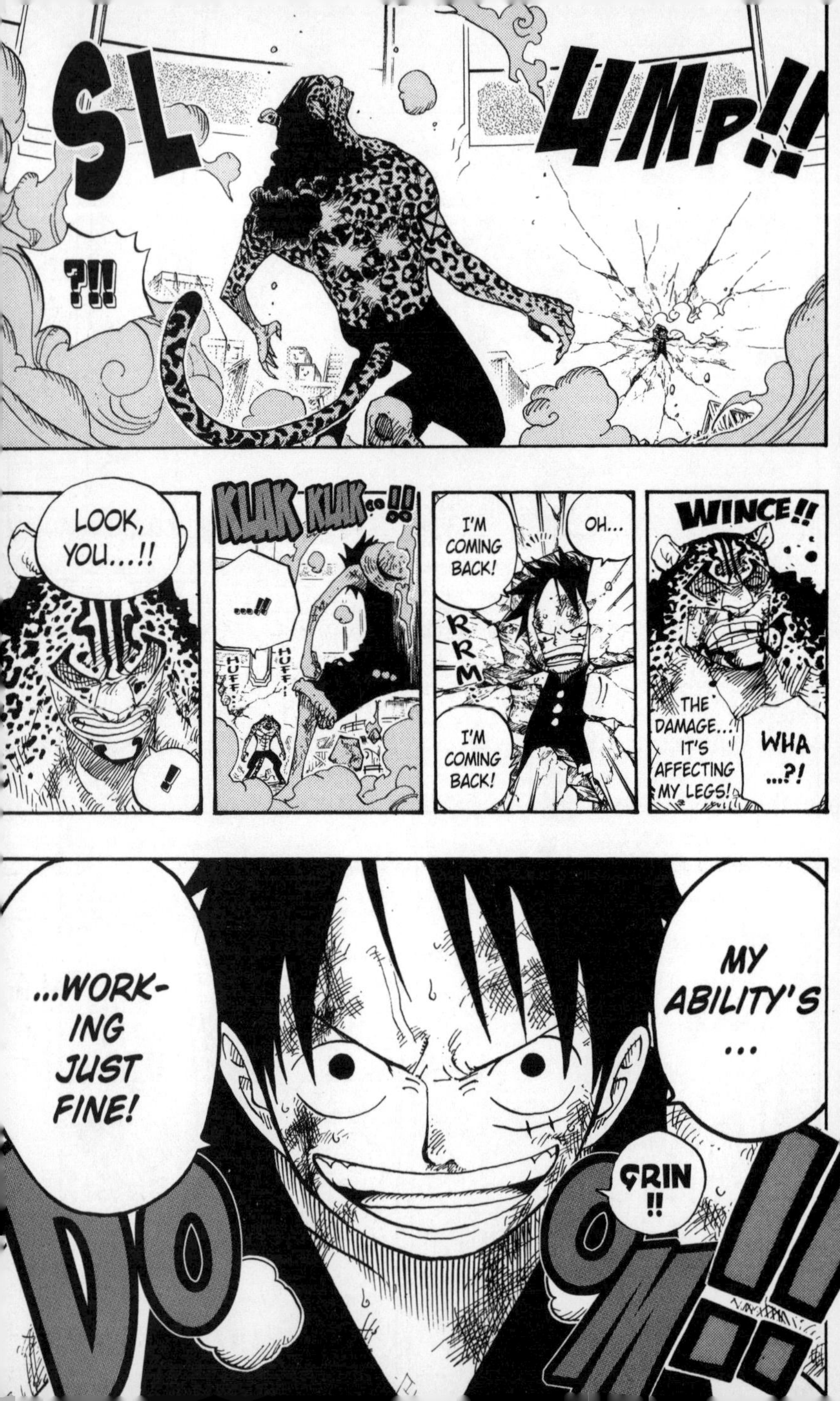
SL UMP!!
?!!
WINCE!!
WHA ...?!
THE DAMAGE... IT'S AFFECTING MY LEGS!
OH...
I'M COMING BACK!
RRM
I'M COMING BACK!
KLAK KLAK!!
...!!
HUFF
HUFF
LOOK, YOU...!!
!
MY ABILITY'S ...
...WORK-ING JUST FINE!
GRIN !!

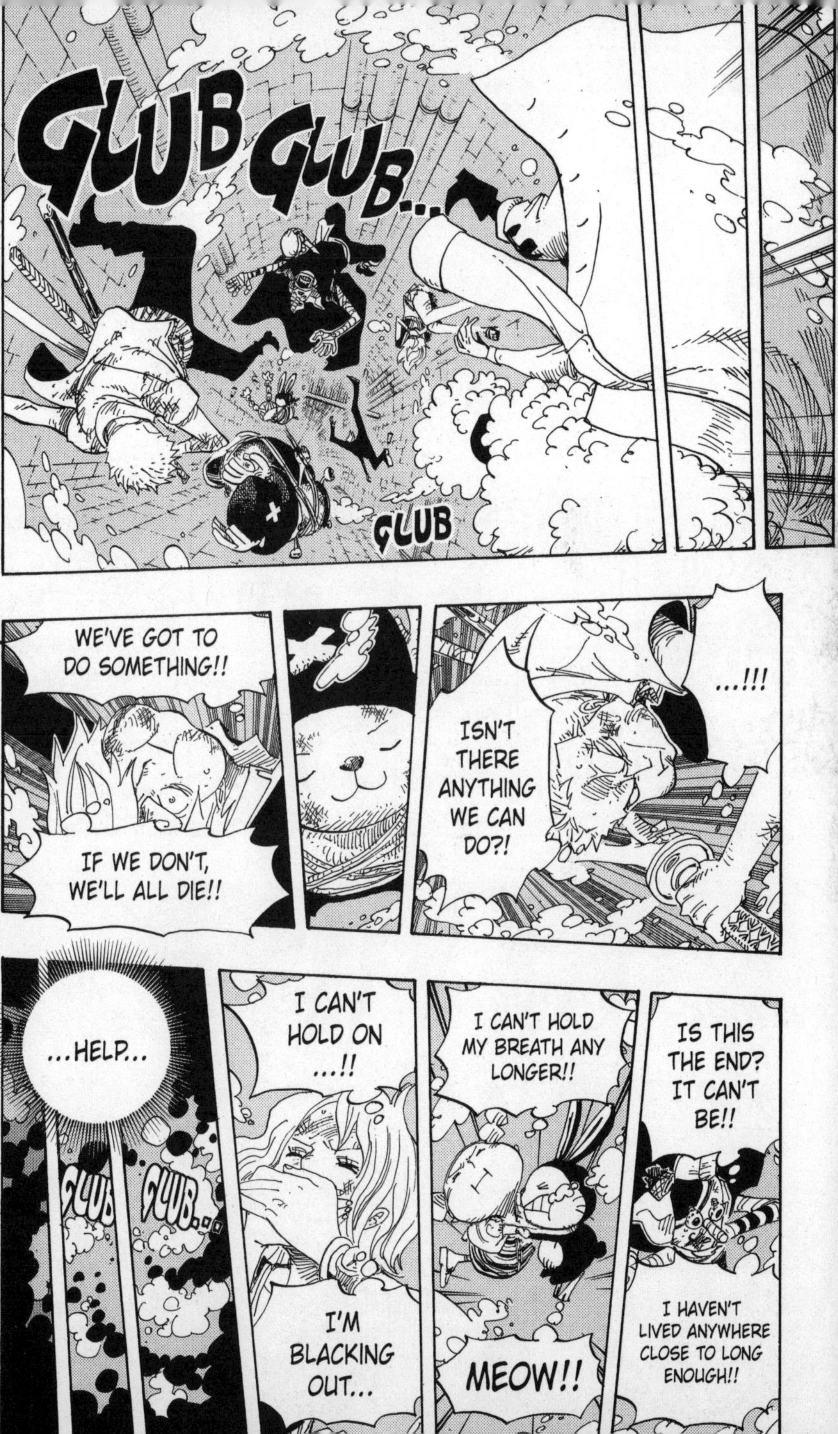
GLUB GLUB...
GLUB
...!!!
ISN'T THERE ANYTHING WE CAN DO?!
WE'VE GOT TO DO SOMETHING!!
IF WE DON'T, WE'LL ALL DIE!!
IS THIS THE END? IT CAN'T BE!!
I HAVEN'T LIVED ANYWHERE CLOSE TO LONG ENOUGH!!
I CAN'T HOLD MY BREATH ANY LONGER!!
MEOW!!
I CAN'T HOLD ON ...!!
I'M BLACKING OUT...
...HELP...
GLUB GLUB...

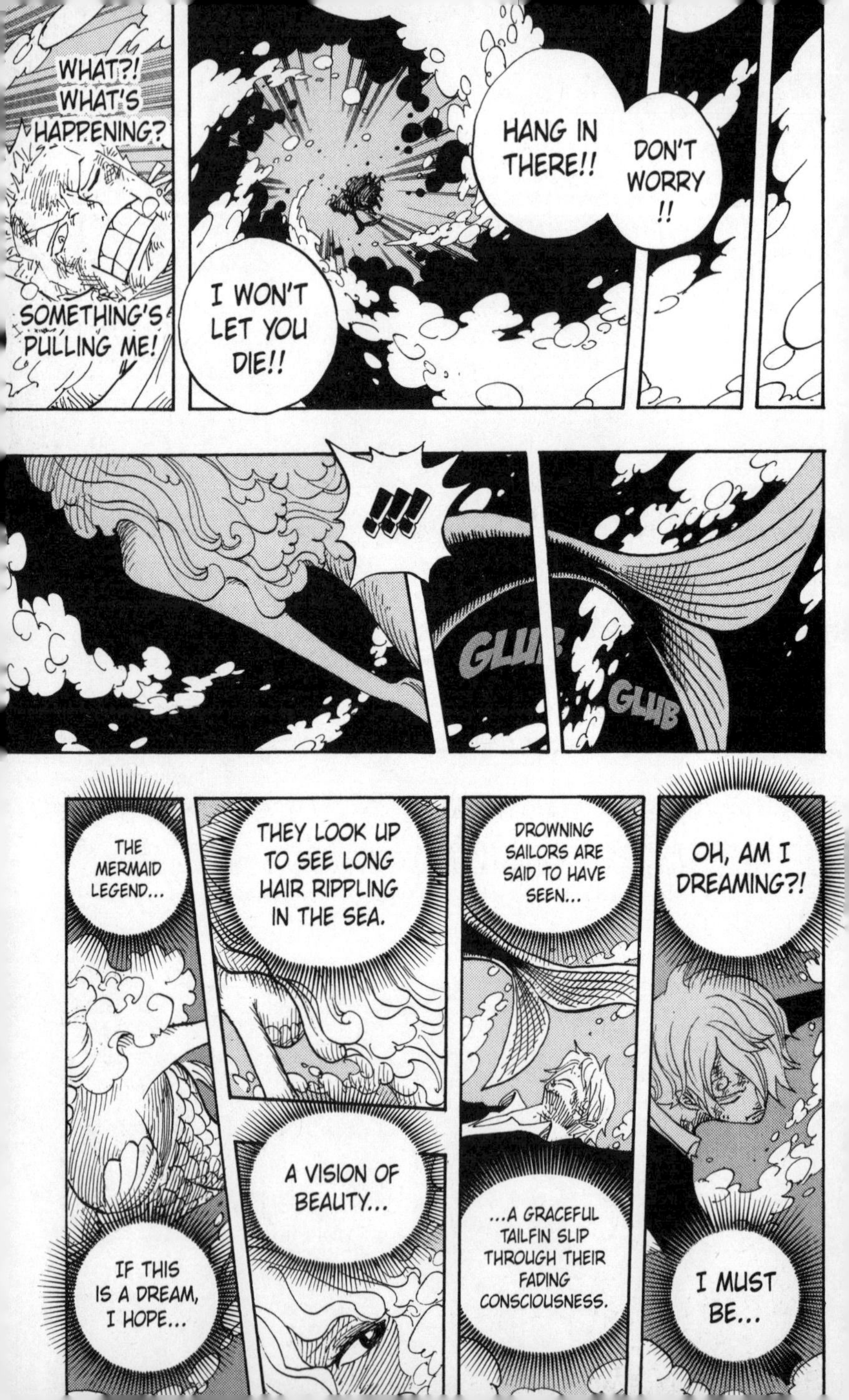
DON'T WORRY !!
HANG IN THERE!!
I WON'T LET YOU DIE!!
WHAT?! WHAT'S HAPPENING?
SOMETHING'S PULLING ME!
GLUB
GLUB
!!!
OH, AM I DREAMING?!
I MUST BE...
DROWNING SAILORS ARE SAID TO HAVE SEEN...
...A GRACEFUL TAILFIN SLIP THROUGH THEIR FADING CONSCIOUSNESS.
THEY LOOK UP TO SEE LONG HAIR RIPPLING IN THE SEA.
A VISION OF BEAUTY...
THE MERMAID LEGEND...
IF THIS IS A DREAM, I HOPE...

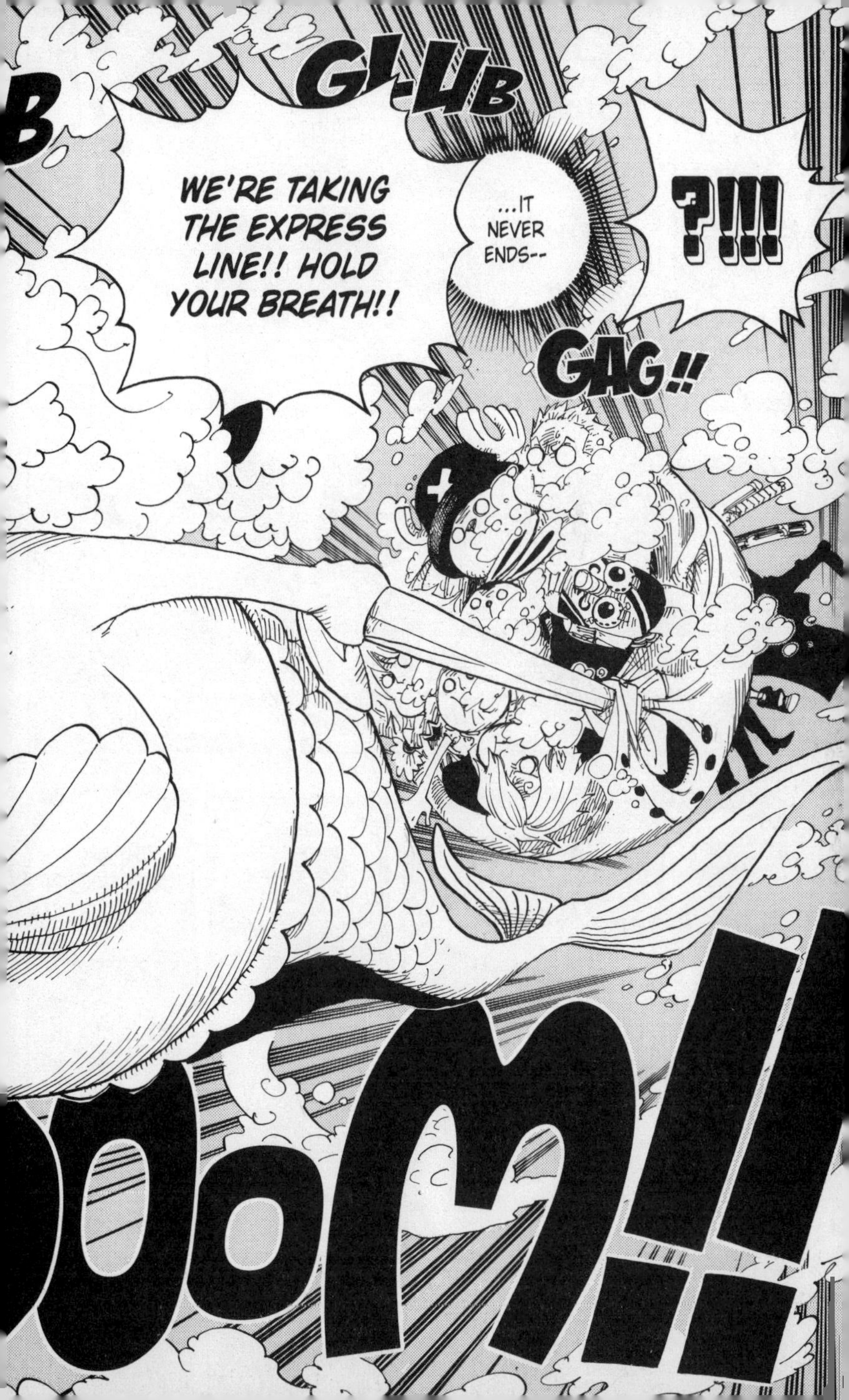
GLUB
B
?!!!
...IT NEVER ENDS--
WE'RE TAKING THE EXPRESS LINE!! HOLD YOUR BREATH!!
GAG!!
DOOM!!

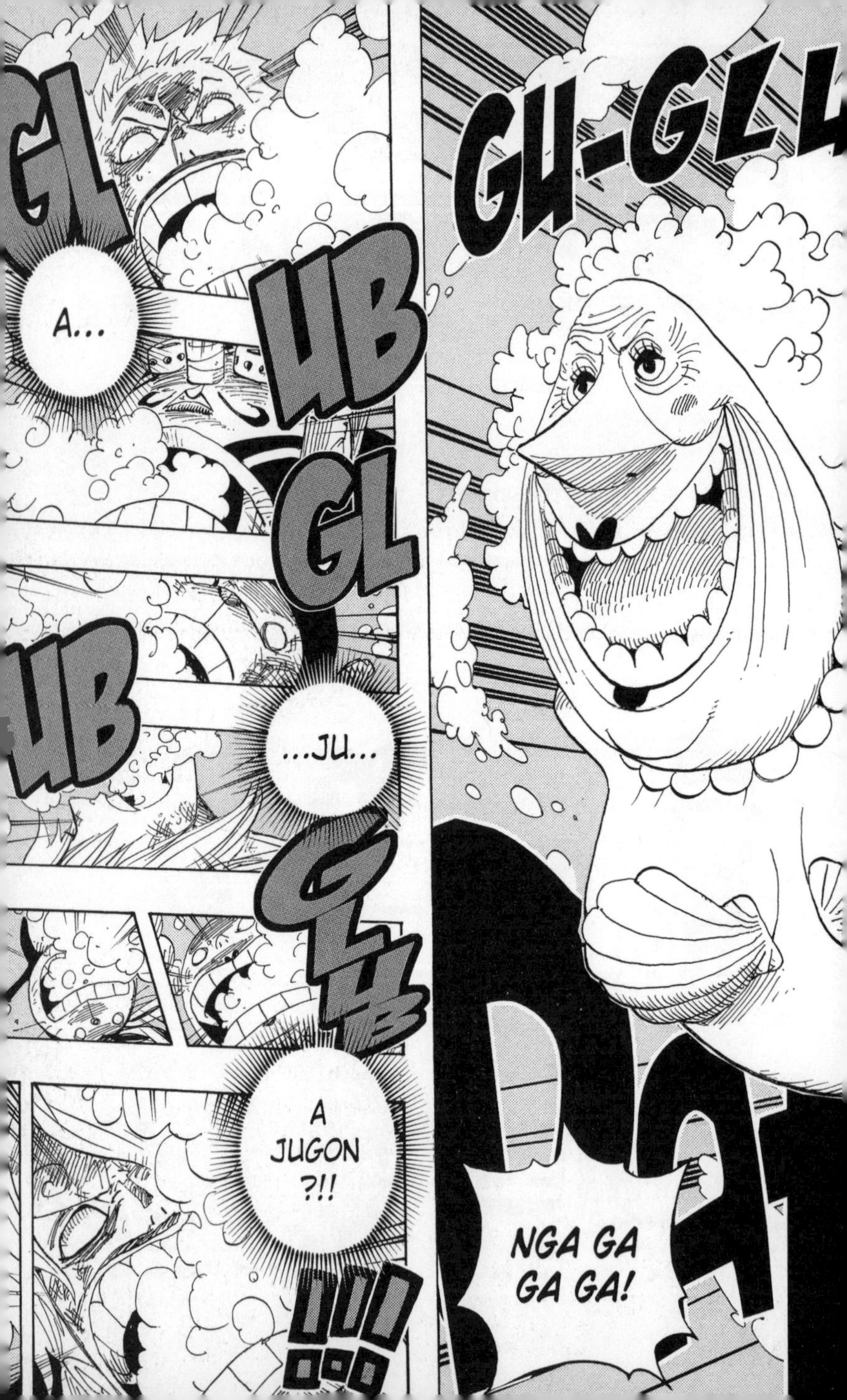
GU-GLL
NGA GA GA GA!
GL
A...
UB
GL
UB
...JU...
GLLB
A JUGON ?!!
!!!

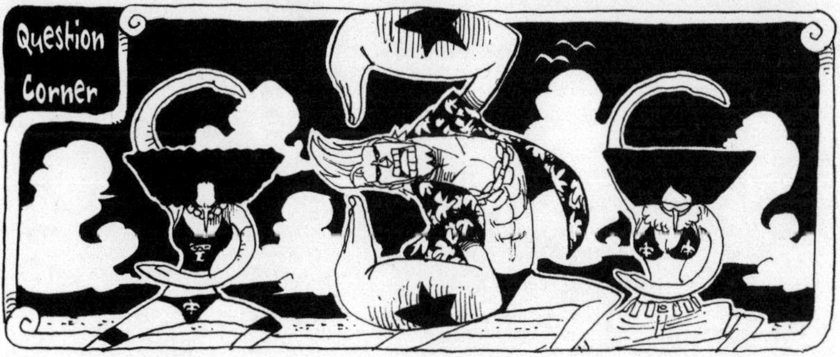
Question Corner

Q: Aargh!! Hewwo?! Ish dish Oda Shensheiiii? Ummm! …! What wazzit again?! I fergot!! Wheee!

--Shoma-kun

A: Are you tipsy?!! Someone get this guy out of here!

Q: Sensei, I absolutely must know what the eight members of CP9 looked like as children (especially Lucci). If you don't mind, would you draw them for me? Please?

--The Sea Is So Vast

A: Okay.

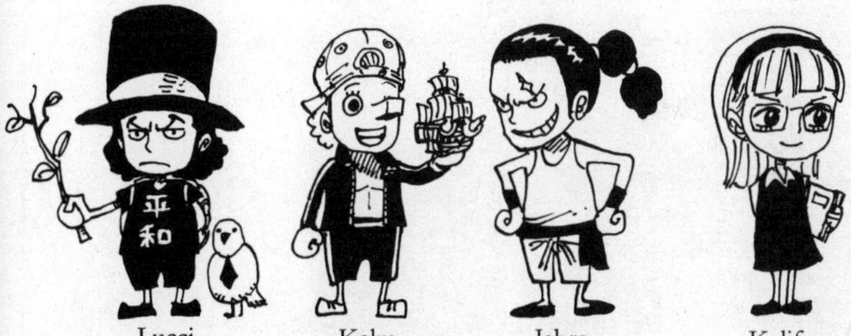

Lucci
SHIRT SAYS "PEACE"--ED.

Kaku

Jabra

Kalifa

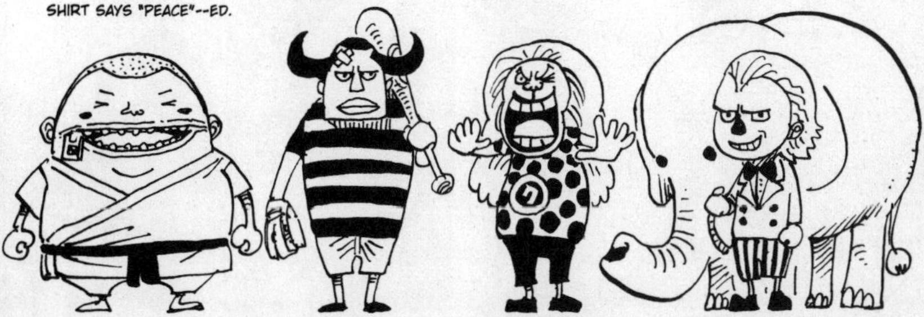

Fukurô

Blueno

Kumadori
SHIRT SAYS "K"--ED.

Spandam

Chapter 424:
ESCAPE SHIP

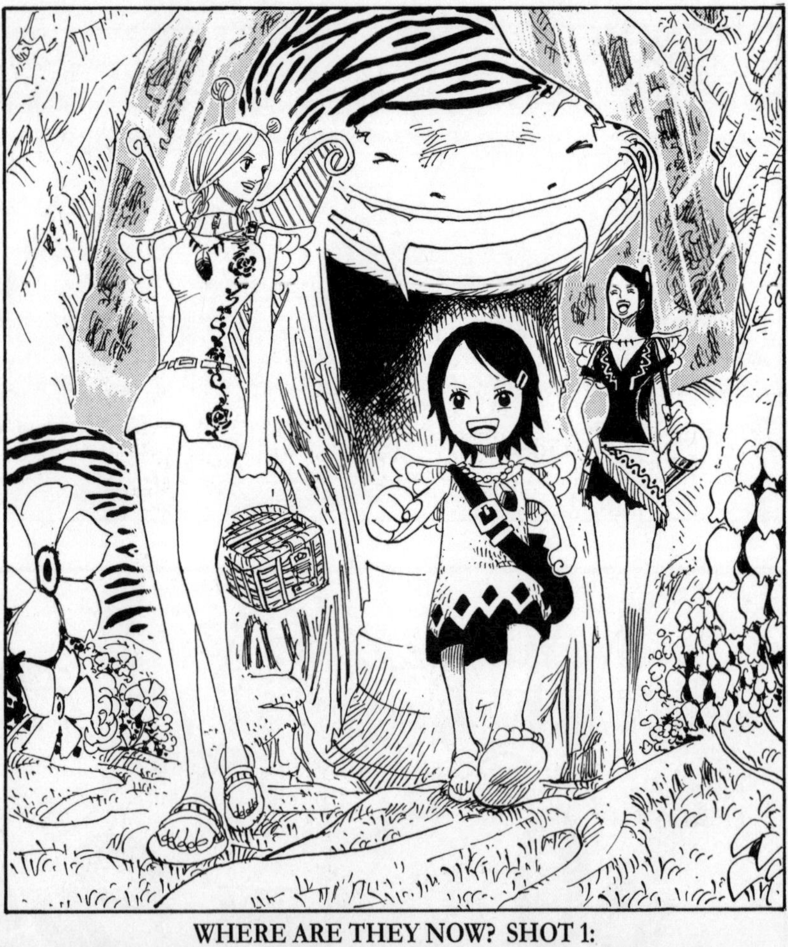

WHERE ARE THEY NOW? SHOT 1:
"CONIS, AISA, RAKI AND NOLA WALK ACROSS THE VARSE"

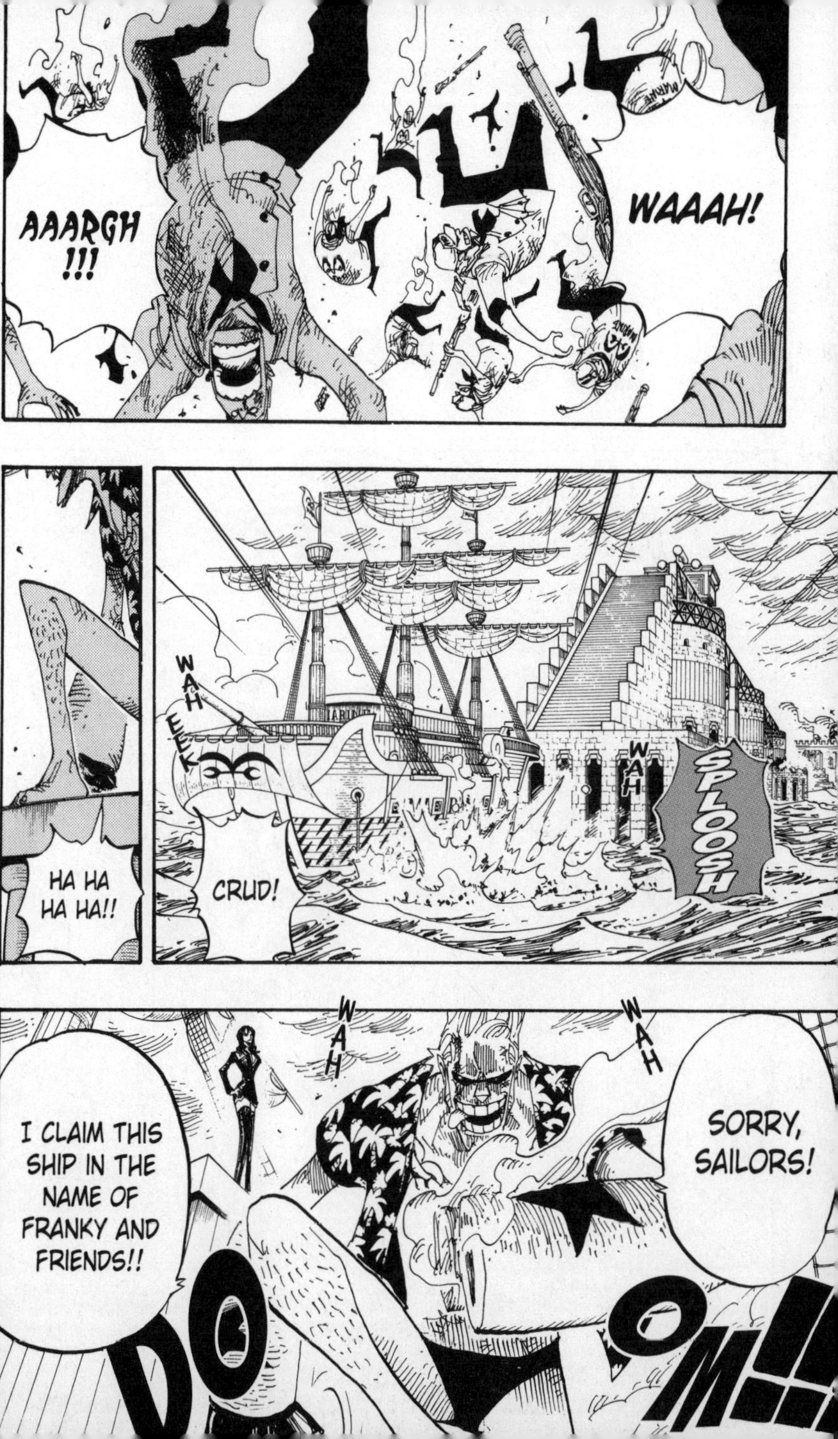
WAAAH!
AAARGH !!!
WAH
EEK
WAH
SPLOOSH
CRUD!
HA HA HA HA!!
WAH
SORRY, SAILORS!
WAH
I CLAIM THIS SHIP IN THE NAME OF FRANKY AND FRIENDS!!
DOOM!!

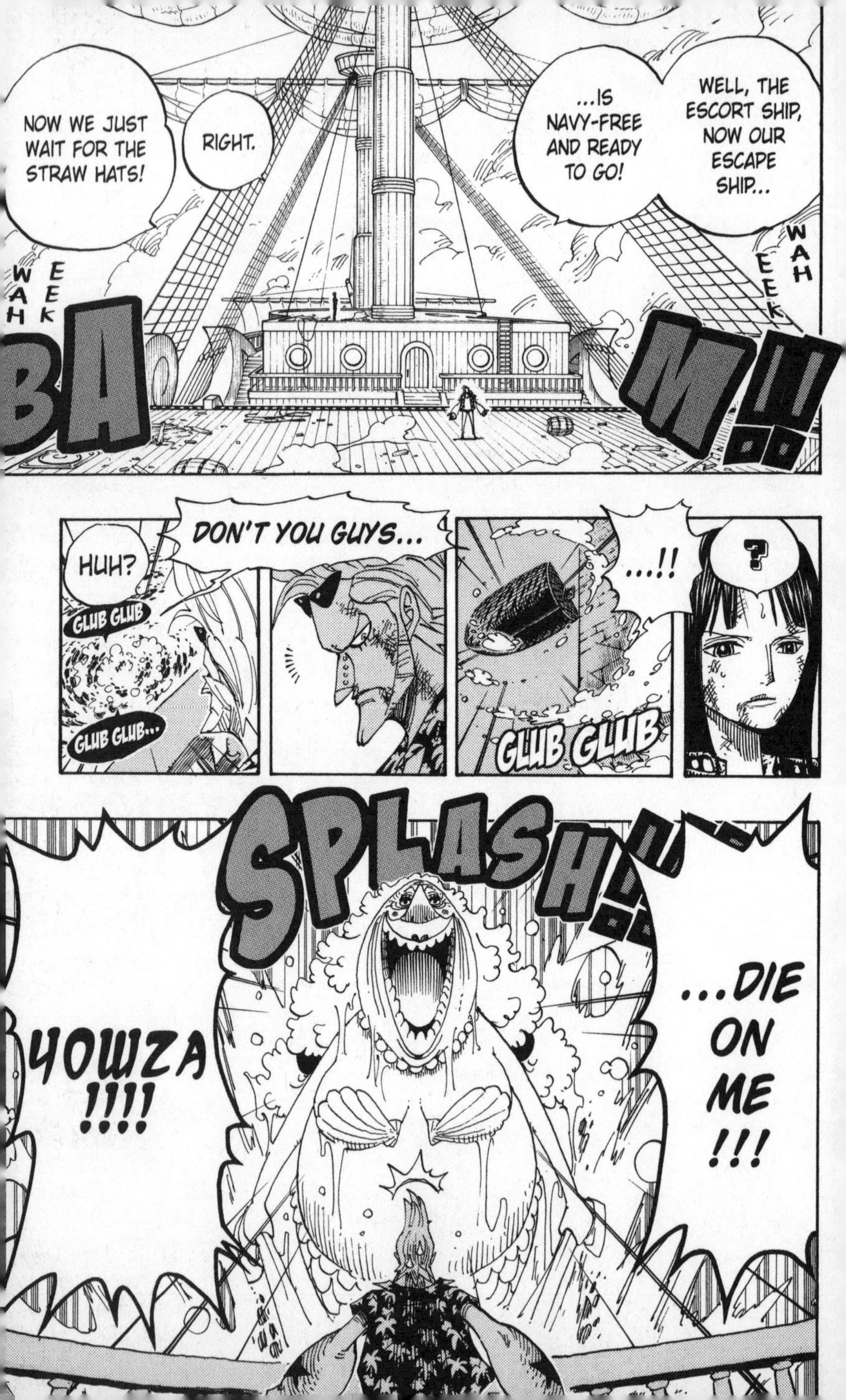
WELL, THE ESCORT SHIP, NOW OUR ESCAPE SHIP...
...IS NAVY-FREE AND READY TO GO!
RIGHT.
NOW WE JUST WAIT FOR THE STRAW HATS!
WAH EEK
WAH EEK
BAM!!
?
...!!
GLUB GLUB
DON'T YOU GUYS...
HUH?
GLUB GLUB
GLUB GLUB...
SPLASH!!
...DIE ON ME!!!
YOWZA!!!!

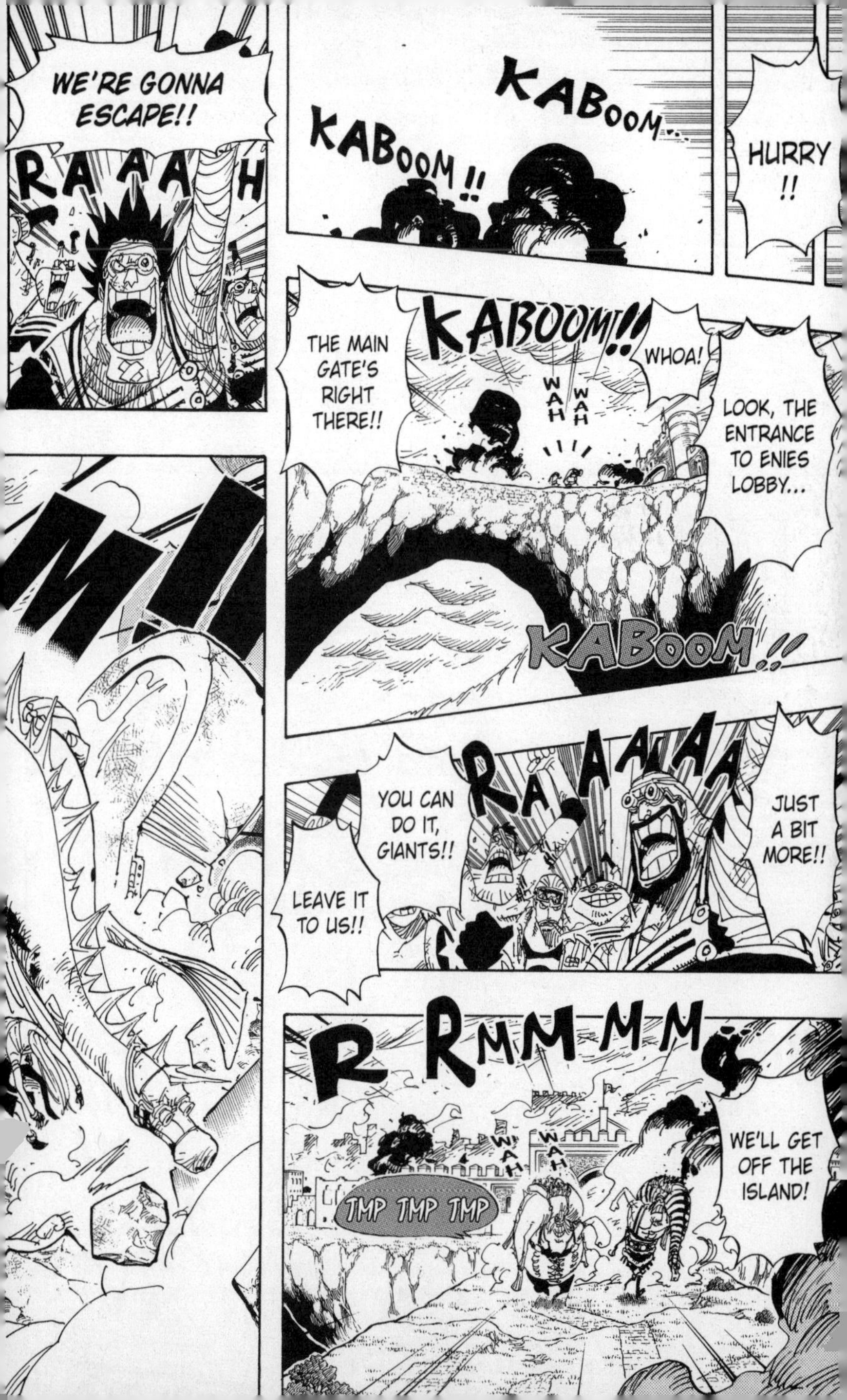
HURRY!!
KABOOM...
KABOOM!!
WE'RE GONNA ESCAPE!!
RAAAH
LOOK, THE ENTRANCE TO ENIES LOBBY...
WHOA!
KABOOM!!
WAH WAH
THE MAIN GATE'S RIGHT THERE!!
KABOOM!!
JUST A BIT MORE!!
RAAAAA
YOU CAN DO IT, GIANTS!!
LEAVE IT TO US!!
WE'LL GET OFF THE ISLAND!
RRMMMM
WAH WAH
TMP TMP TMP
M!!

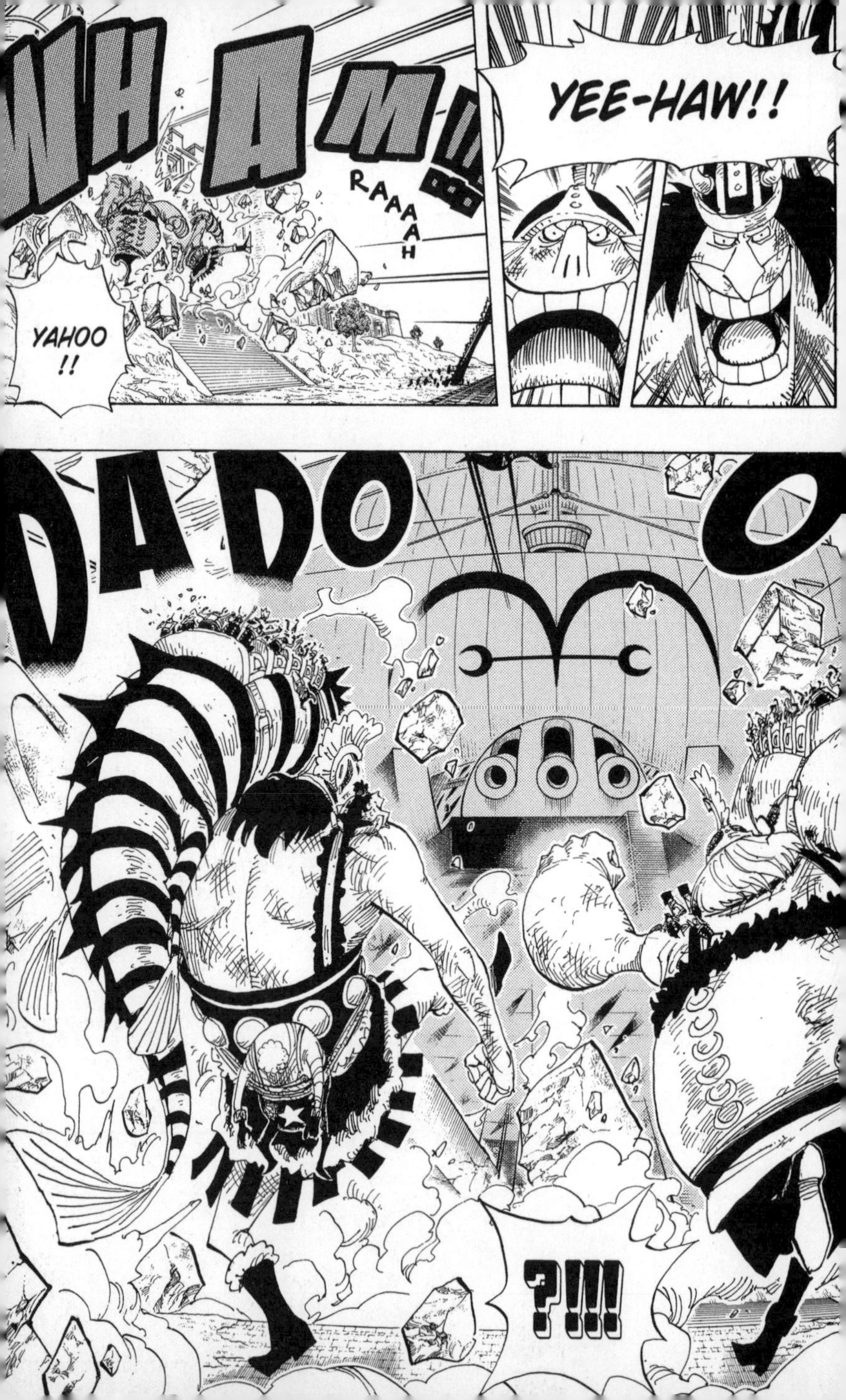
YEE-HAW!!
WHAM!!
RAAAAAH
YAHOO!!
DADOO
?!!!

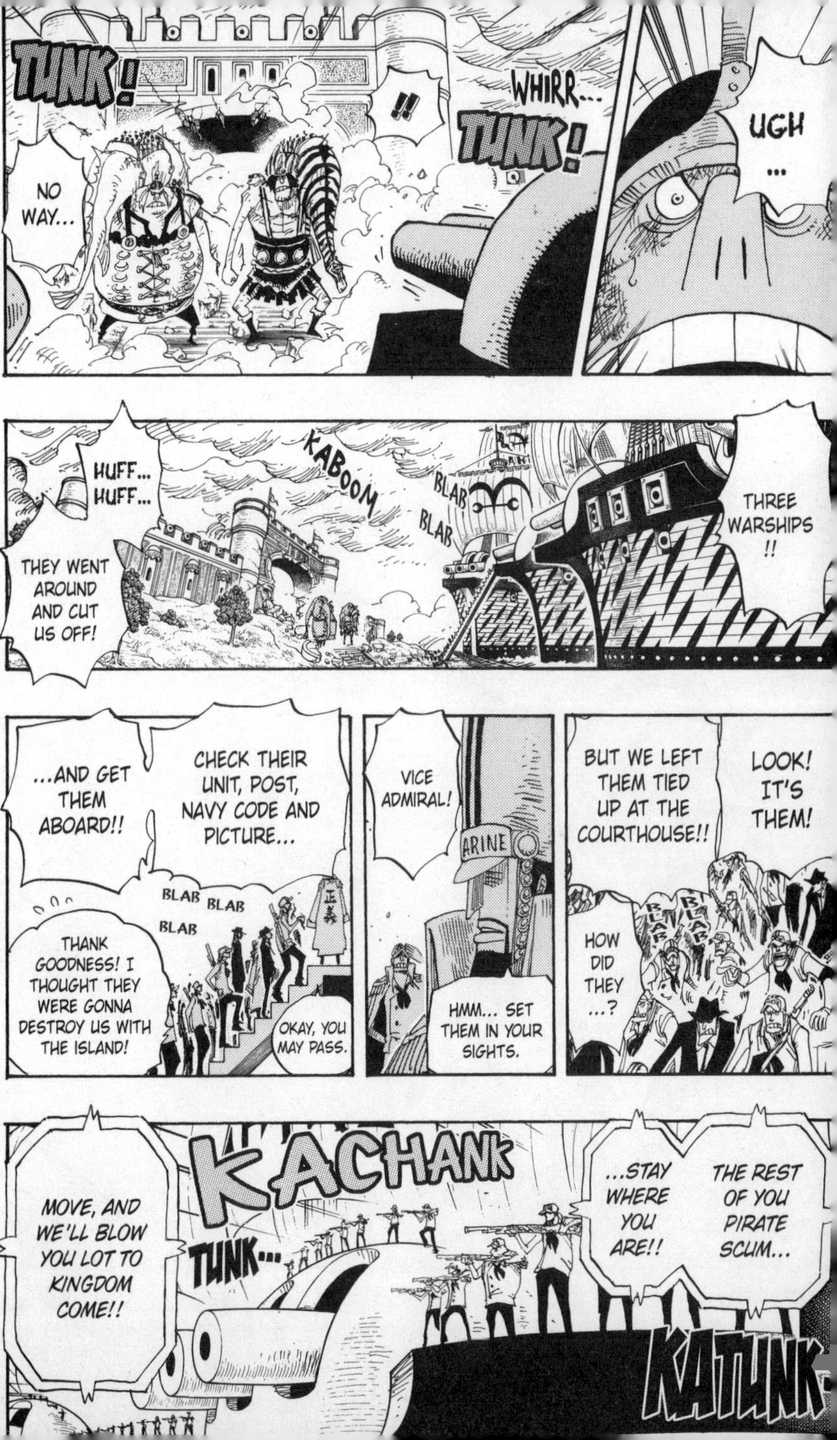
UGH ...
WHIRR...
TUNK!
!!
TUNK!
NO WAY...
THREE WARSHIPS !!
BLAB
BLAB
KABOOM
HUFF... HUFF...
THEY WENT AROUND AND CUT US OFF!
LOOK! IT'S THEM!
BUT WE LEFT THEM TIED UP AT THE COURTHOUSE!!
BLAB
BLAB
HOW DID THEY ...?
VICE ADMIRAL!
HMM... SET THEM IN YOUR SIGHTS.
CHECK THEIR UNIT, POST, NAVY CODE AND PICTURE...
...AND GET THEM ABOARD!!
BLAB BLAB
BLAB
OKAY, YOU MAY PASS.
THANK GOODNESS! I THOUGHT THEY WERE GONNA DESTROY US WITH THE ISLAND!
THE REST OF YOU PIRATE SCUM...
...STAY WHERE YOU ARE!!
KACHANK
KATUNK
TUNK...
MOVE, AND WE'LL BLOW YOU LOT TO KINGDOM COME!!

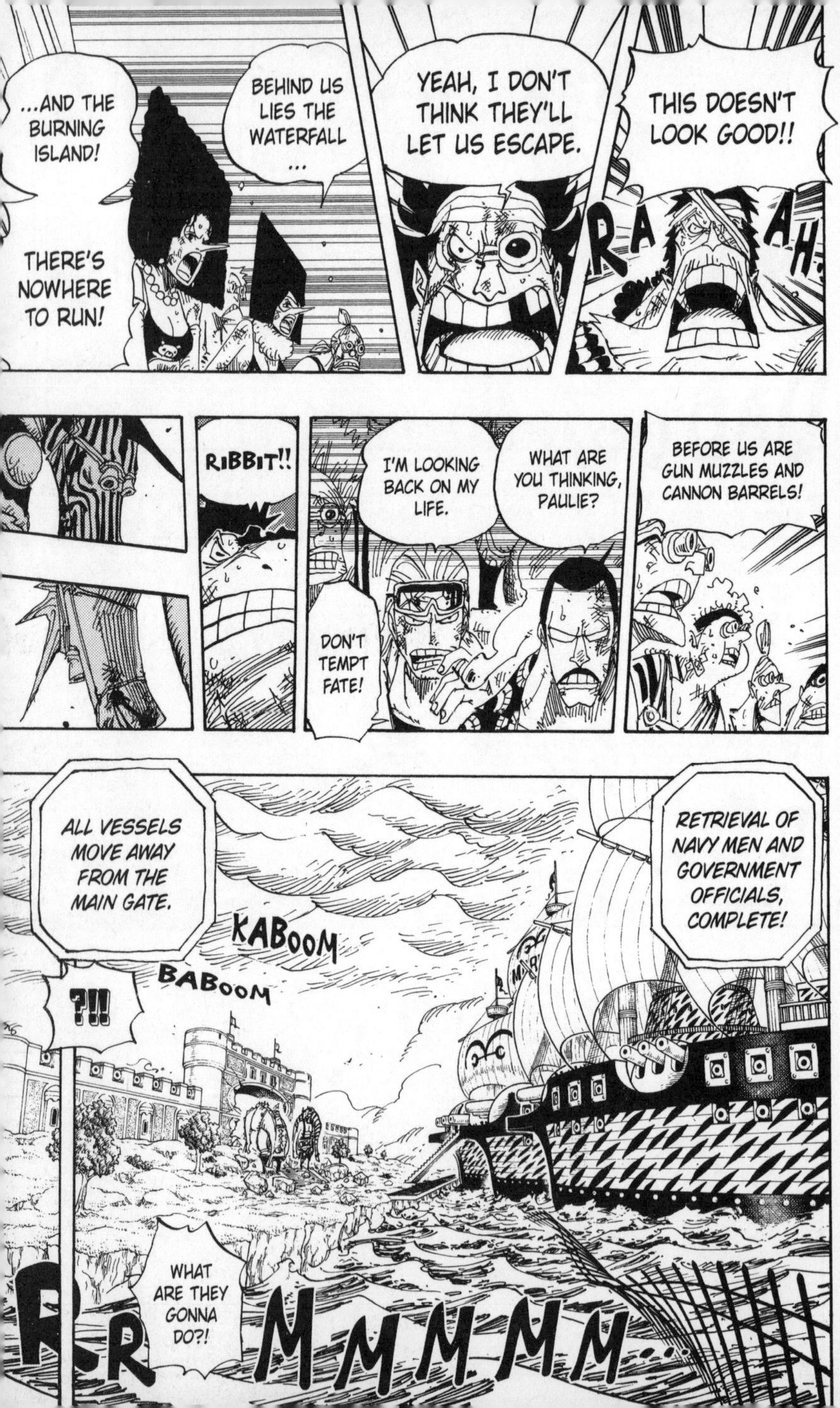
THIS DOESN'T LOOK GOOD!!
RAAH
YEAH, I DON'T THINK THEY'LL LET US ESCAPE.
BEHIND US LIES THE WATERFALL ...
...AND THE BURNING ISLAND!
THERE'S NOWHERE TO RUN!
BEFORE US ARE GUN MUZZLES AND CANNON BARRELS!
WHAT ARE YOU THINKING, PAULIE?
I'M LOOKING BACK ON MY LIFE.
DON'T TEMPT FATE!
RIBBIT!!
RETRIEVAL OF NAVY MEN AND GOVERNMENT OFFICIALS, COMPLETE!
ALL VESSELS MOVE AWAY FROM THE MAIN GATE.
KABOOM
BABOOM
?!!
WHAT ARE THEY GONNA DO?!
RRMMMMMM...

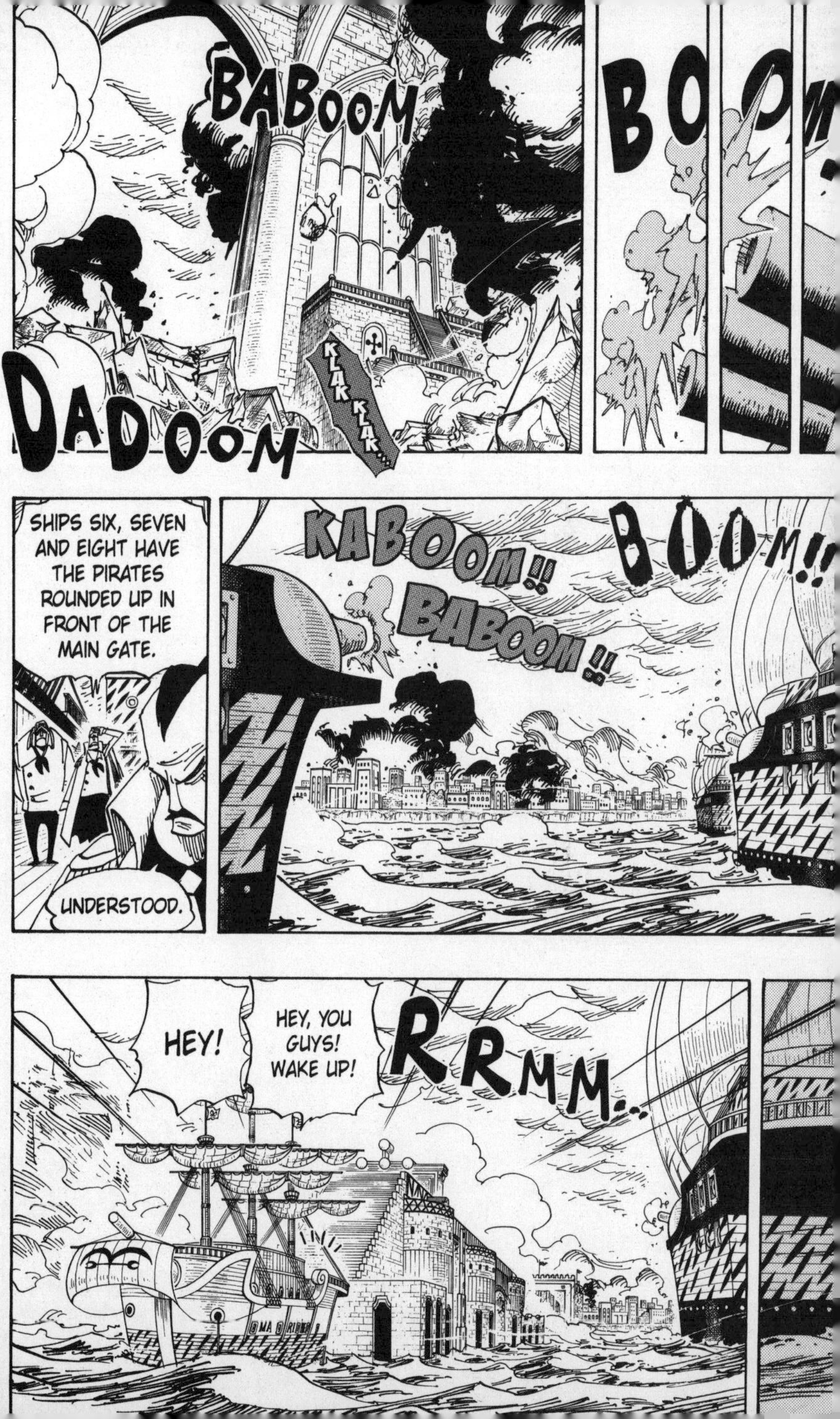
BOOM
BABOOM
KLAK KLAK...
DADOOM
BOOM!!
KABOOM!!
BABOOM!!
SHIPS SIX, SEVEN AND EIGHT HAVE THE PIRATES ROUNDED UP IN FRONT OF THE MAIN GATE.
UNDERSTOOD.
RRMM...
HEY, YOU GUYS! WAKE UP!
HEY!

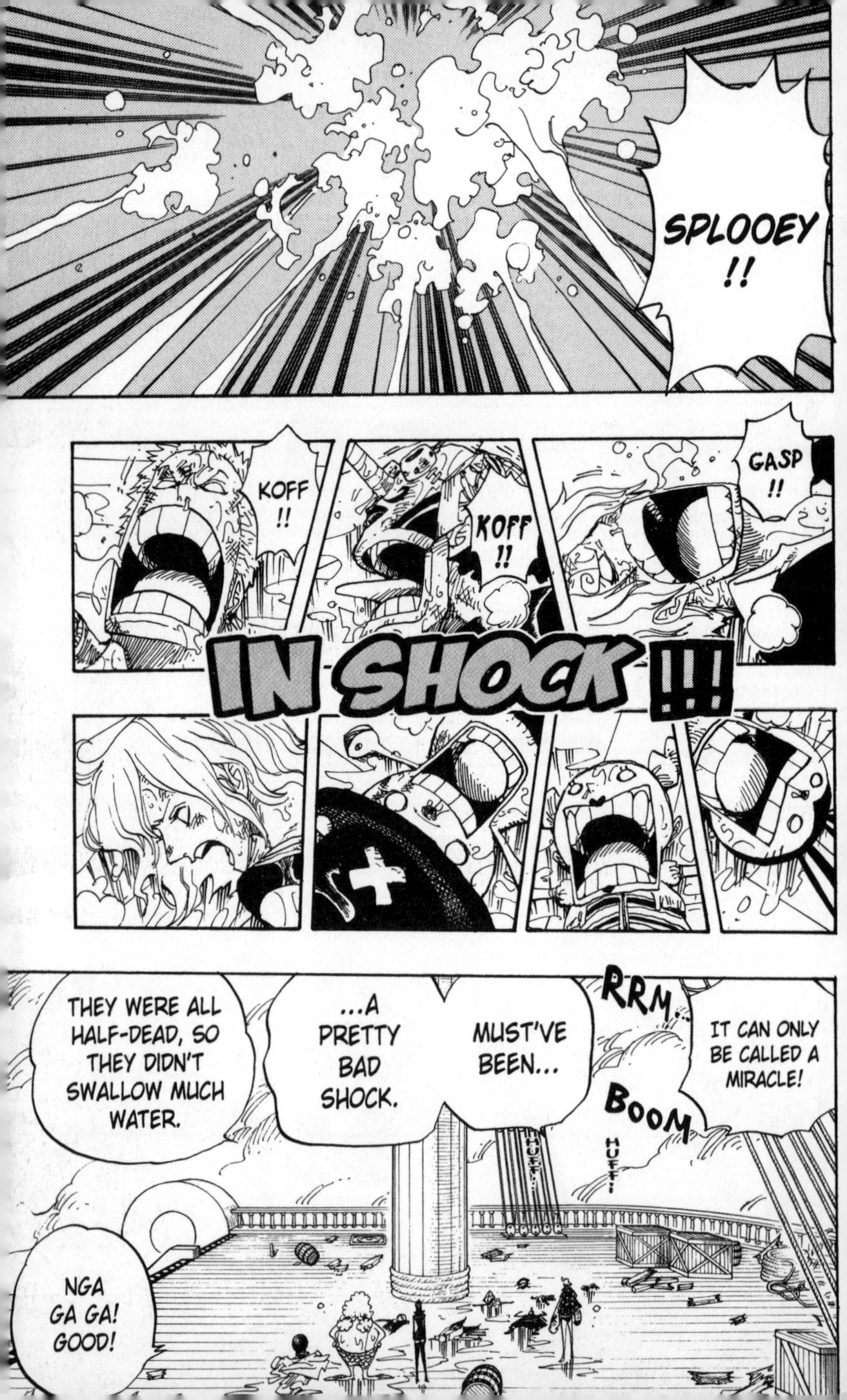
SPLOOEY!!
GASP!!
KOFF!!
KOFF!!
IN SHOCK!!!
IT CAN ONLY BE CALLED A MIRACLE!
RRM...
BOOM
HUFF!
HUFF!
MUST'VE BEEN...
...A PRETTY BAD SHOCK.
THEY WERE ALL HALF-DEAD, SO THEY DIDN'T SWALLOW MUCH WATER.
NGA GA GA! GOOD!

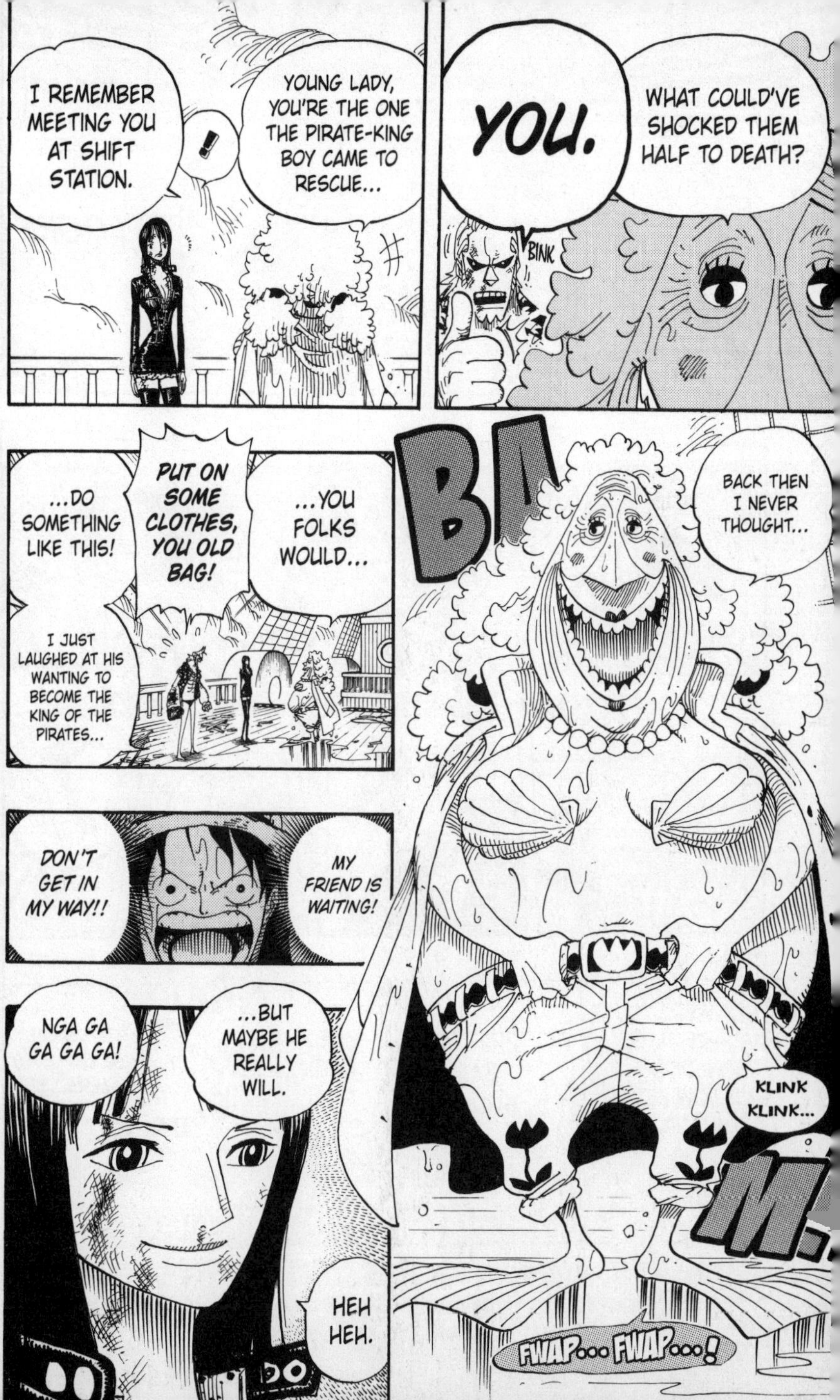
WHAT COULD'VE SHOCKED THEM HALF TO DEATH?
YOU.
BINK
YOUNG LADY, YOU'RE THE ONE THE PIRATE-KING BOY CAME TO RESCUE...
!
I REMEMBER MEETING YOU AT SHIFT STATION.
BA
BACK THEN I NEVER THOUGHT...
KLINK KLINK...
M..
FWAP... FWAP...!
...YOU FOLKS WOULD...
PUT ON SOME CLOTHES, YOU OLD BAG!
...DO SOMETHING LIKE THIS!
I JUST LAUGHED AT HIS WANTING TO BECOME THE KING OF THE PIRATES...
MY FRIEND IS WAITING!
DON'T GET IN MY WAY!!
...BUT MAYBE HE REALLY WILL.
NGA GA GA GA GA!
HEH HEH.

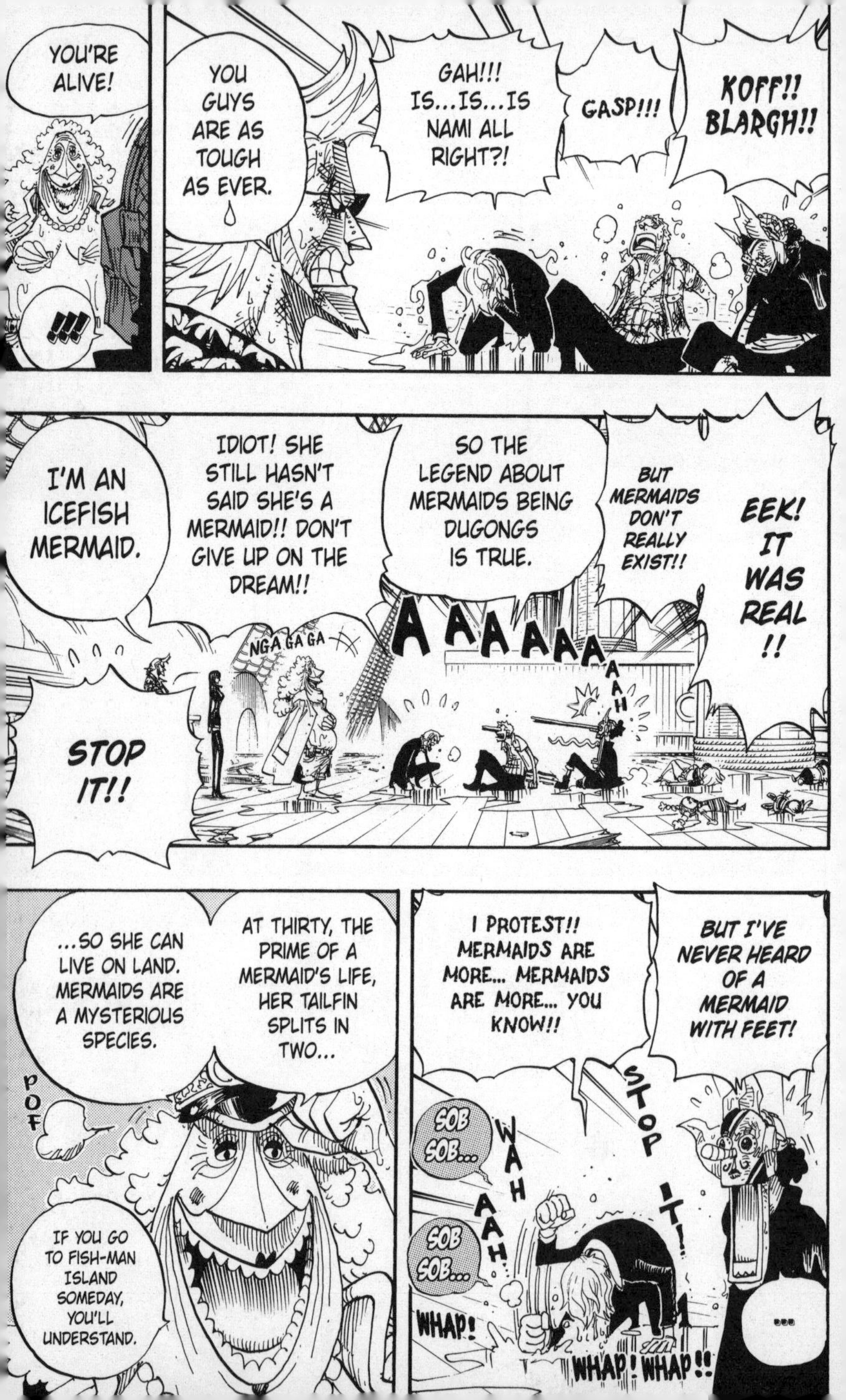
KOFF!! BLARGH!!
GASP!!!
GAH!!! IS...IS...IS NAMI ALL RIGHT?!
YOU GUYS ARE AS TOUGH AS EVER.
YOU'RE ALIVE!
!!!
EEK! IT WAS REAL!!
BUT MERMAIDS DON'T REALLY EXIST!!
SO THE LEGEND ABOUT MERMAIDS BEING DUGONGS IS TRUE.
IDIOT! SHE STILL HASN'T SAID SHE'S A MERMAID!! DON'T GIVE UP ON THE DREAM!!
I'M AN ICEFISH MERMAID.
AAAAAAAAH
NGA GA GA
STOP IT!!
BUT I'VE NEVER HEARD OF A MERMAID WITH FEET!
I PROTEST!! MERMAIDS ARE MORE... MERMAIDS ARE MORE... YOU KNOW!!
STOP IT!!
WAH AAH...
SOB SOB...
SOB SOB...
...
WHAP!
WHAP! WHAP!!
AT THIRTY, THE PRIME OF A MERMAID'S LIFE, HER TAILFIN SPLITS IN TWO...
...SO SHE CAN LIVE ON LAND. MERMAIDS ARE A MYSTERIOUS SPECIES.
POF
IF YOU GO TO FISH-MAN ISLAND SOMEDAY, YOU'LL UNDERSTAND.

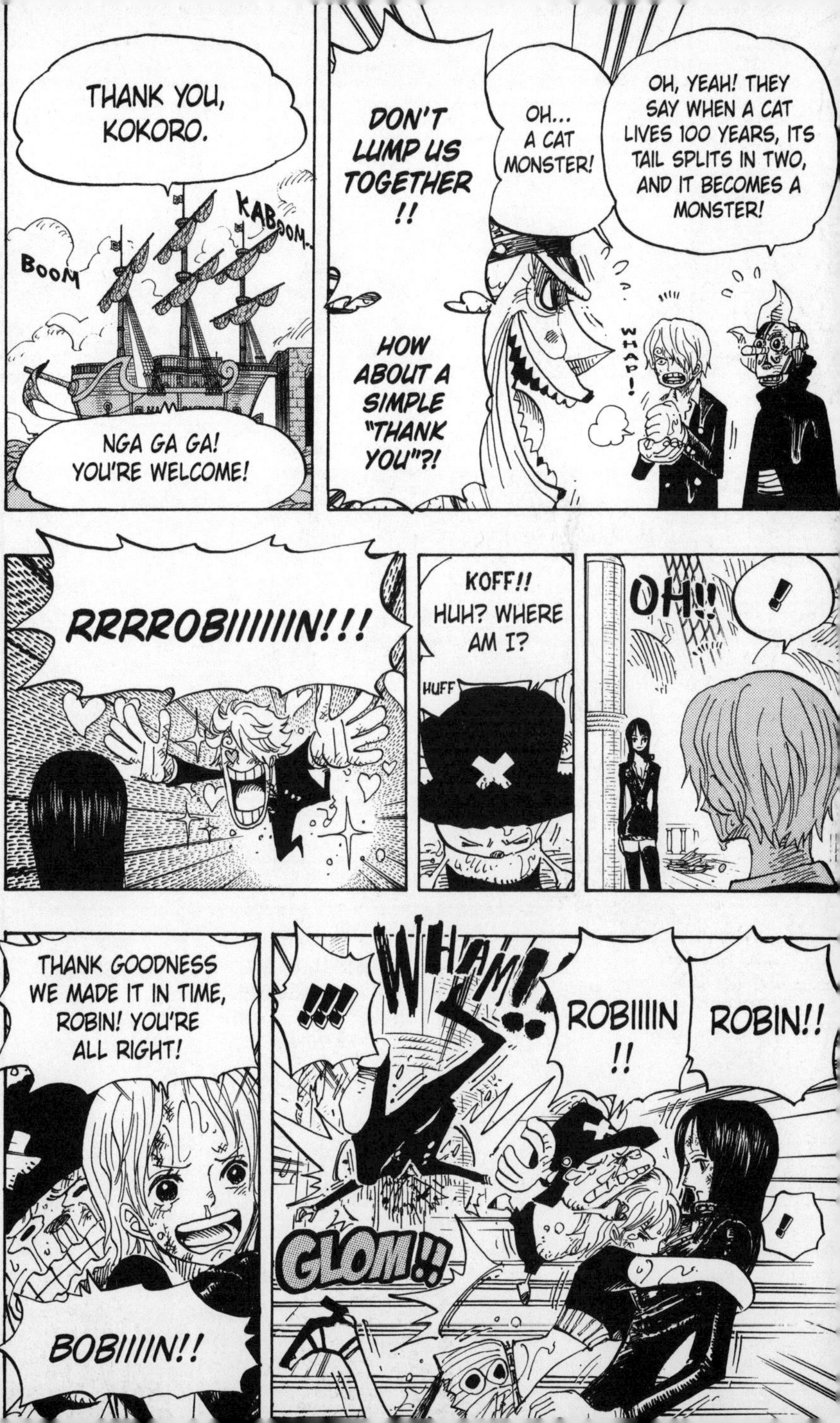
OH... A CAT MONSTER!
OH, YEAH! THEY SAY WHEN A CAT LIVES 100 YEARS, ITS TAIL SPLITS IN TWO, AND IT BECOMES A MONSTER!
WHAP!
DON'T LUMP US TOGETHER!!
HOW ABOUT A SIMPLE "THANK YOU"?!
THANK YOU, KOKORO.
KABOOM
BOOM
NGA GA GA! YOU'RE WELCOME!
OH!!
!
KOFF!! HUH? WHERE AM I?
HUFF
RRRROBIIIIIIN!!!
ROBIN!!
ROBIIIIN!!
WHAM!
!!!
GLOM!!
!
THANK GOODNESS WE MADE IT IN TIME, ROBIN! YOU'RE ALL RIGHT!
BOBIIIIN!!

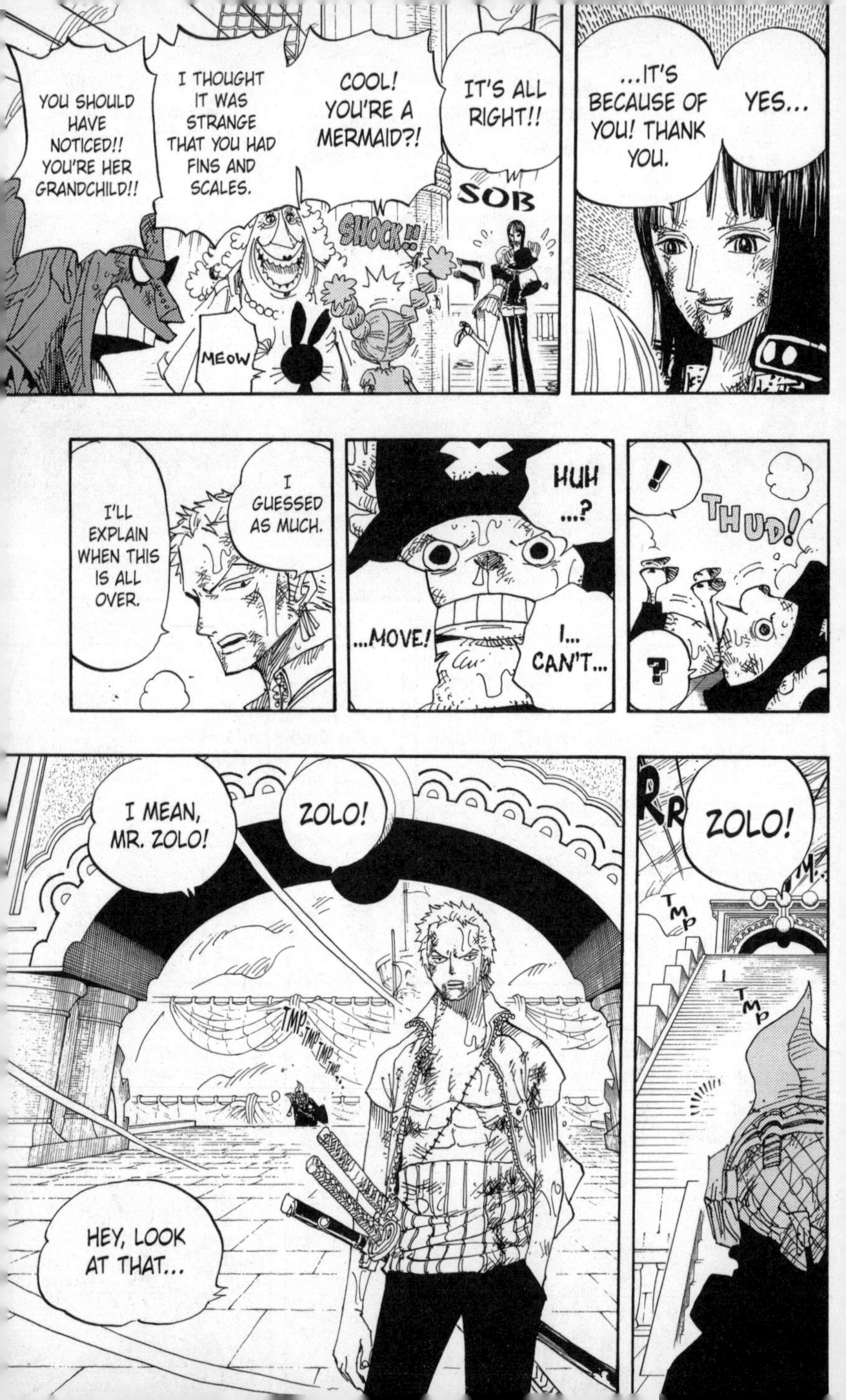
YES...
...IT'S BECAUSE OF YOU! THANK YOU.
IT'S ALL RIGHT!!
SOB
COOL! YOU'RE A MERMAID?!
SHOCK!!
I THOUGHT IT WAS STRANGE THAT YOU HAD FINS AND SCALES.
YOU SHOULD HAVE NOTICED!! YOU'RE HER GRANDCHILD!!
MEOW
!
THUD!
?
HUH ...?
I... CAN'T...
...MOVE!
I GUESSED AS MUCH.
I'LL EXPLAIN WHEN THIS IS ALL OVER.
ZOLO!
RR
TMP
TMP
ZOLO!
I MEAN, MR. ZOLO!
TMP TMP TMP TMP
HEY, LOOK AT THAT...

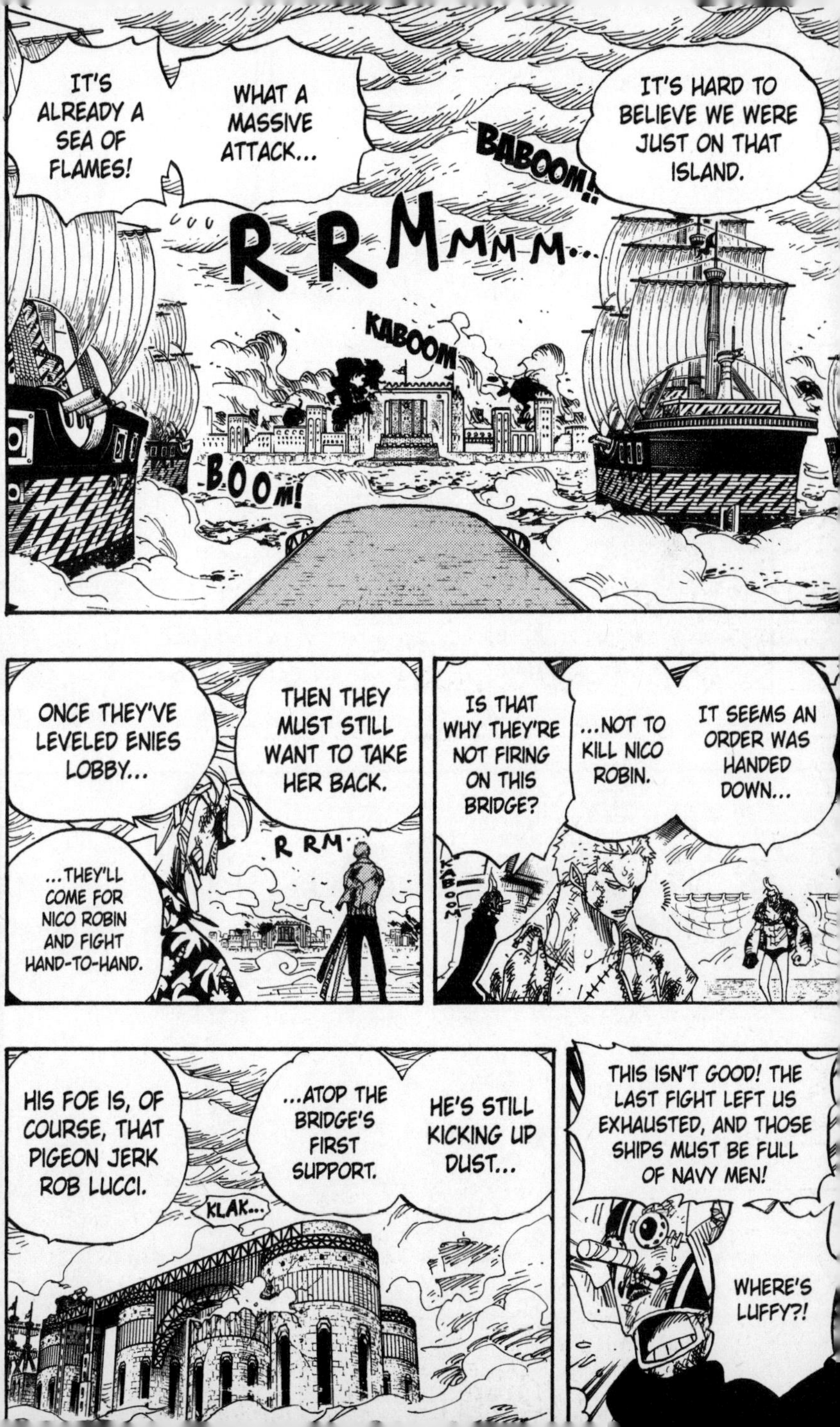
IT'S HARD TO BELIEVE WE WERE JUST ON THAT ISLAND.
BABOOM!!
WHAT A MASSIVE ATTACK...
IT'S ALREADY A SEA OF FLAMES!
RRMMMM...
KABOOM
BOOM!
IT SEEMS AN ORDER WAS HANDED DOWN...
...NOT TO KILL NICO ROBIN.
IS THAT WHY THEY'RE NOT FIRING ON THIS BRIDGE?
KABOOM
THEN THEY MUST STILL WANT TO TAKE HER BACK.
ONCE THEY'VE LEVELED ENIES LOBBY...
...THEY'LL COME FOR NICO ROBIN AND FIGHT HAND-TO-HAND.
RRM...
THIS ISN'T GOOD! THE LAST FIGHT LEFT US EXHAUSTED, AND THOSE SHIPS MUST BE FULL OF NAVY MEN!
WHERE'S LUFFY?!
HE'S STILL KICKING UP DUST...
...ATOP THE BRIDGE'S FIRST SUPPORT.
HIS FOE IS, OF COURSE, THAT PIGEON JERK ROB LUCCI.
KLAK...

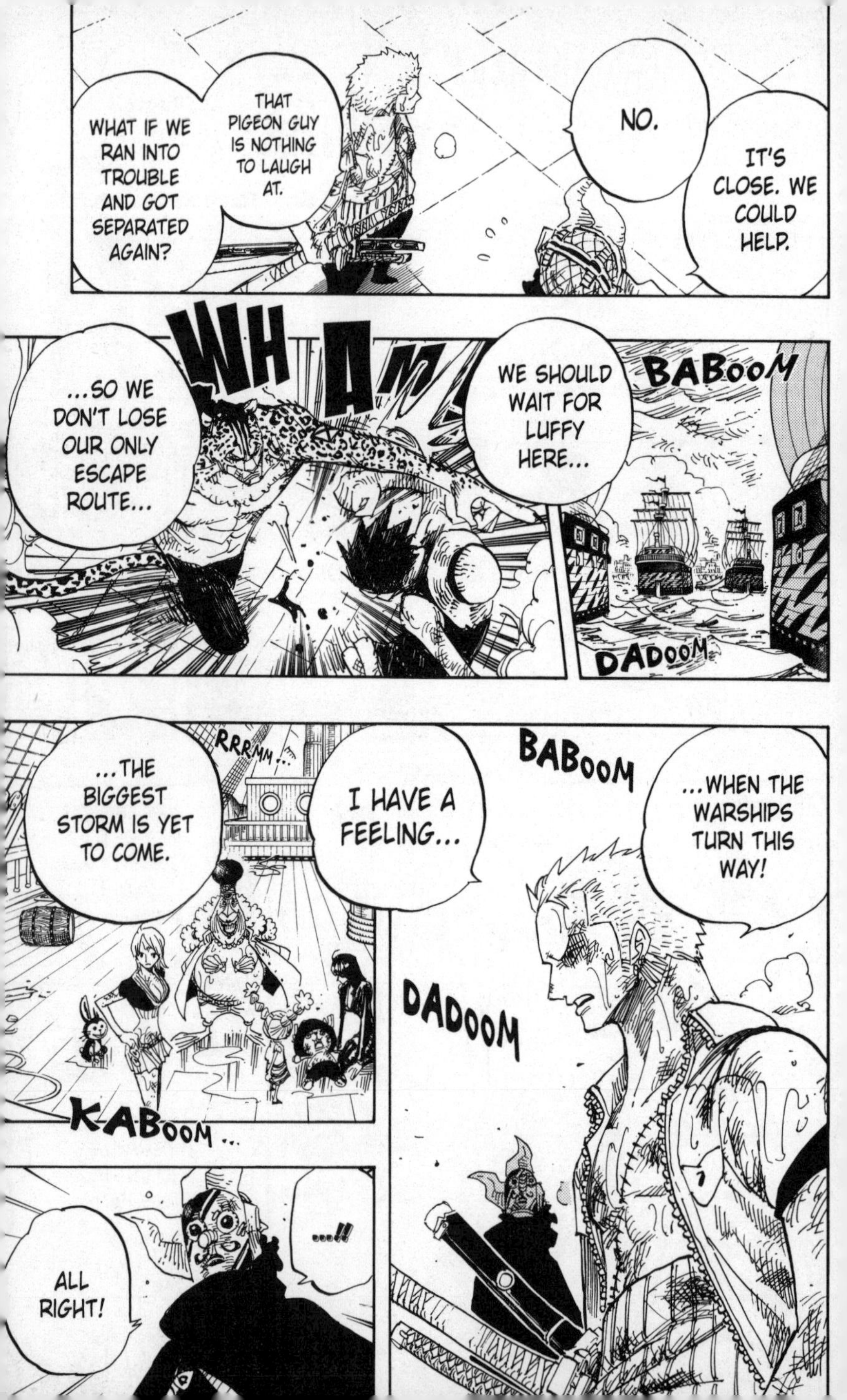
IT'S CLOSE. WE COULD HELP.
NO.
THAT PIGEON GUY IS NOTHING TO LAUGH AT.
WHAT IF WE RAN INTO TROUBLE AND GOT SEPARATED AGAIN?
BABOOM
WE SHOULD WAIT FOR LUFFY HERE...
DADOOM
WHAM
...SO WE DON'T LOSE OUR ONLY ESCAPE ROUTE...
...WHEN THE WARSHIPS TURN THIS WAY!
BABOOM
I HAVE A FEELING...
DADOOM
RRRMM...
...THE BIGGEST STORM IS YET TO COME.
KABOOM...
...!!
ALL RIGHT!

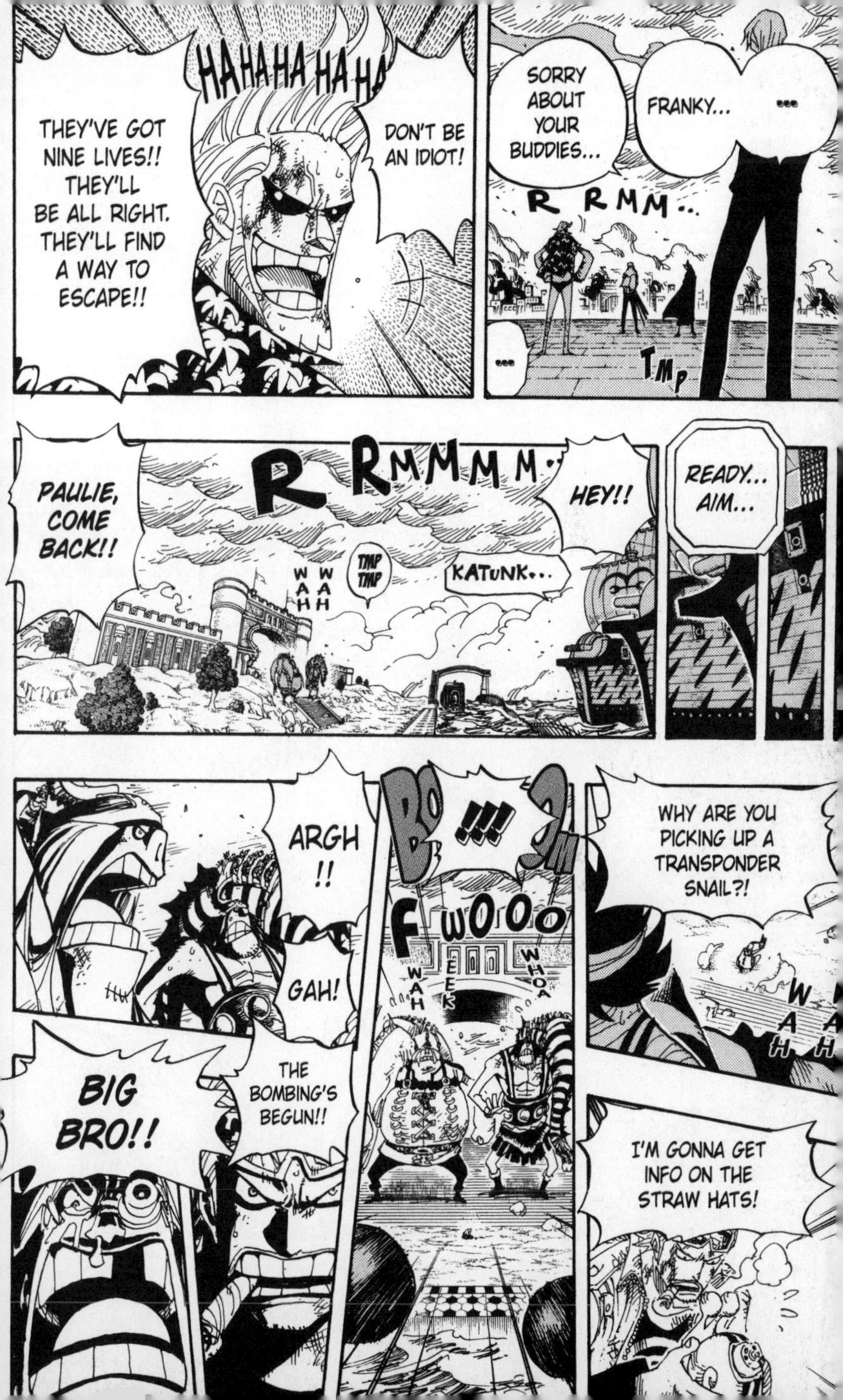
...
FRANKY...
SORRY ABOUT YOUR BUDDIES...
R RMM..
TMP
...
HAHAHA HA HA
DON'T BE AN IDIOT!
THEY'VE GOT NINE LIVES!! THEY'LL BE ALL RIGHT. THEY'LL FIND A WAY TO ESCAPE!!
READY... AIM...
HEY!!
R RMMMM..
KATUNK...
TMP TMP
WAH WAH
PAULIE, COME BACK!!
WHY ARE YOU PICKING UP A TRANSPONDER SNAIL?!
WAH WAH
I'M GONNA GET INFO ON THE STRAW HATS!
BOOM!!!
FWOOO
WHOA
EEEK
WAH
ARGH!!
GAH!
THE BOMBING'S BEGUN!!
BIG BRO!!

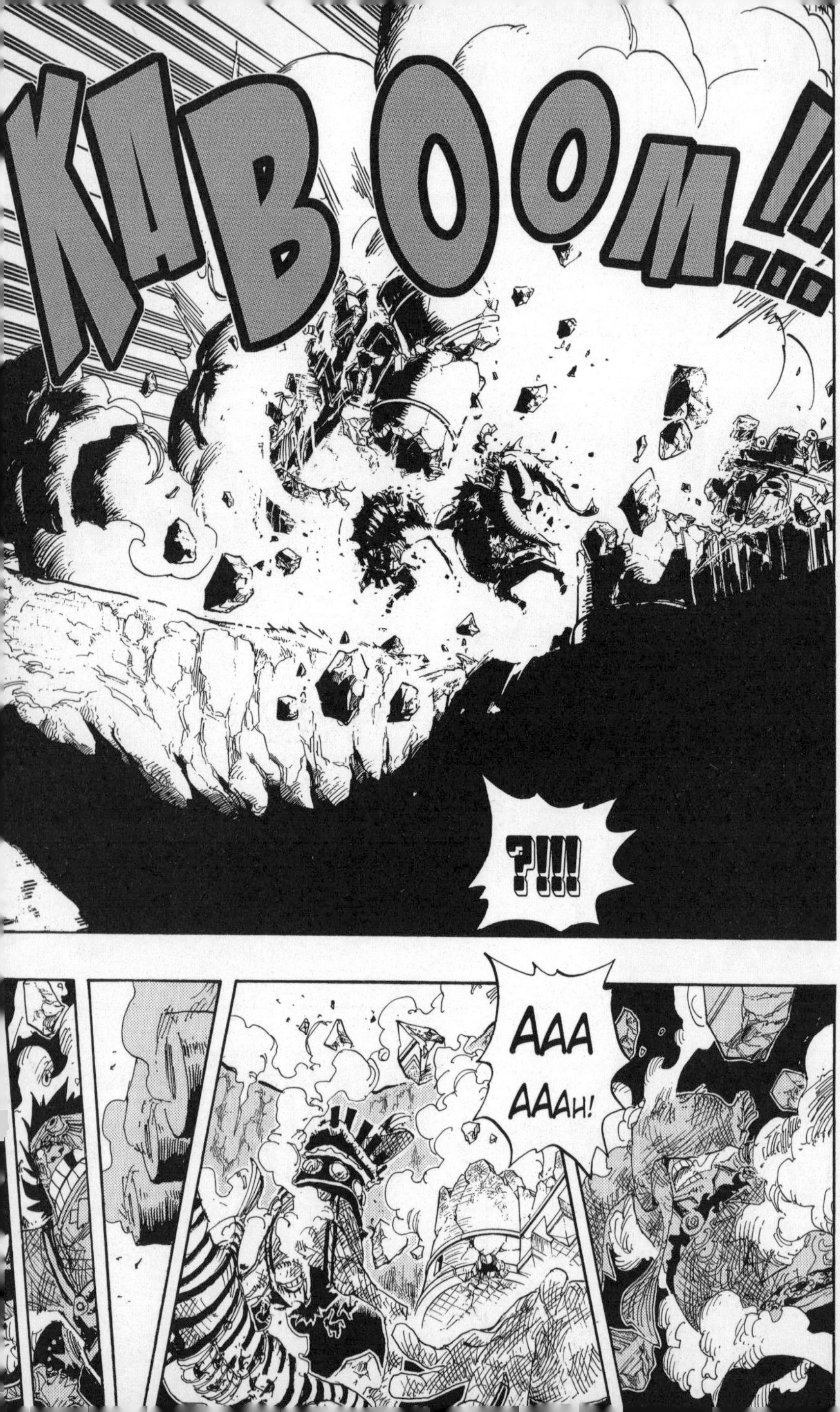
KABOOM...!!!
?!!!
AAA AAAH!

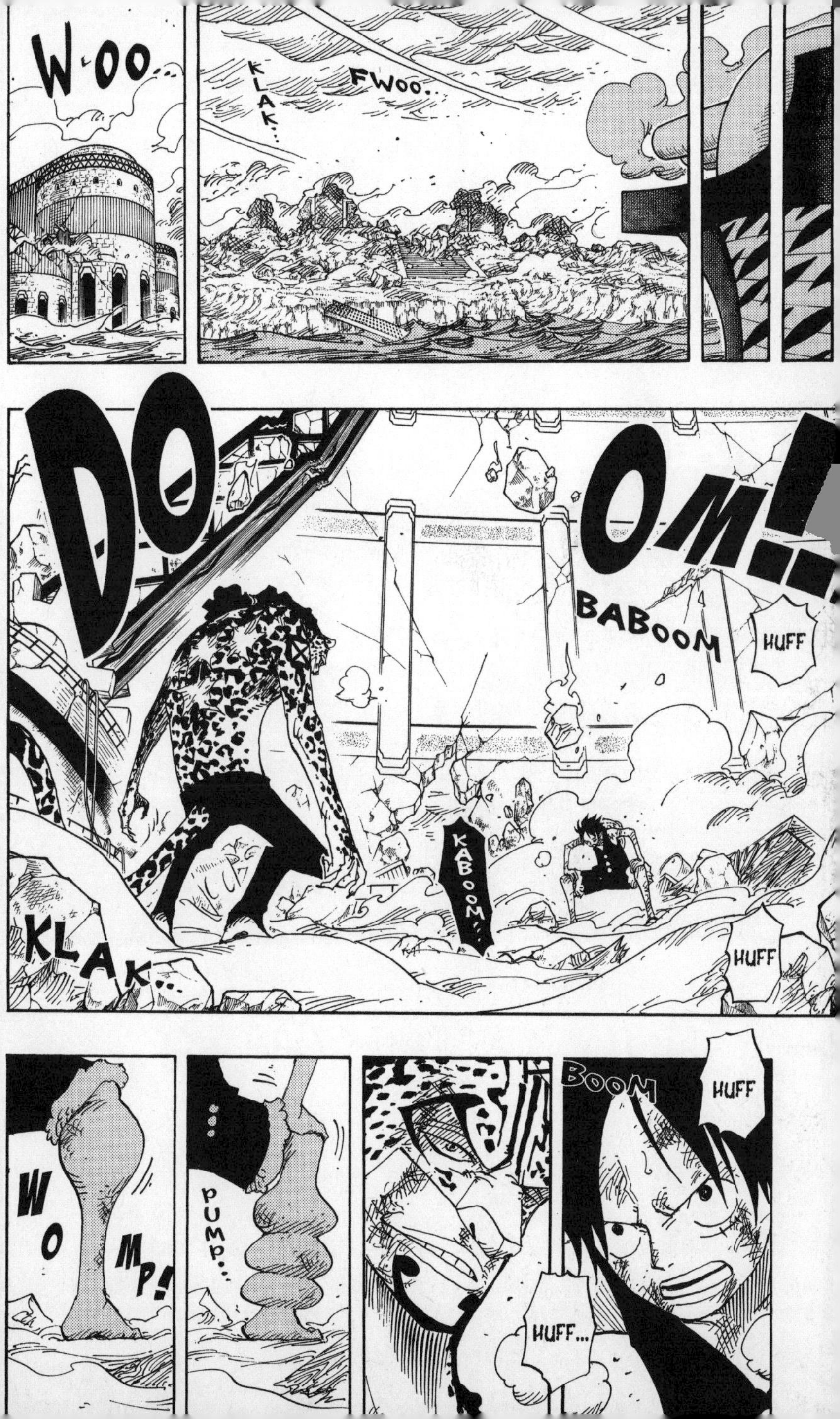
FWOO...
KLAK...
W-OO...
DO-OM!!
BABOOM
HUFF
KABOOM...
HUFF
KLAK...
HUFF
BOOM
HUFF...
PUMP...
WOMP!

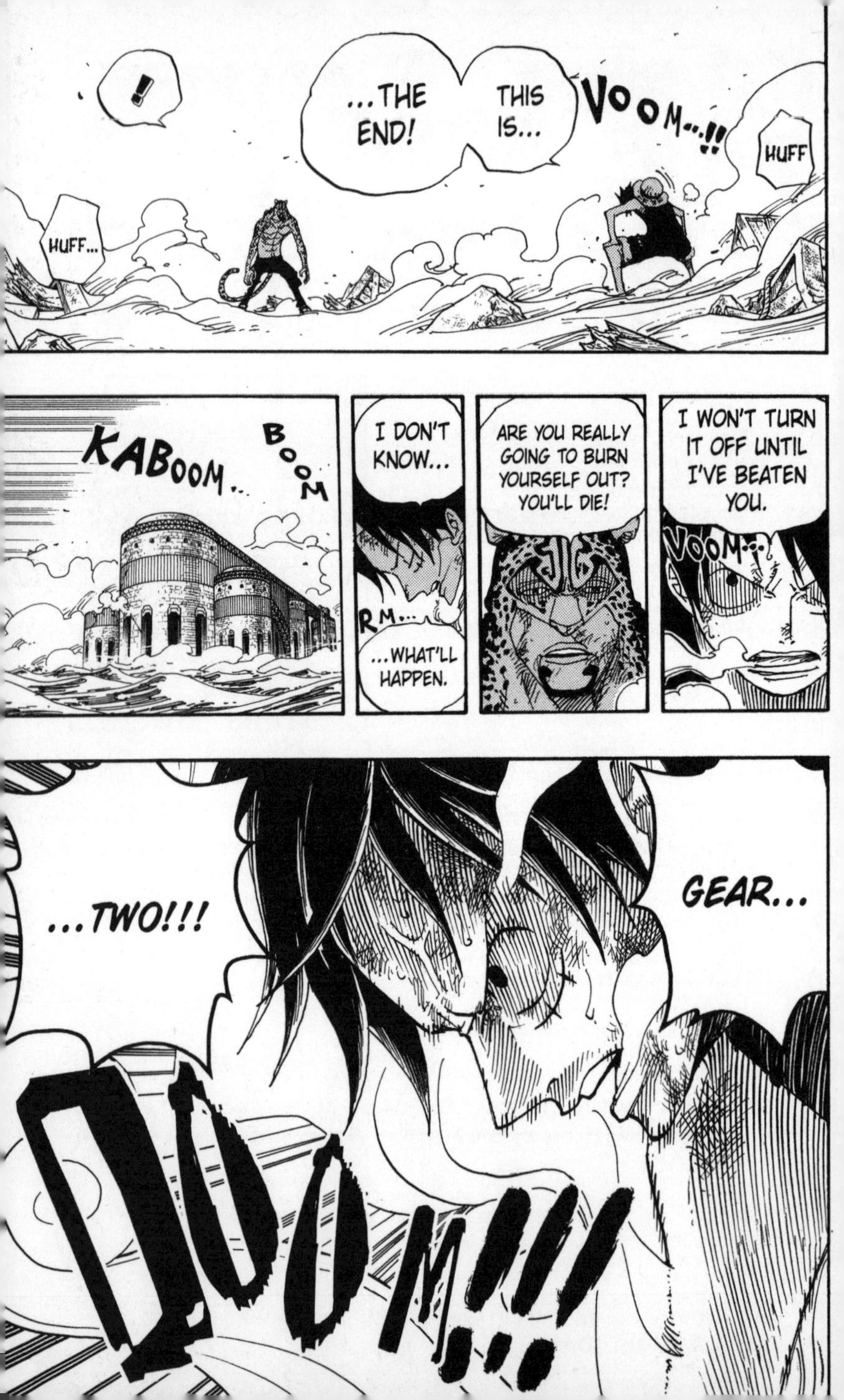
HUFF
VOOM--!!
THIS IS...
...THE END!
!
HUFF...
I WON'T TURN IT OFF UNTIL I'VE BEATEN YOU.
VOOM--
ARE YOU REALLY GOING TO BURN YOURSELF OUT? YOU'LL DIE!
I DON'T KNOW...
RM...
...WHAT'LL HAPPEN.
KABOOM..
BOOM
GEAR...
...TWO!!!
DOOM!!!...

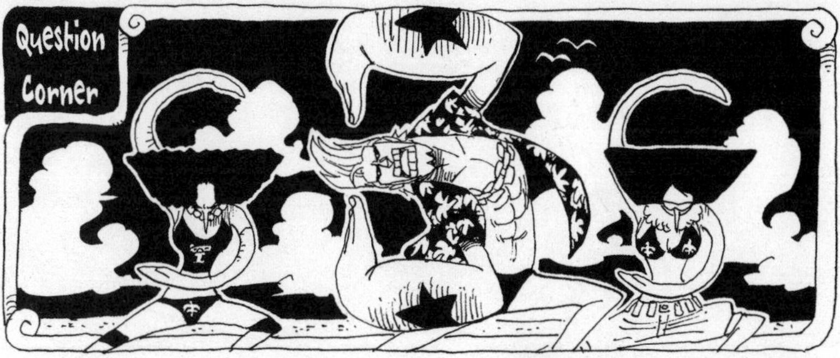
Question Corner

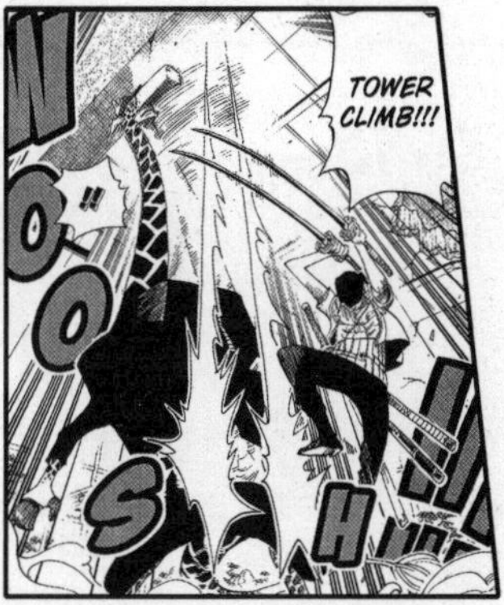
TOWER CLIMB!!!

Q: Odacchi, hello! I noticed something. It's the secret of Zolo's techniques during his battle against Kaku in volume 43. The attacks have a double meaning in Japanese!
Nigiri → Nigiri (sushi)
Tower Climb (tôrô) → Fatty tuna (toro)
Tower Climb Return (ôtôrô) → Big fatty tuna (ôtoro, fattier than toro)
Flash (hirameki) → Flounder (hirame)
Ripple (samon) → Salmon (samon)

What a focus on sushi… Has Zolo even eaten sushi before?!

--Susshi

Here, the way each attack is pronounced in Japanese suggests a particular type of fish or sushi. The Japanese pronunciation appears in parentheses.--Ed.

A: Well, well, well! Once again it appears charges have been leveled at you, Zolo! It must hurt to have people accuse you of such shameless puns! Come out and say it's not true, Zolo!

Zolo: **Hey, now! Listen up, Susshi. I-it isn't...isn't...**

A: You're not lying well!

Q: Dear Oda Sensei. Does Santa really exist?

--Kinoko

A: Yes!! He totally exists!! One time, I wanted to see him, and was waiting with my eyes open, but I fell asleep. He's really hard to see! Argh!

Q: Oda Sensei! I've got a serious question. Aren't you ever going to draw Luffy's father?

--Mr. Unii, 16 years old

A: His father? I already drew him. He'll be in the next volume. Look forward to it!

Chapter 425:

BRIDGE OF MORTAL COMBAT

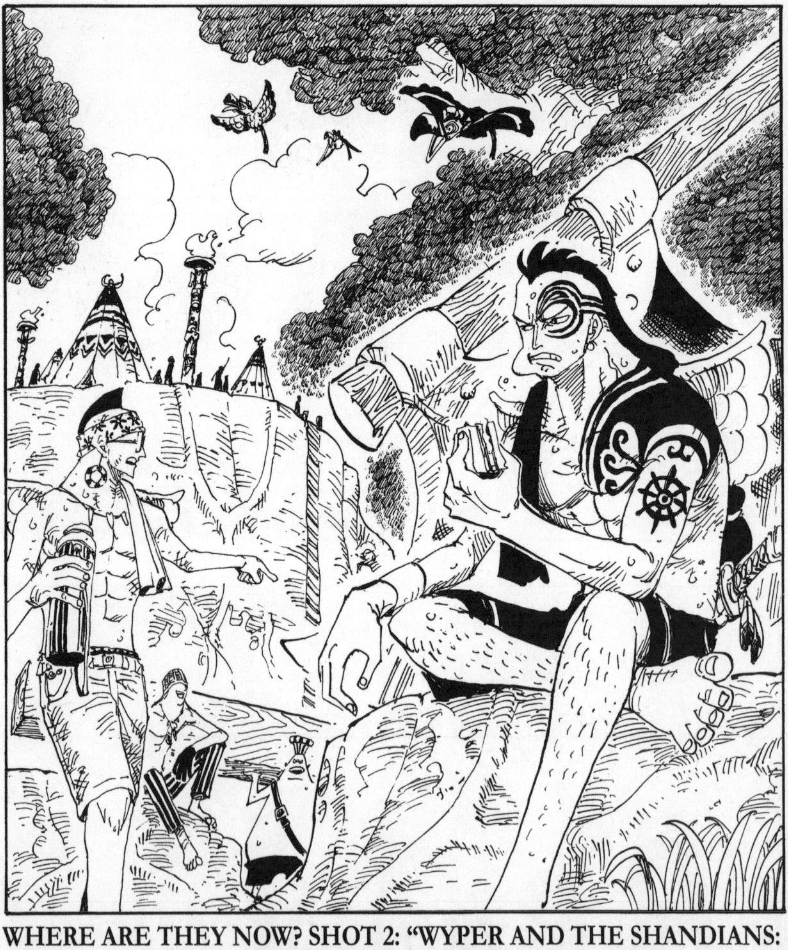

WHERE ARE THEY NOW? SHOT 2: "WYPER AND THE SHANDIANS: THE FOREST FRONTIER"

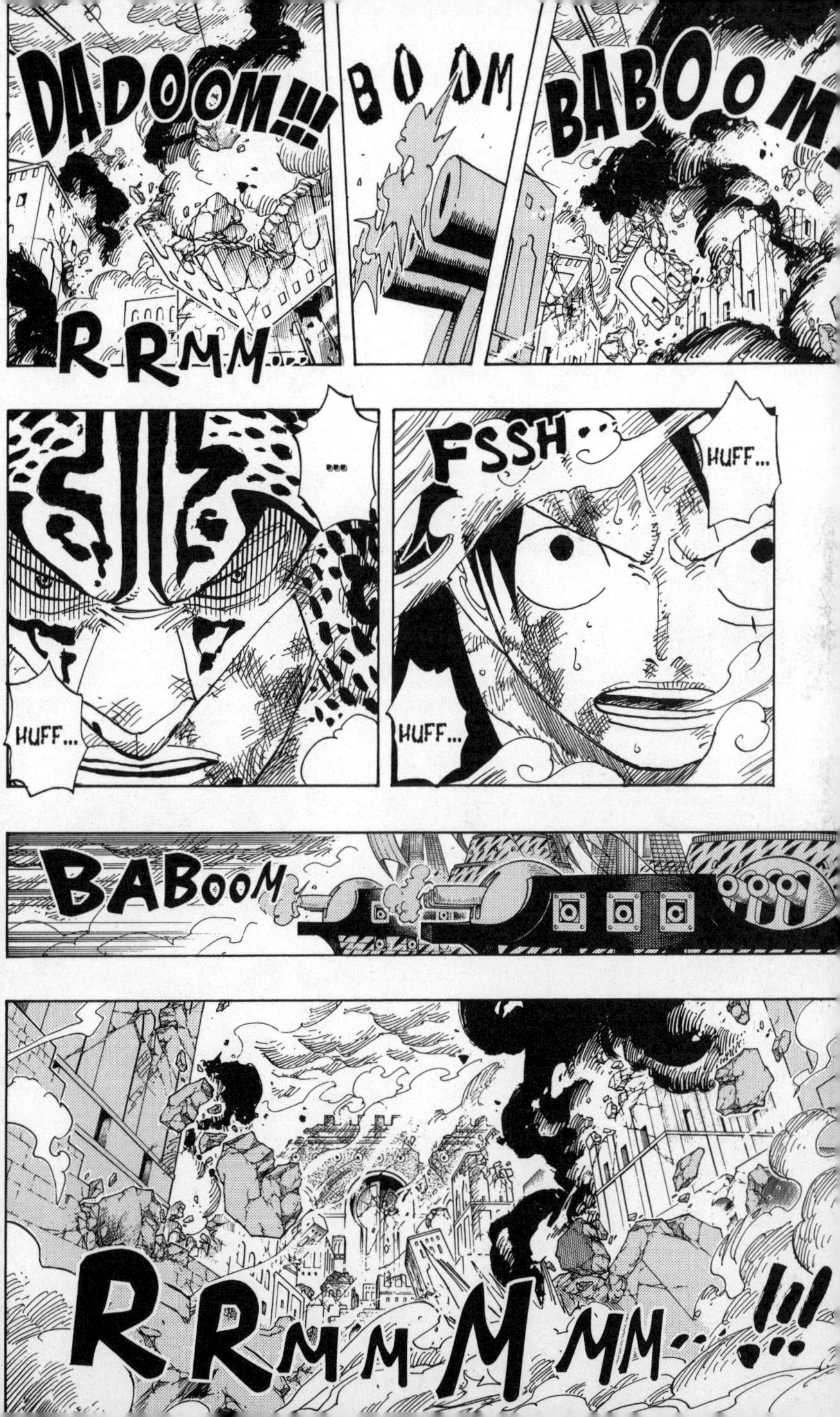
BABOOM
BOOM
DADOOM!!!
RRMM
HUFF...
FSSH
HUFF...
...
HUFF...
BABOOM
RRMMMMMM...!!!

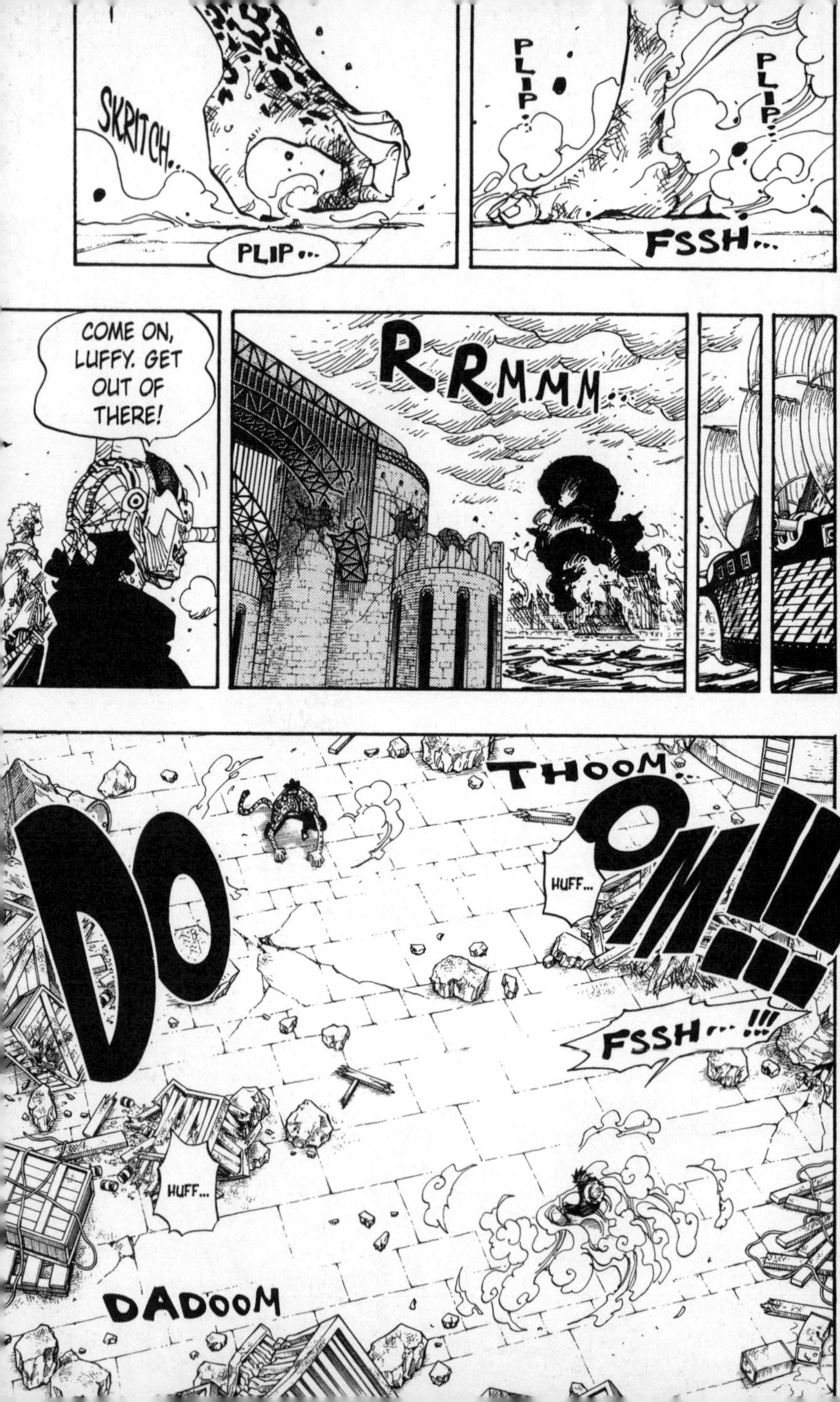
PLIP
PLIP
FSSH...
SKRITCH...
PLIP...
RRMMM...
COME ON, LUFFY. GET OUT OF THERE!
THOOM...
DOOM!!!
HUFF...
FSSH...!!!
HUFF...
DADOOM

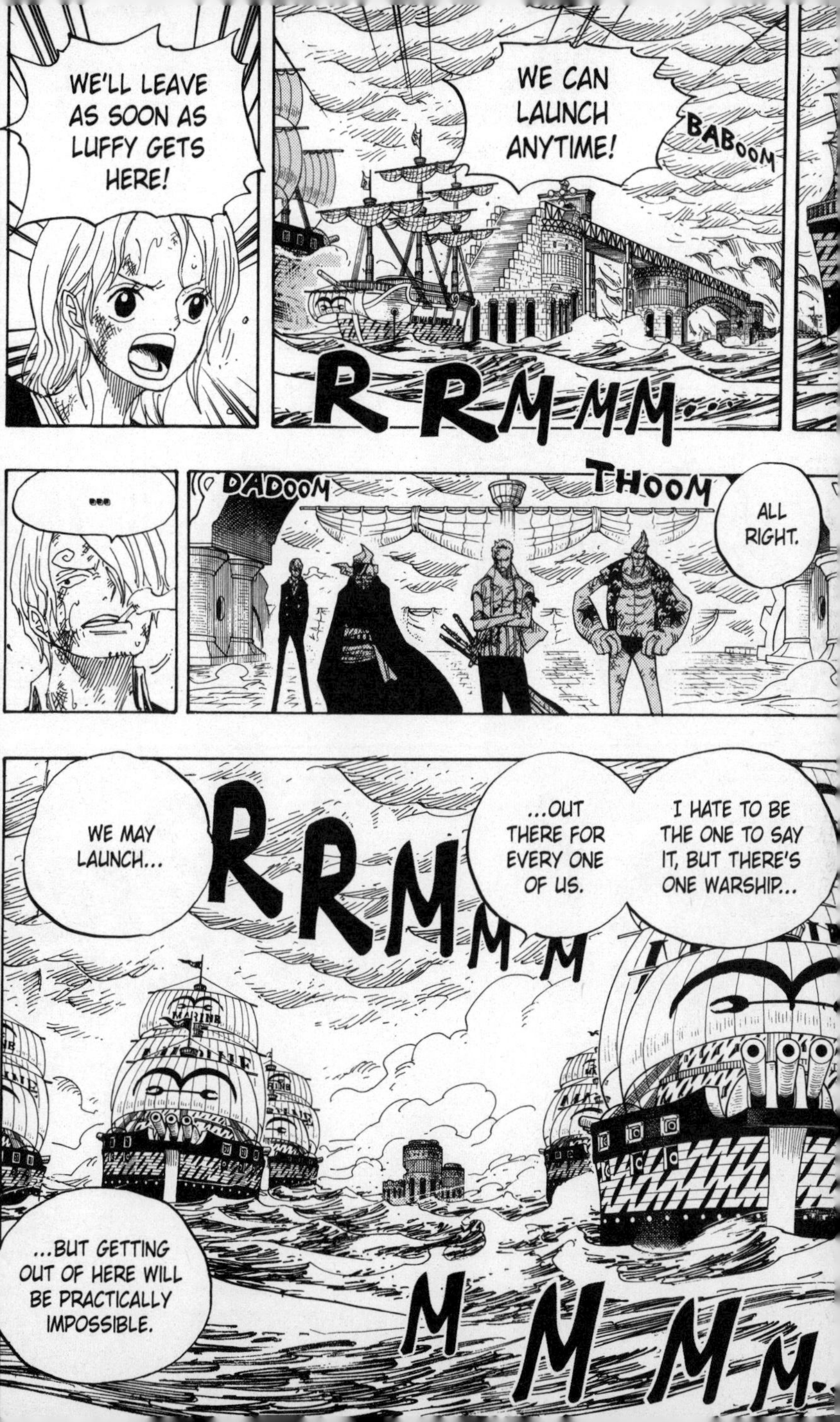
WE CAN LAUNCH ANYTIME!
BABOOM
RRMMM...
WE'LL LEAVE AS SOON AS LUFFY GETS HERE!
ALL RIGHT.
THOOM
DADOOM
...
I HATE TO BE THE ONE TO SAY IT, BUT THERE'S ONE WARSHIP...
...OUT THERE FOR EVERY ONE OF US.
RRMMM
WE MAY LAUNCH...
...BUT GETTING OUT OF HERE WILL BE PRACTICALLY IMPOSSIBLE.
MMMM.

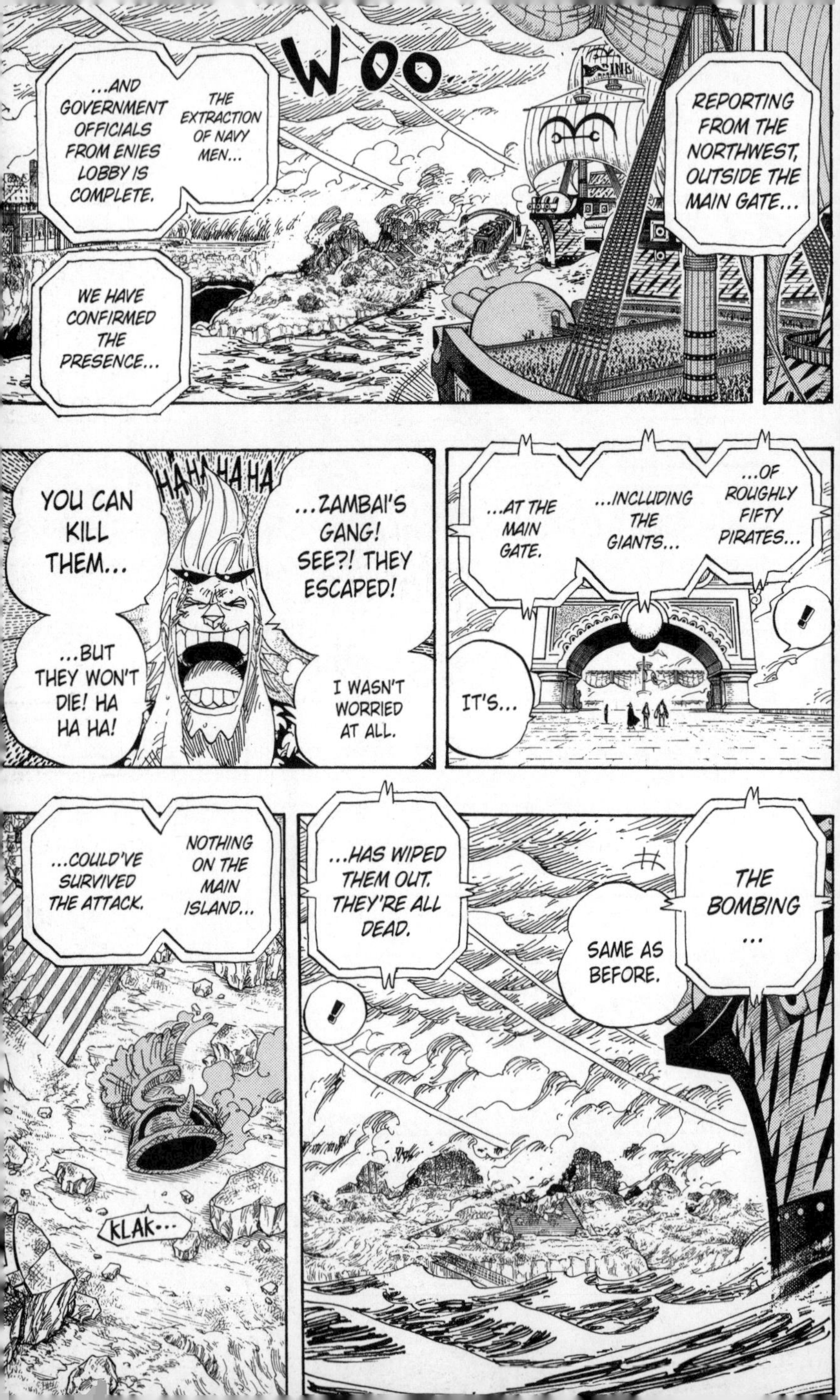
REPORTING FROM THE NORTHWEST, OUTSIDE THE MAIN GATE...
WOO
THE EXTRACTION OF NAVY MEN...
...AND GOVERNMENT OFFICIALS FROM ENIES LOBBY IS COMPLETE.
WE HAVE CONFIRMED THE PRESENCE...
...OF ROUGHLY FIFTY PIRATES...
...INCLUDING THE GIANTS...
...AT THE MAIN GATE.
!
IT'S...
...ZAMBAI'S GANG! SEE?! THEY ESCAPED!
I WASN'T WORRIED AT ALL.
HA HA HA HA
YOU CAN KILL THEM...
...BUT THEY WON'T DIE! HA HA HA!
THE BOMBING ...
SAME AS BEFORE.
...HAS WIPED THEM OUT. THEY'RE ALL DEAD.
!
NOTHING ON THE MAIN ISLAND...
...COULD'VE SURVIVED THE ATTACK.
KLAK...

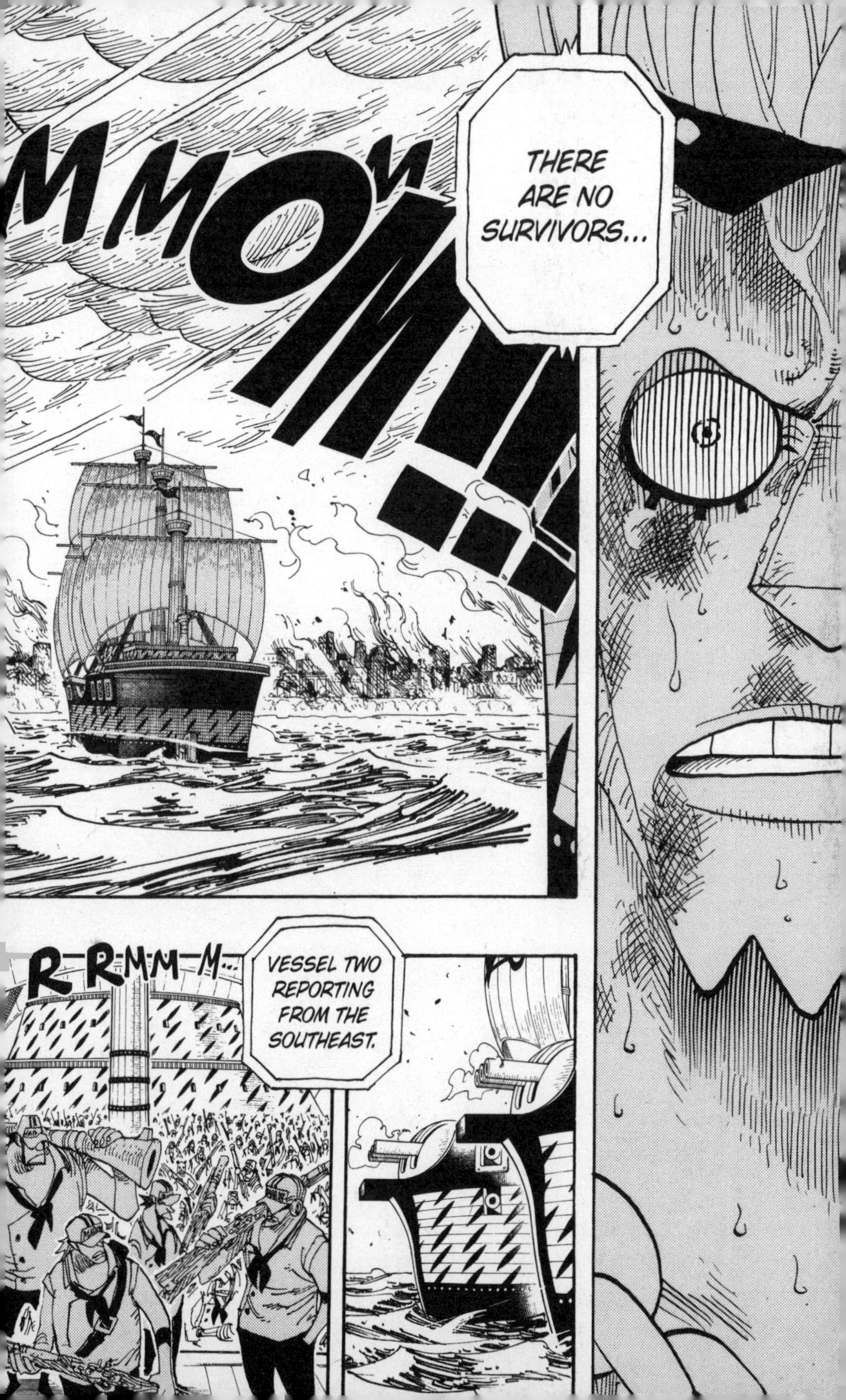
THERE ARE NO SURVIVORS...
MMOM!!
VESSEL TWO REPORTING FROM THE SOUTHEAST.
R-RMM-M...

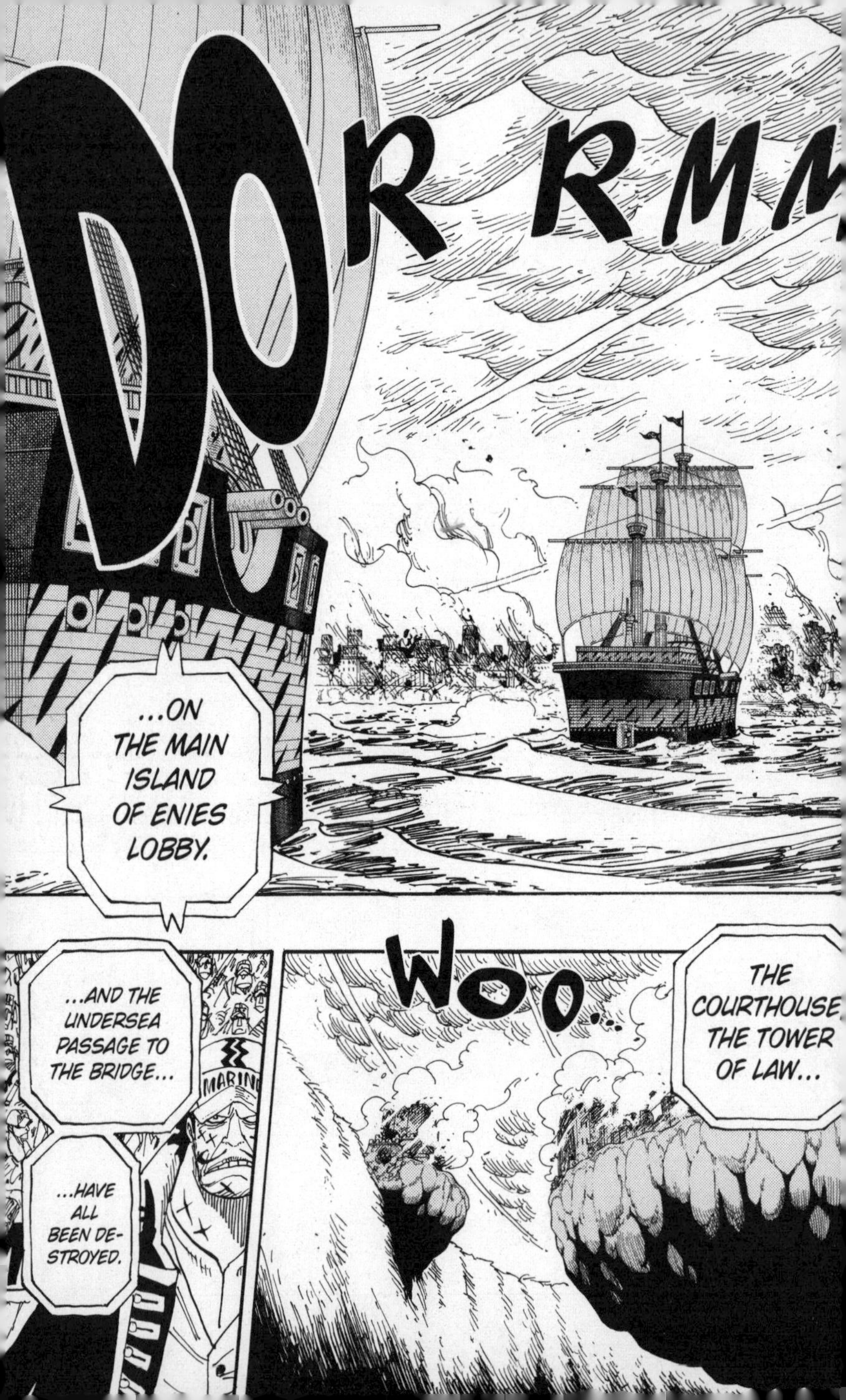
DOORMM
...ON THE MAIN ISLAND OF ENIES LOBBY.
WOO...
THE COURTHOUSE, THE TOWER OF LAW...
...AND THE UNDERSEA PASSAGE TO THE BRIDGE...
...HAVE ALL BEEN DE-STROYED.
MARINE

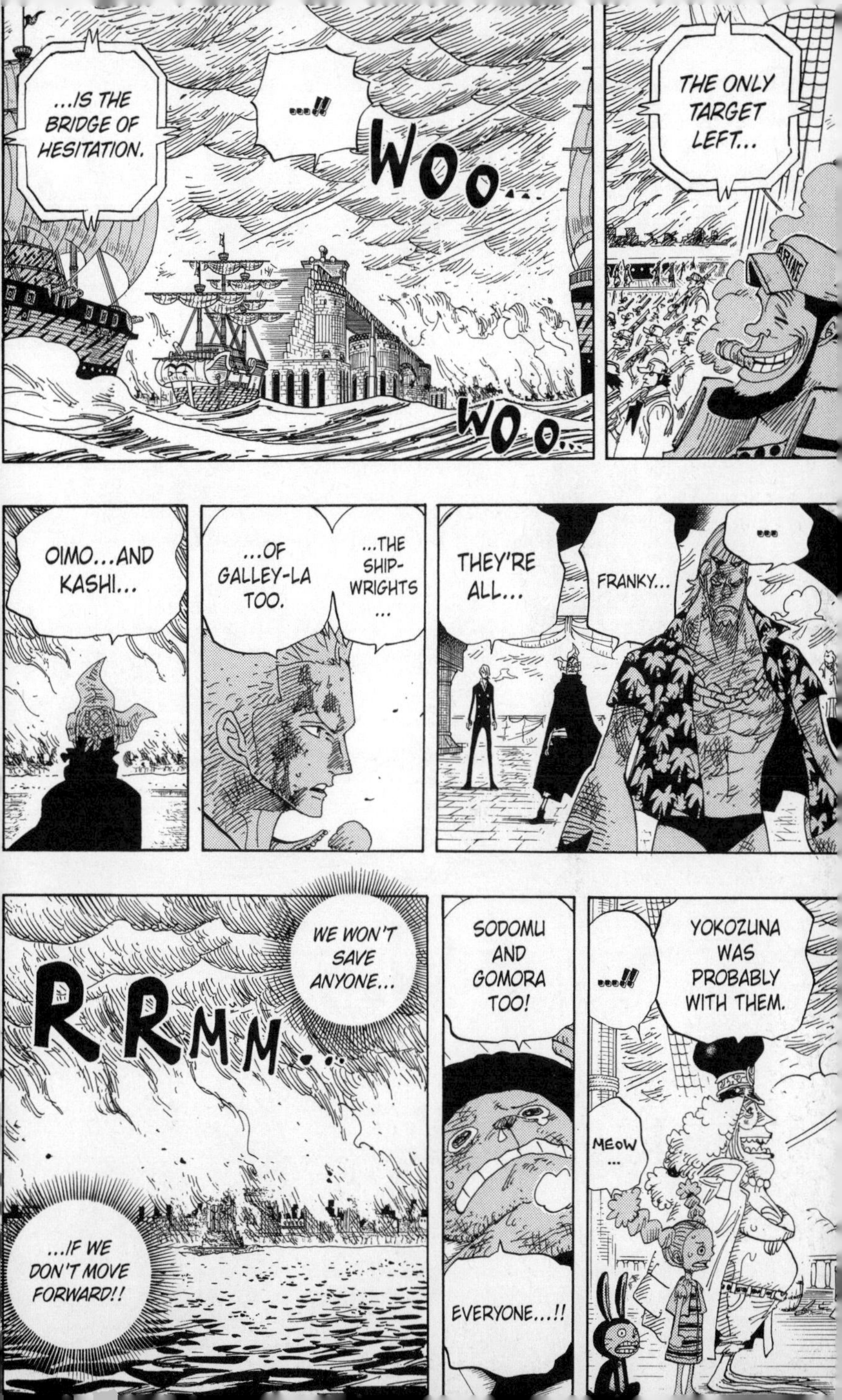
THE ONLY TARGET LEFT...
...IS THE BRIDGE OF HESITATION.
...!!
WOO...
WOO...
...
FRANKY...
THEY'RE ALL...
...THE SHIP-WRIGHTS ...
...OF GALLEY-LA TOO.
OIMO...AND KASHI...
YOKOZUNA WAS PROBABLY WITH THEM.
...!!
MEOW ...
SODOMU AND GOMORA TOO!
EVERYONE...!!
WE WON'T SAVE ANYONE...
RRMM...
...IF WE DON'T MOVE FORWARD!!

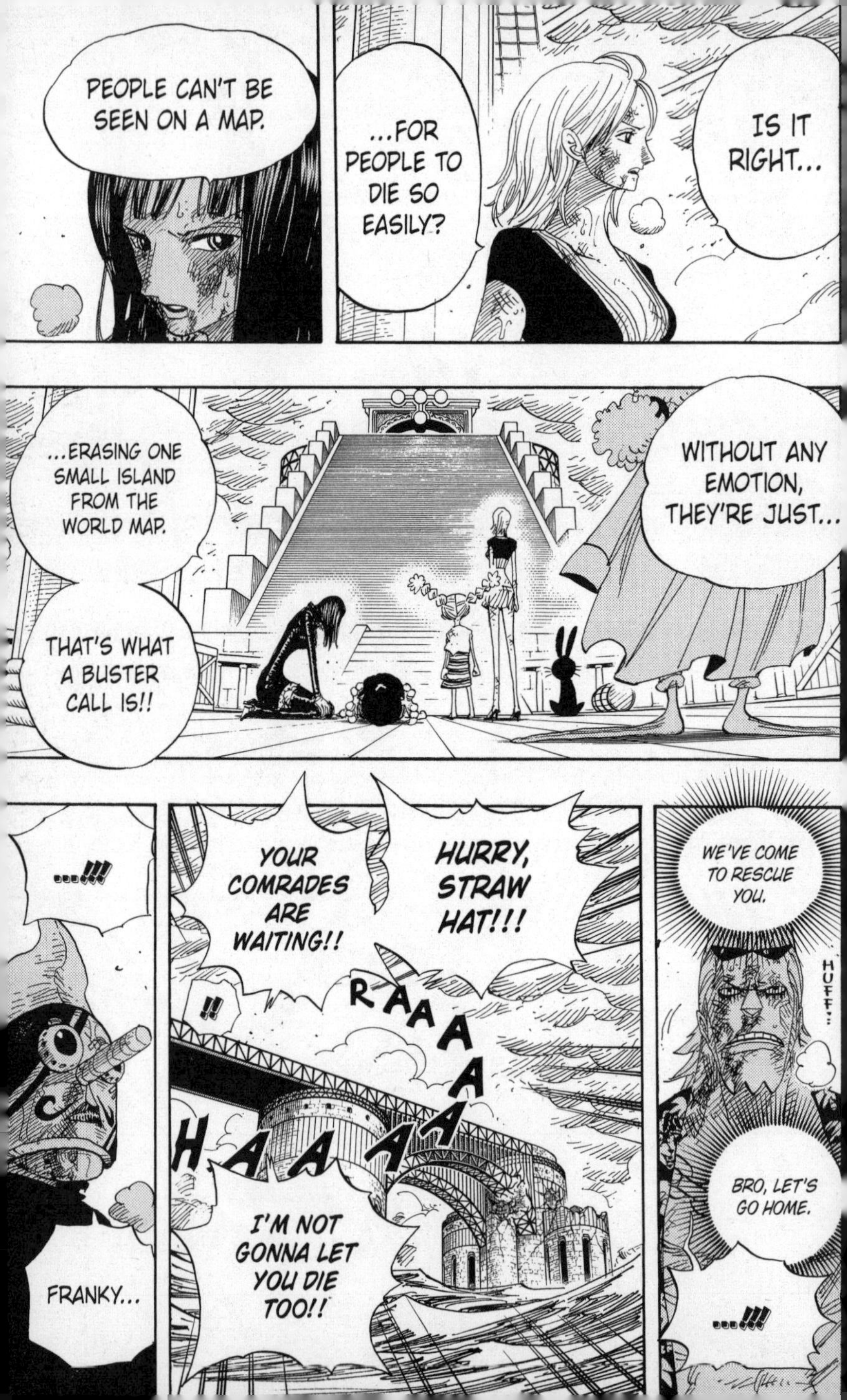
IS IT RIGHT...
...FOR PEOPLE TO DIE SO EASILY?
PEOPLE CAN'T BE SEEN ON A MAP.
WITHOUT ANY EMOTION, THEY'RE JUST...
...ERASING ONE SMALL ISLAND FROM THE WORLD MAP.
THAT'S WHAT A BUSTER CALL IS!!
WE'VE COME TO RESCUE YOU.
HUFF
BRO, LET'S GO HOME.
...!!!
HURRY, STRAW HAT!!!
YOUR COMRADES ARE WAITING!!
!!
RAAAAAAAAH
I'M NOT GONNA LET YOU DIE TOO!!
...!!!
FRANKY...

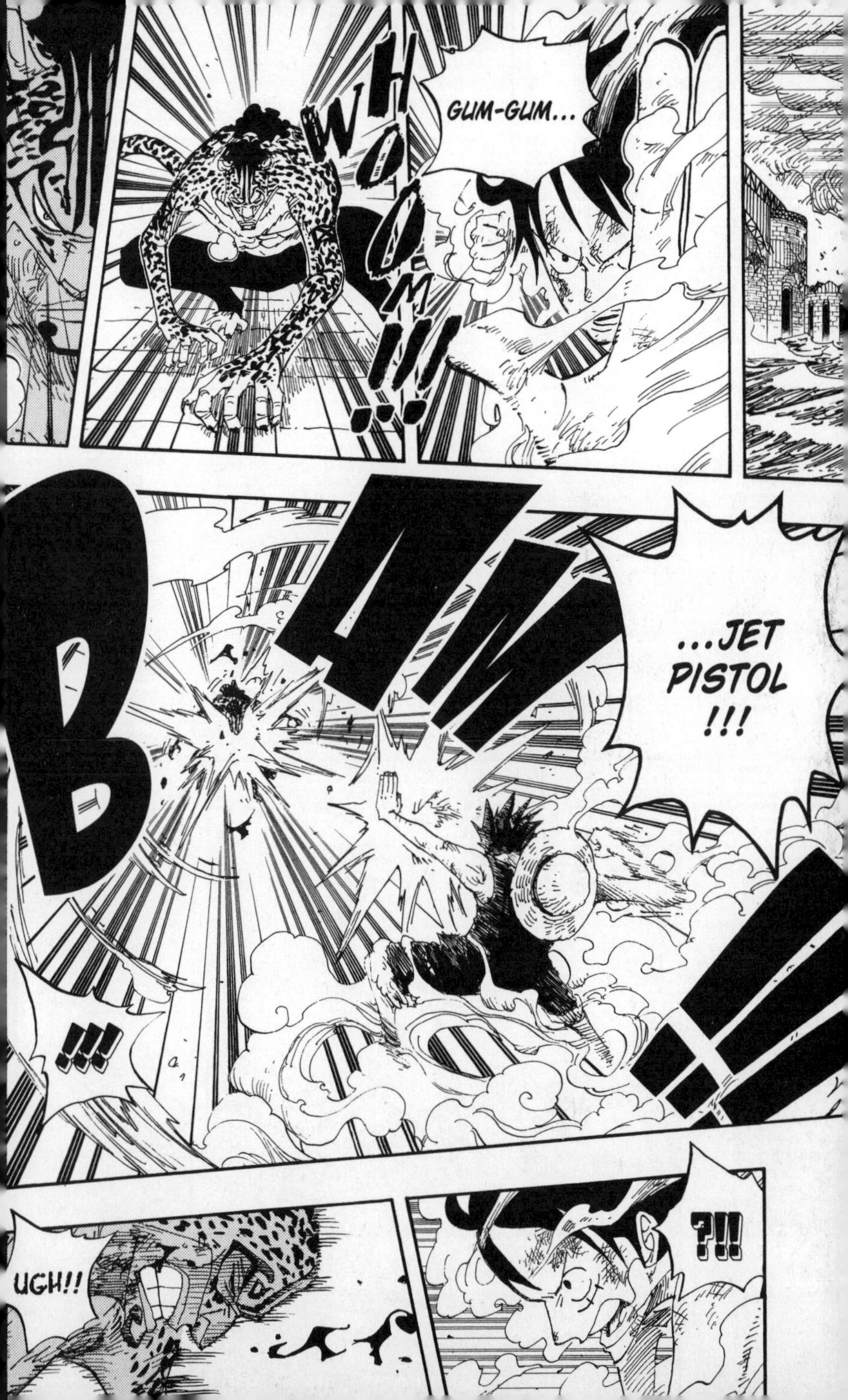
GUM-GUM...
WHOOM!!
...JET PISTOL !!!
BAM!!!
!!!
?!!
UGH!!

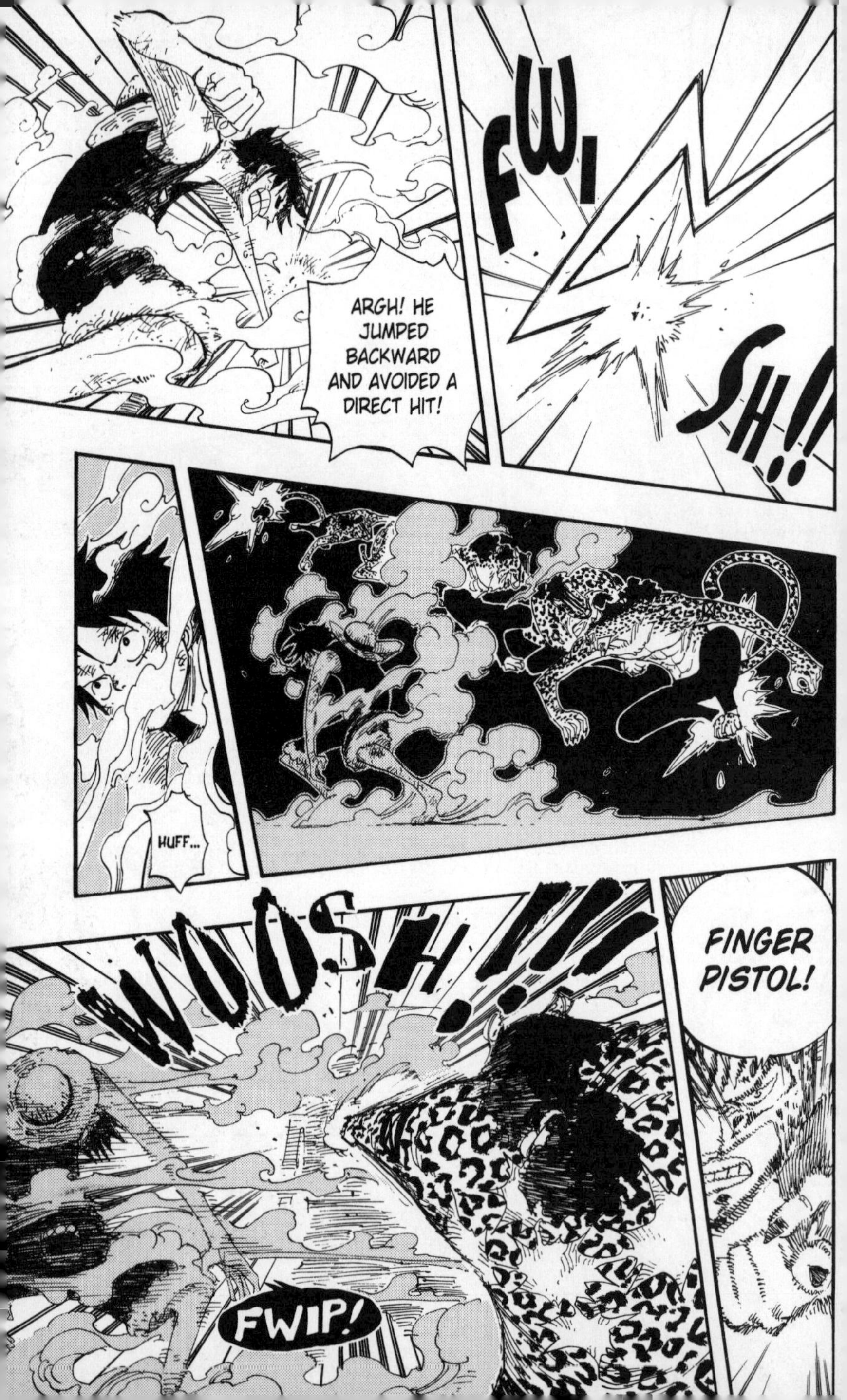
FWISH!!
ARGH! HE JUMPED BACKWARD AND AVOIDED A DIRECT HIT!
HUFF...
FINGER PISTOL!
WOOSH!!!
FWIP!

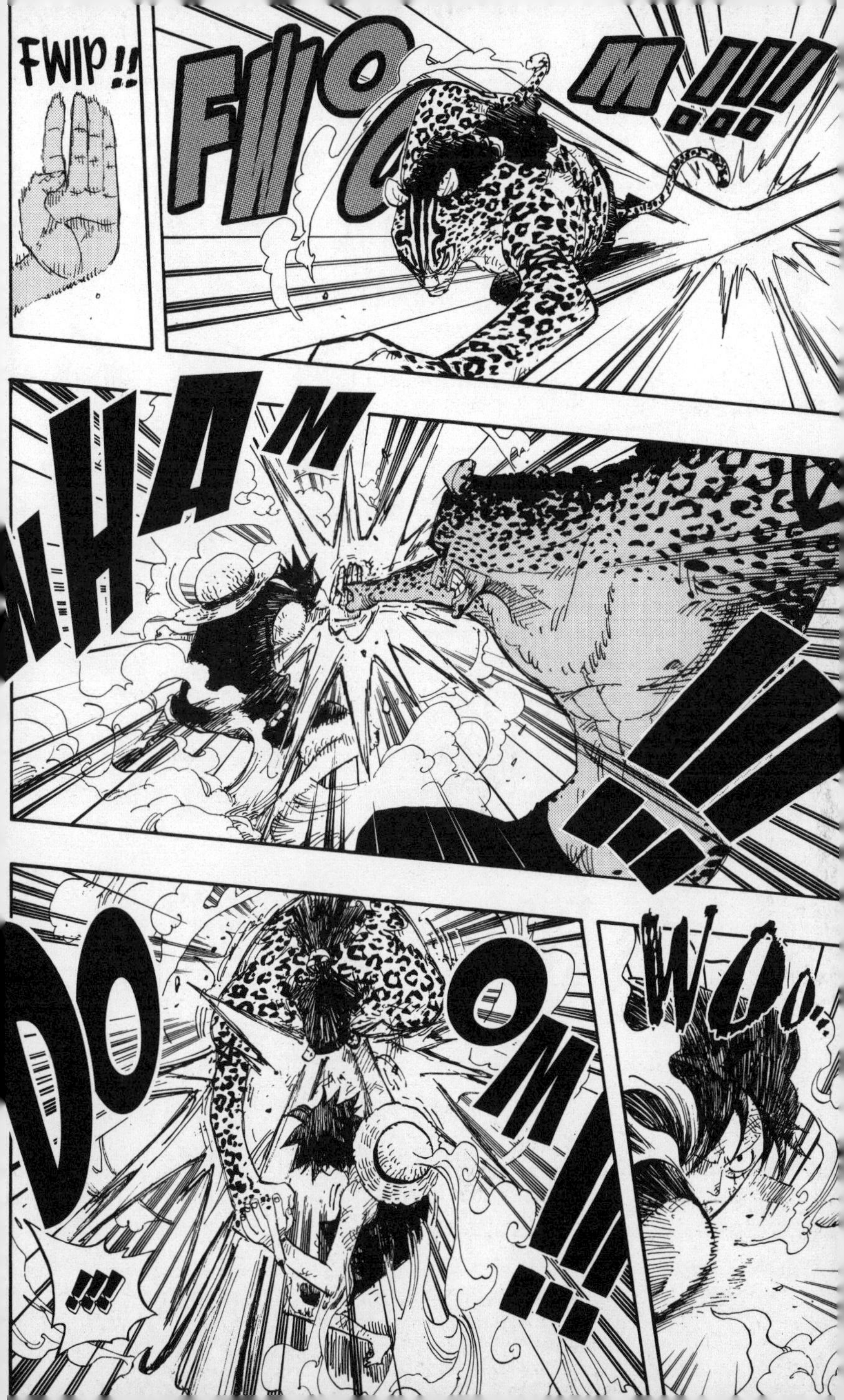
FWOOM!!!
FWIP!!
WHAM!!!
WOO..
DOOM!!!

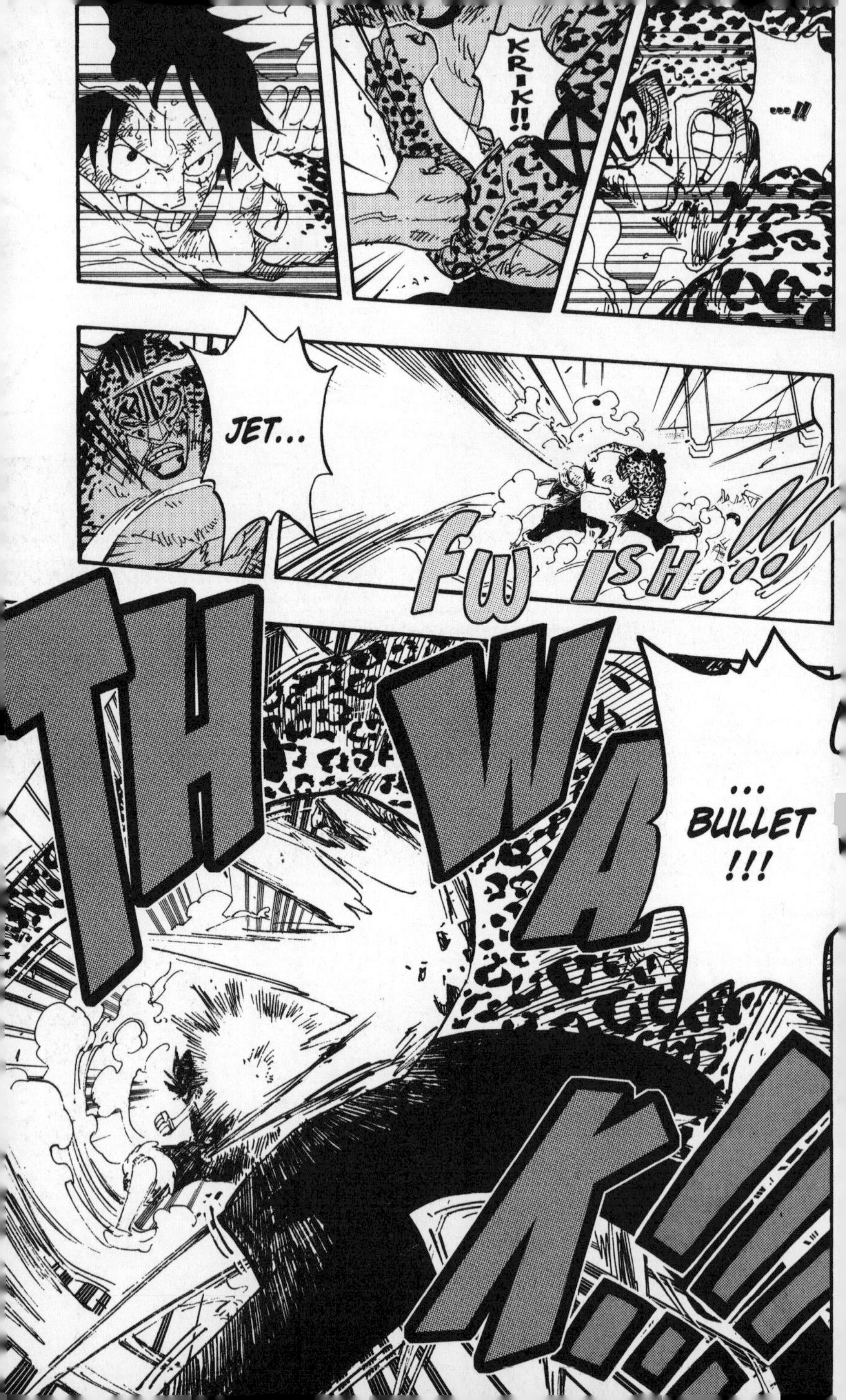
...!!
KRIK!!
JET...
FWISH...!!
...BULLET!!!
THWAK!!

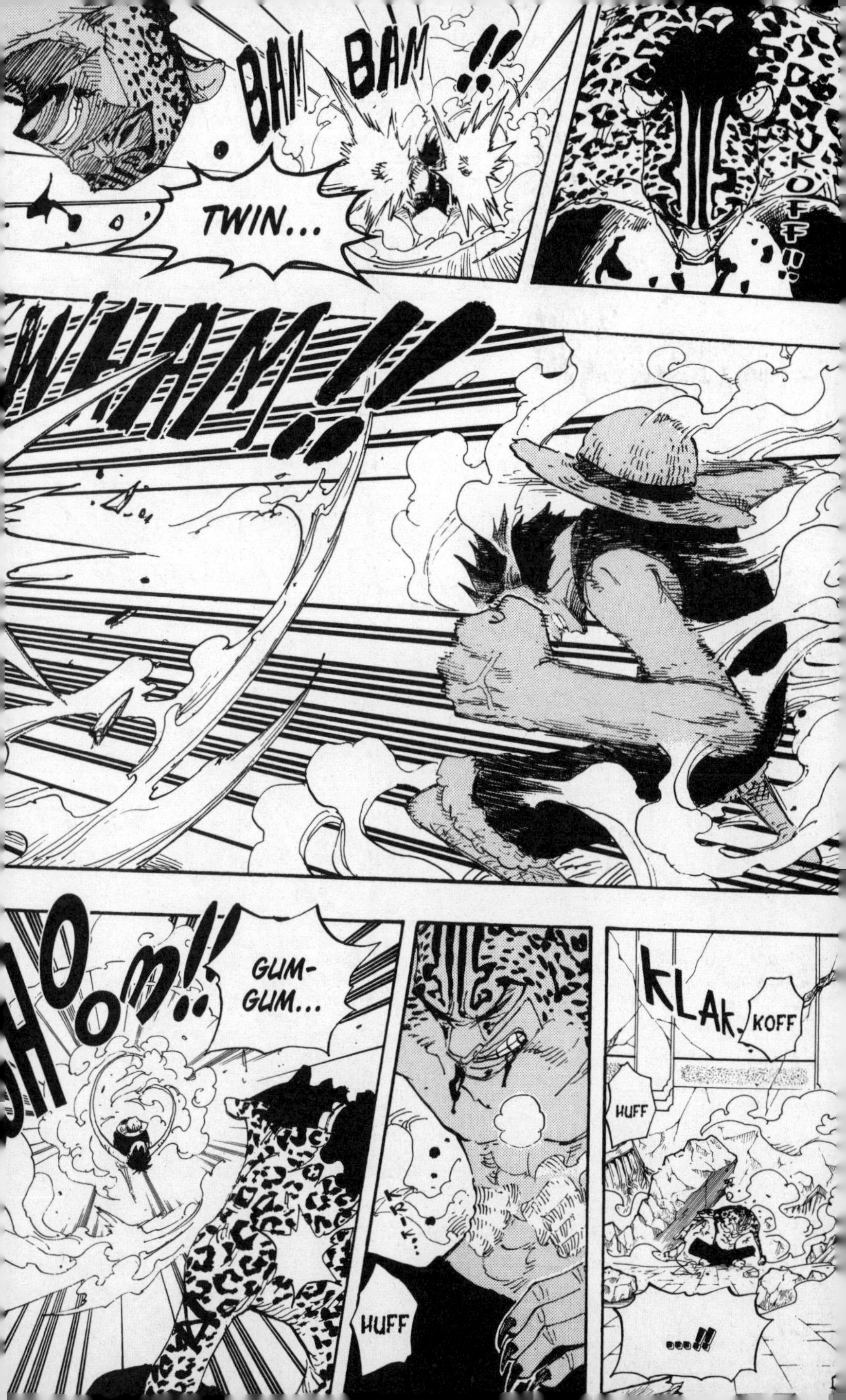

KOFF!!
BAM BAM!!
TWIN...
WHAM!!
KLAK.
KOFF
HUFF
...!!
KRIK...
HUFF
GUM-GUM...
SHOOM!!

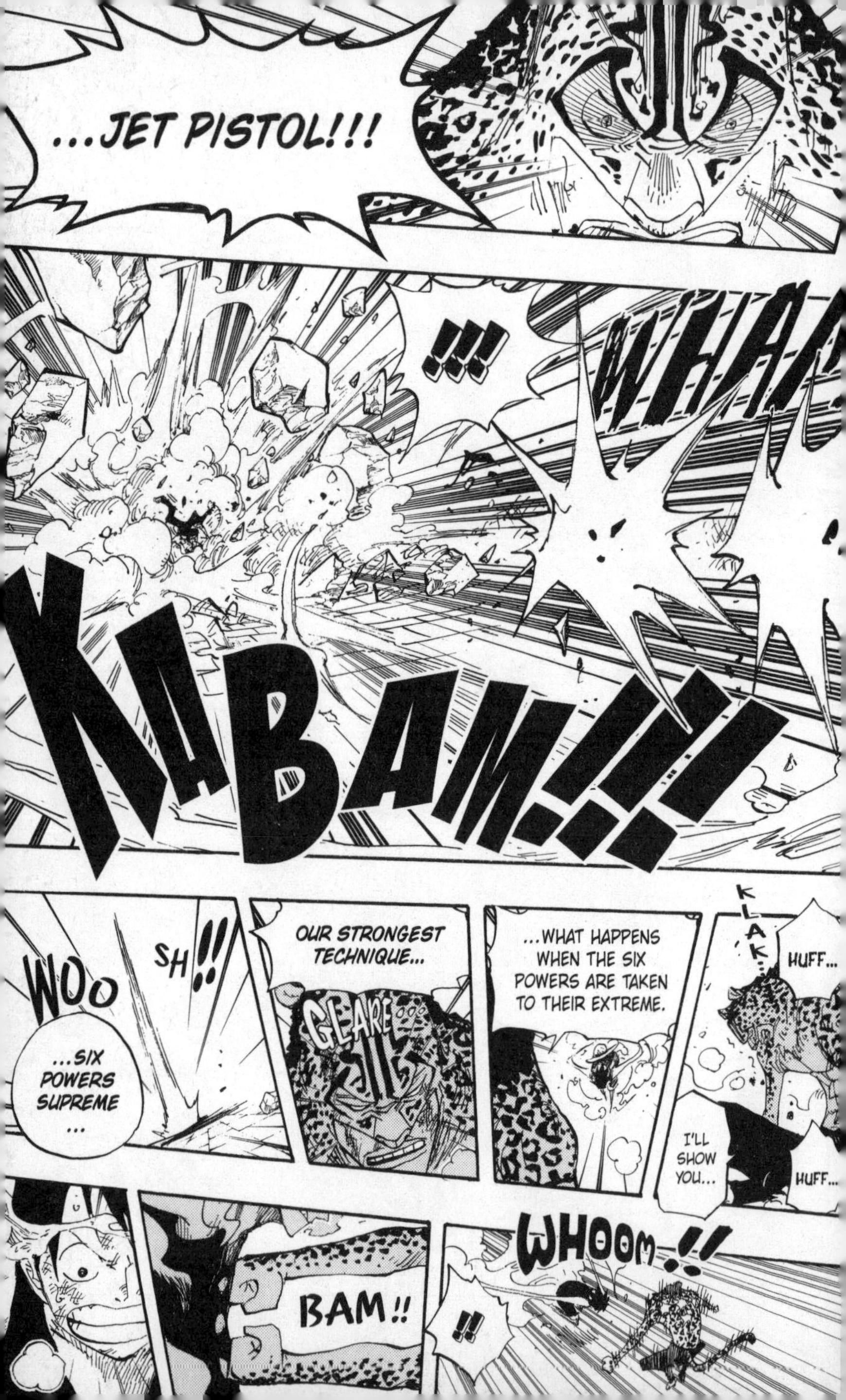

...JET PISTOL!!!
WHA
!!!
KABAM!!!
KLAK...
HUFF...
I'LL SHOW YOU...
HUFF...
...WHAT HAPPENS WHEN THE SIX POWERS ARE TAKEN TO THEIR EXTREME.
OUR STRONGEST TECHNIQUE...
GLARE
SH!!
WOO
...SIX POWERS SUPREME ...
WHOOM..!!
!!
BAM!!

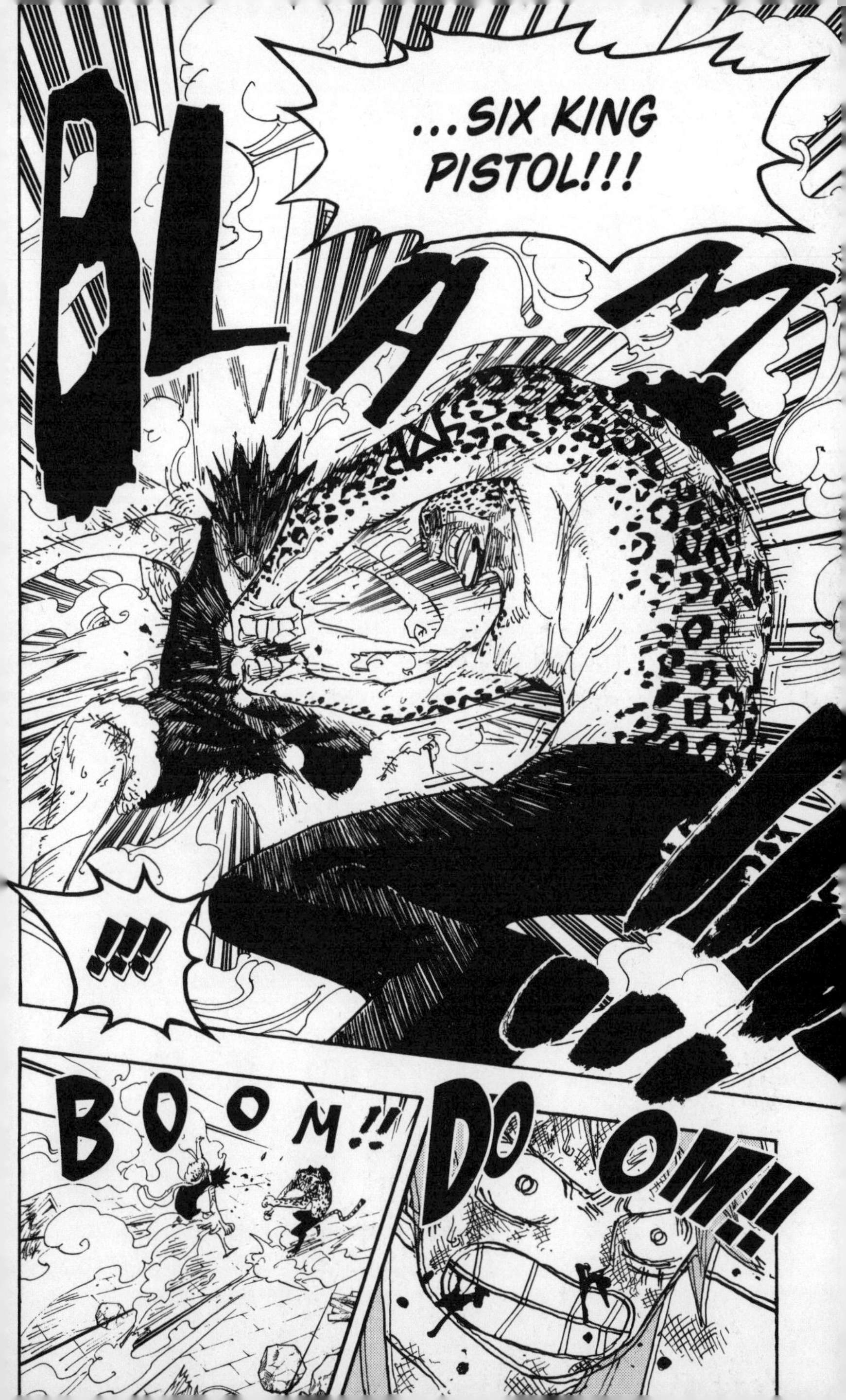
...SIX KING
PISTOL!!!
BLAM
!!!
BOOM!!
DOOM!!

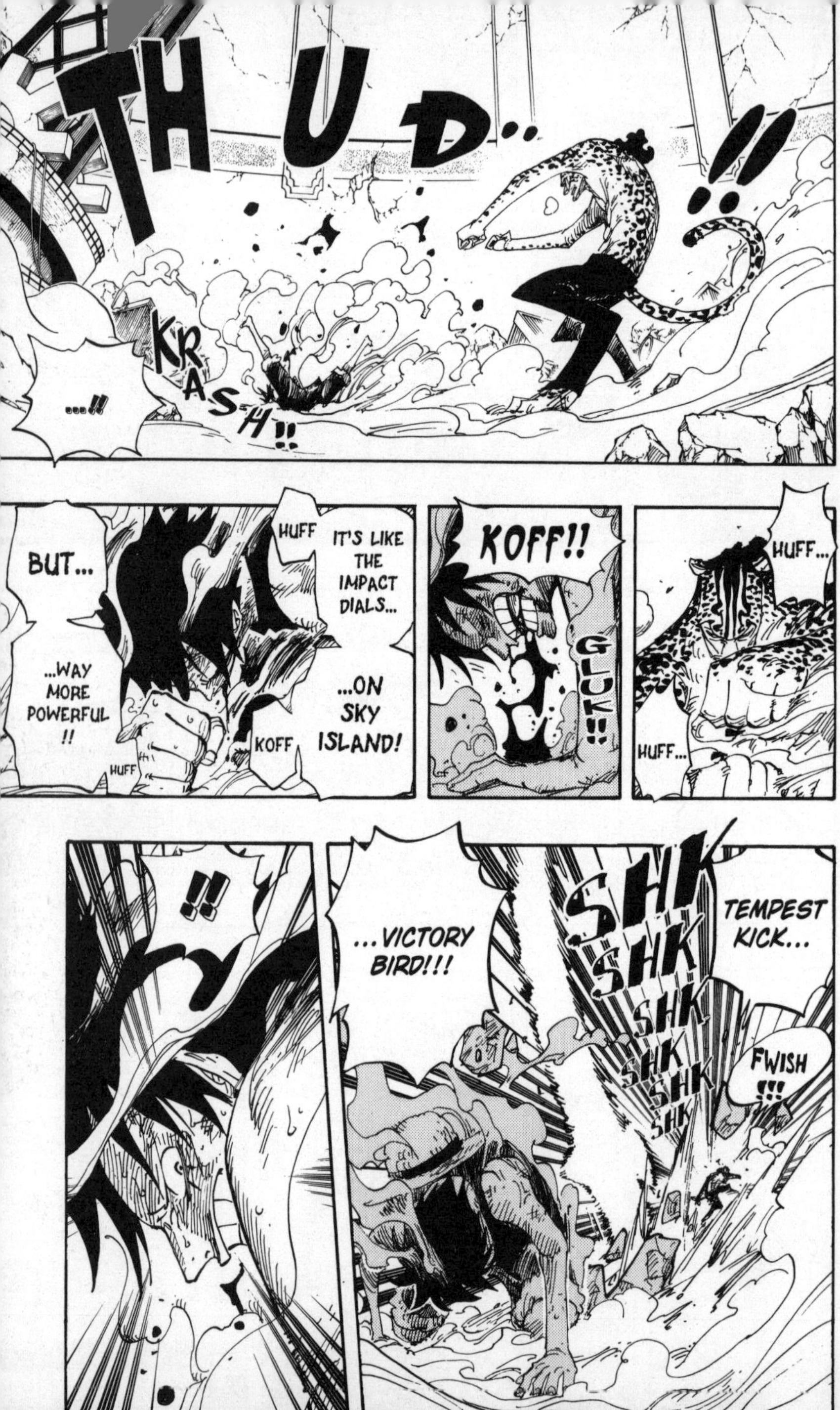
THUD..!!
KRASH!!
...!!
HUFF...
HUFF...
KOFF!!
GLUK!!
HUFF
IT'S LIKE THE IMPACT DIALS...
...ON SKY ISLAND!
KOFF
BUT...
...WAY MORE POWERFUL!!
HUFF
TEMPEST KICK...
SHK SHK SHK SHK SHK SHK SHK
FWISH!!!
...VICTORY BIRD!!!
!!

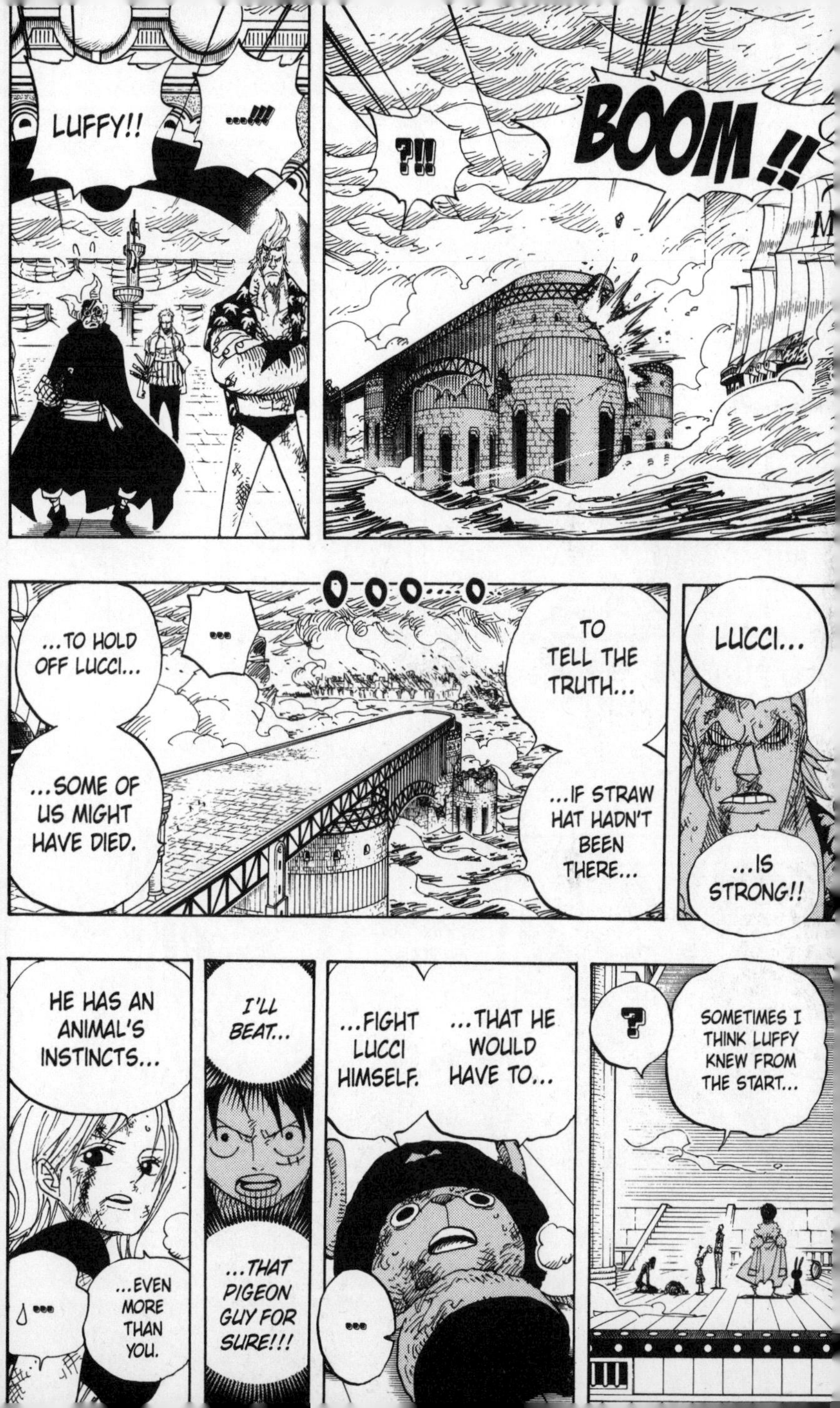
BOOM!!
?!!
...!!!
LUFFY!!
LUCCI...
...IS STRONG!!
O O O...O
TO TELL THE TRUTH...
...IF STRAW HAT HADN'T BEEN THERE...
...
...TO HOLD OFF LUCCI...
...SOME OF US MIGHT HAVE DIED.
?
SOMETIMES I THINK LUFFY KNEW FROM THE START...
...THAT HE WOULD HAVE TO...
...FIGHT LUCCI HIMSELF.
...
I'LL BEAT...
...THAT PIGEON GUY FOR SURE!!!
HE HAS AN ANIMAL'S INSTINCTS...
...EVEN MORE THAN YOU.
...

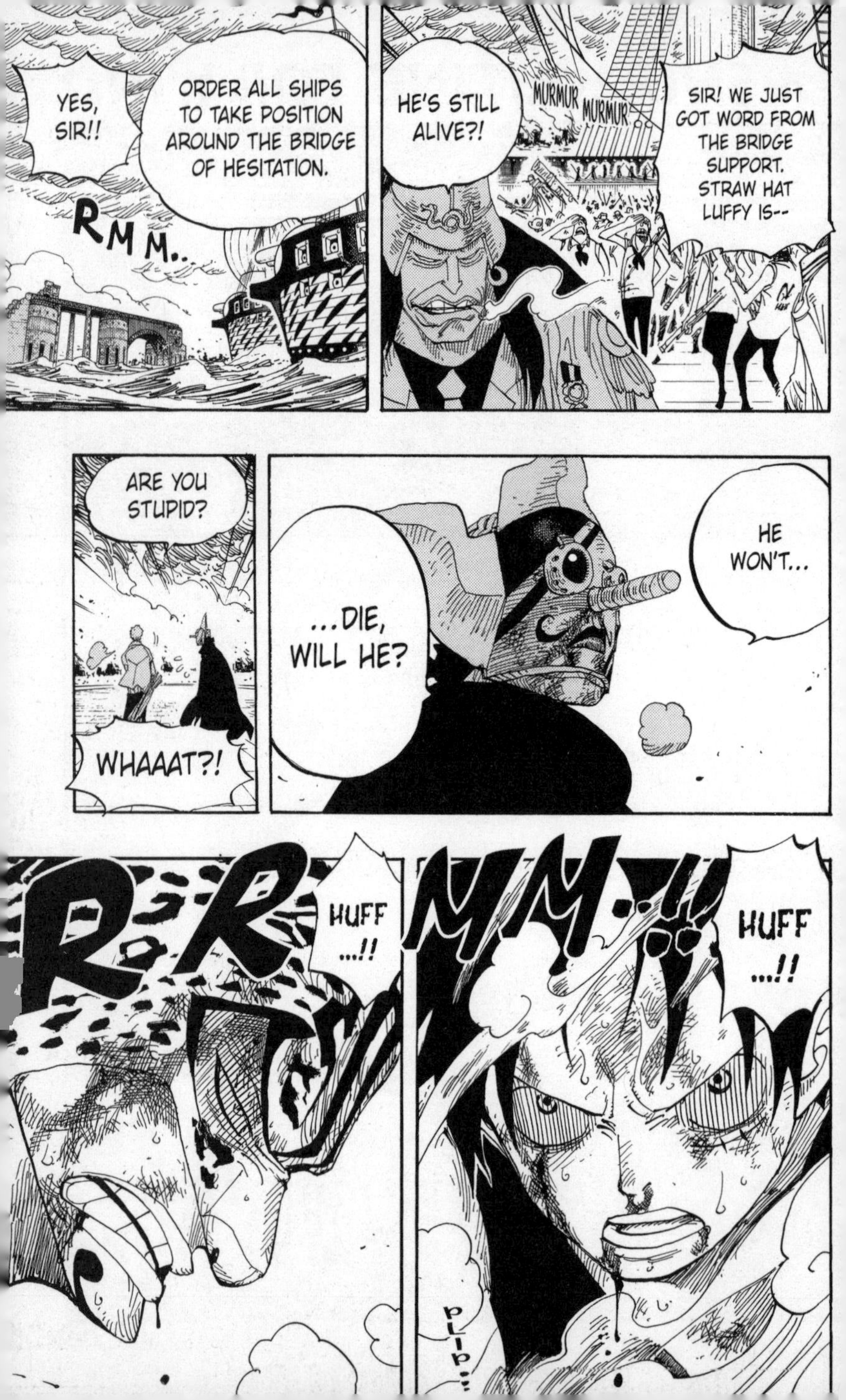
SIR! WE JUST GOT WORD FROM THE BRIDGE SUPPORT. STRAW HAT LUFFY IS--
MURMUR
MURMUR
HE'S STILL ALIVE?!
ORDER ALL SHIPS TO TAKE POSITION AROUND THE BRIDGE OF HESITATION.
YES, SIR!!
RMM..
HE WON'T...
...DIE, WILL HE?
ARE YOU STUPID?
WHAAAT?!
RRMM!!
HUFF ...!!
PLIP
HUFF ...!!

A SHIP WAITING FOR WIND

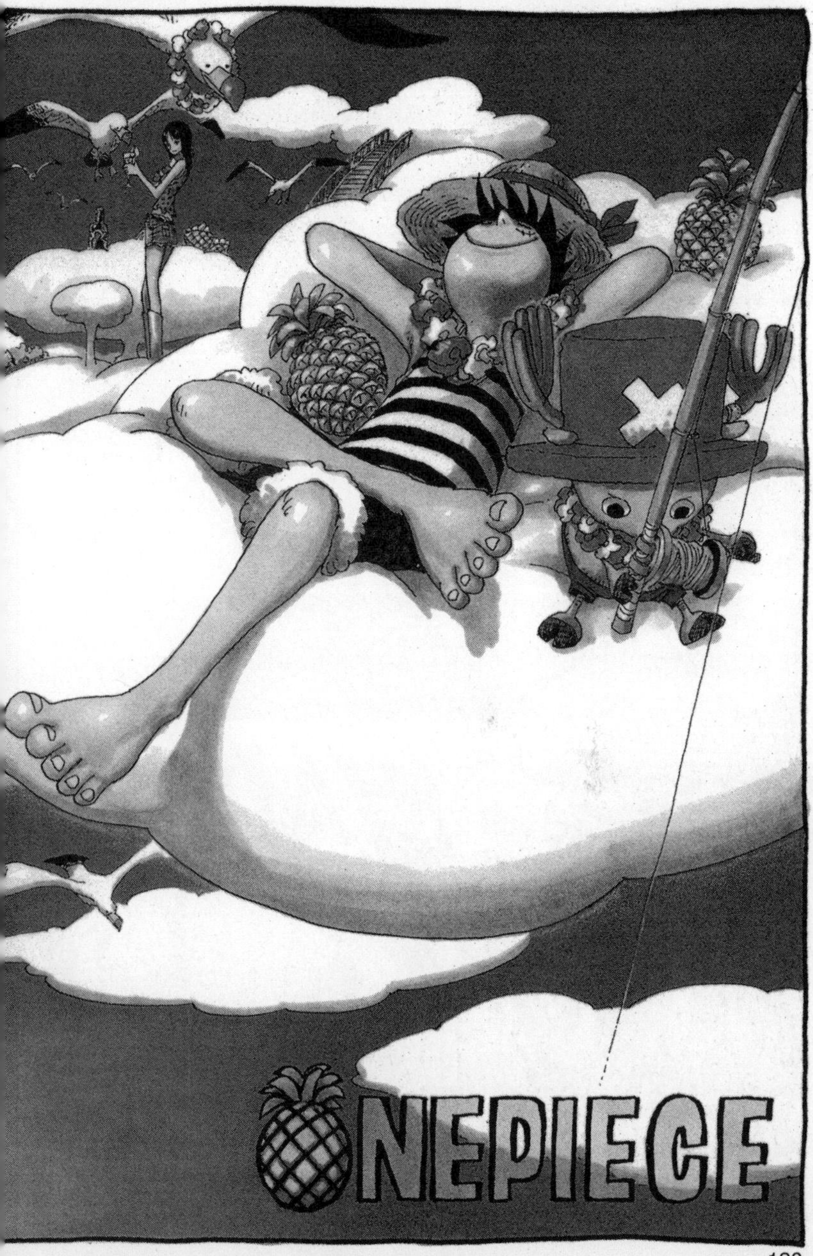
ONE PIECE

Chapter 426:

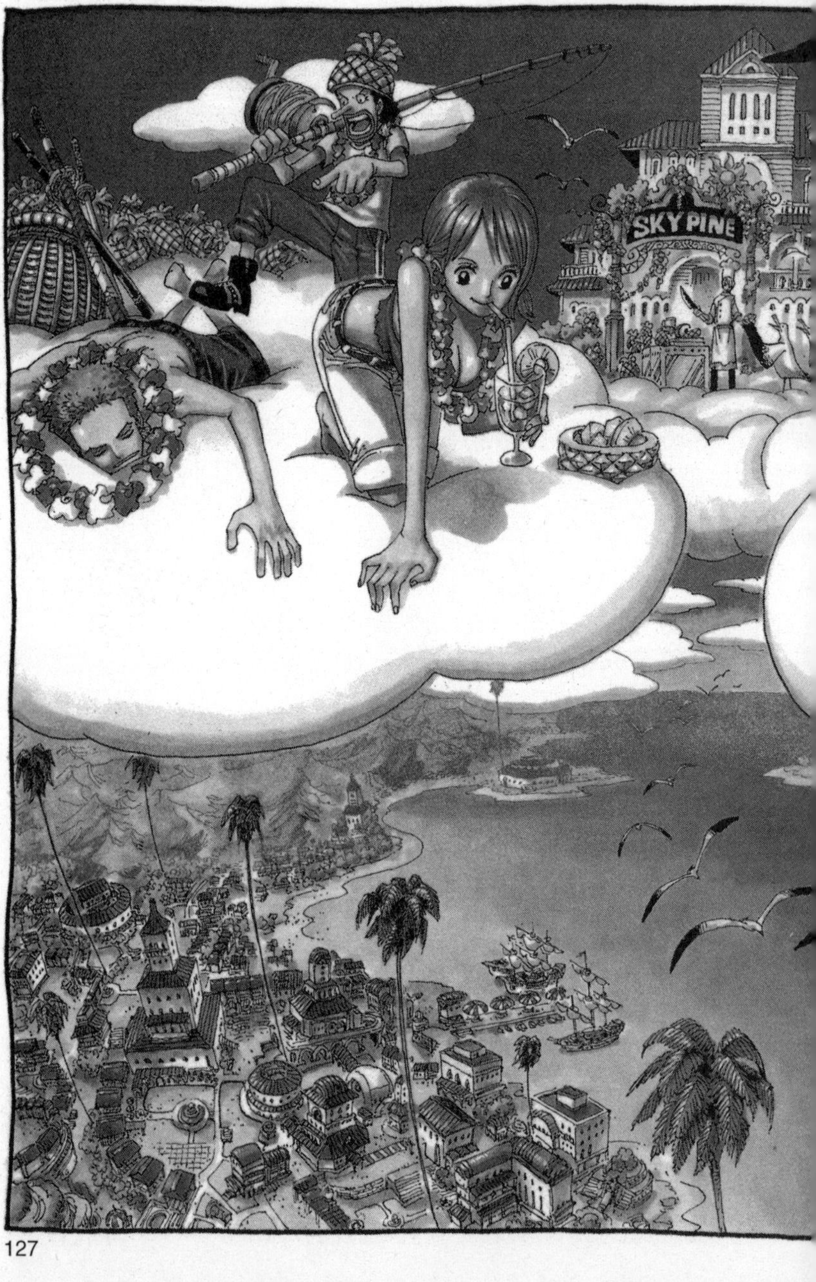
SKYPINE

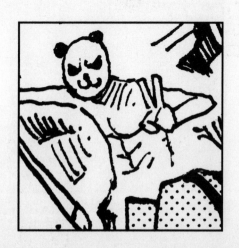

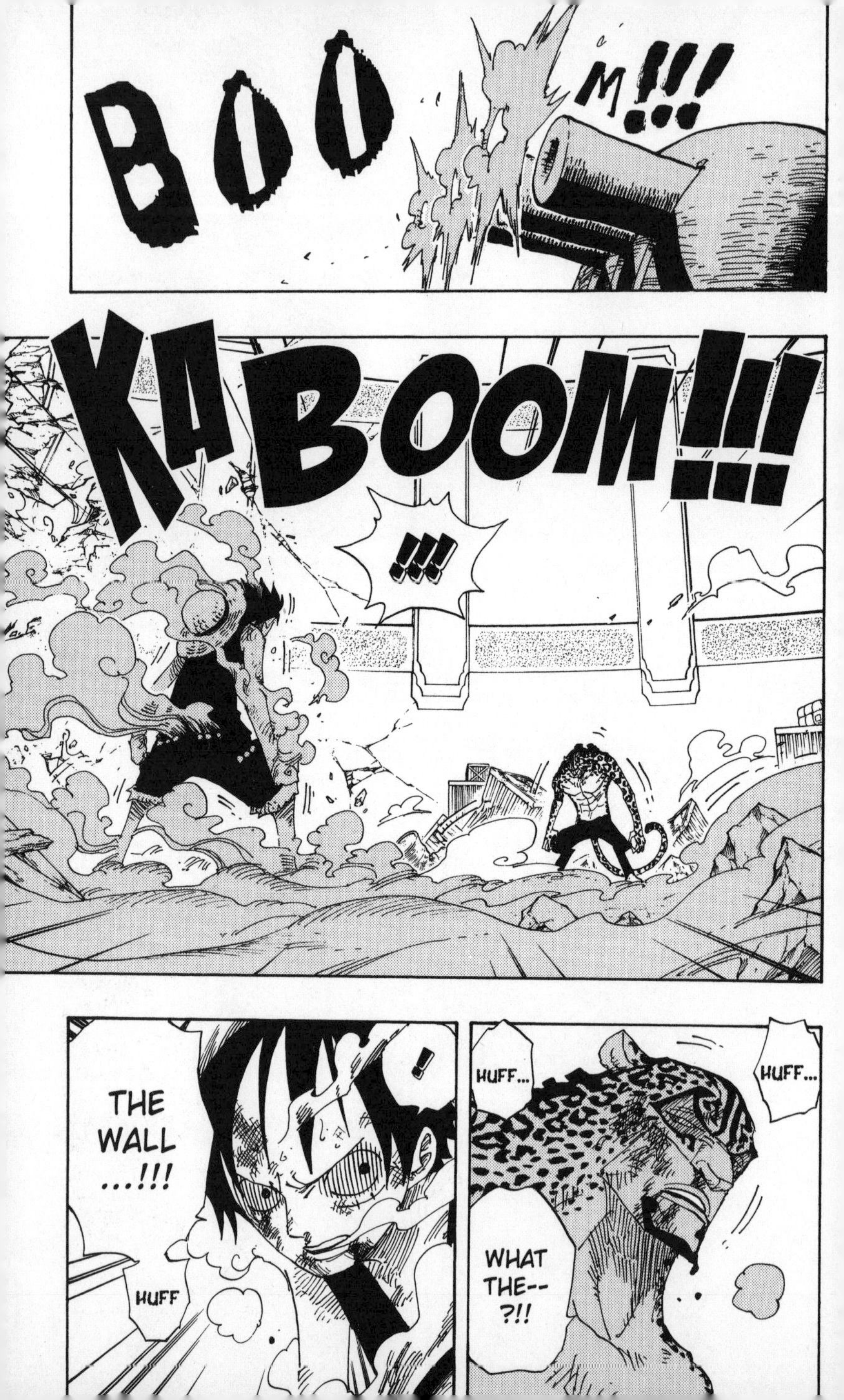
BOOOM!!!
KABOOM!!!
!!!
HUFF...
HUFF...
WHAT THE--?!!
!
THE WALL...!!!
HUFF

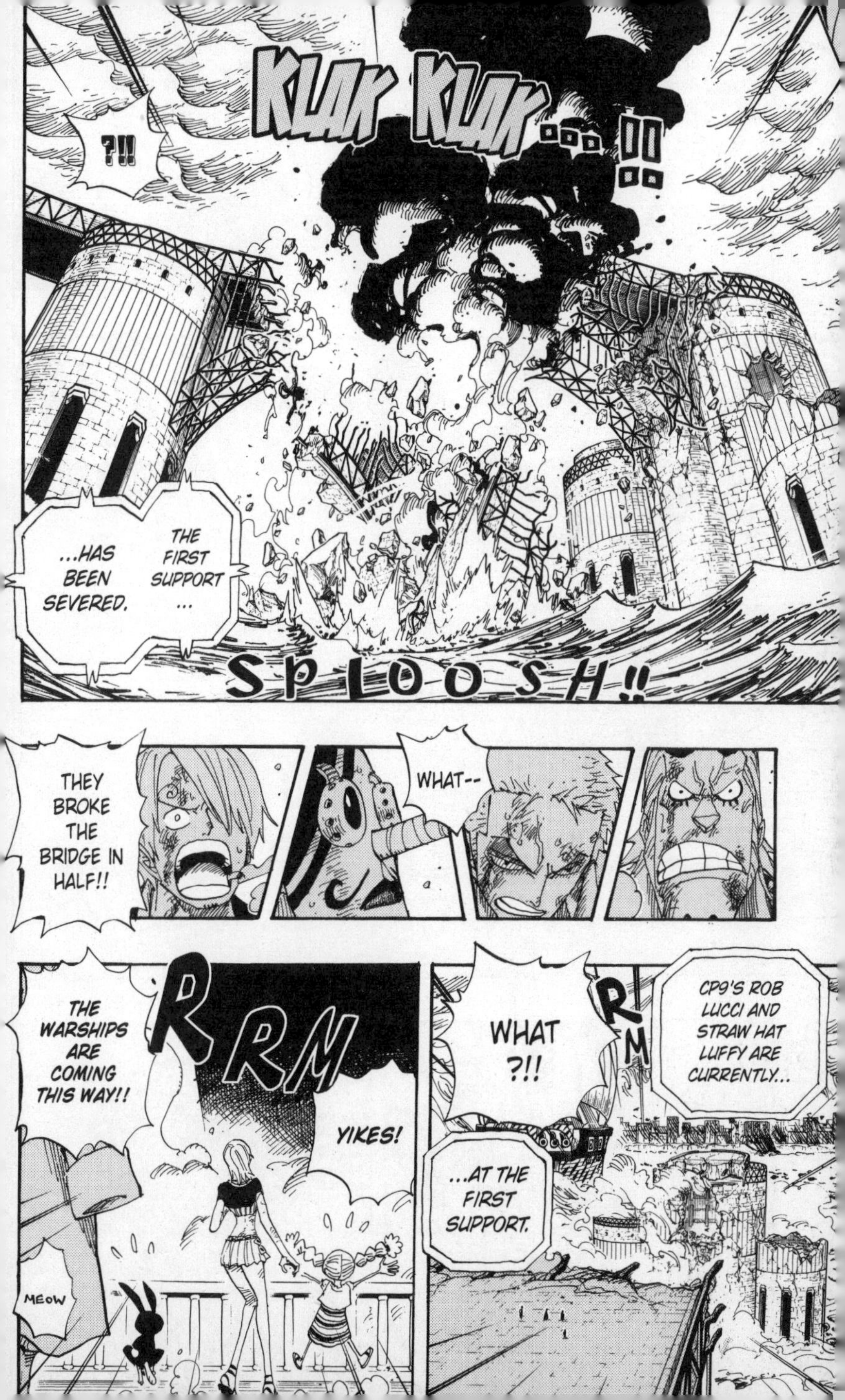
KLAK KLAK...!!
?!!
THE FIRST SUPPORT...
...HAS BEEN SEVERED.
SPLOOSH!!
WHAT--
THEY BROKE THE BRIDGE IN HALF!!
CP9'S ROB LUCCI AND STRAW HAT LUFFY ARE CURRENTLY...
...AT THE FIRST SUPPORT.
WHAT ?!!
RM
RRM
THE WARSHIPS ARE COMING THIS WAY!!
YIKES!
MEOW

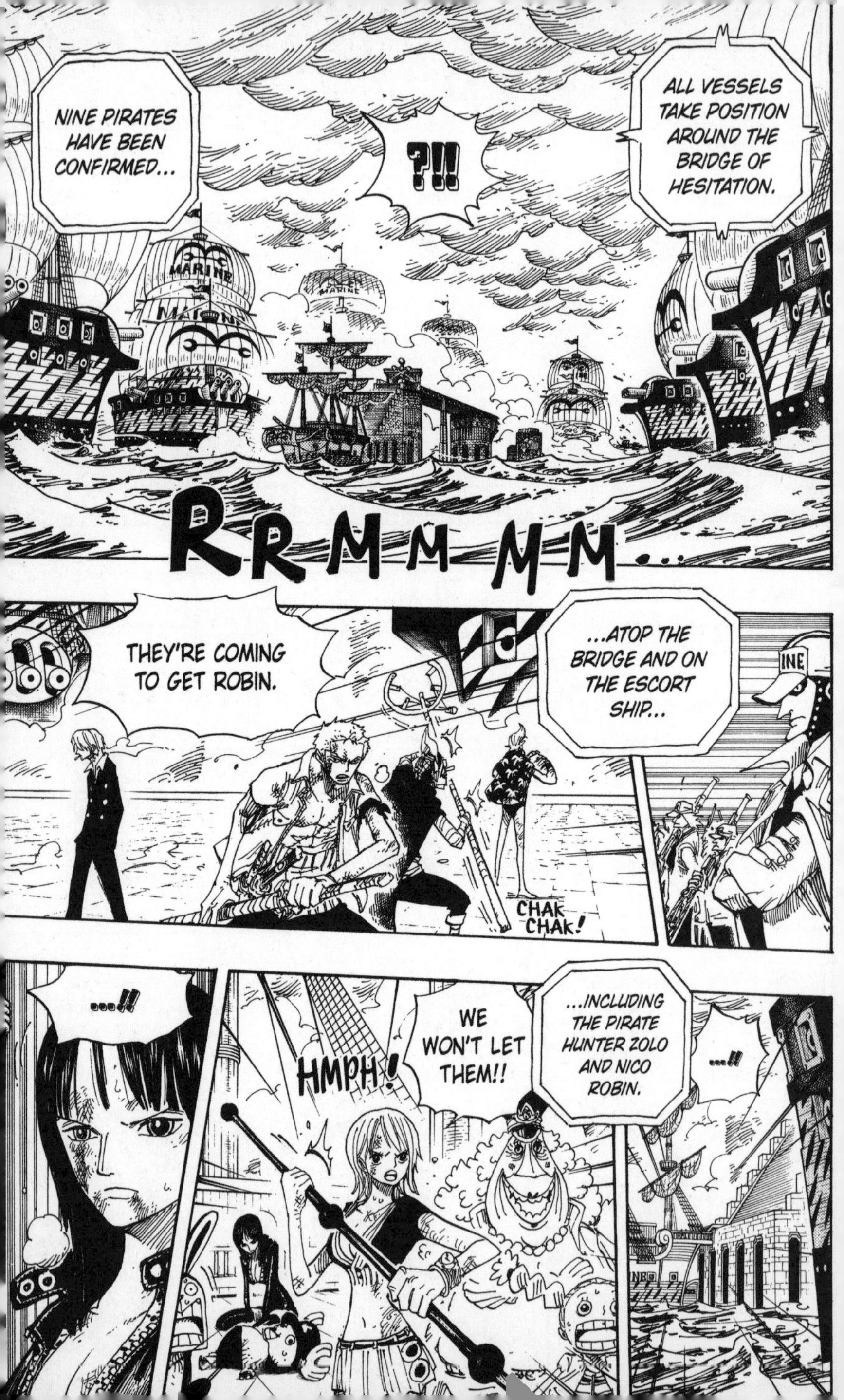
ALL VESSELS TAKE POSITION AROUND THE BRIDGE OF HESITATION.
?!!
NINE PIRATES HAVE BEEN CONFIRMED...
RRMMM MM...
...ATOP THE BRIDGE AND ON THE ESCORT SHIP...
THEY'RE COMING TO GET ROBIN.
CHAK CHAK!
...!!
...INCLUDING THE PIRATE HUNTER ZOLO AND NICO ROBIN.
WE WON'T LET THEM!!
HMPH!
...!!

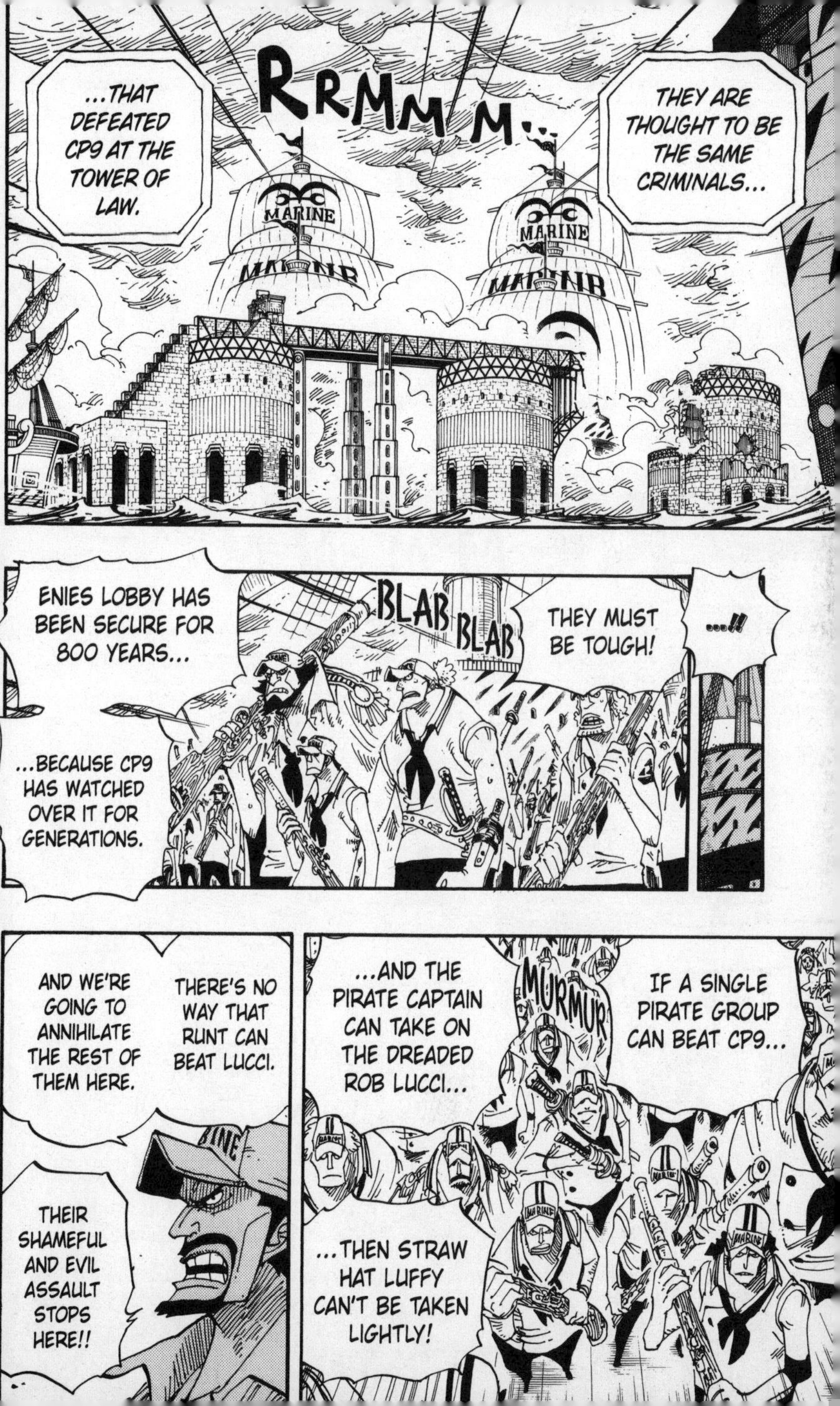
THEY ARE THOUGHT TO BE THE SAME CRIMINALS...
RRMMM M...
...THAT DEFEATED CP9 AT THE TOWER OF LAW.
...!!
THEY MUST BE TOUGH!
BLAB BLAB
ENIES LOBBY HAS BEEN SECURE FOR 800 YEARS...
...BECAUSE CP9 HAS WATCHED OVER IT FOR GENERATIONS.
IF A SINGLE PIRATE GROUP CAN BEAT CP9...
MURMUR
...AND THE PIRATE CAPTAIN CAN TAKE ON THE DREADED ROB LUCCI...
...THEN STRAW HAT LUFFY CAN'T BE TAKEN LIGHTLY!
THERE'S NO WAY THAT RUNT CAN BEAT LUCCI.
AND WE'RE GOING TO ANNIHILATE THE REST OF THEM HERE.
THEIR SHAMEFUL AND EVIL ASSAULT STOPS HERE!!

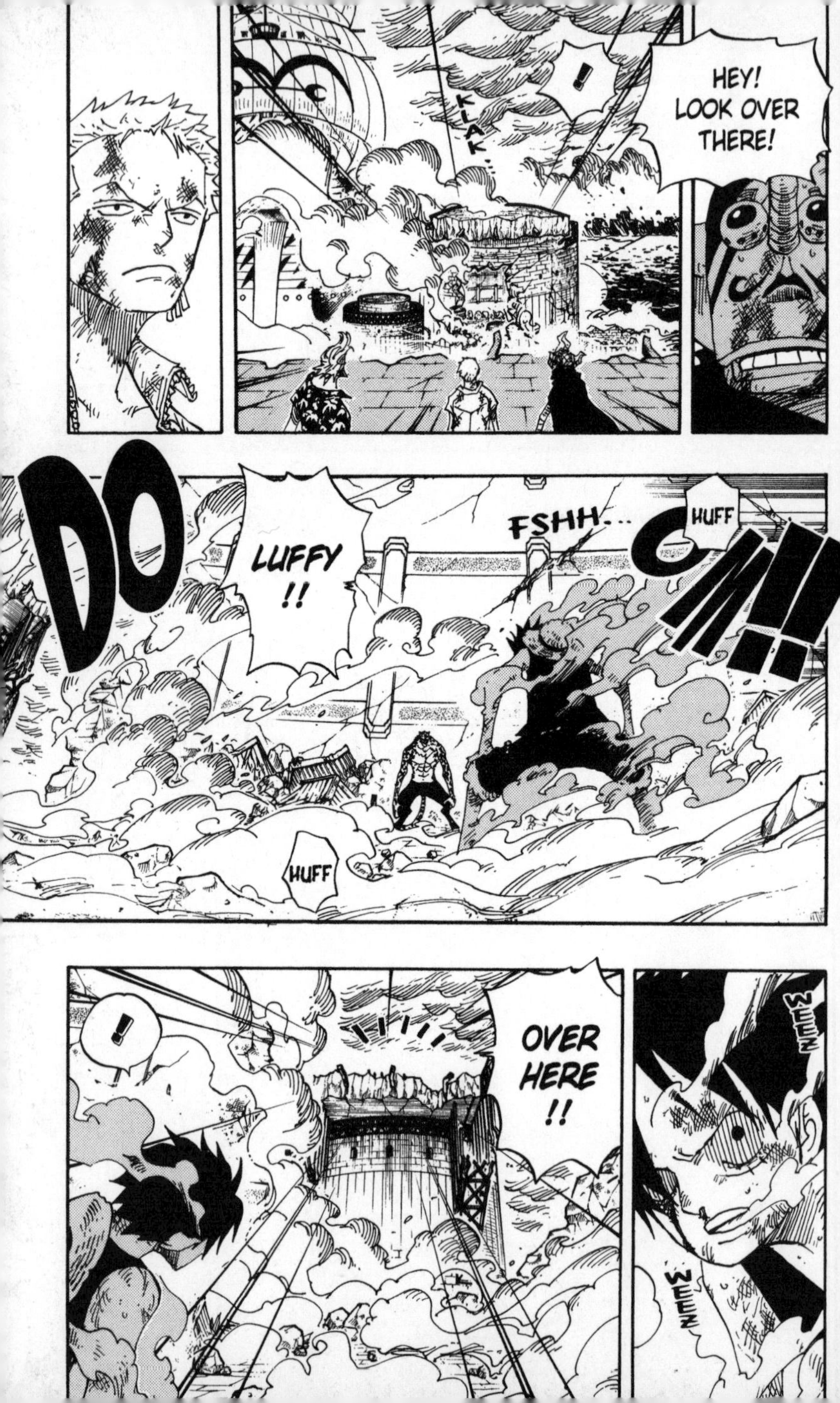
HEY! LOOK OVER THERE!
!
KLAK...
HUFF
FSHH...
LUFFY!!
DO
HUFF
WEEZ
WEEZ
OVER HERE!!
!

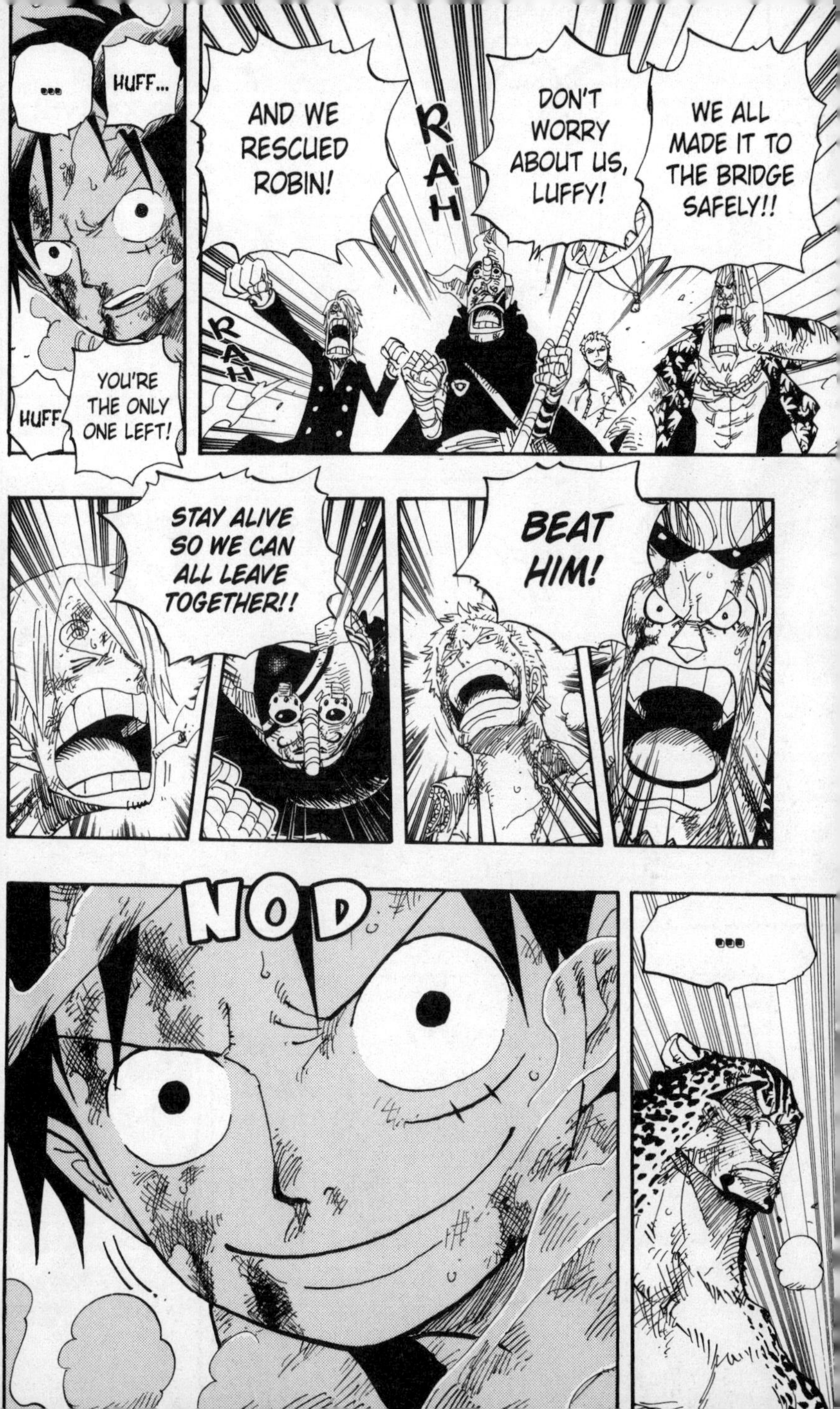
WE ALL MADE IT TO THE BRIDGE SAFELY!!
DON'T WORRY ABOUT US, LUFFY!
RAH
AND WE RESCUED ROBIN!
RAH
HUFF...
...
YOU'RE THE ONLY ONE LEFT!
HUFF
BEAT HIM!
STAY ALIVE SO WE CAN ALL LEAVE TOGETHER!!
...
NOD

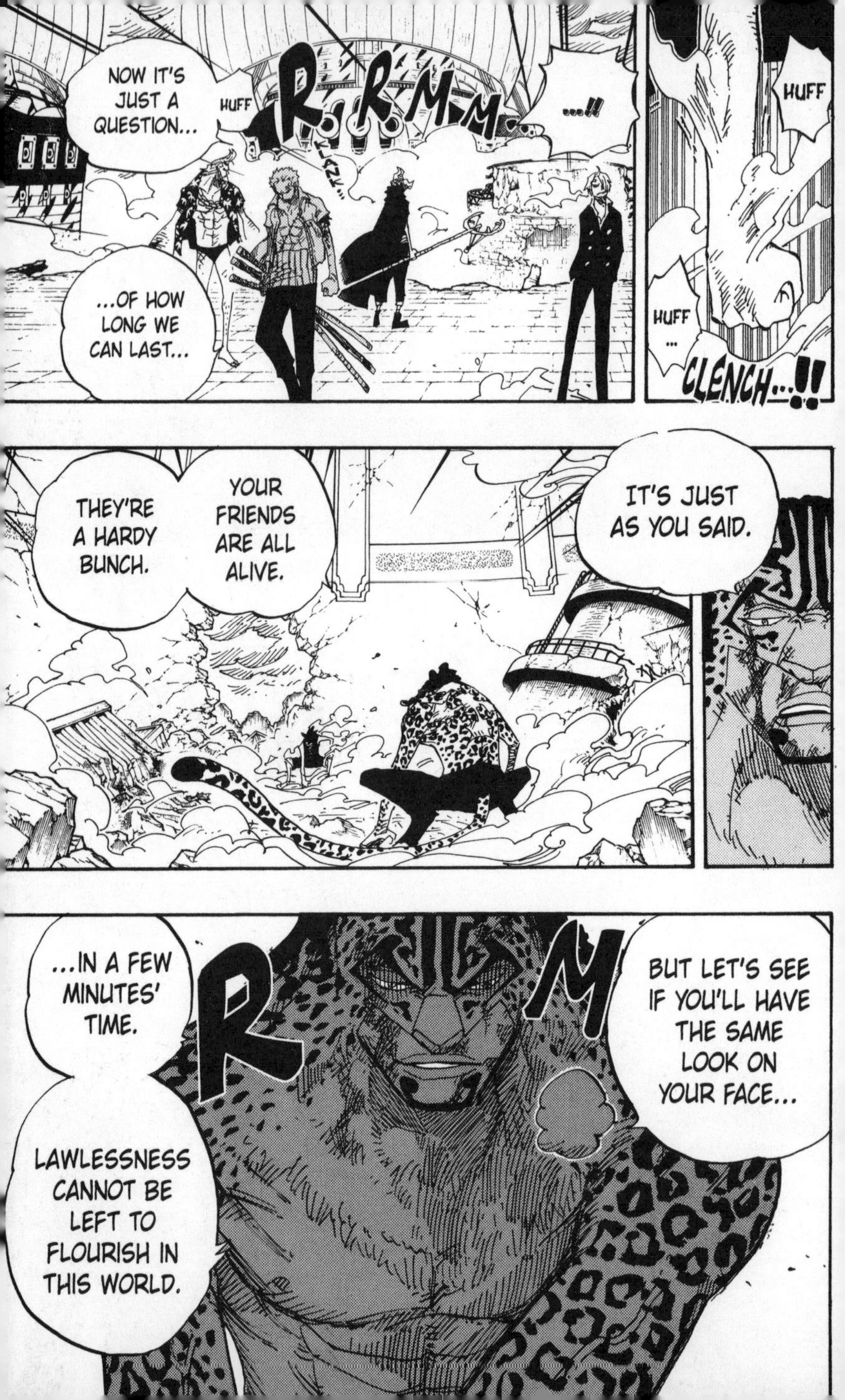
HUFF
HUFF ...
CLENCH...!!
NOW IT'S JUST A QUESTION...
HUFF
RRMM
...!!
KLANK...
...OF HOW LONG WE CAN LAST...
IT'S JUST AS YOU SAID.
YOUR FRIENDS ARE ALL ALIVE.
THEY'RE A HARDY BUNCH.
RM
BUT LET'S SEE IF YOU'LL HAVE THE SAME LOOK ON YOUR FACE...
...IN A FEW MINUTES' TIME.
LAWLESSNESS CANNOT BE LEFT TO FLOURISH IN THIS WORLD.

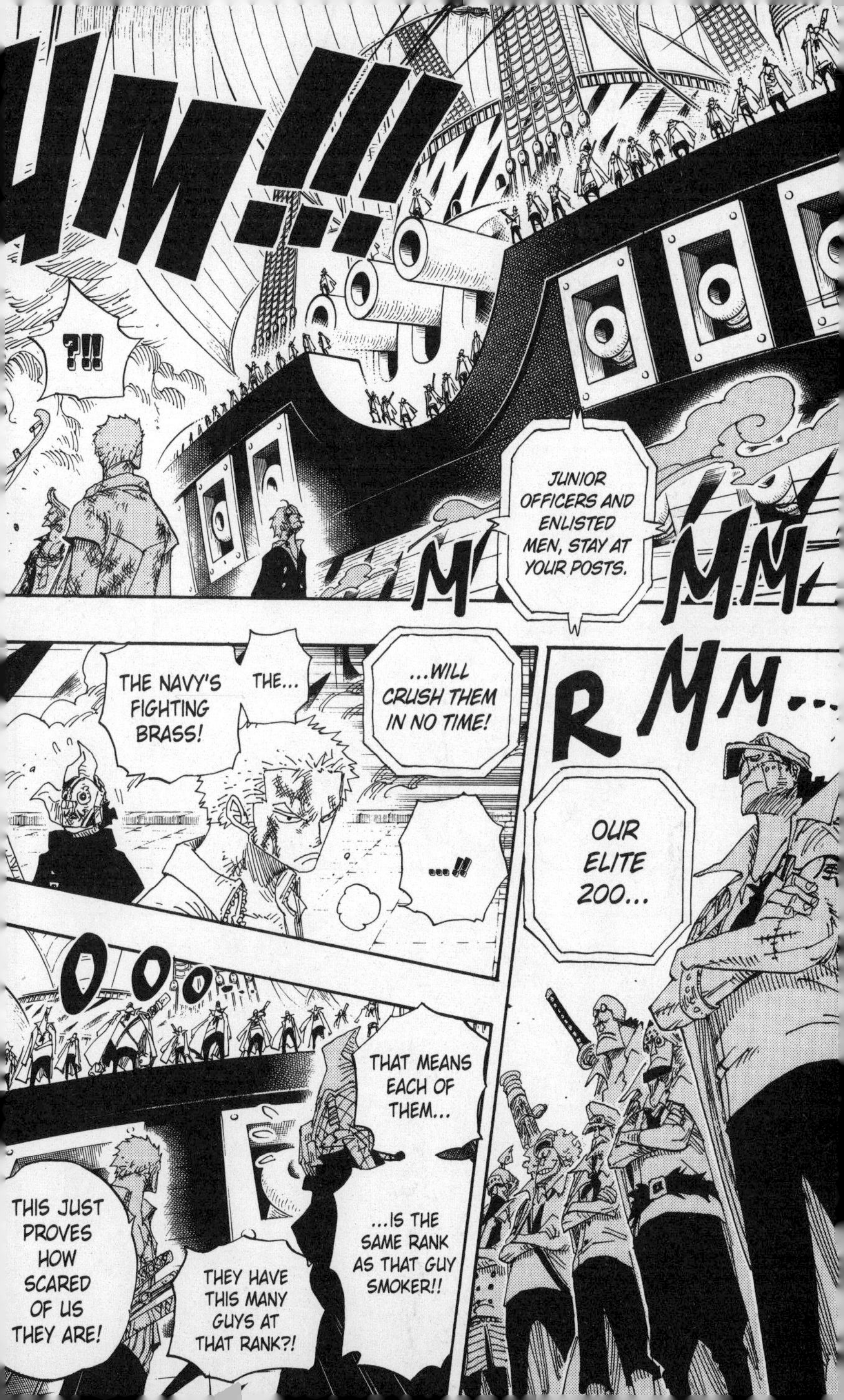
UM!!
JUNIOR OFFICERS AND ENLISTED MEN, STAY AT YOUR POSTS.
?!!
M MMM
RMM...
OUR ELITE 200...
...WILL CRUSH THEM IN NO TIME!
THE...
THE NAVY'S FIGHTING BRASS!
...!!
OOO
THAT MEANS EACH OF THEM...
...IS THE SAME RANK AS THAT GUY SMOKER!!
THEY HAVE THIS MANY GUYS AT THAT RANK?!
THIS JUST PROVES HOW SCARED OF US THEY ARE!

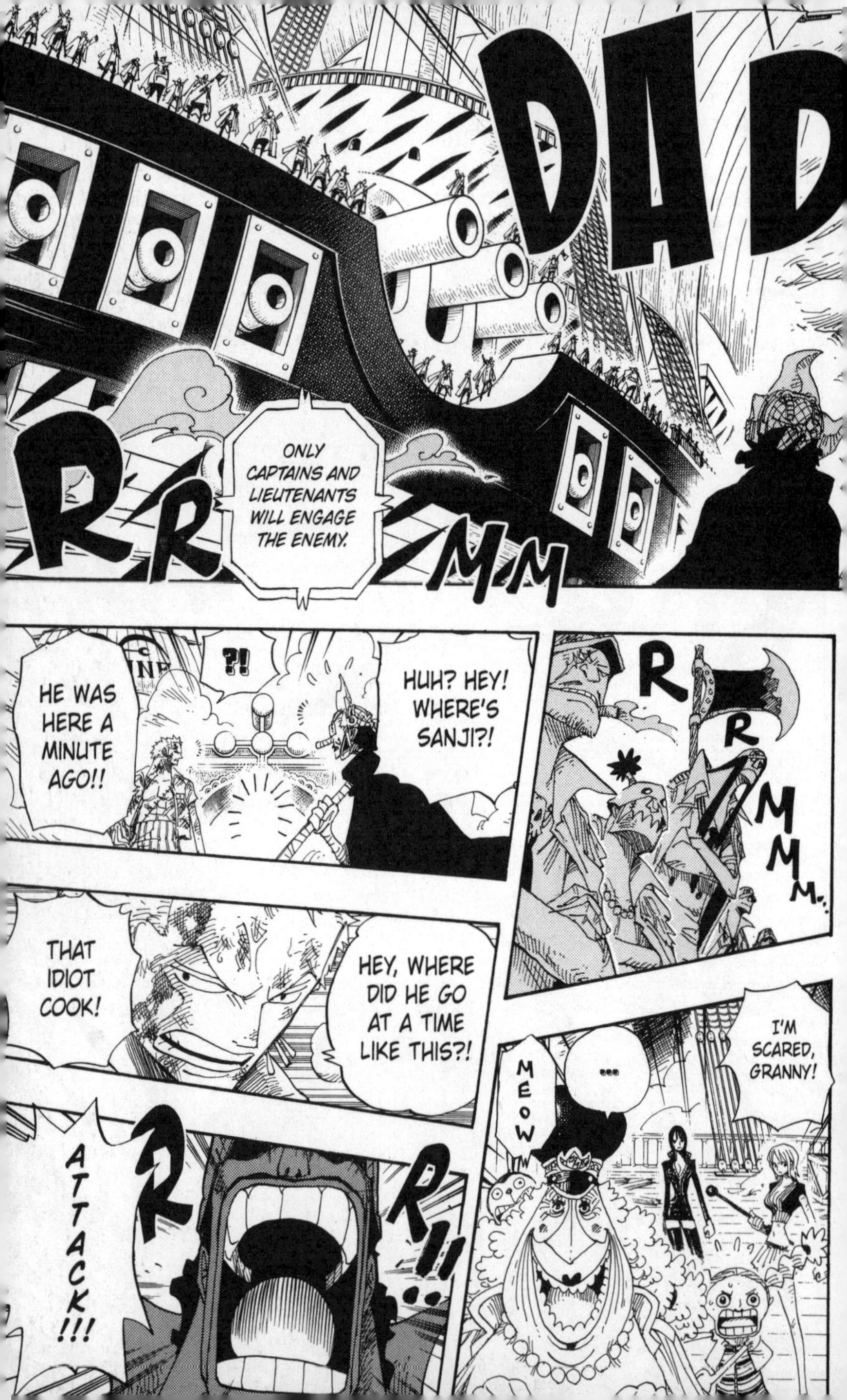
DAD
RRRMM
ONLY CAPTAINS AND LIEUTENANTS WILL ENGAGE THE ENEMY.
RRMMMM..
HUH? HEY! WHERE'S SANJI?!
?!
HE WAS HERE A MINUTE AGO!!
HEY, WHERE DID HE GO AT A TIME LIKE THIS?!
THAT IDIOT COOK!
I'M SCARED, GRANNY!
...
MEOW
RR!!
ATTACK!!!

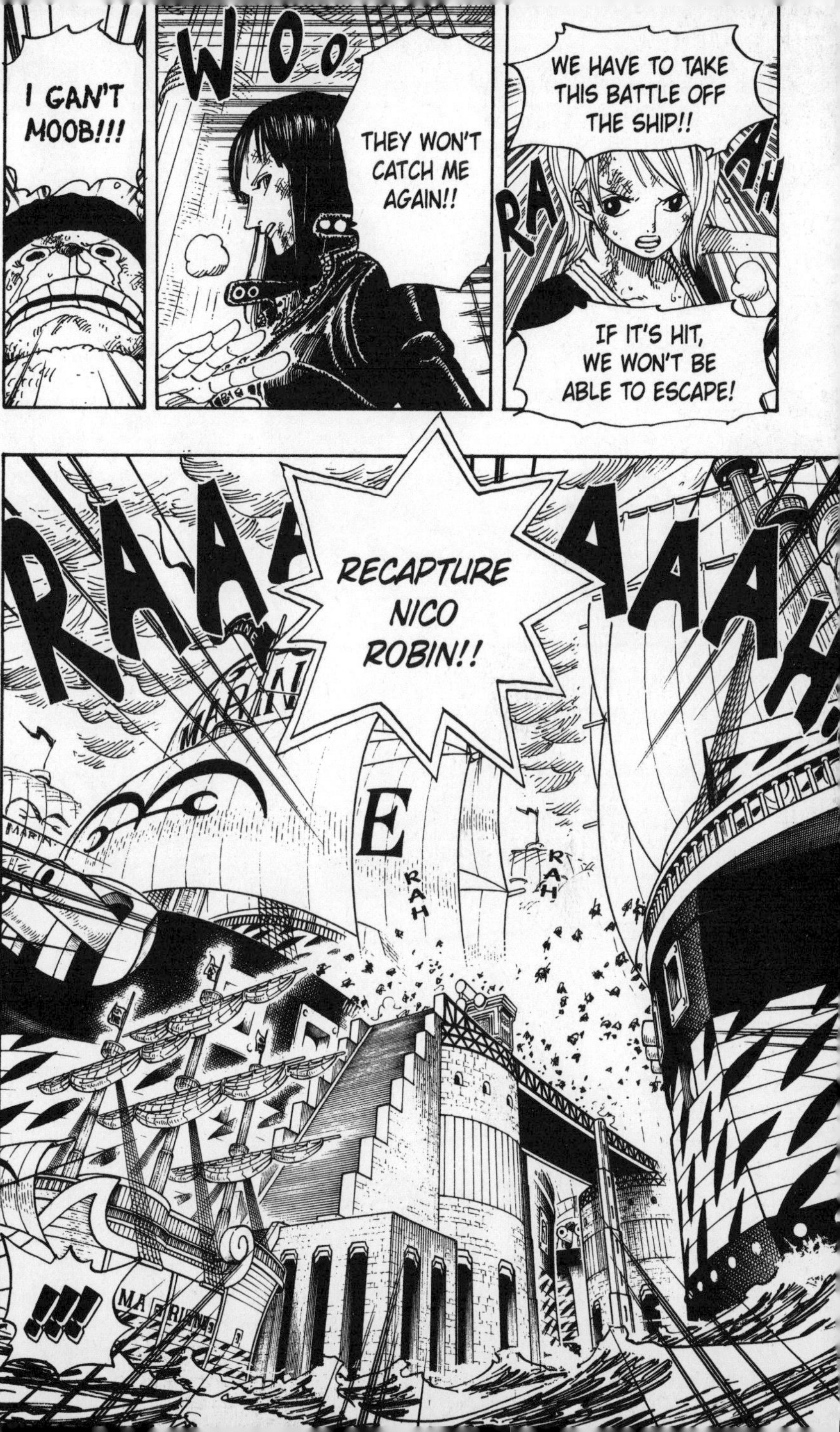
RA AH
WE HAVE TO TAKE THIS BATTLE OFF THE SHIP!!
IF IT'S HIT, WE WON'T BE ABLE TO ESCAPE!
WOO
THEY WON'T CATCH ME AGAIN!!
I GAN'T MOOB!!!
RAAA AAAH!!
RECAPTURE NICO ROBIN!!
E
RAH
RAH
!!!

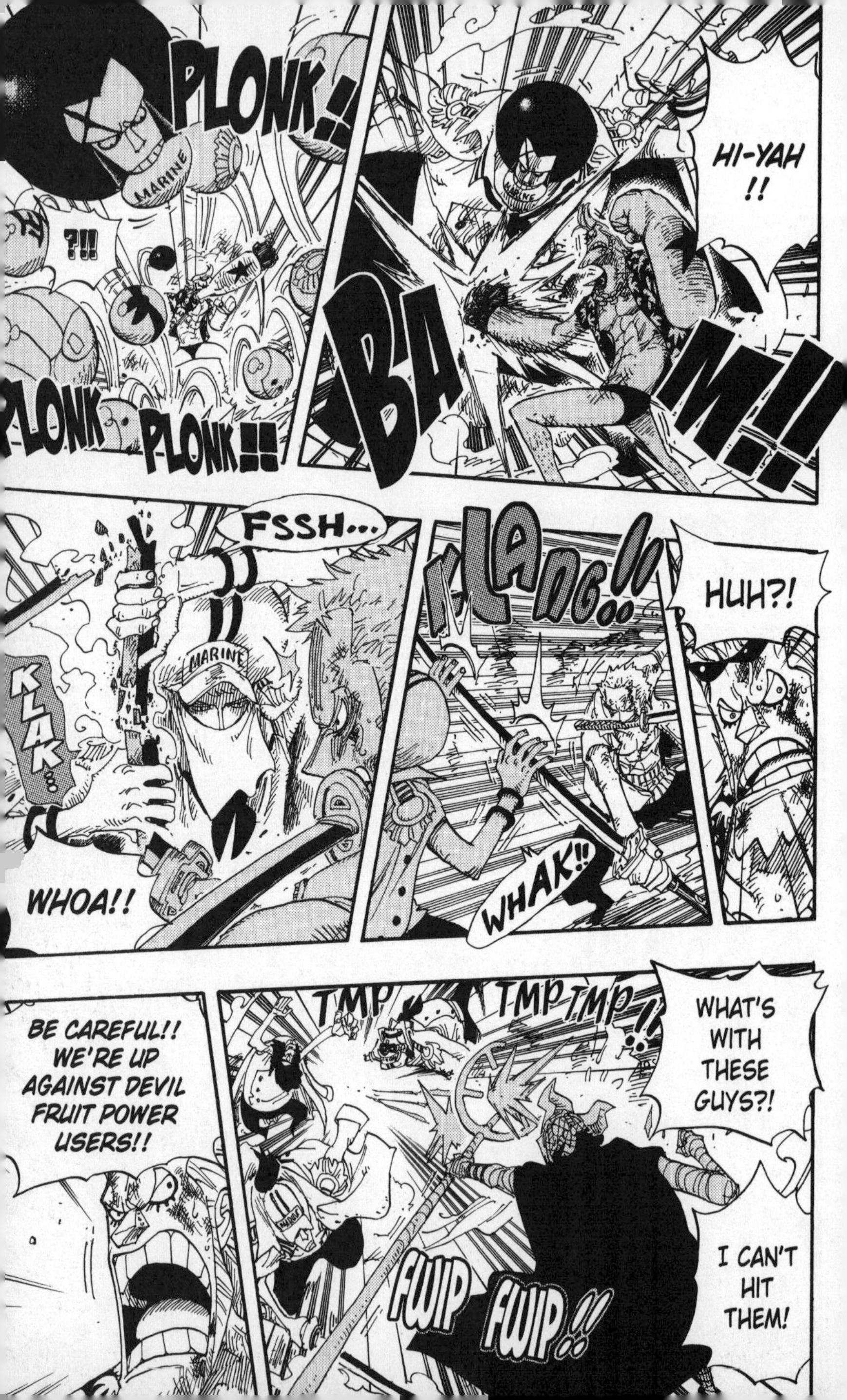
HI-YAH !!
BAM!!
PLONK!!
?!!
PLONK
PLONK!!
HUH?!
KLANG!!
WHAK!!
FSSH...
KLAK...
WHOA!!
WHAT'S WITH THESE GUYS?!
I CAN'T HIT THEM!
TMP TMP TMP
FWIP FWIP!!
BE CAREFUL!! WE'RE UP AGAINST DEVIL FRUIT POWER USERS!!

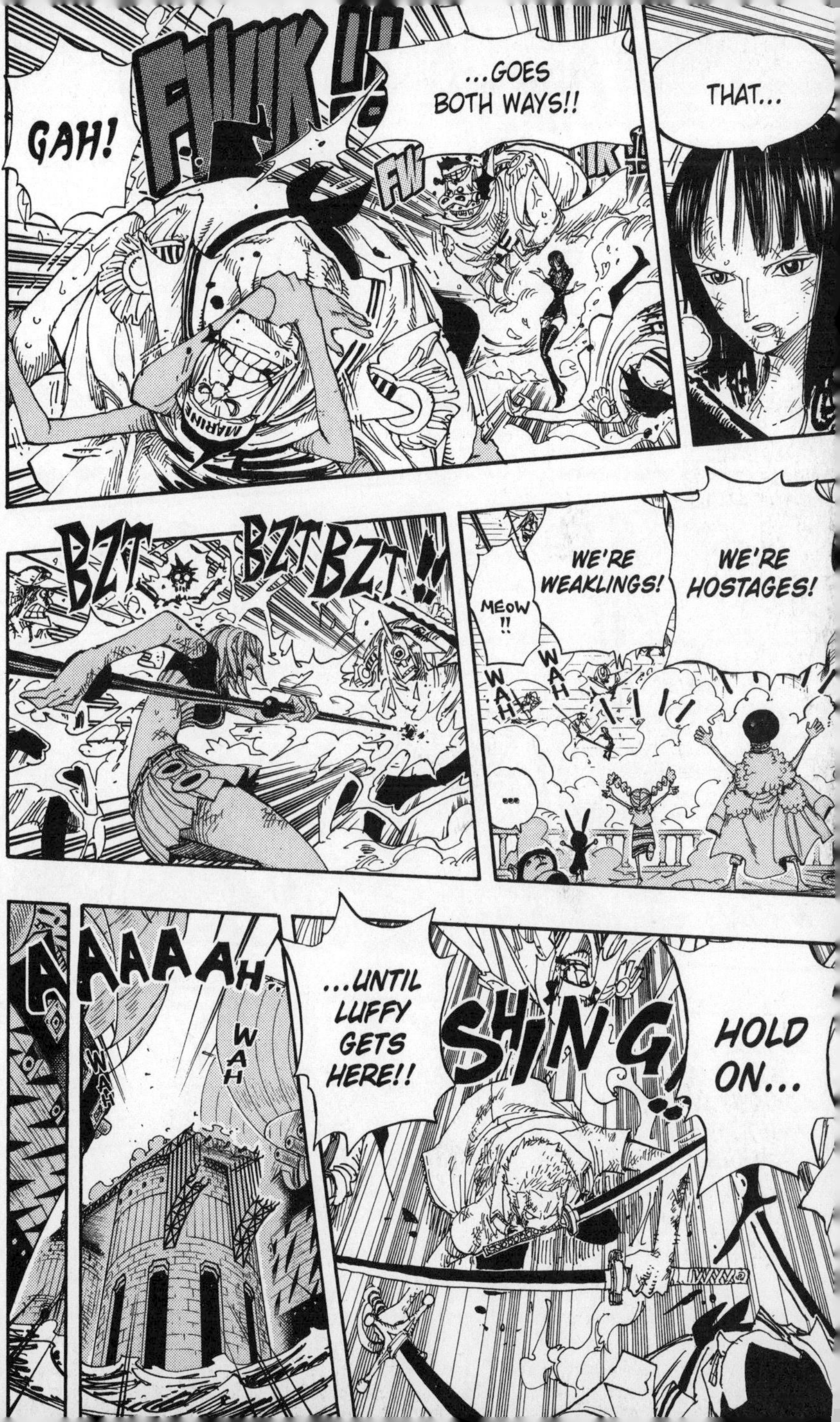
THAT...
...GOES BOTH WAYS!!
FWK!!
GAH!
FWK!!
WE'RE HOSTAGES!
WE'RE WEAKLINGS!
MEOW!!
WAH
WAH
...
BZT
BZTBZT!!
HOLD ON...
SHING!!
...UNTIL LUFFY GETS HERE!!
AAAAAH
WAH
WAH

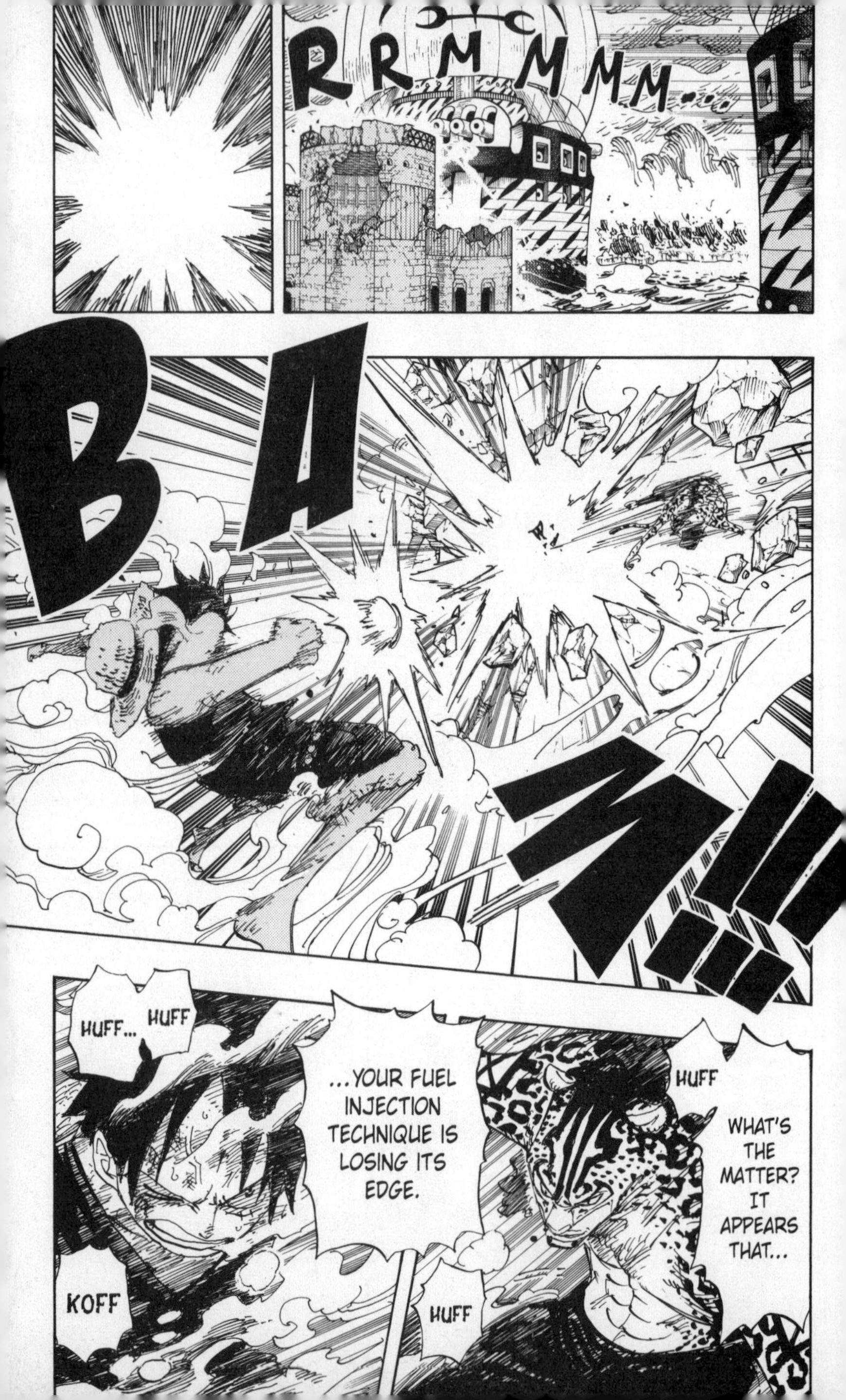
RRMMMM...
BAM!!!
HUFF
WHAT'S THE MATTER? IT APPEARS THAT...
...YOUR FUEL INJECTION TECHNIQUE IS LOSING ITS EDGE.
HUFF... HUFF
KOFF
HUFF

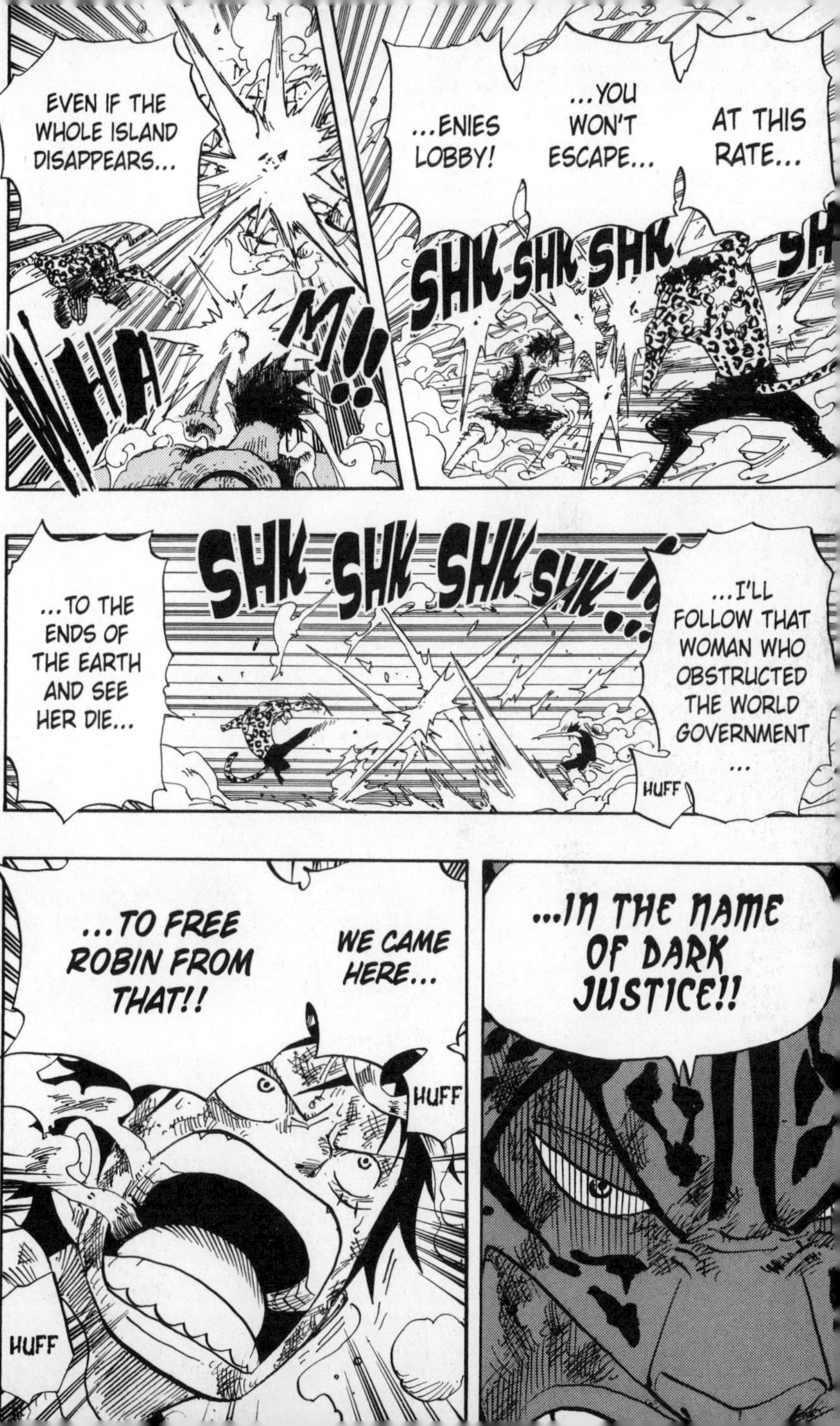

AT THIS RATE...
...YOU WON'T ESCAPE...
...ENIES LOBBY!
SHK SHK SHK SH
EVEN IF THE WHOLE ISLAND DISAPPEARS...
WHAM!!
...I'LL FOLLOW THAT WOMAN WHO OBSTRUCTED THE WORLD GOVERNMENT...
HUFF
SHK SHK SHK SHK!!
...TO THE ENDS OF THE EARTH AND SEE HER DIE...
...IN THE NAME OF DARK JUSTICE!!
HUFF
WE CAME HERE...
...TO FREE ROBIN FROM THAT!!
HUFF

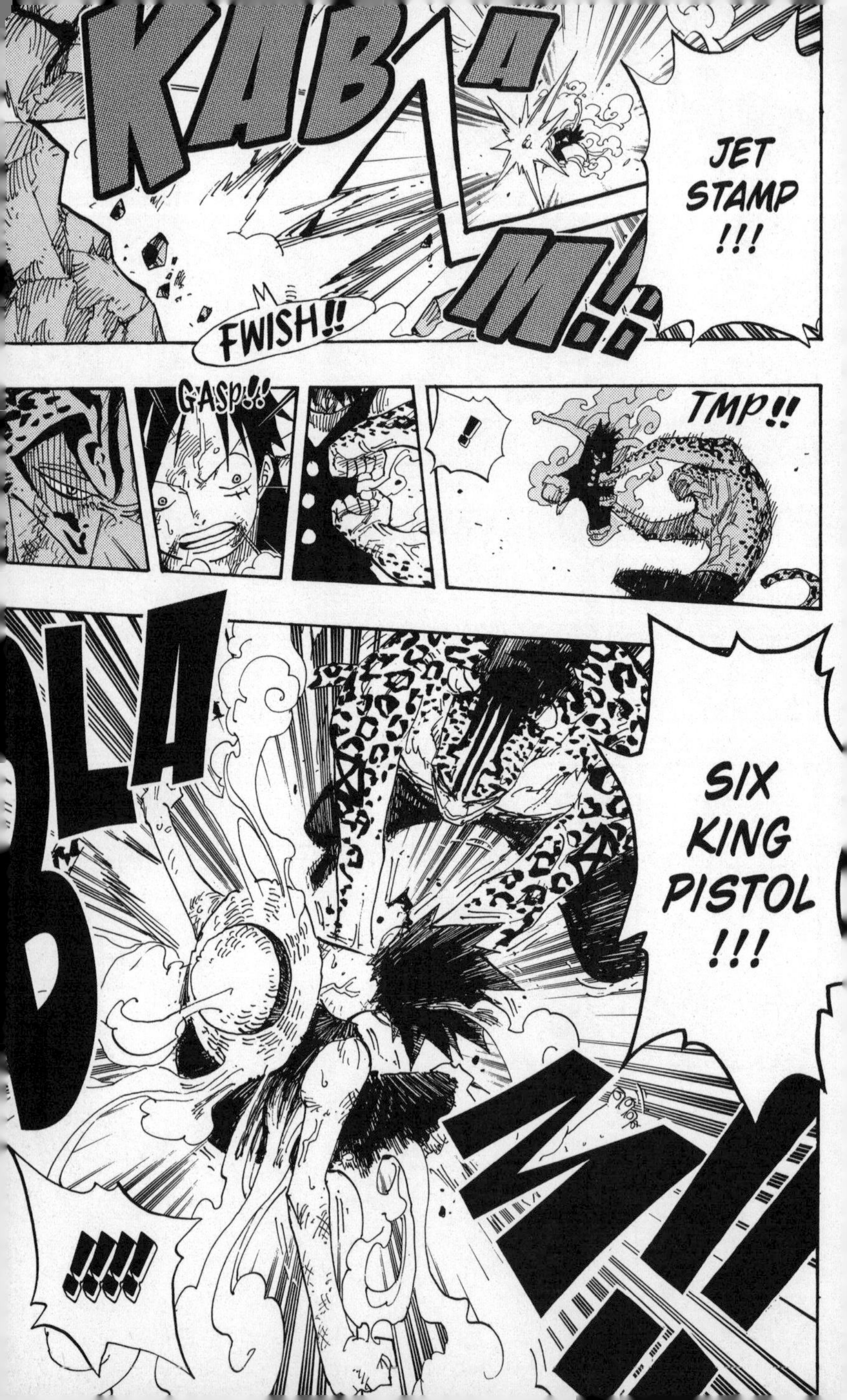
JET STAMP !!!
KABAM!!
FWISH!!
TMP!!
!
GASP!!
SIX KING PISTOL !!!
BLAM
!!!!!

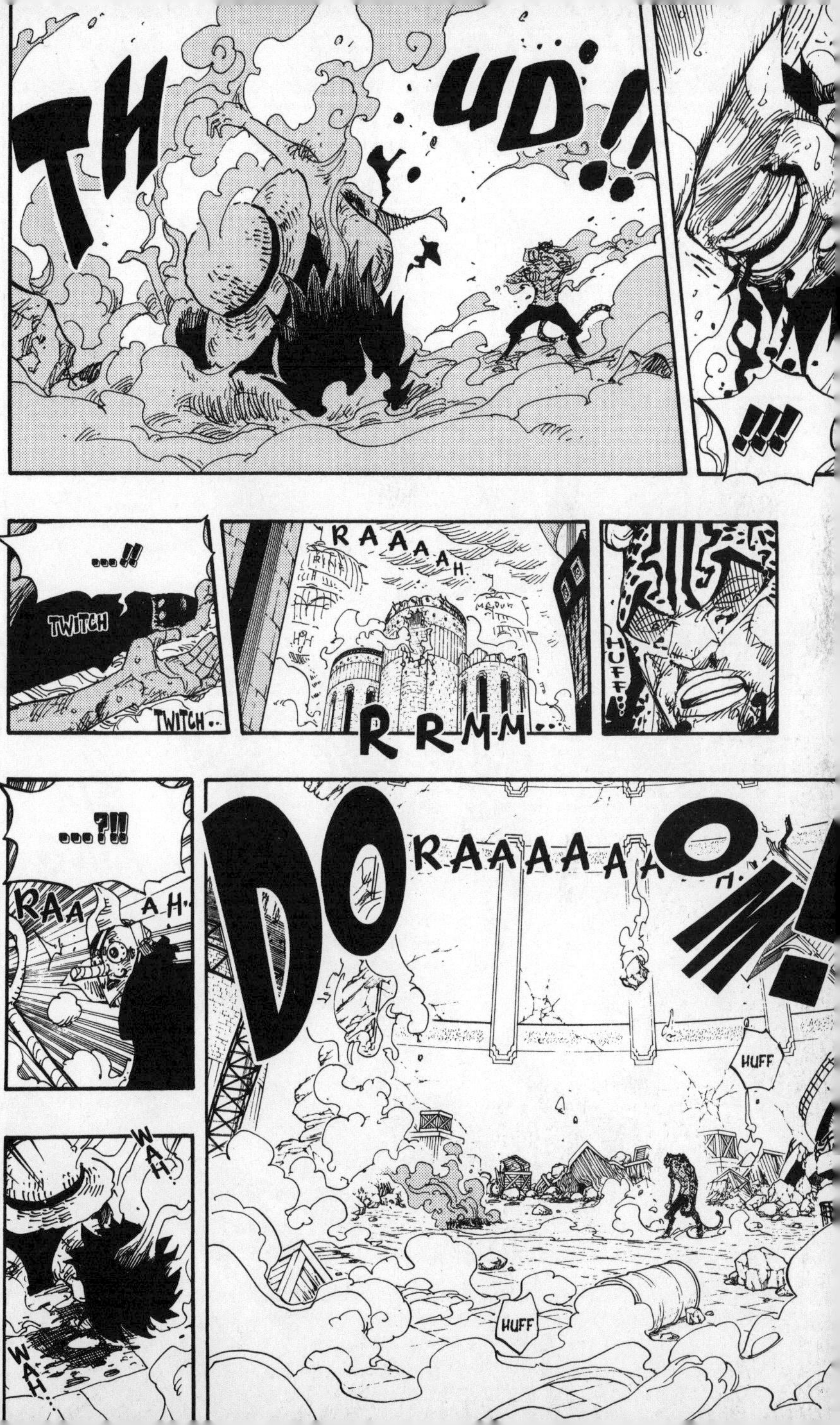
!!!
THUD!!
HUFF...
RAAAAAH
RRMM...
...!!
TWITCH
TWITCH...
DORAAAAAAOM..!!
HUFF
HUFF
...?!!
RAA AH
WAH
WAH...

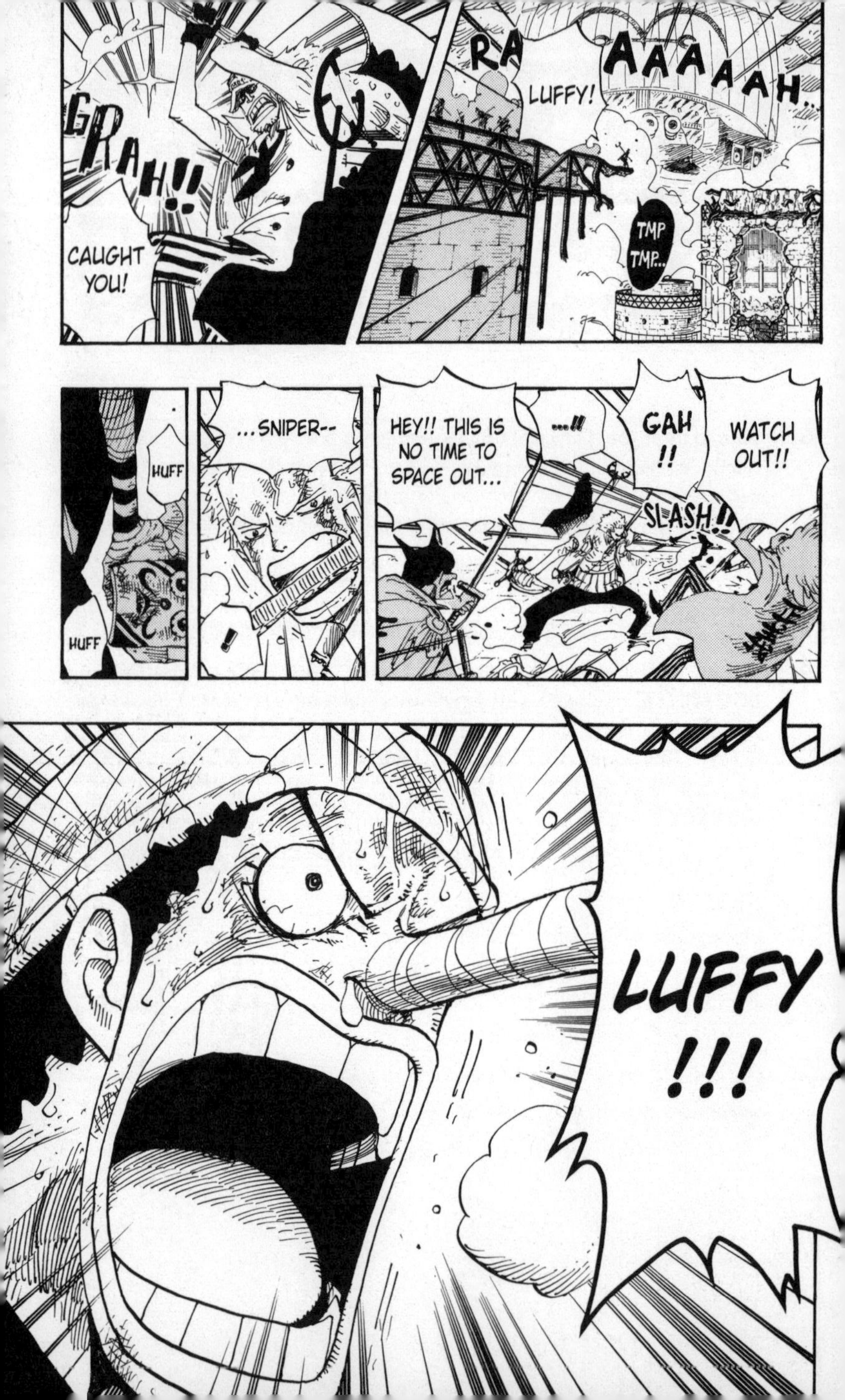
RA AAAAAAH...
LUFFY!
TMP TMP...
GRAH!!
CAUGHT YOU!
WATCH OUT!!
GAH!!
SLASH!!
...!!
HEY!! THIS IS NO TIME TO SPACE OUT...
...SNIPER--
!
HUFF
HUFF
LUFFY!!!

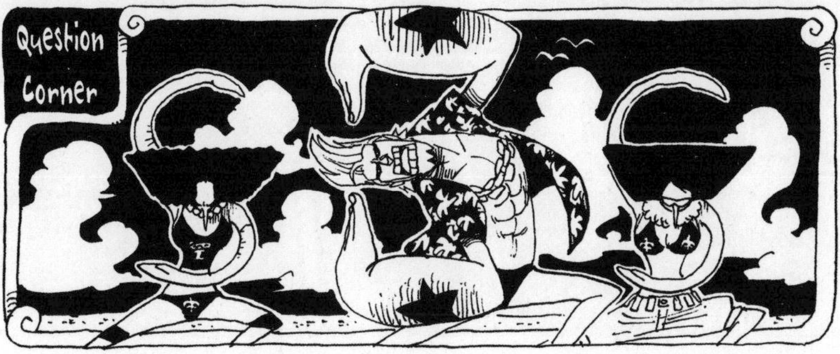
Question Corner

Q: Nice to meet you, Odacchi! I finally sent you a postcard! The question is serious, so please give me a proper answer. It's about the technique that Sanji used to defeat Jabra. Shouldn't the heat have been incredible given the effect it had on Jabra?!! Does Sanji ever think to himself, "Ow! That's hot!!"? Tell me!

--Geiichiro Oda

A: What are you talking about? What are you talking about?! Can't you see anything? What were you looking at during the fight?! That Sanji's feet were hot?! They weren't that hot! I mean, come on, Sanji's heart was burning way hotter!!

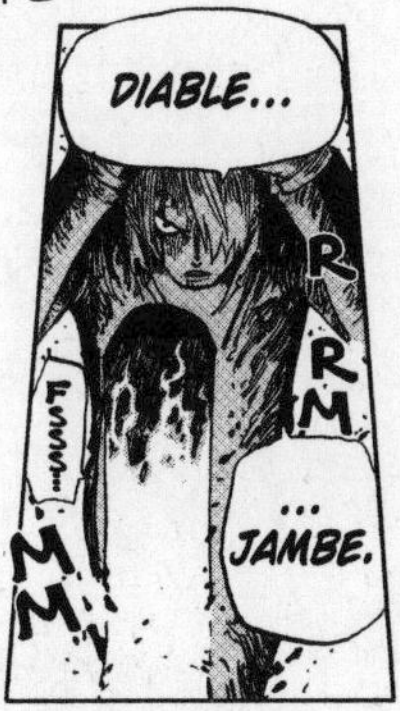
DIABLE...
RRM
...JAMBE.
MM

Q: Hope you're having a propitious summer.

--Naoko-chan

A: Uh...right. The same to you. (Do you mean an auspicious summer?!)

Chapter 427:
THIS ISN'T THE AFTERLIFE

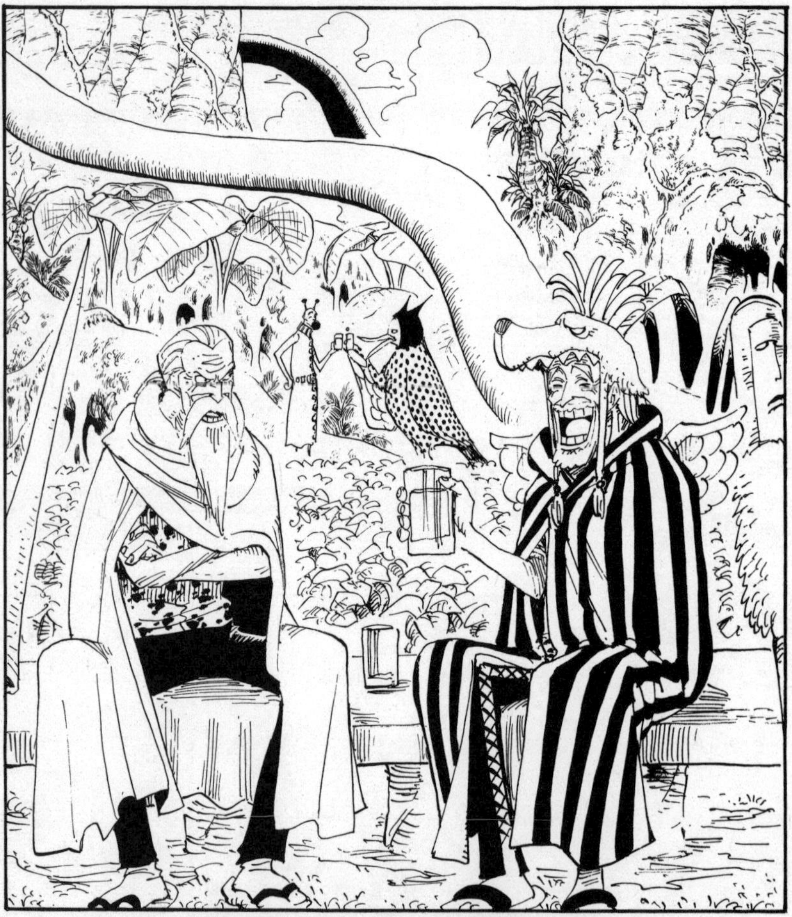

WHERE ARE THEY NOW? SHOT 3:
"GANFOR AND CHIEF'S BRILLIANT PUMPKIN PLAN"

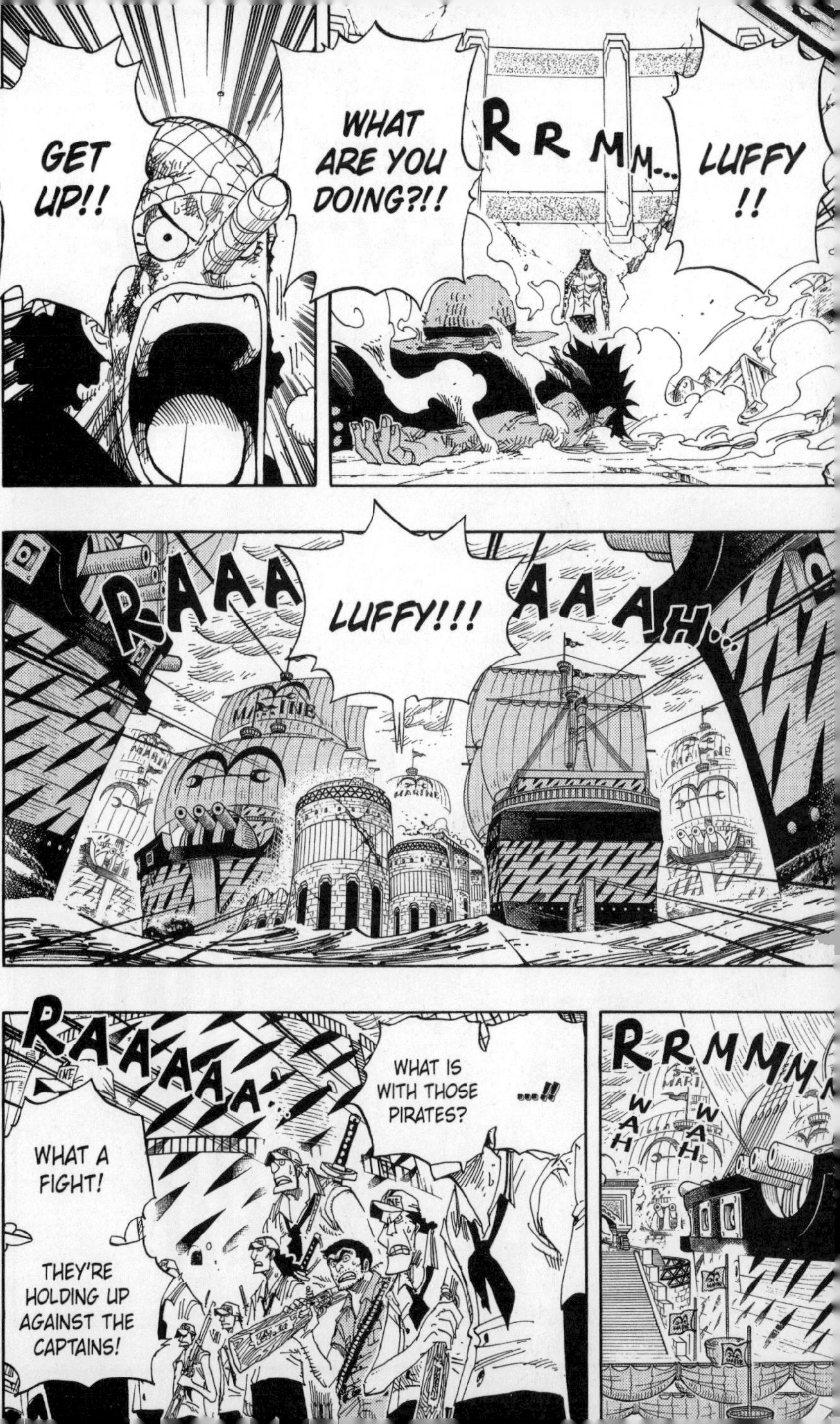
LUFFY !!
RRMMM...
WHAT ARE YOU DOING?!!
GET UP!!
RAAA
LUFFY!!!
AAAH...
RRMMMM
WAH
WAH
RAAAAA...
WHAT IS WITH THOSE PIRATES?
...!!
WHAT A FIGHT!
THEY'RE HOLDING UP AGAINST THE CAPTAINS!

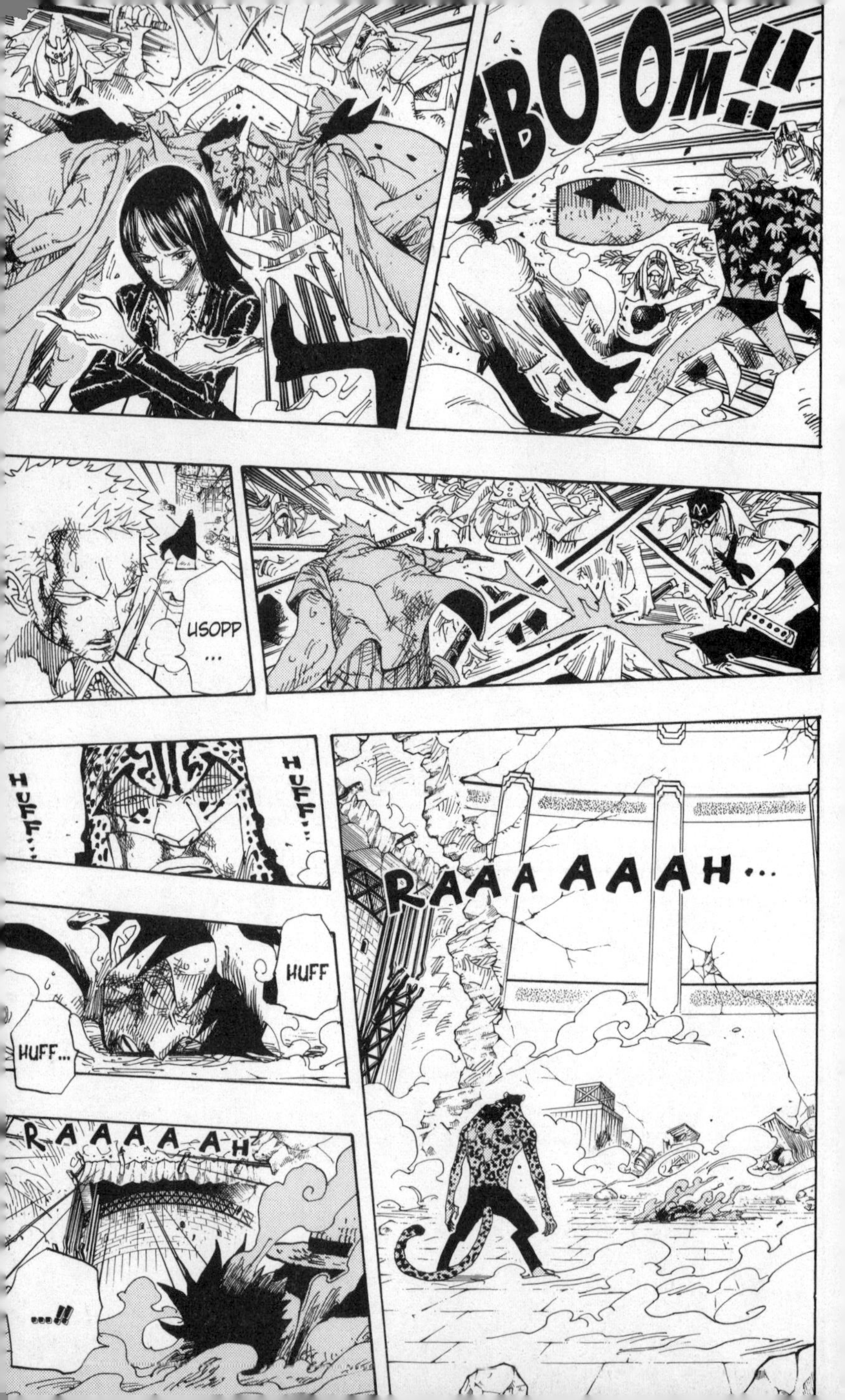
BOOM!!
USOPP ...
RAAAAAAH...
HUFF...
HUFF...
HUFF
HUFF...
RAAAAAH
...!!

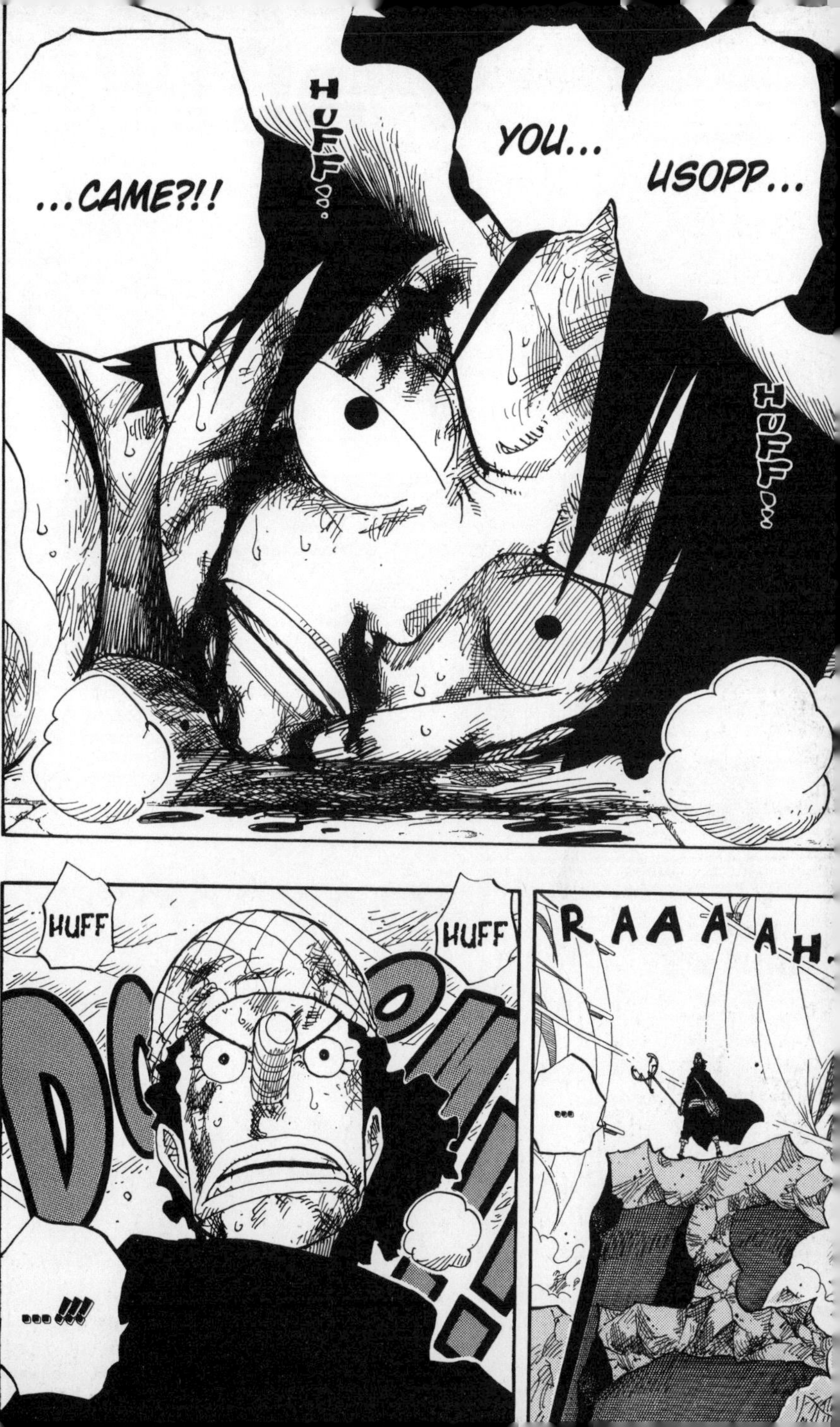
USOPP...
YOU...
HUFF..
...CAME?!!
HUFF..
RAAAAH..
...
HUFF
HUFF
...!!!

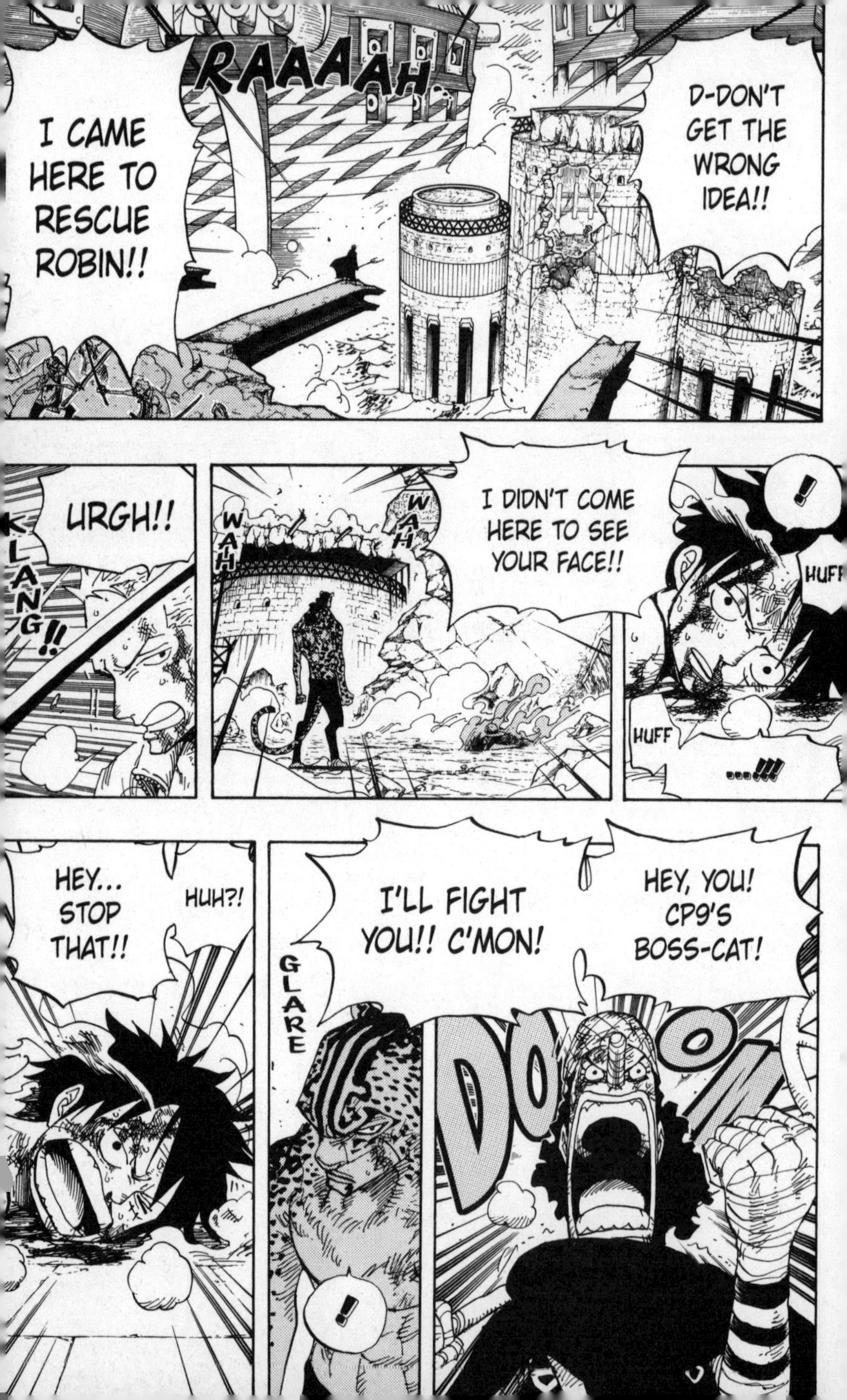
D-DON'T GET THE WRONG IDEA!!
RAAAAH
I CAME HERE TO RESCUE ROBIN!!
!
HUFF
HUFF
...!!!
I DIDN'T COME HERE TO SEE YOUR FACE!!
WAH
WAH
URGH!!
KLANG!!
HEY, YOU! CP9'S BOSS-CAT!
I'LL FIGHT YOU!! C'MON!
GLARE
!
HUH?!
HEY... STOP THAT!!

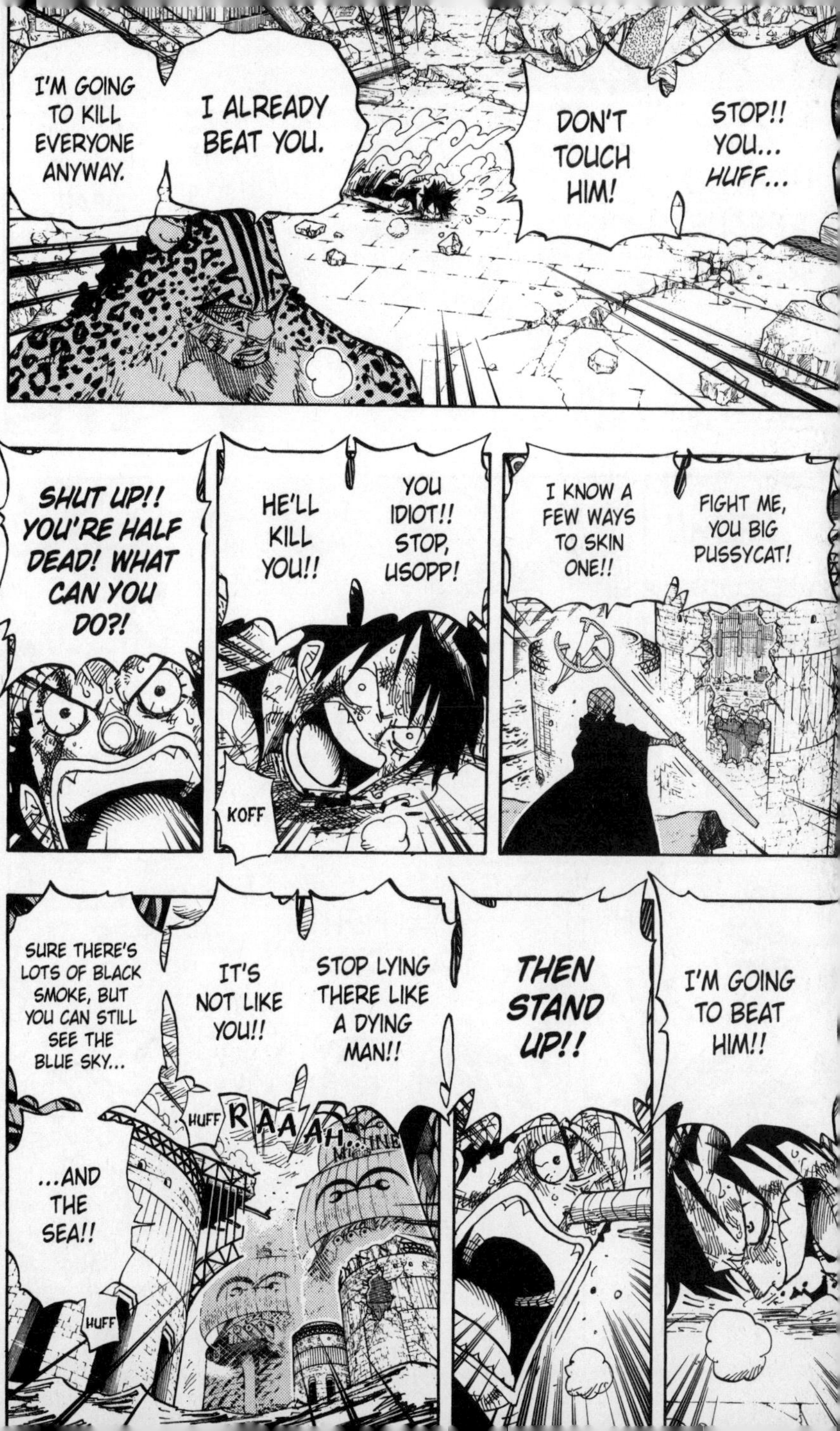
STOP!! YOU... HUFF...
DON'T TOUCH HIM!
I ALREADY BEAT YOU.
I'M GOING TO KILL EVERYONE ANYWAY.
FIGHT ME, YOU BIG PUSSYCAT!
I KNOW A FEW WAYS TO SKIN ONE!!
YOU IDIOT!! STOP, USOPP!
HE'LL KILL YOU!!
KOFF
SHUT UP!! YOU'RE HALF DEAD! WHAT CAN YOU DO?!
I'M GOING TO BEAT HIM!!
THEN STAND UP!!
STOP LYING THERE LIKE A DYING MAN!!
IT'S NOT LIKE YOU!!
HUFF
RAAAH
SURE THERE'S LOTS OF BLACK SMOKE, BUT YOU CAN STILL SEE THE BLUE SKY...
...AND THE SEA!!
HUFF

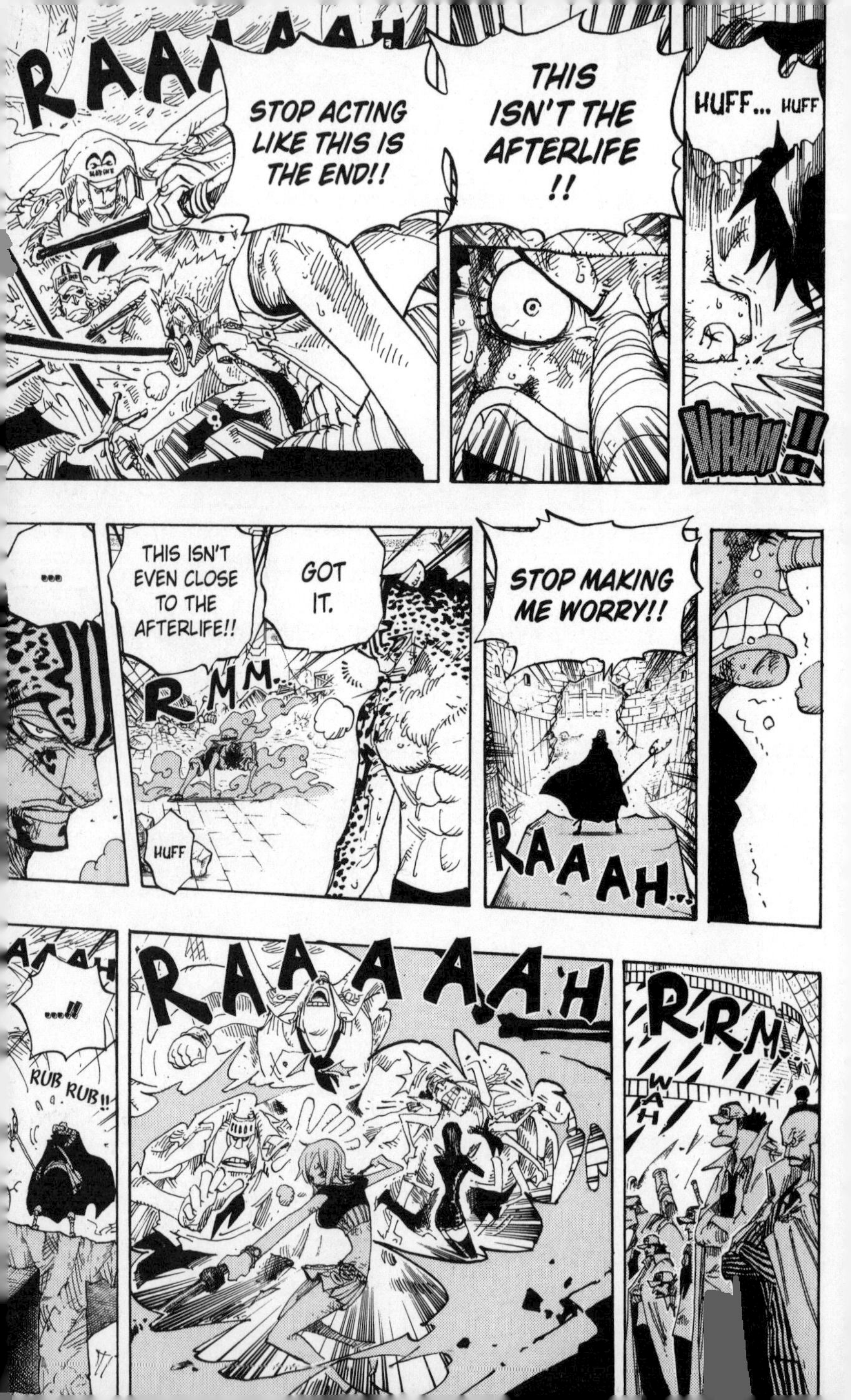
HUFF... HUFF
THIS ISN'T THE AFTERLIFE !!
STOP ACTING LIKE THIS IS THE END!!
RAAAAAAH
STOP MAKING ME WORRY!!
RAAAH...
GOT IT.
THIS ISN'T EVEN CLOSE TO THE AFTERLIFE!!
RMM...
HUFF
...
RRRM...
WAH
RAAAAAAH
...!!
RUB RUB!!

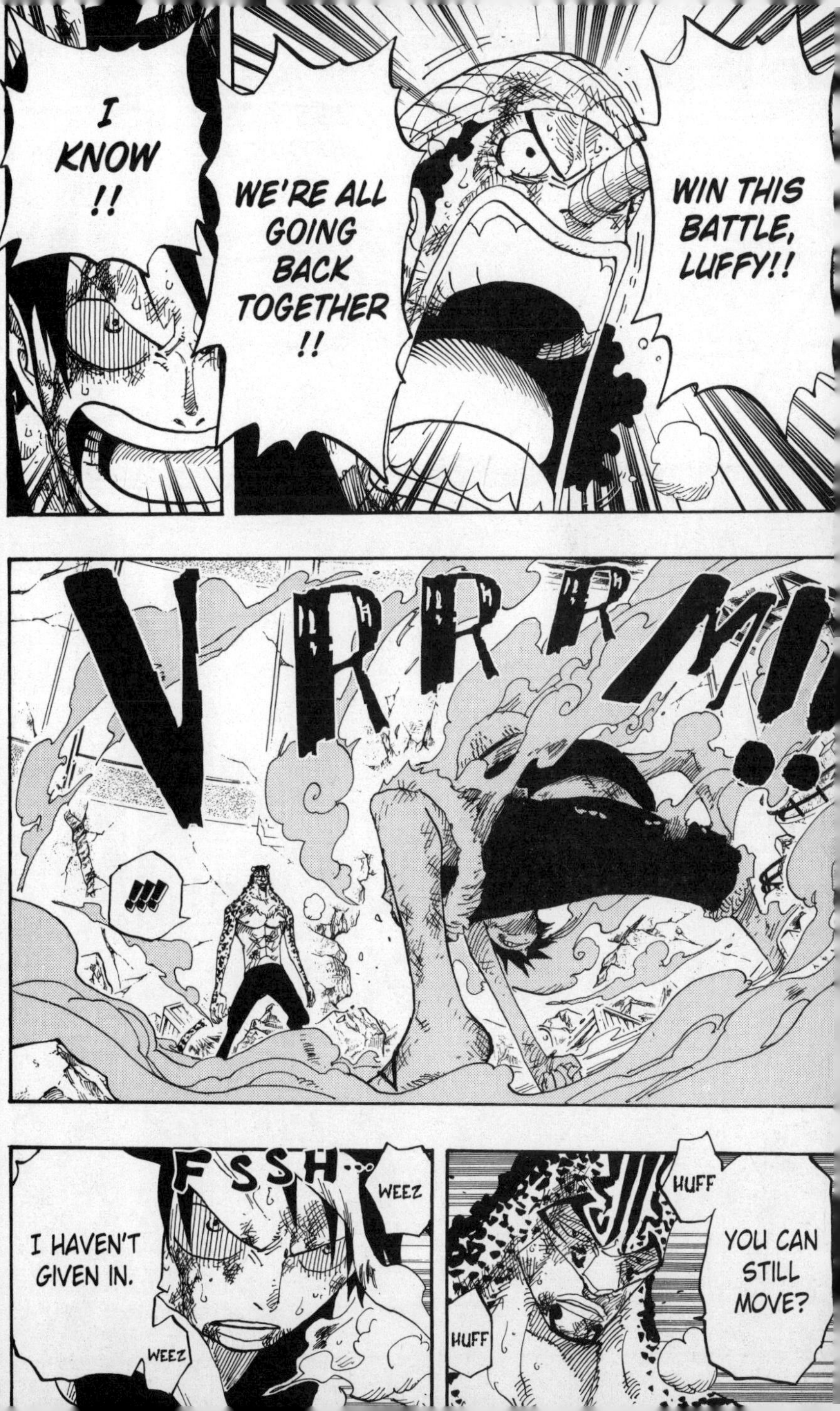
WIN THIS BATTLE, LUFFY!!
WE'RE ALL GOING BACK TOGETHER!!
I KNOW!!
VRRRM
!!!
HUFF
YOU CAN STILL MOVE?
HUFF
FSSH
WEEZ
I HAVEN'T GIVEN IN.
WEEZ

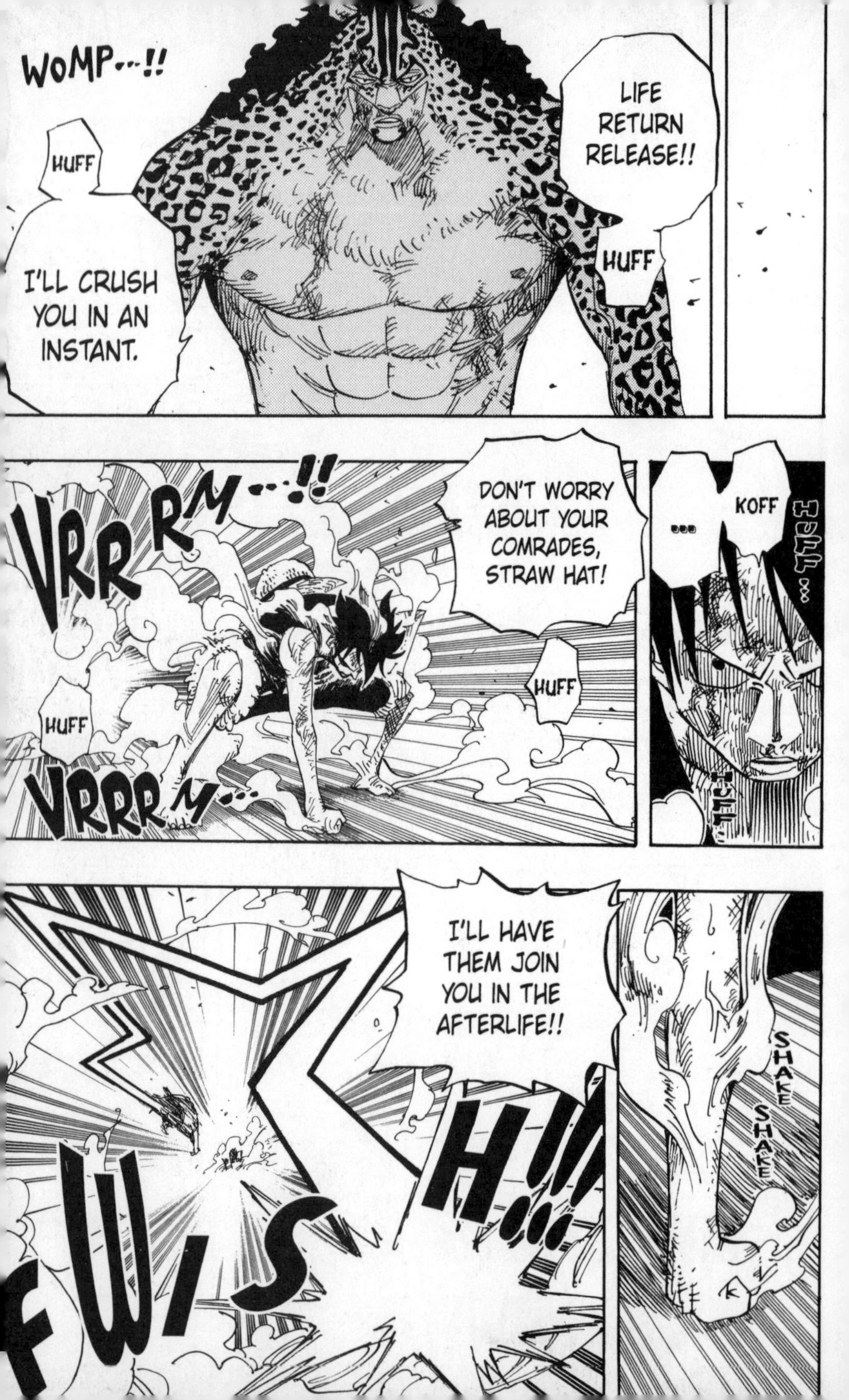
LIFE RETURN RELEASE!!
HUFF
WOMP...!!
HUFF
I'LL CRUSH YOU IN AN INSTANT.
KOFF
...
HUFF...
HUFF
DON'T WORRY ABOUT YOUR COMRADES, STRAW HAT!
HUFF
VRRRM...!!
HUFF
VRRRM...
SHAKE
SHAKE
I'LL HAVE THEM JOIN YOU IN THE AFTERLIFE!!
FWISH!!...

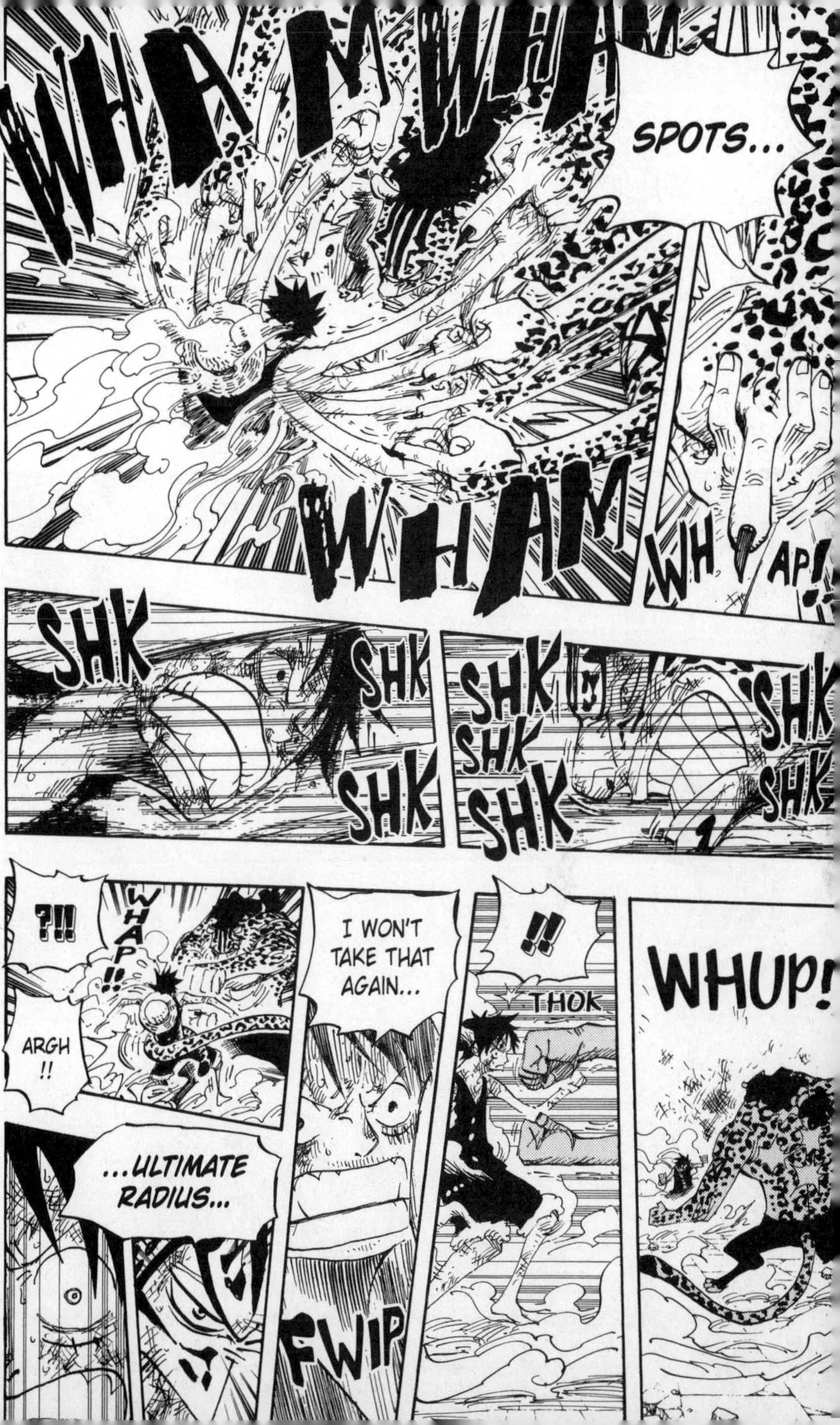
SPOTS...
WHAP!!
WHAM WHAM
WHAM
SHK
SHK
SHK SHK SHK SHK
SHK SHK SHK
WHUP!
!!
THOK
I WON'T TAKE THAT AGAIN...
FWIP
?!!
WHAP!!
ARGH !!
...ULTIMATE RADIUS...

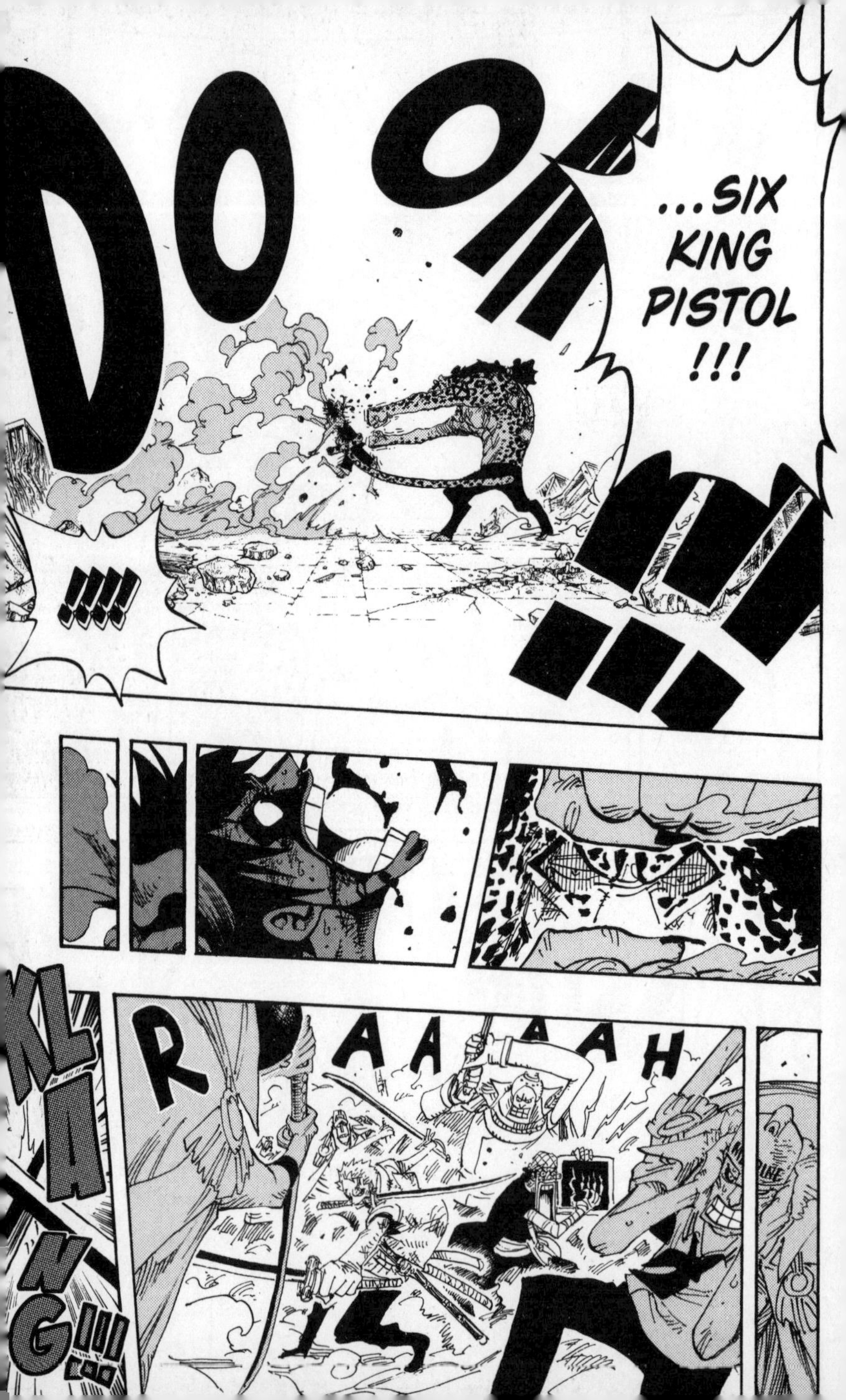
...SIX KING PISTOL !!!
DOOM!!!
!!!!
RAAAH
KLANG!!!

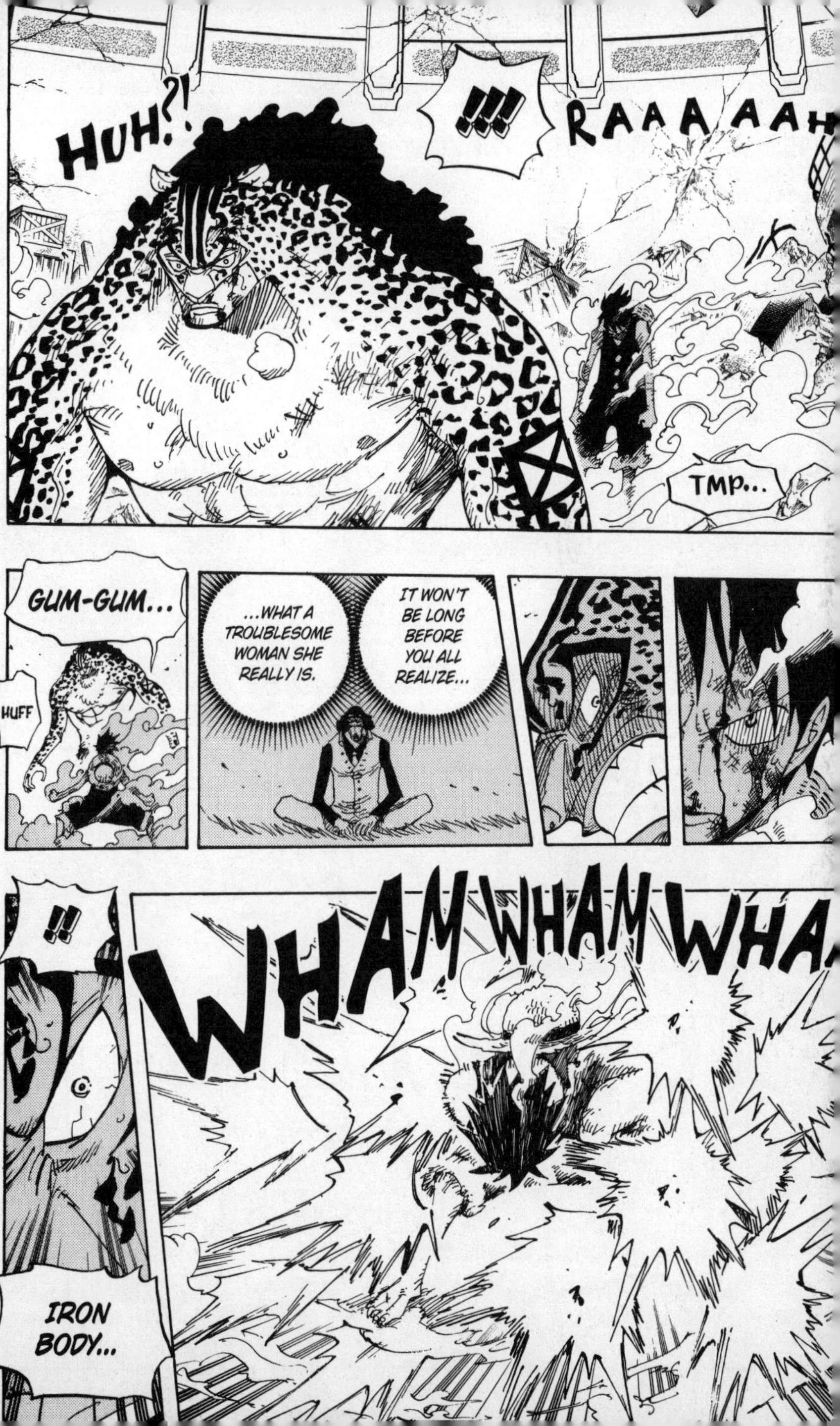
RAAAAAH
!!!
HUH?!
TMP...
IT WON'T BE LONG BEFORE YOU ALL REALIZE...
...WHAT A TROUBLESOME WOMAN SHE REALLY IS.
GUM-GUM...
HUFF
WHAM WHAM WHA
!!
IRON BODY...

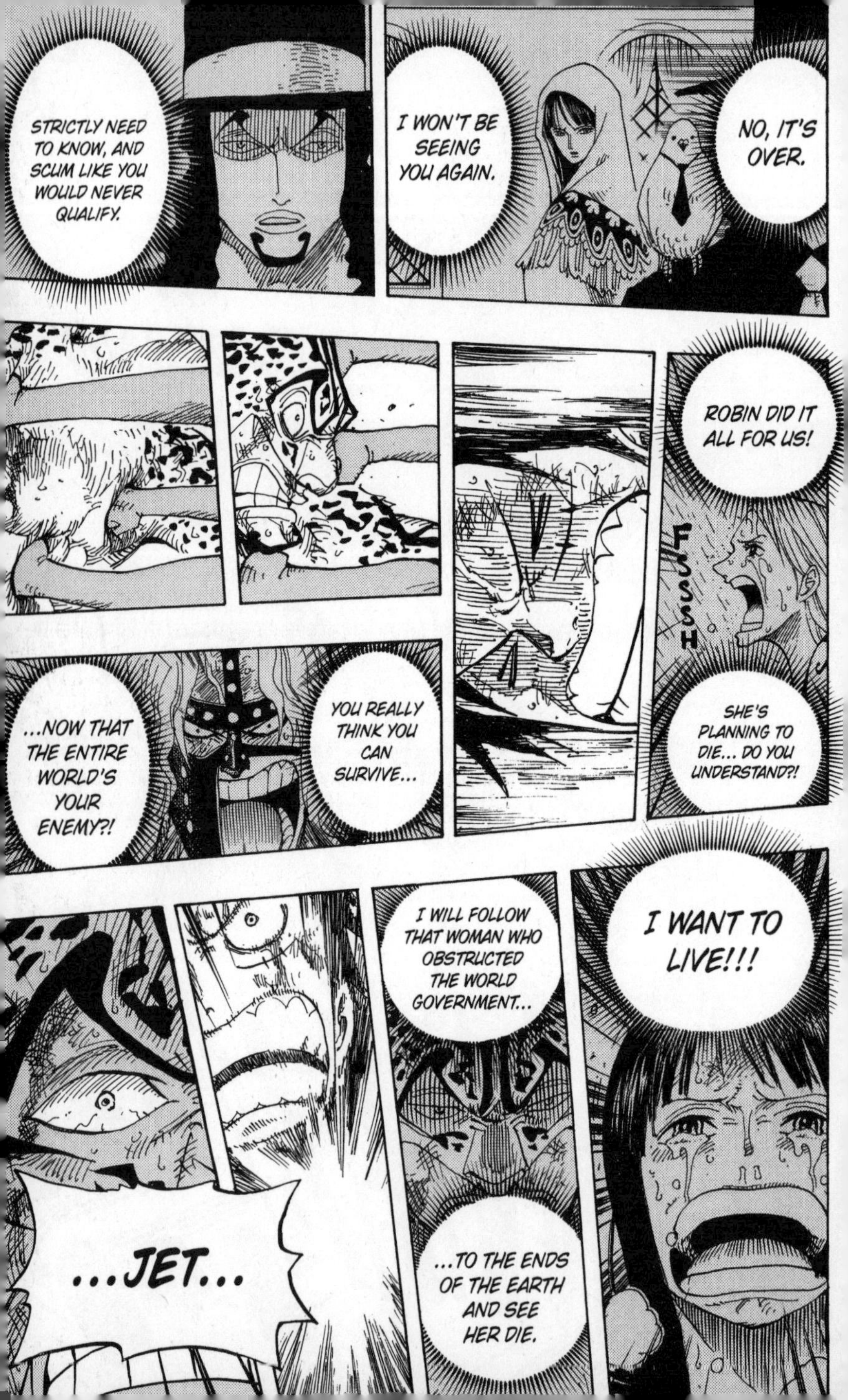
NO, IT'S OVER.
I WON'T BE SEEING YOU AGAIN.
STRICTLY NEED TO KNOW, AND SCUM LIKE YOU WOULD NEVER QUALIFY.
ROBIN DID IT ALL FOR US!
FSSSH
SHE'S PLANNING TO DIE... DO YOU UNDERSTAND?!
YOU REALLY THINK YOU CAN SURVIVE...
...NOW THAT THE ENTIRE WORLD'S YOUR ENEMY?!
I WANT TO LIVE!!!
I WILL FOLLOW THAT WOMAN WHO OBSTRUCTED THE WORLD GOVERNMENT...
...TO THE ENDS OF THE EARTH AND SEE HER DIE.
...JET...

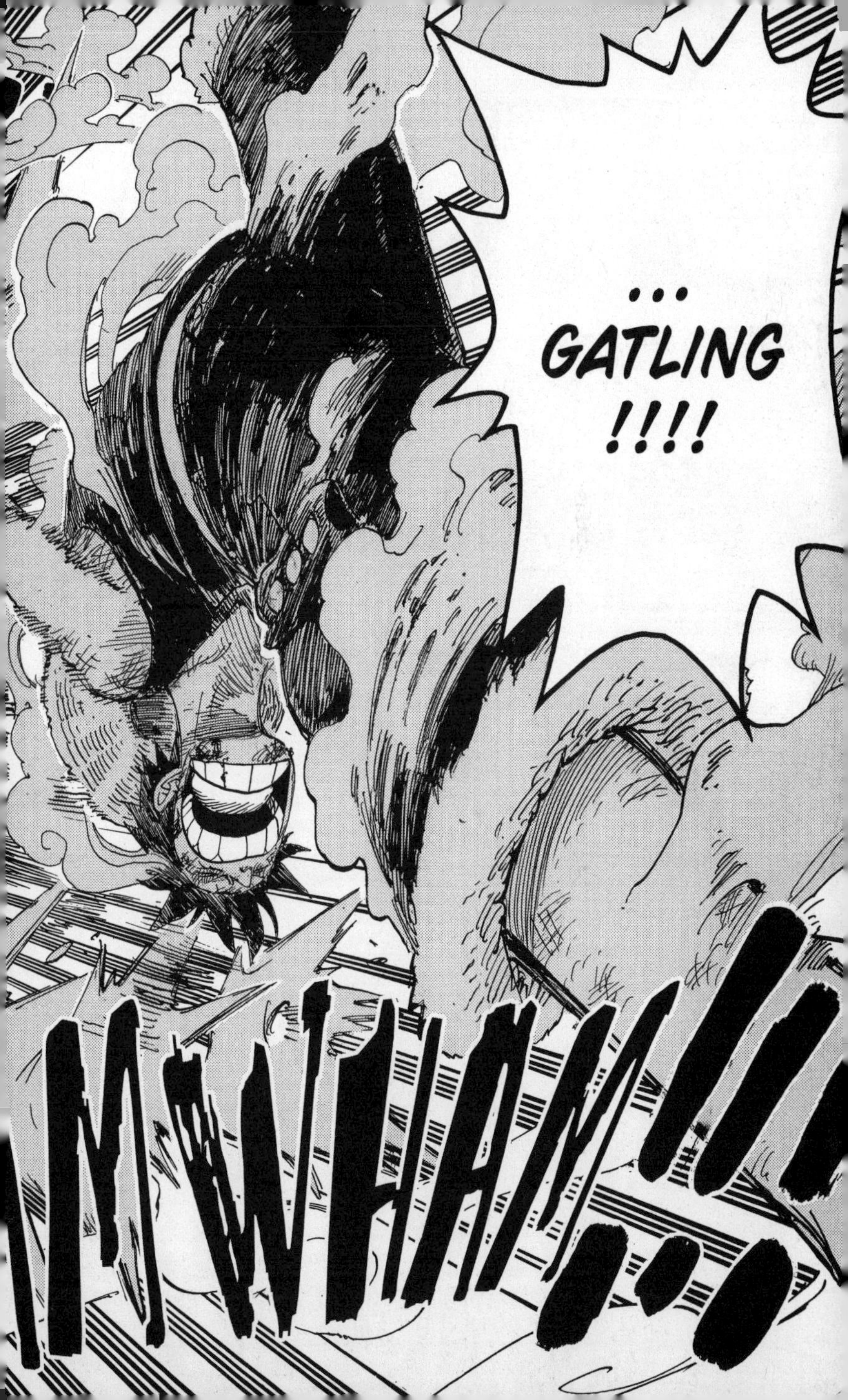
... GATLING !!!!
WHAM!!

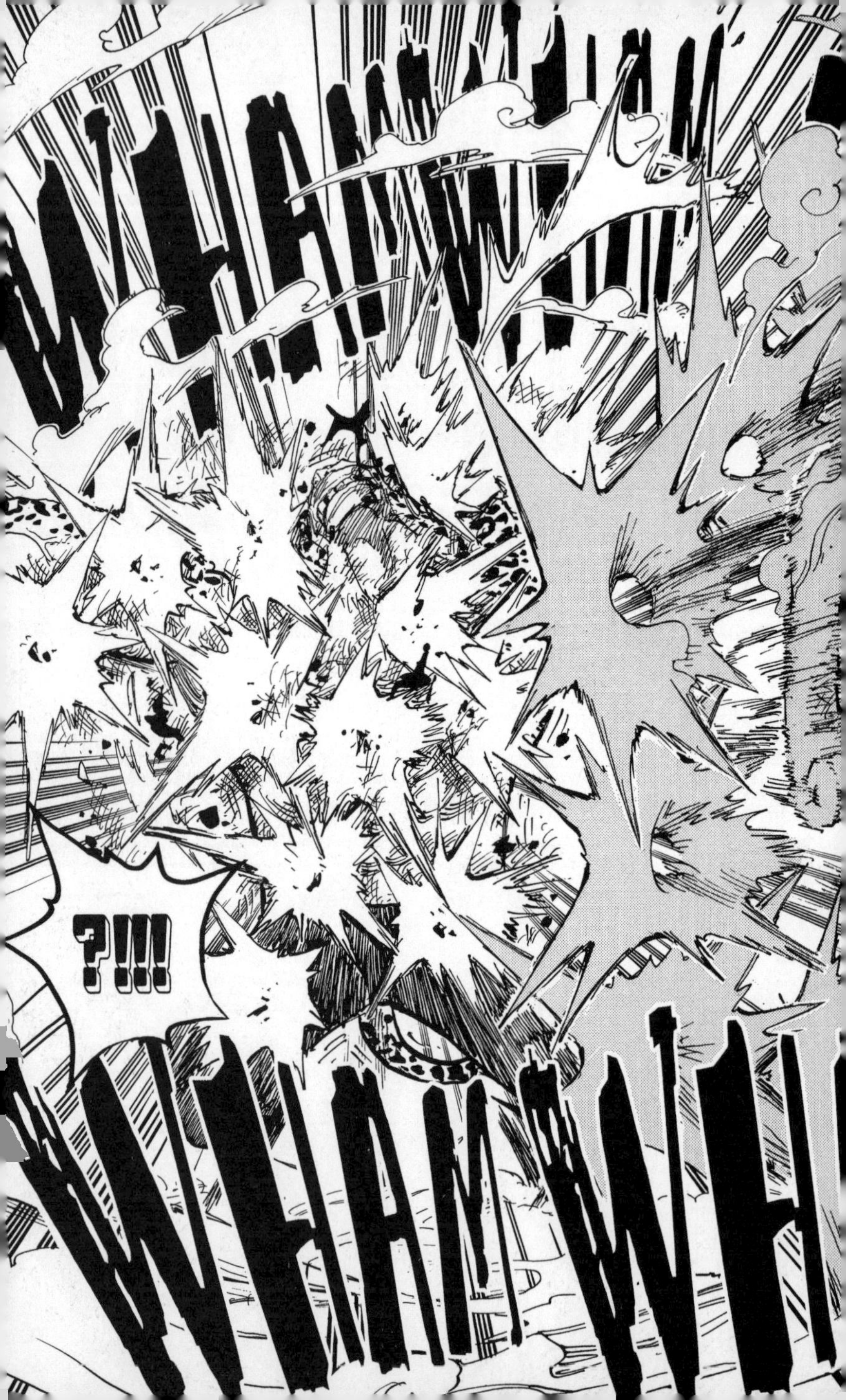
?!!!

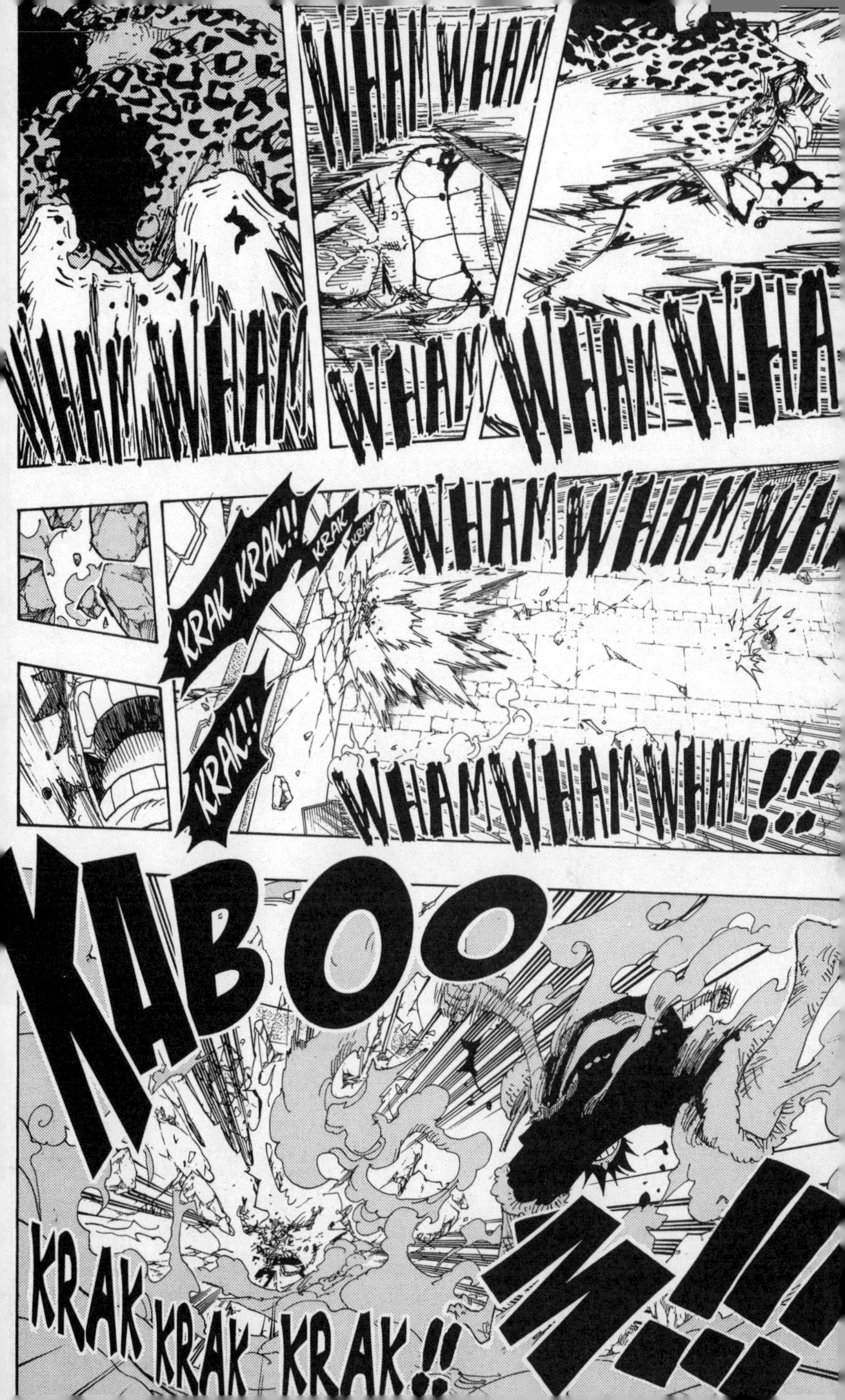

WHAM WHAM
WHAM WHA
WHAM
WHAM WHAM
WHAM WHAM WHA
KRAK KRAK!!
KRAK
KRAK
KRAK!!
WHAM WHAM WHAM!!
KABOOM!!
KRAK KRAK KRAK!!

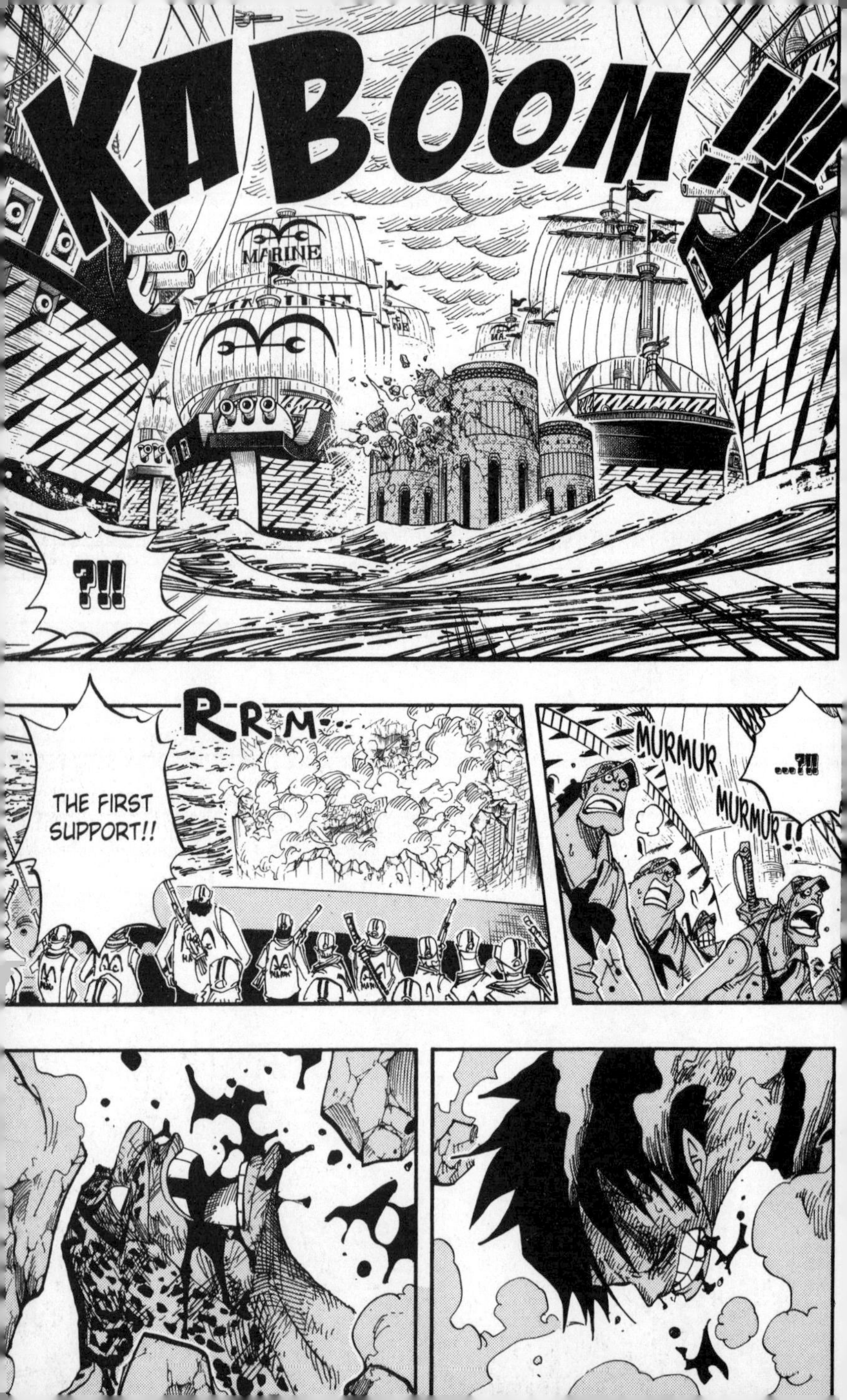
KABOOM!!!
MARINE
?!!
...?!!
MURMUR
MURMUR!!
RRM
THE FIRST SUPPORT!!

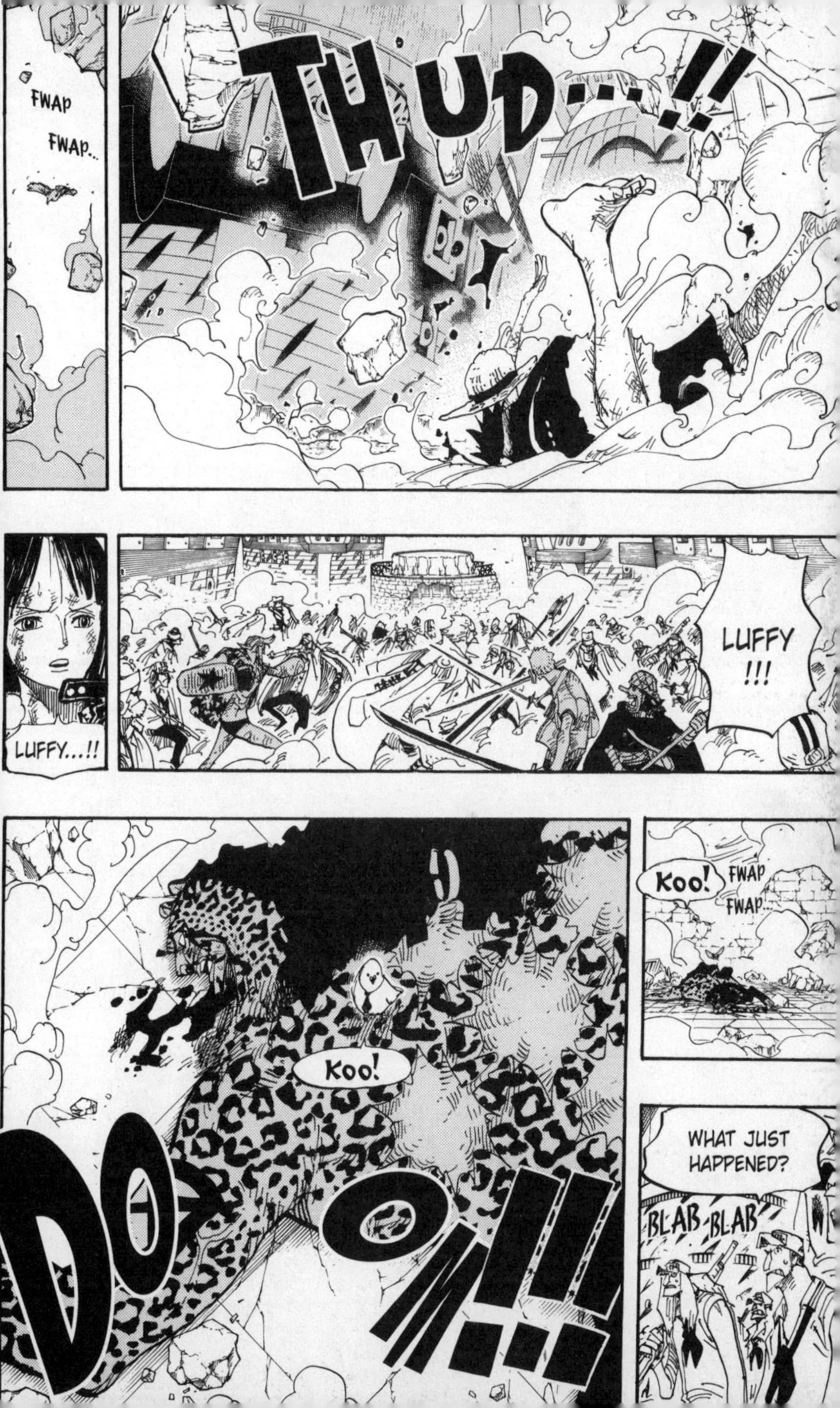
THUD...!!
FWAP
FWAP...
LUFFY !!!
LUFFY...!!
Koo!
FWAP
FWAP...
WHAT JUST HAPPENED?
BLAB BLAB
Koo!
DOOM...!!

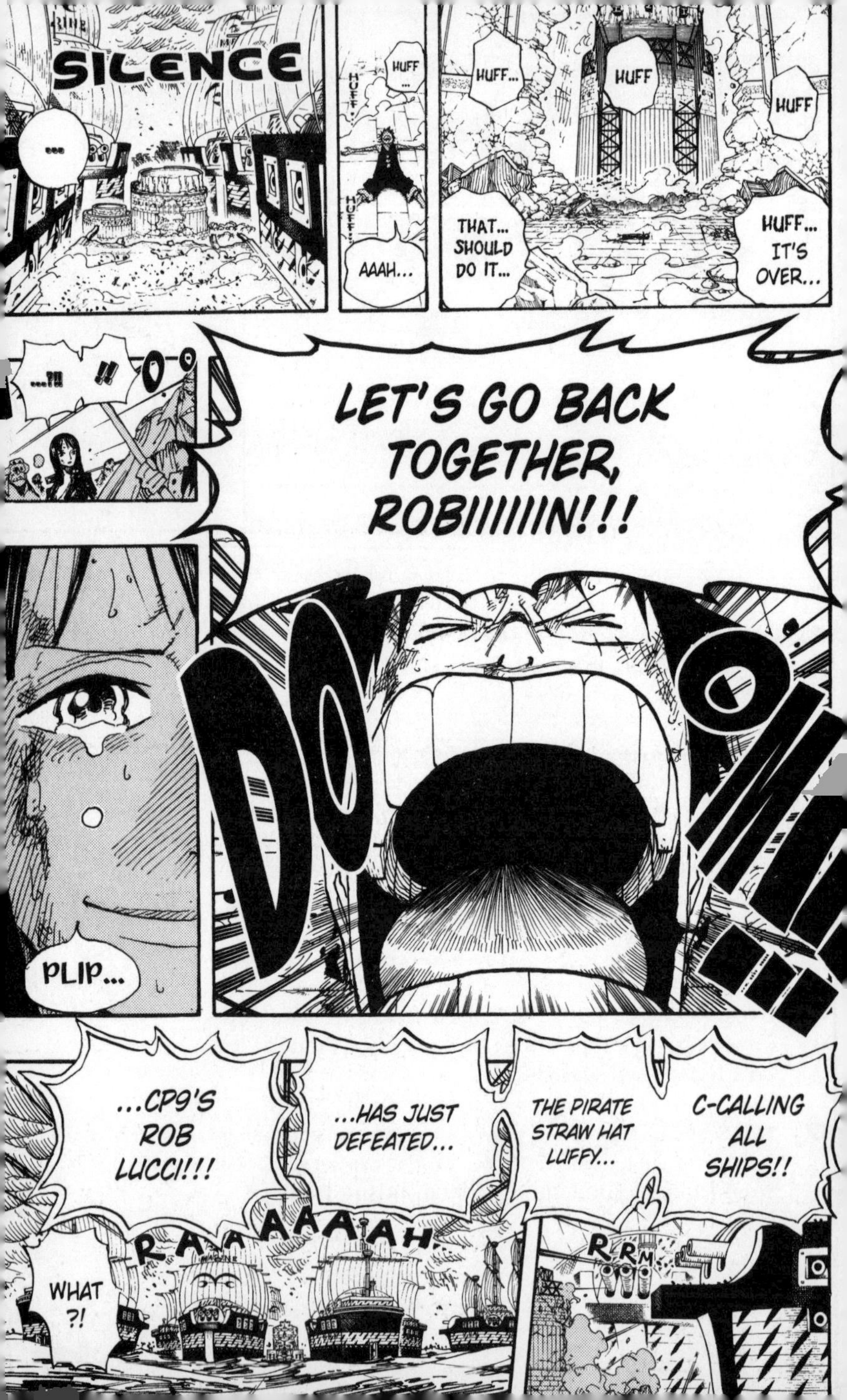
HUFF
HUFF...
HUFF
HUFF... IT'S OVER...
THAT... SHOULD DO IT...
HUFF...
HUFF...
HUFF...
AAAH...
SILENCE
...
LET'S GO BACK TOGETHER, ROBIIIIIIIN!!!
DOOM
...?!!
!!
PLIP...
C-CALLING ALL SHIPS!!
THE PIRATE STRAW HAT LUFFY...
...HAS JUST DEFEATED...
...CP9'S ROB LUCCI!!!
RRM
RAAAAAAH
WHAT?!

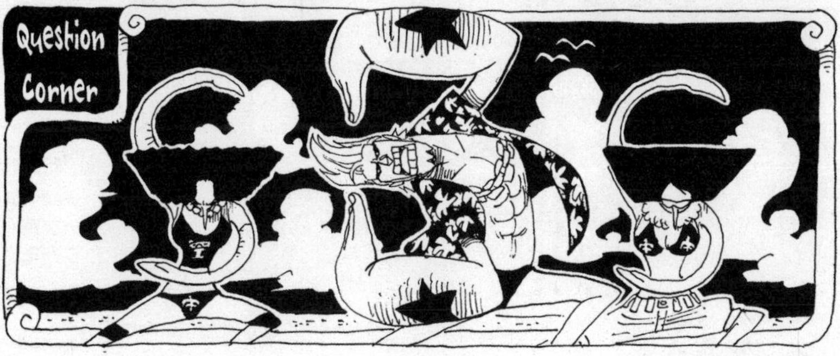
Question Corner

Q: Please pass me the *ponzu* sauce!!

--W-what the?!!

A: Here you go.

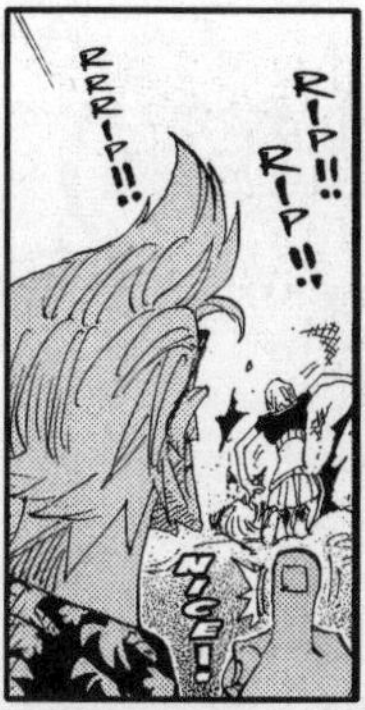
RRRIP!!
RIP!!
RIP!!
NICE!

Q: After she defeated Kalifa, Nami was ripping at her clothes looking for the key. In the end, where was it?

--Udon Powder

A: W-where was it? I couldn't reveal something so private! (Blush) I mean, it was there! That wily Kalifa!

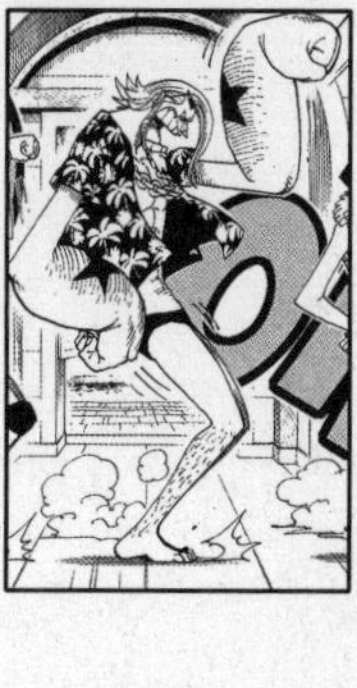

Q: Um, I'd like to talk to you about Franky. He was found when he was 10 years old. He began building the Sea Train at 12 and completed it ten years later. Then four years after that he was involved in the so-called incident that happened eight years ago, so…is he 34 years old?! Should he be so hyper at that age? I took him for about 18 until I worked it out…

--Young Iceberg Is Too Cool!!

A: I see. You worked it out. You're right. Franky is 34. That's why he's so cool! And he's a die-hard weirdo.

Q: Oda Sensei, I've got to talk to you about something! It's about… uh, first would you put on some clothes?! Are you wearing pants now? Good! Now to what I wanted. Could you lend me that swimsuit catalog?

--Chanman

A: No! This is reference material! For manga!!

Chapter 428:
LET'S GO BACK

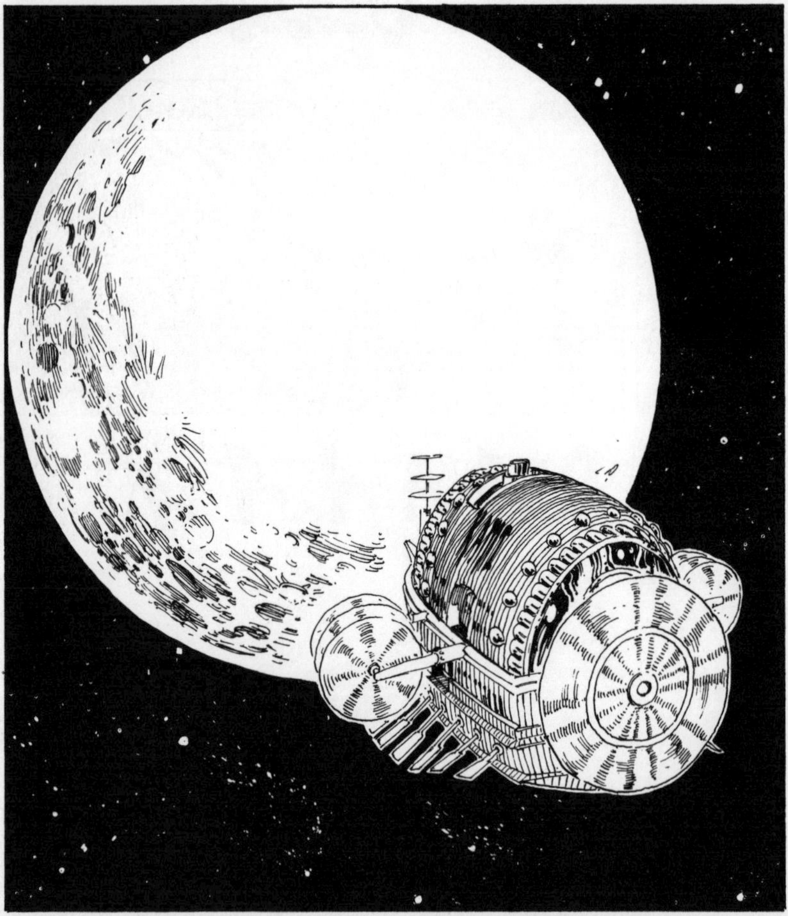

LIMITED COVER SERIES, NO. 9: "ENDLESS VARSE"

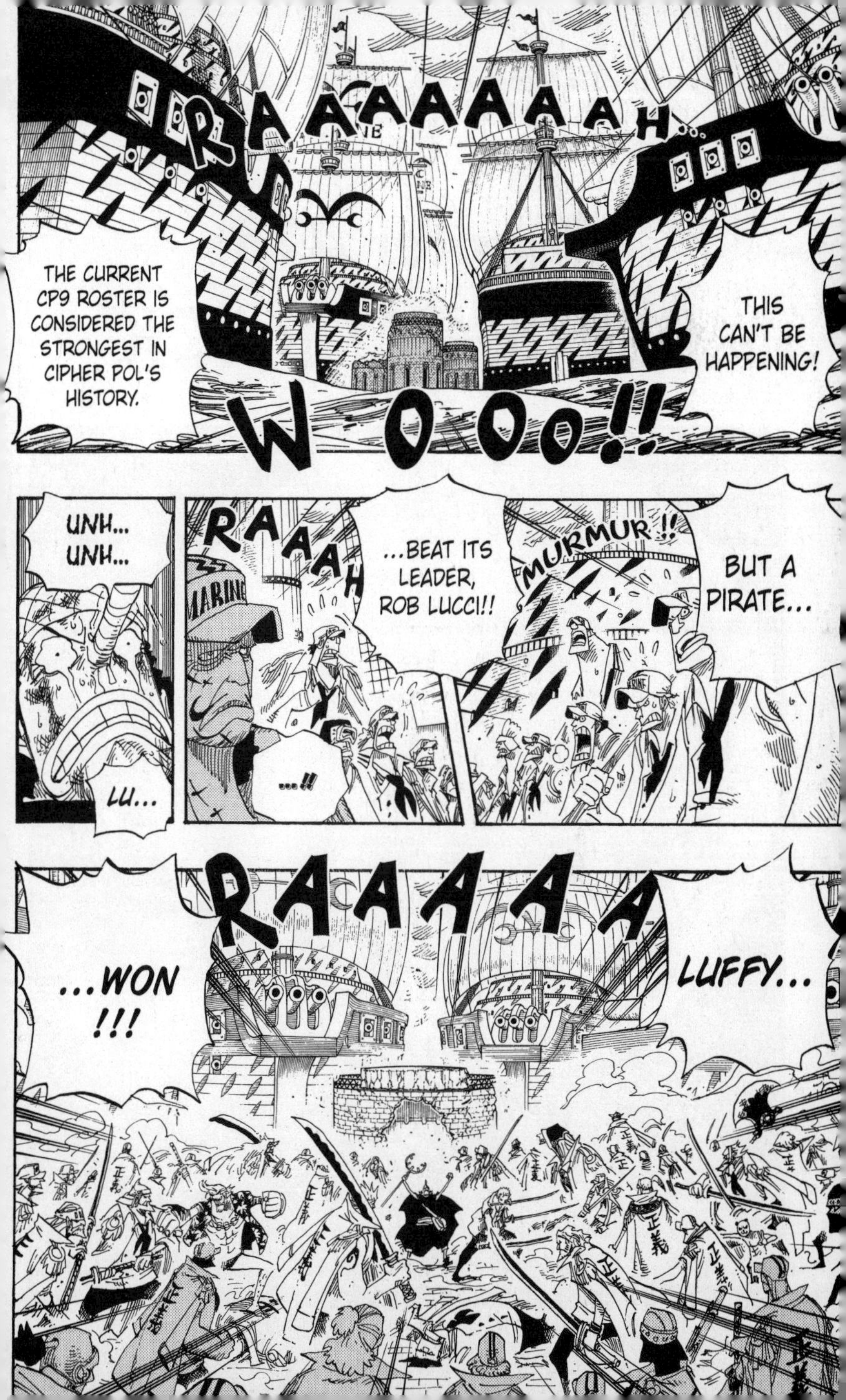
RAAAAAAAH
THIS CAN'T BE HAPPENING!
THE CURRENT CP9 ROSTER IS CONSIDERED THE STRONGEST IN CIPHER POL'S HISTORY.
WOOO!!
BUT A PIRATE...
MURMUR!!
...BEAT ITS LEADER, ROB LUCCI!!
RAAAH
...!!
UNH... UNH...
LU...
RAAAAA
LUFFY...
...WON !!!

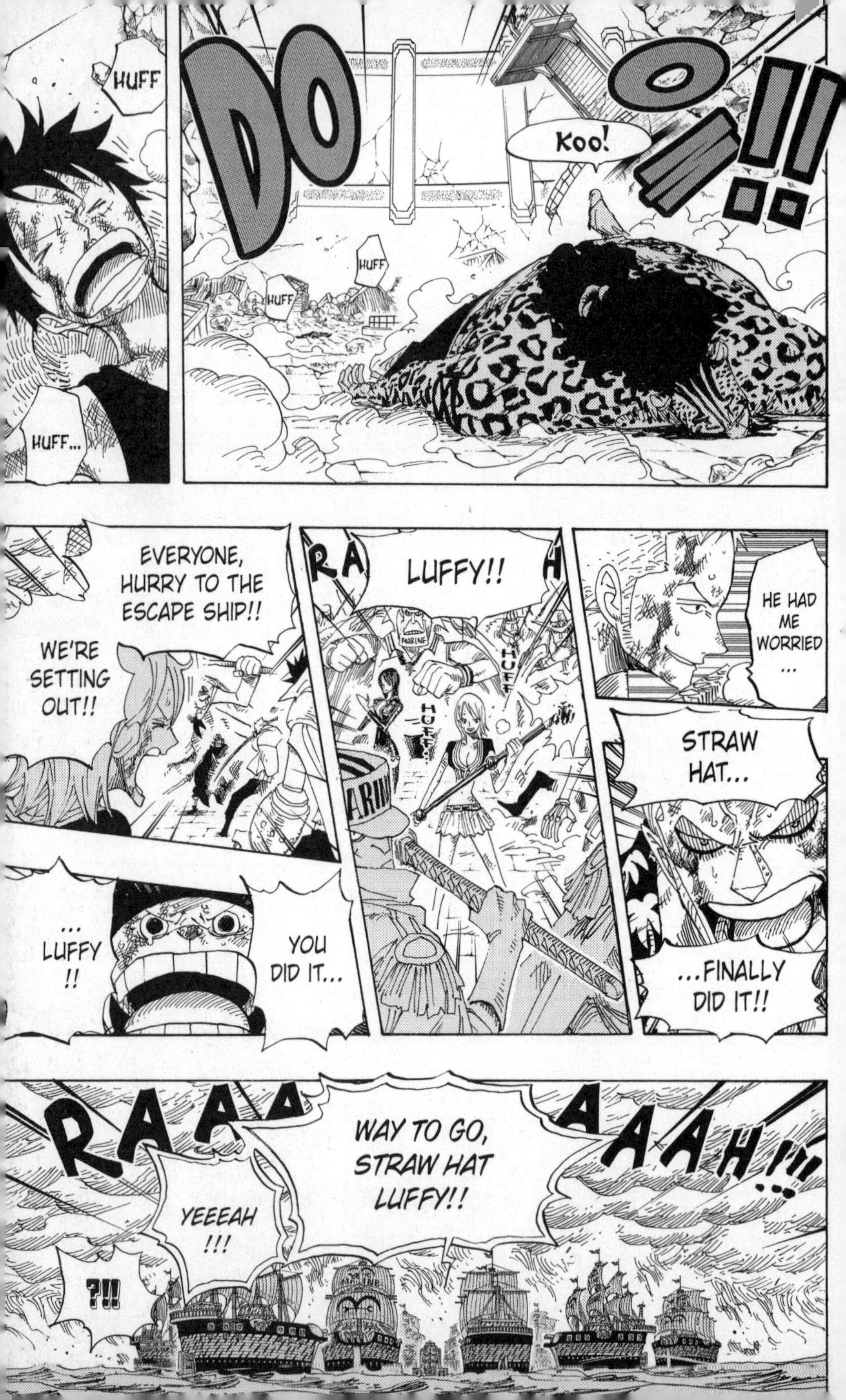
DOO!!
KOO!
HUFF
HUFF
HUFF
HUFF...
HE HAD ME WORRIED...
STRAW HAT...
...FINALLY DID IT!!
RA...H
LUFFY!!
HUFF
HUFF...
EVERYONE, HURRY TO THE ESCAPE SHIP!!
WE'RE SETTING OUT!!
YOU DID IT...
...LUFFY!!
RAAAAAAH!!!
WAY TO GO, STRAW HAT LUFFY!!
YEEEAH!!!
?!!

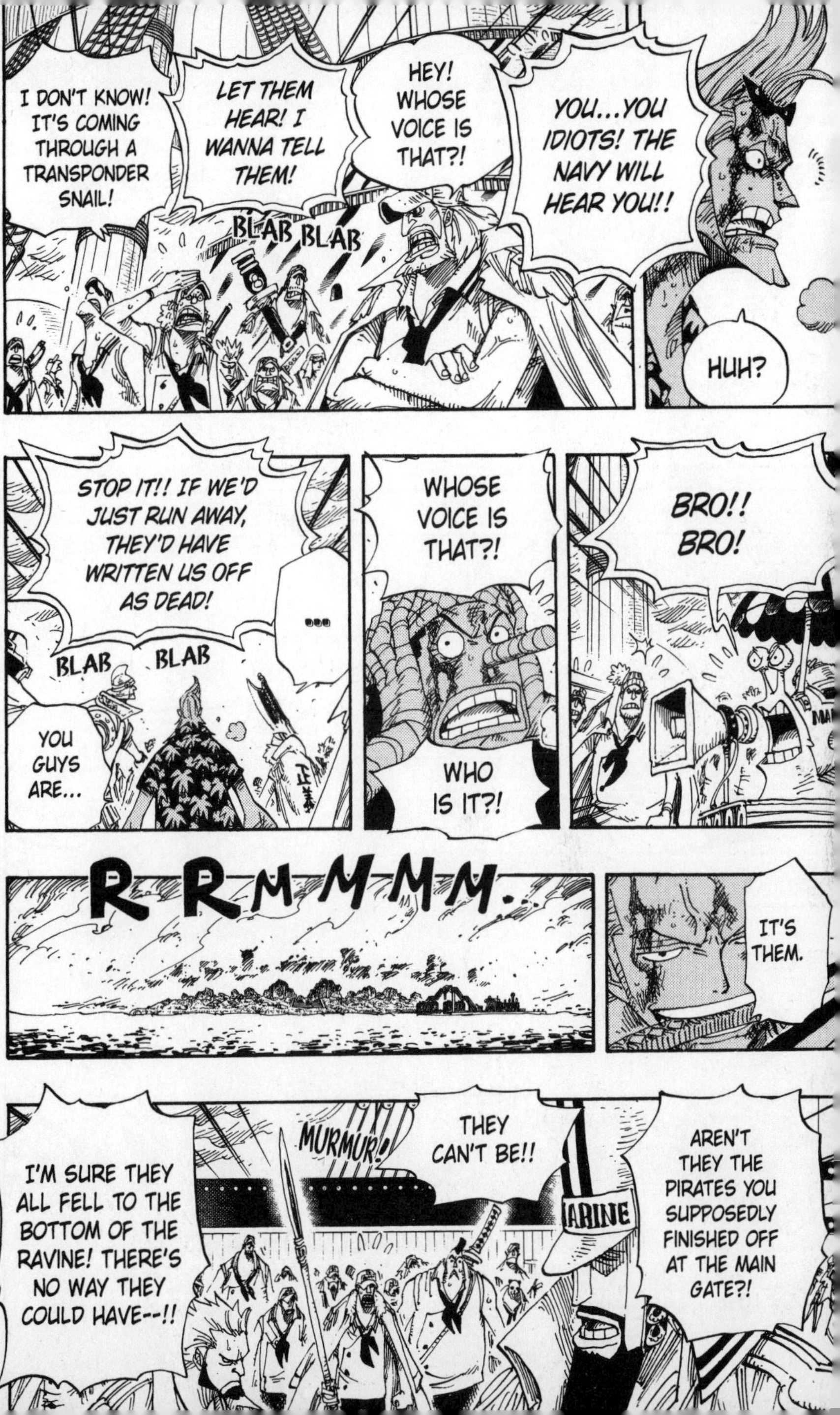
HUH?
YOU...YOU IDIOTS! THE NAVY WILL HEAR YOU!!
HEY! WHOSE VOICE IS THAT?!
LET THEM HEAR! I WANNA TELL THEM!
I DON'T KNOW! IT'S COMING THROUGH A TRANSPONDER SNAIL!
BLAB BLAB
BRO!! BRO!
WHOSE VOICE IS THAT?!
WHO IS IT?!
STOP IT!! IF WE'D JUST RUN AWAY, THEY'D HAVE WRITTEN US OFF AS DEAD!
...
BLAB BLAB
YOU GUYS ARE...
IT'S THEM.
R R M M M M
AREN'T THEY THE PIRATES YOU SUPPOSEDLY FINISHED OFF AT THE MAIN GATE?!
THEY CAN'T BE!!
MURMUR
I'M SURE THEY ALL FELL TO THE BOTTOM OF THE RAVINE! THERE'S NO WAY THEY COULD HAVE--!!

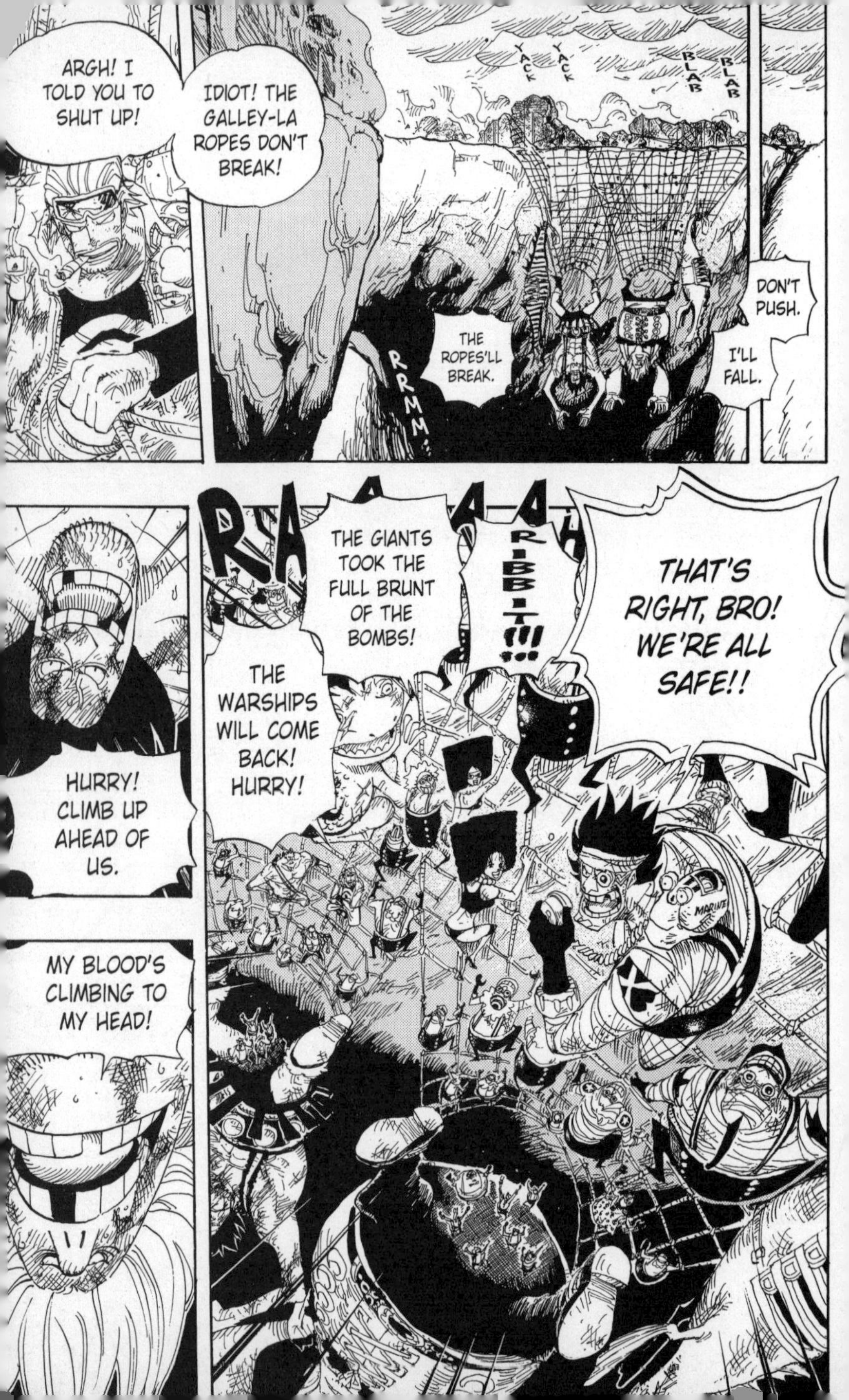
DON'T PUSH.
I'LL FALL.
BLAB BLAB
YACK YACK
THE ROPES'LL BREAK.
RRMM
IDIOT! THE GALLEY-LA ROPES DON'T BREAK!
ARGH! I TOLD YOU TO SHUT UP!
RAAAAH
THAT'S RIGHT, BRO! WE'RE ALL SAFE!!
RIBBIT!!!
THE GIANTS TOOK THE FULL BRUNT OF THE BOMBS!
THE WARSHIPS WILL COME BACK! HURRY!
MARINE
HURRY! CLIMB UP AHEAD OF US.
MY BLOOD'S CLIMBING TO MY HEAD!

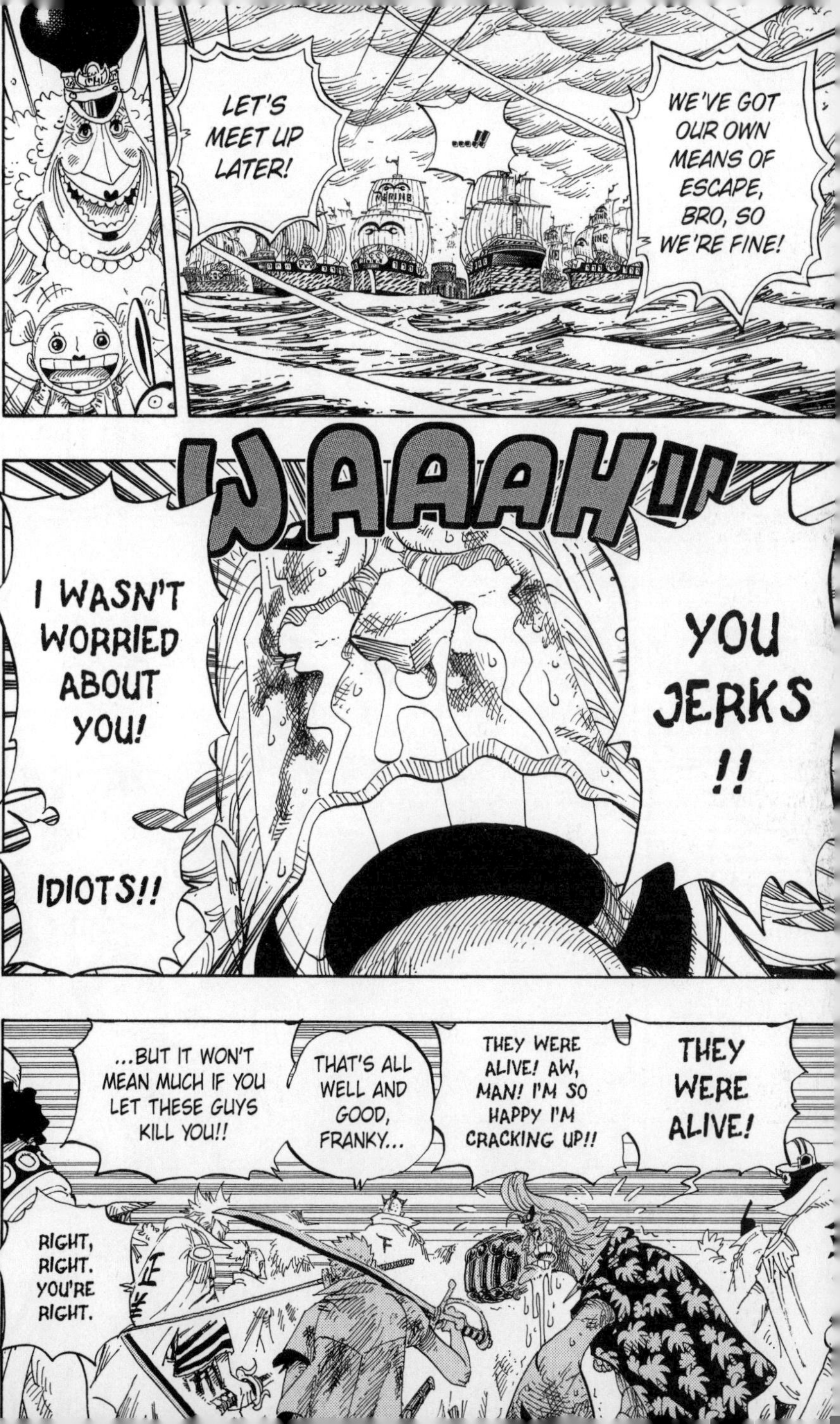
WE'VE GOT OUR OWN MEANS OF ESCAPE, BRO, SO WE'RE FINE!
...!!
LET'S MEET UP LATER!
WAAAH!!
YOU JERKS!!
I WASN'T WORRIED ABOUT YOU!
IDIOTS!!
THEY WERE ALIVE!
THEY WERE ALIVE! AW, MAN! I'M SO HAPPY I'M CRACKING UP!!
THAT'S ALL WELL AND GOOD, FRANKY...
...BUT IT WON'T MEAN MUCH IF YOU LET THESE GUYS KILL YOU!!
RIGHT, RIGHT. YOU'RE RIGHT.

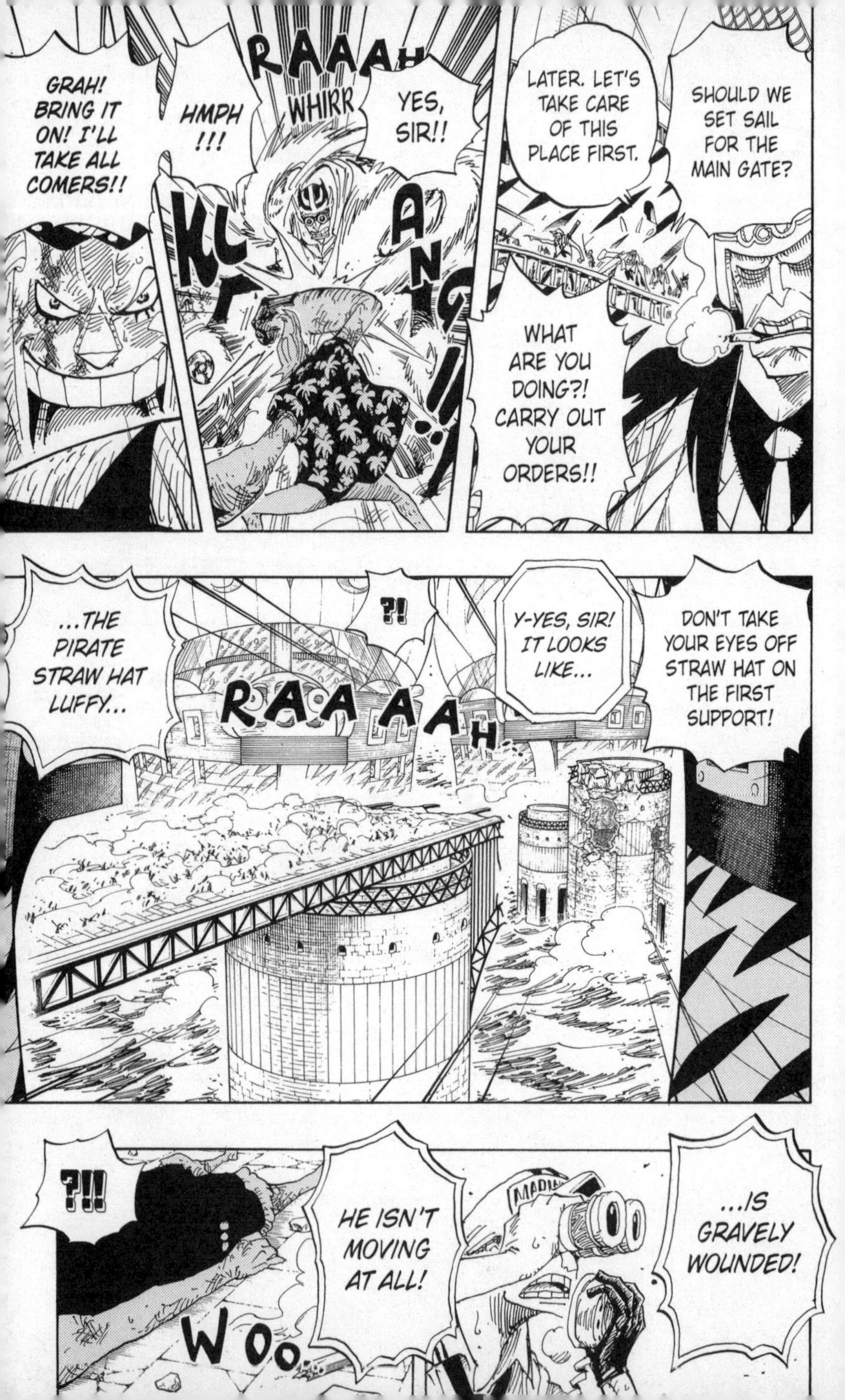
SHOULD WE SET SAIL FOR THE MAIN GATE?
LATER. LET'S TAKE CARE OF THIS PLACE FIRST.
WHAT ARE YOU DOING?! CARRY OUT YOUR ORDERS!!
RAAAAH
WHIRR
YES, SIR!!
KLANG!!
HMPH!!!
GRAH! BRING IT ON! I'LL TAKE ALL COMERS!!
DON'T TAKE YOUR EYES OFF STRAW HAT ON THE FIRST SUPPORT!
Y-YES, SIR! IT LOOKS LIKE...
?!
RAAAAH
...THE PIRATE STRAW HAT LUFFY...
...IS GRAVELY WOUNDED!
HE ISN'T MOVING AT ALL!
?!!
WOO

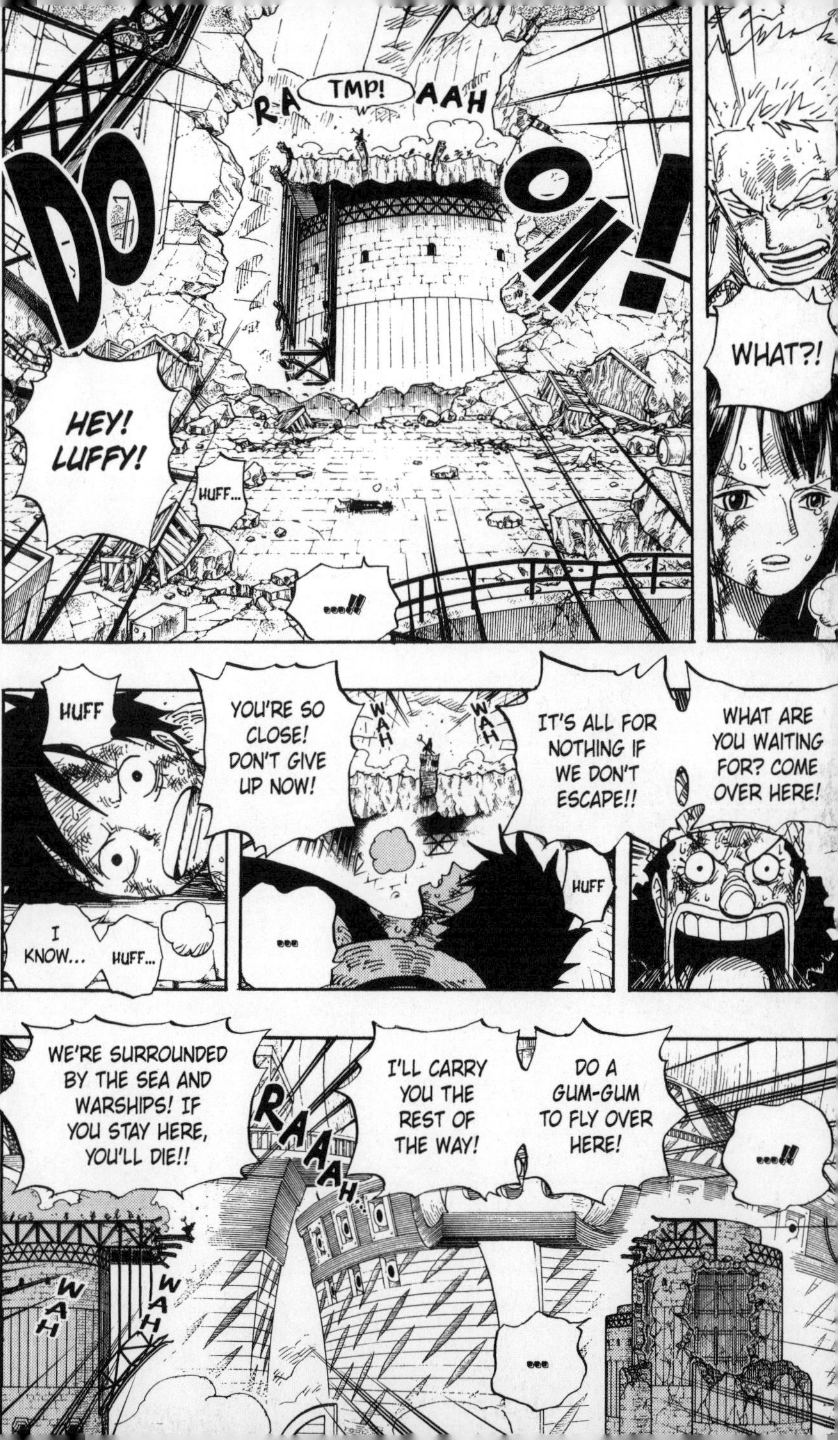
WHAT?!
RA TMP! AAH
DOOM!
HEY! LUFFY!
HUFF...
...!!
WHAT ARE YOU WAITING FOR? COME OVER HERE!
IT'S ALL FOR NOTHING IF WE DON'T ESCAPE!!
WAH WAH
YOU'RE SO CLOSE! DON'T GIVE UP NOW!
HUFF
...
HUFF
I KNOW...
HUFF...
...!!
DO A GUM-GUM TO FLY OVER HERE!
I'LL CARRY YOU THE REST OF THE WAY!
WE'RE SURROUNDED BY THE SEA AND WARSHIPS! IF YOU STAY HERE, YOU'LL DIE!!
RAAAAH...
WAH WAH
...

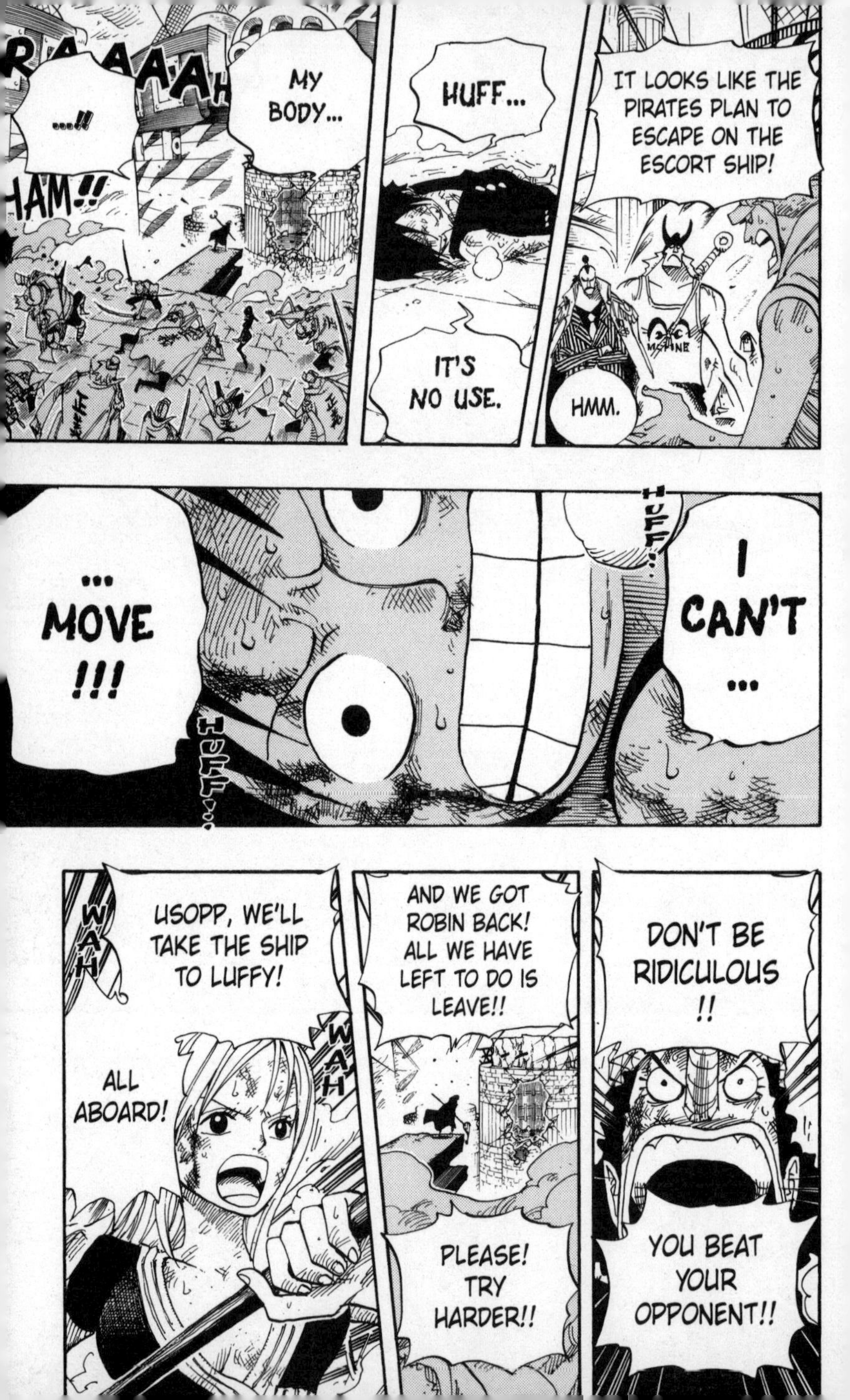
IT LOOKS LIKE THE PIRATES PLAN TO ESCAPE ON THE ESCORT SHIP!
HMM.
HUFF...
IT'S NO USE.
MY BODY...
...!!
RAAAAAH
HAM!!
I CAN'T ...
HUFF...
...MOVE!!!
HUFF...
DON'T BE RIDICULOUS!!
YOU BEAT YOUR OPPONENT!!
AND WE GOT ROBIN BACK! ALL WE HAVE LEFT TO DO IS LEAVE!!
PLEASE! TRY HARDER!!
WAH
USOPP, WE'LL TAKE THE SHIP TO LUFFY!
WAH
ALL ABOARD!

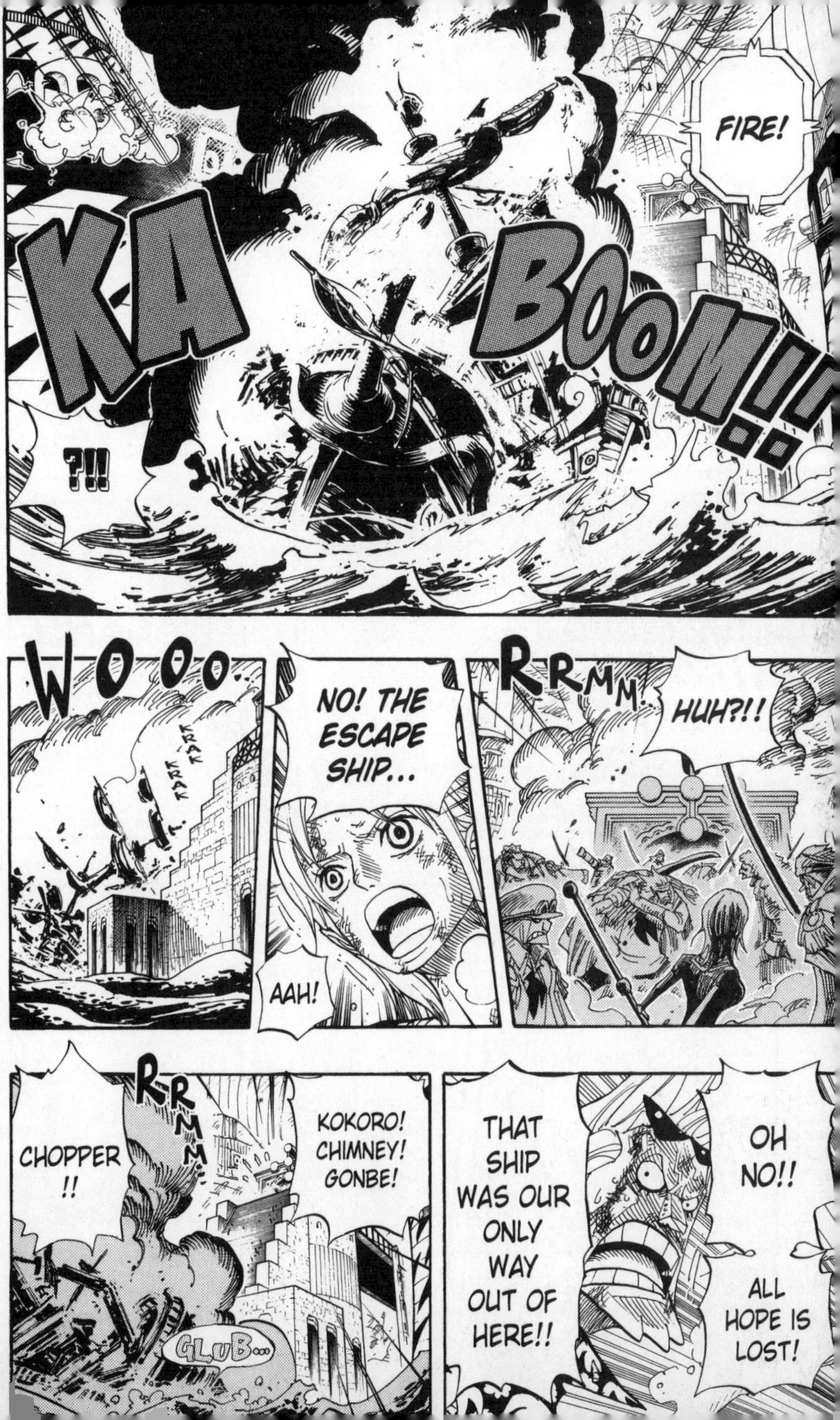
FIRE!
KA BOOM!!
?!!
RRMM...
HUH?!!
NO! THE ESCAPE SHIP...
AAH!
WOOO
KRAK KRAK
OH NO!!
ALL HOPE IS LOST!
THAT SHIP WAS OUR ONLY WAY OUT OF HERE!!
KOKORO! CHIMNEY! GONBE!
CHOPPER !!
RRMM
GLUB...

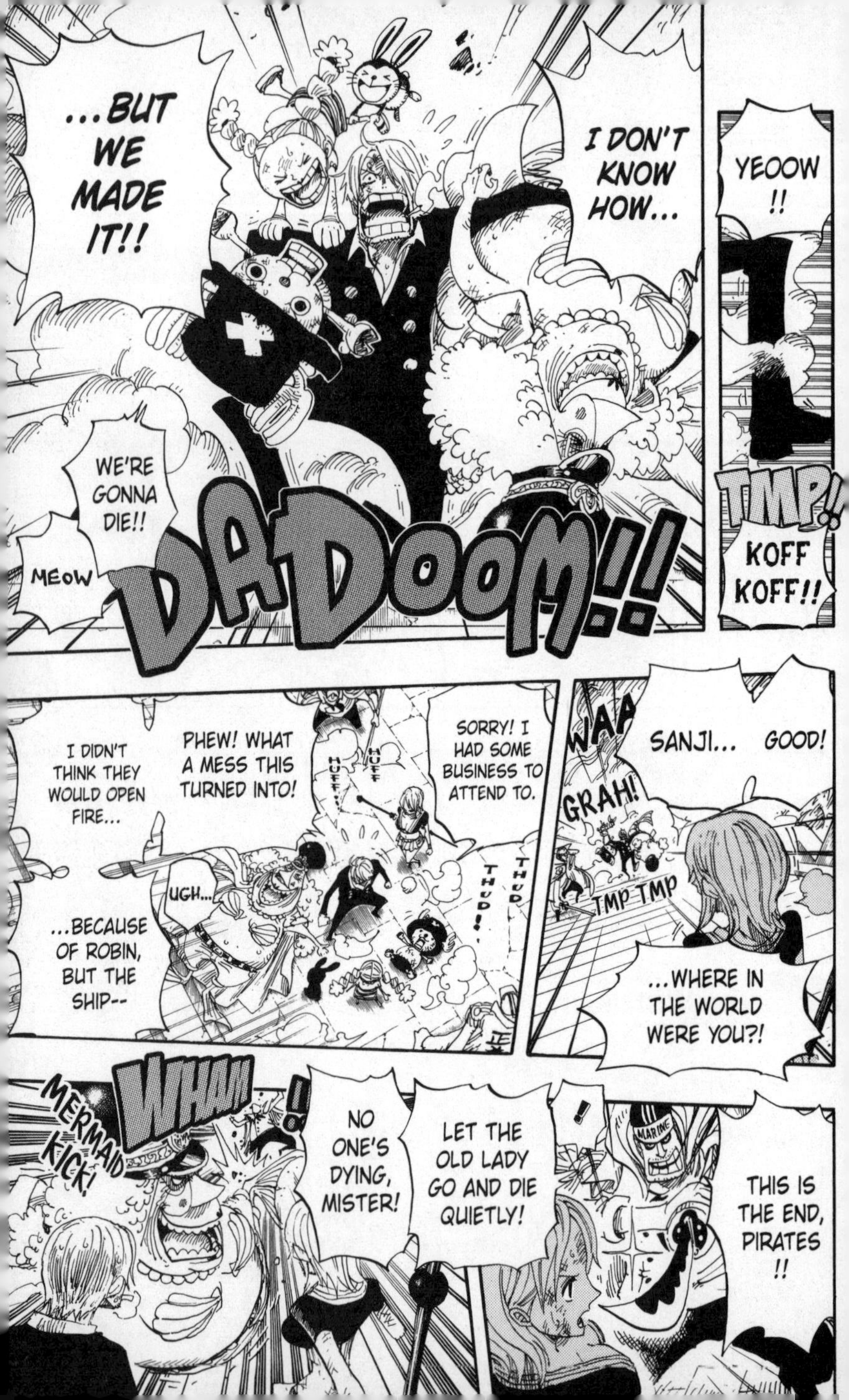
YEOOW!!
TMP!!
KOFF KOFF!!
I DON'T KNOW HOW...
...BUT WE MADE IT!!
WE'RE GONNA DIE!!
MEOW
DADOOM!!
SANJI... GOOD!
WAP
GRAH!
TMP TMP
...WHERE IN THE WORLD WERE YOU?!
SORRY! I HAD SOME BUSINESS TO ATTEND TO.
HUFF HUFF
THUD! THUD!
PHEW! WHAT A MESS THIS TURNED INTO!
I DIDN'T THINK THEY WOULD OPEN FIRE...
UGH...
...BECAUSE OF ROBIN, BUT THE SHIP--
THIS IS THE END, PIRATES!!
MARINE
!
LET THE OLD LADY GO AND DIE QUIETLY!
NO ONE'S DYING, MISTER!
!
WHAM
MERMAID KICK!

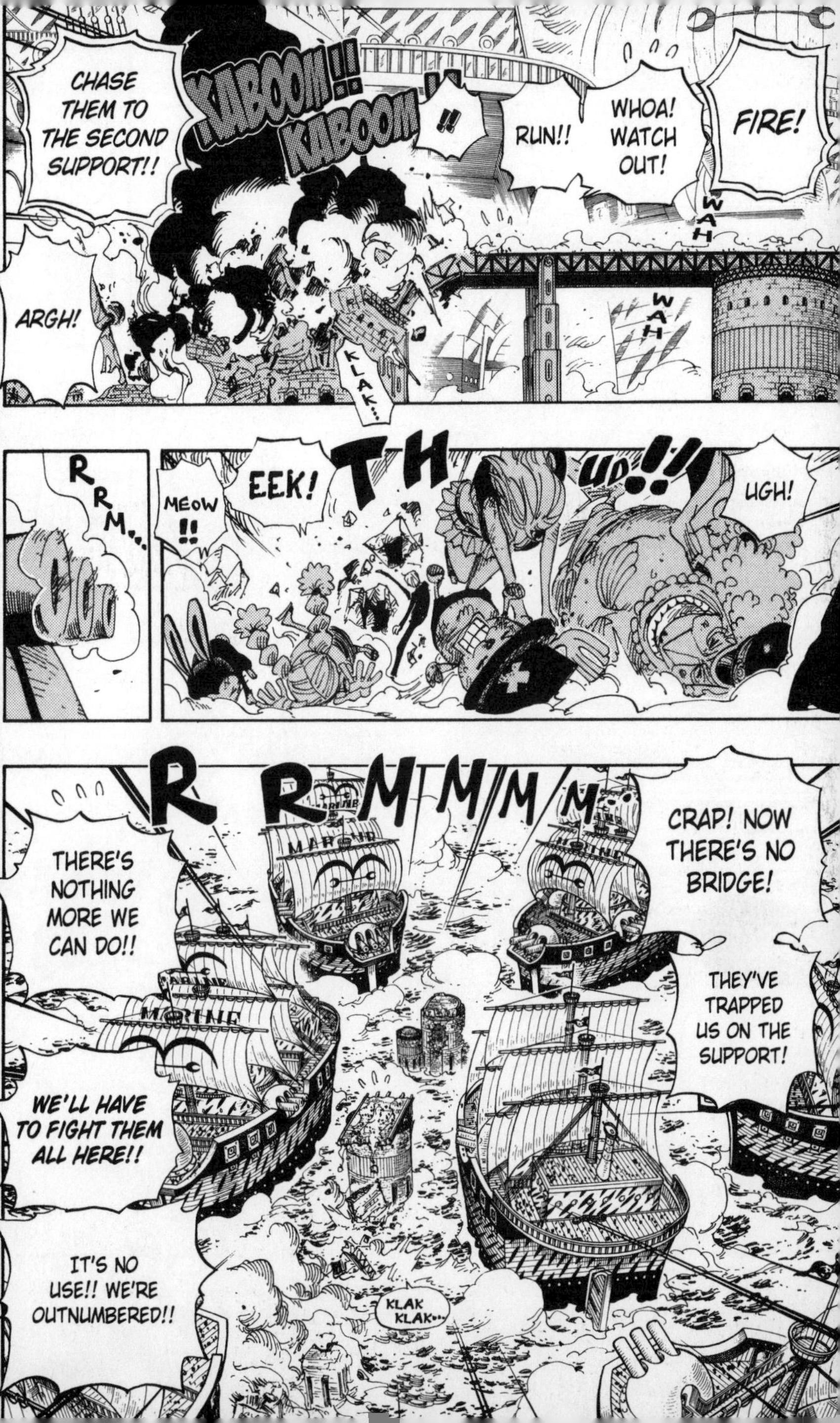
FIRE!
WHOA! WATCH OUT!
RUN!!
!!
KABOOM!!
KABOOM!!
CHASE THEM TO THE SECOND SUPPORT!!
WAH
WAH
KLAK...
ARGH!
UGH!
THUD!!
EEK!
MEOW !!
RRM...
CRAP! NOW THERE'S NO BRIDGE!
RRMMMM
THERE'S NOTHING MORE WE CAN DO!!
THEY'VE TRAPPED US ON THE SUPPORT!
WE'LL HAVE TO FIGHT THEM ALL HERE!!
KLAK KLAK...
IT'S NO USE!! WE'RE OUTNUMBERED!!

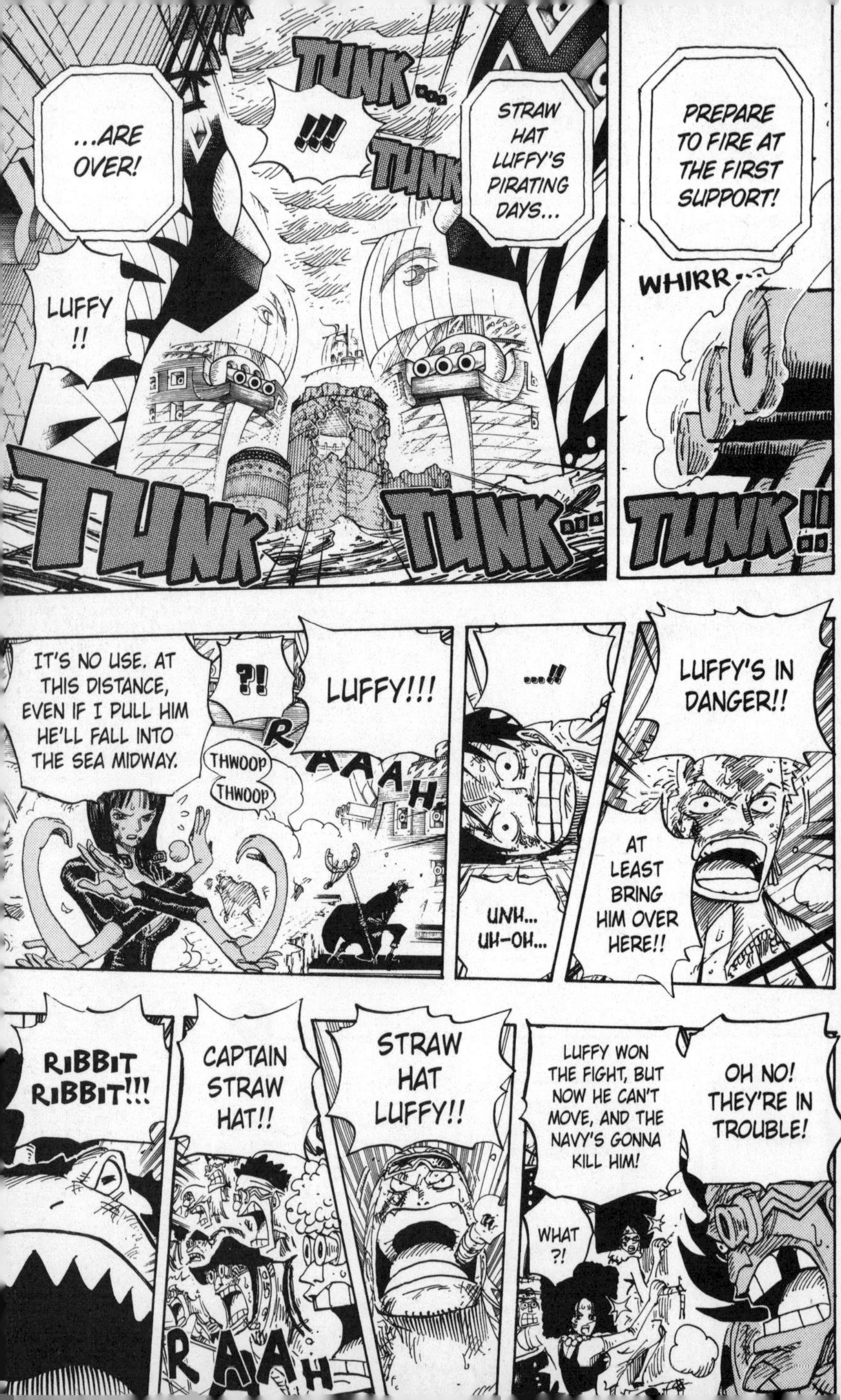
PREPARE TO FIRE AT THE FIRST SUPPORT!
WHIRR...
TUNK!!
STRAW HAT LUFFY'S PIRATING DAYS...
TUNK...
!!!
TUNK
...ARE OVER!
LUFFY !!
TUNK...
TUNK
LUFFY'S IN DANGER!!
AT LEAST BRING HIM OVER HERE!!
...!!
UNH... UH-OH...
LUFFY!!!
RAAAH
?!
THWOOP
THWOOP
IT'S NO USE. AT THIS DISTANCE, EVEN IF I PULL HIM HE'LL FALL INTO THE SEA MIDWAY.
OH NO! THEY'RE IN TROUBLE!
LUFFY WON THE FIGHT, BUT NOW HE CAN'T MOVE, AND THE NAVY'S GONNA KILL HIM!
WHAT ?!
STRAW HAT LUFFY!!
CAPTAIN STRAW HAT!!
RAAAH
RIBBIT RIBBIT!!!

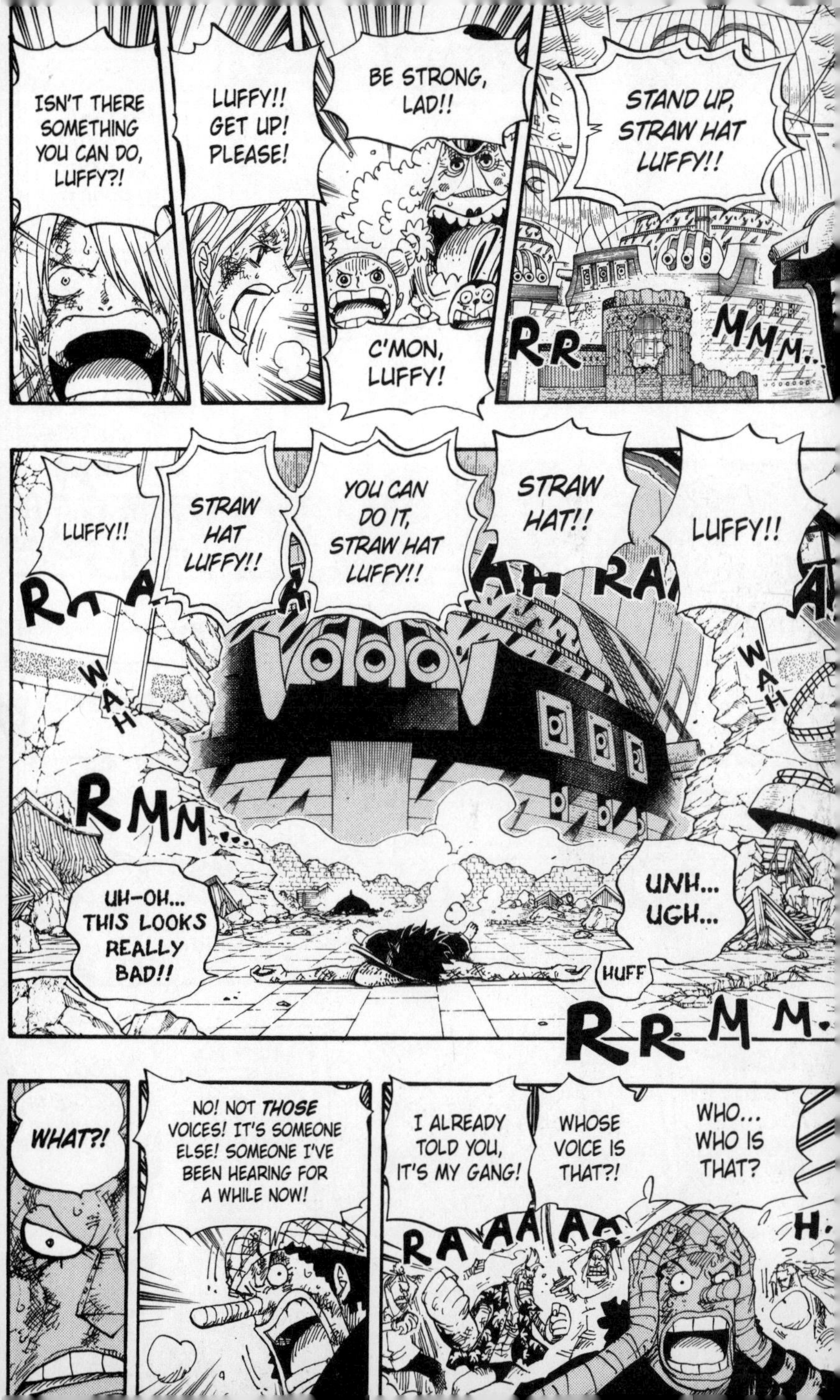
STAND UP, STRAW HAT LUFFY!!
R-R
MMM..
BE STRONG, LAD!!
C'MON, LUFFY!
LUFFY!! GET UP! PLEASE!
ISN'T THERE SOMETHING YOU CAN DO, LUFFY?!
LUFFY!!
STRAW HAT!!
YOU CAN DO IT, STRAW HAT LUFFY!!
STRAW HAT LUFFY!!
LUFFY!!
WAH
WAH
RMM..
UNH... UGH...
HUFF
UH-OH... THIS LOOKS REALLY BAD!!
RRMMM.
WHO... WHO IS THAT?
WHOSE VOICE IS THAT?!
I ALREADY TOLD YOU, IT'S MY GANG!
RAAAAA
H.
NO! NOT *THOSE* VOICES! IT'S SOMEONE ELSE! SOMEONE I'VE BEEN HEARING FOR A WHILE NOW!
WHAT?!

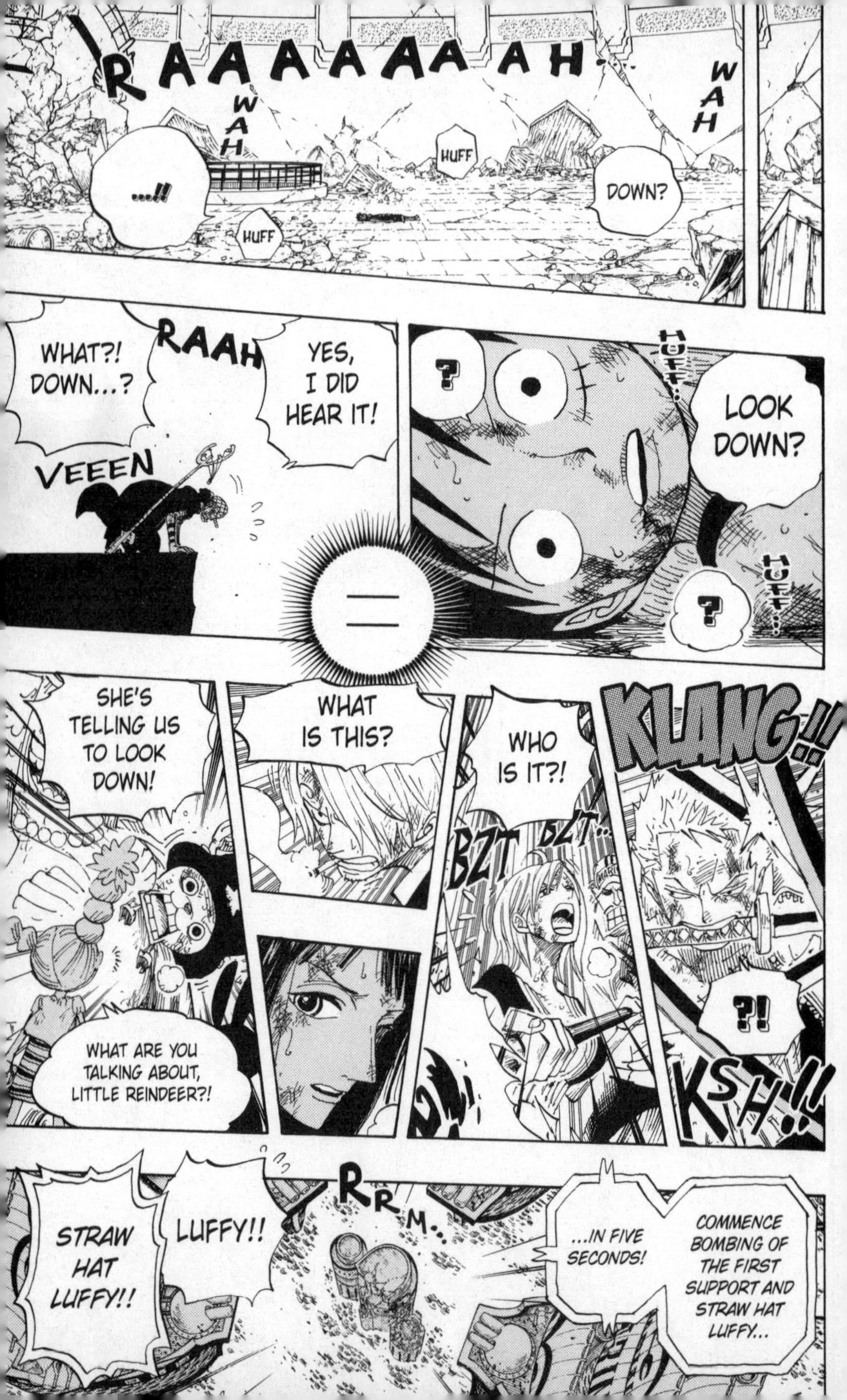
WAH
DOWN?
HUFF
RAAAAAAAAH
WAH
...!!
HUFF
HUFF...
LOOK DOWN?
?
?
HUFF...
YES, I DID HEAR IT!
RAAH
WHAT?! DOWN...?
VEEEN
KLANG!!
?!
KSH!!
WHO IS IT?!
BZT BZT...
WHAT IS THIS?
SHE'S TELLING US TO LOOK DOWN!
WHAT ARE YOU TALKING ABOUT, LITTLE REINDEER?!
COMMENCE BOMBING OF THE FIRST SUPPORT AND STRAW HAT LUFFY...
...IN FIVE SECONDS!
RRM...
LUFFY!!
STRAW HAT LUFFY!!

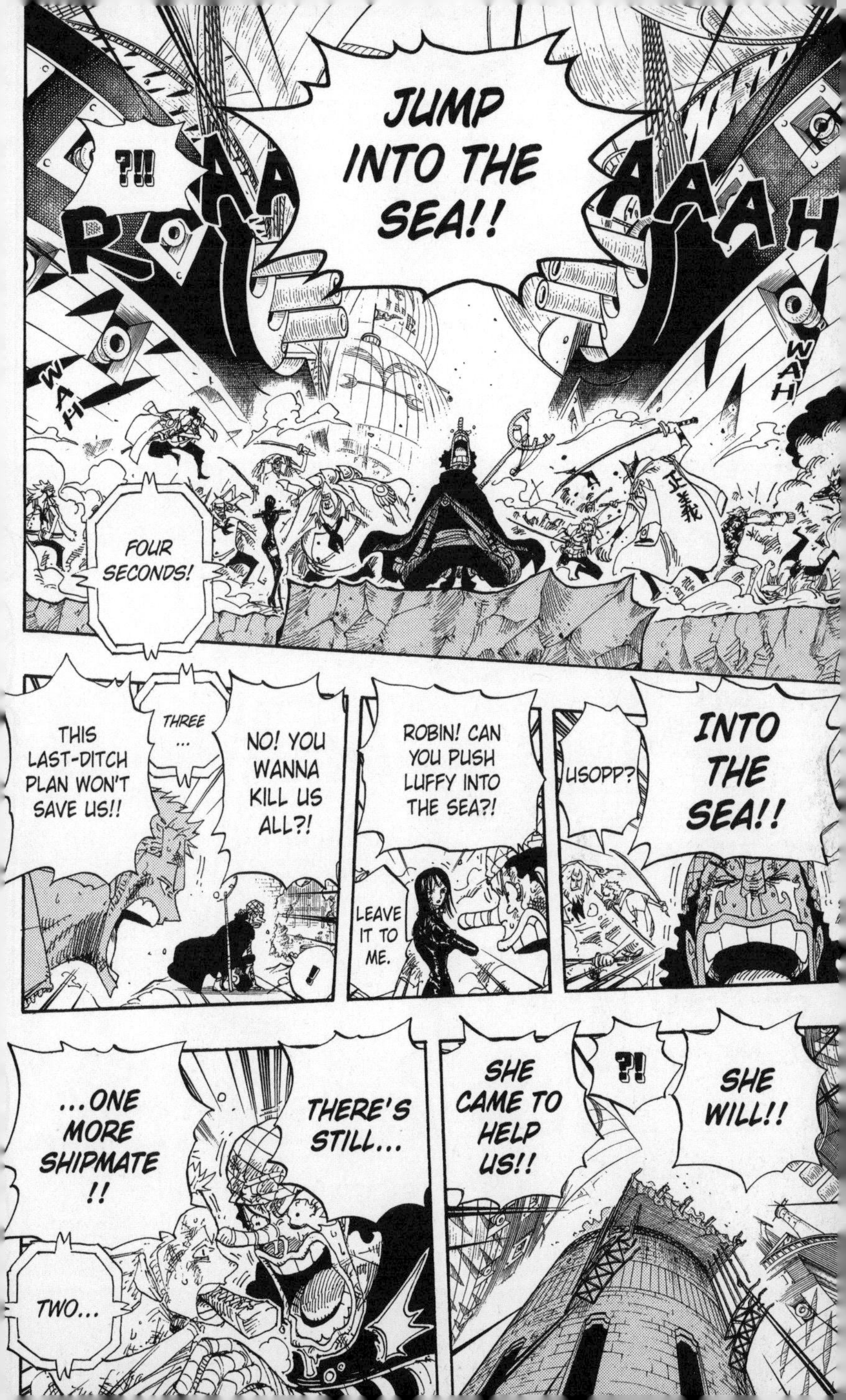
AAAH
WAH
JUMP INTO THE SEA!!
?!!
WAH
FOUR SECONDS!
INTO THE SEA!!
USOPP?
ROBIN! CAN YOU PUSH LUFFY INTO THE SEA?!
LEAVE IT TO ME.
NO! YOU WANNA KILL US ALL?!
THREE ...
THIS LAST-DITCH PLAN WON'T SAVE US!!
!
SHE WILL!!
?!
SHE CAME TO HELP US!!
THERE'S STILL...
...ONE MORE SHIPMATE !!
TWO...

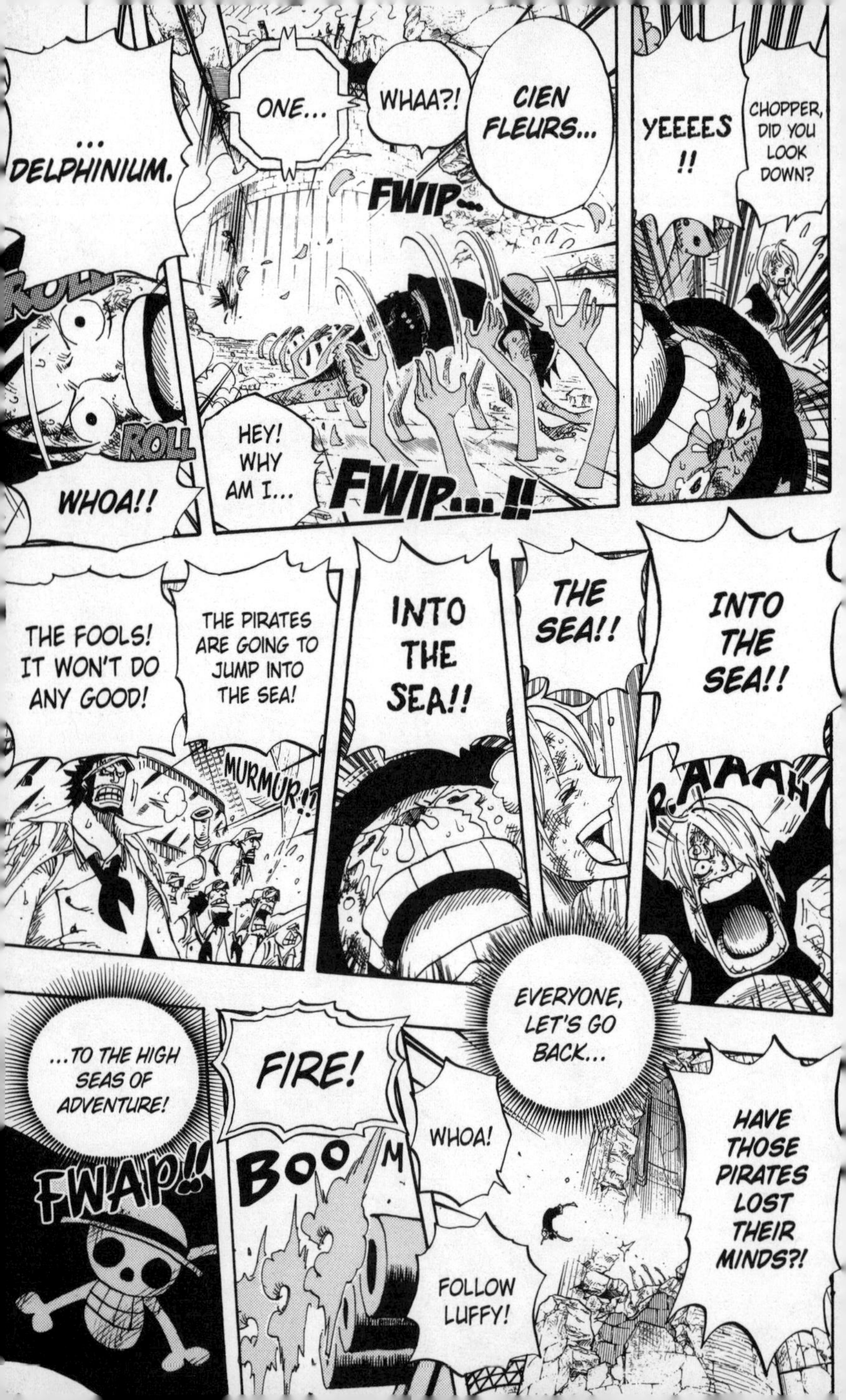

CHOPPER, DID YOU LOOK DOWN?
YEEEES !!
CIEN FLEURS...
WHAA?!
ONE...
FWIP...
HEY! WHY AM I...
FWIP...!!
...DELPHINIUM.
ROLL
WHOA!!
INTO THE SEA!!
THE SEA!!
INTO THE SEA!!
THE PIRATES ARE GOING TO JUMP INTO THE SEA!
THE FOOLS! IT WON'T DO ANY GOOD!
MURMUR!!
HAVE THOSE PIRATES LOST THEIR MINDS?!
EVERYONE, LET'S GO BACK...
WHOA!
FOLLOW LUFFY!
FIRE!
BOOM
...TO THE HIGH SEAS OF ADVENTURE!
FWAP!!

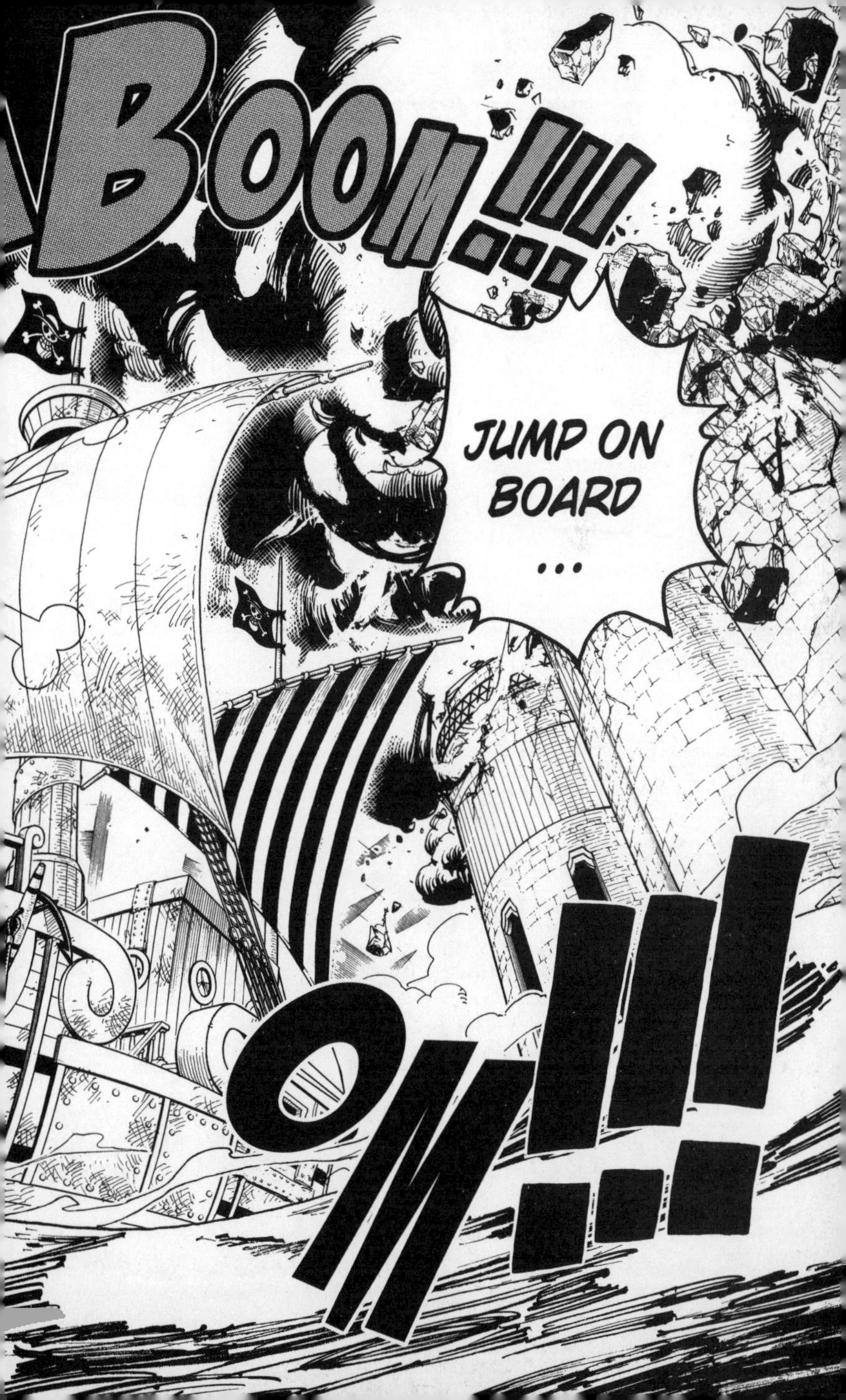
BOOM...!!!
JUMP ON BOARD ...
OM..!!!

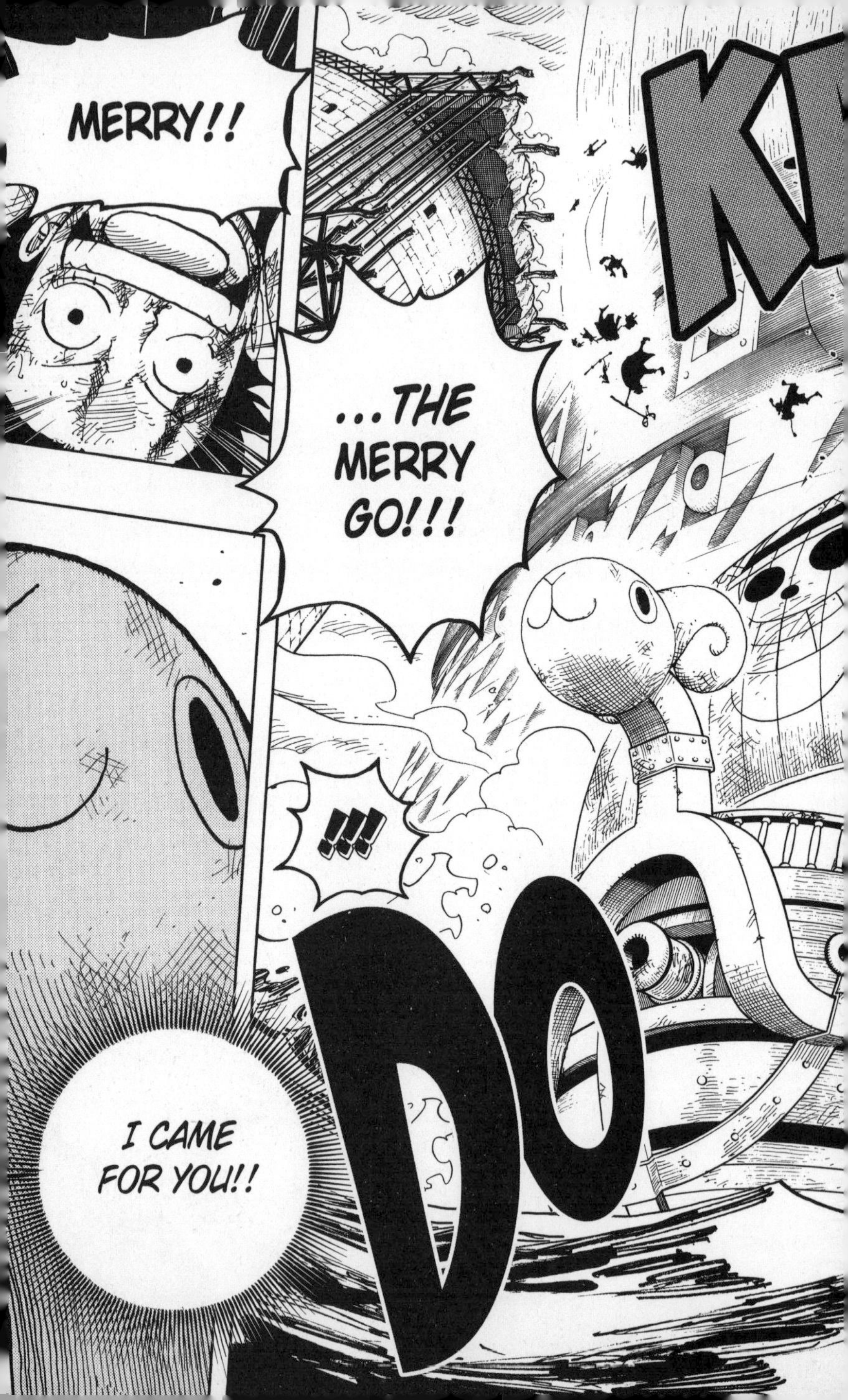
MERRY!!
...THE MERRY GO!!!
!!!
DO
I CAME FOR YOU!!

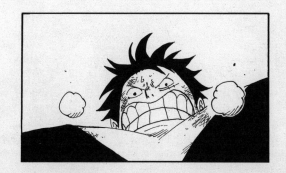

Chapter 429:
UTTER DEFEAT

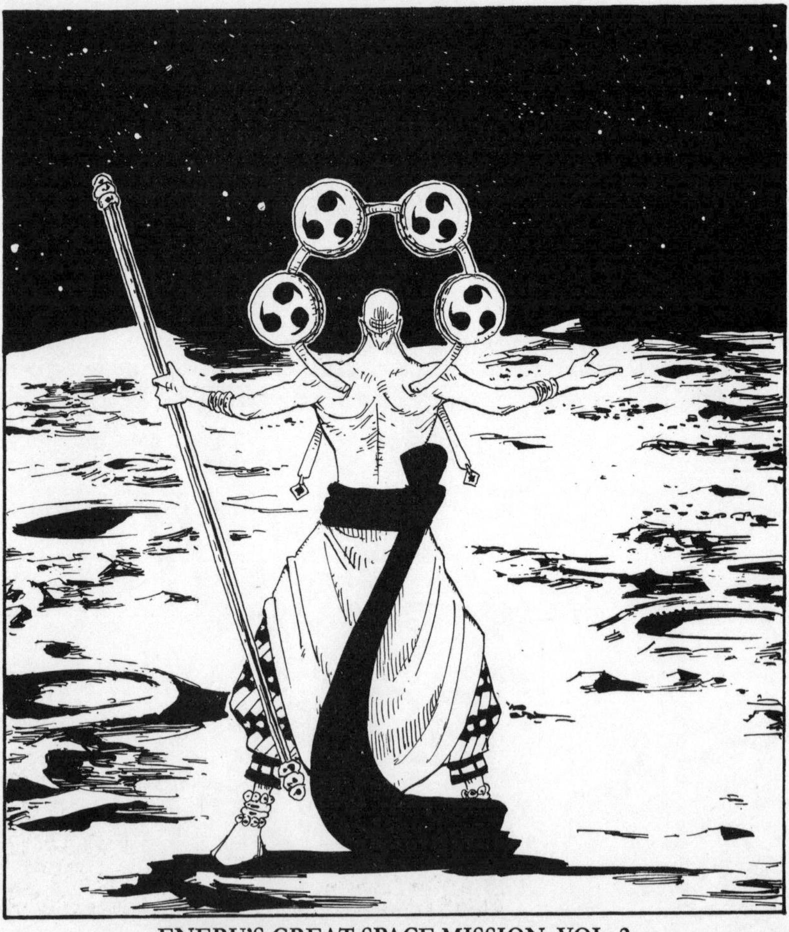

ENERU'S GREAT SPACE MISSION, VOL. 2:
"ARRIVAL AT THE ENDLESS VARSE"

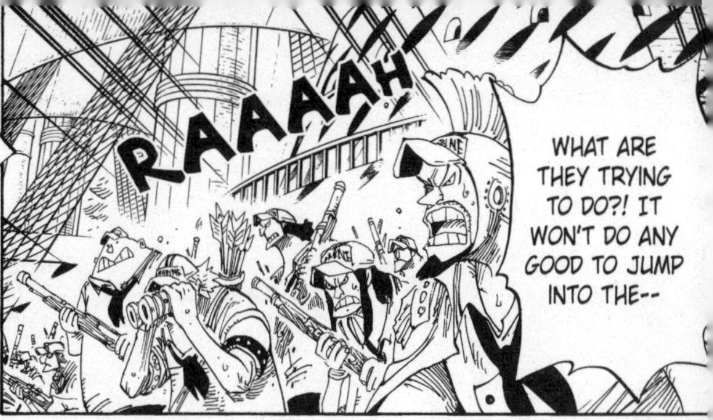
RAAAAH
WHAT ARE THEY TRYING TO DO?! IT WON'T DO ANY GOOD TO JUMP INTO THE--

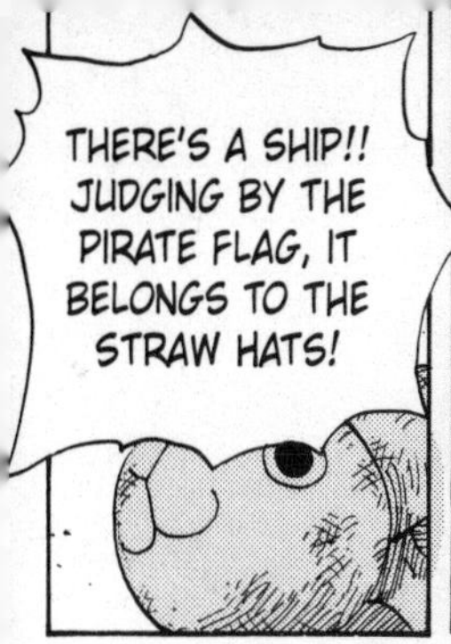
THERE'S A SHIP!! JUDGING BY THE PIRATE FLAG, IT BELONGS TO THE STRAW HATS!

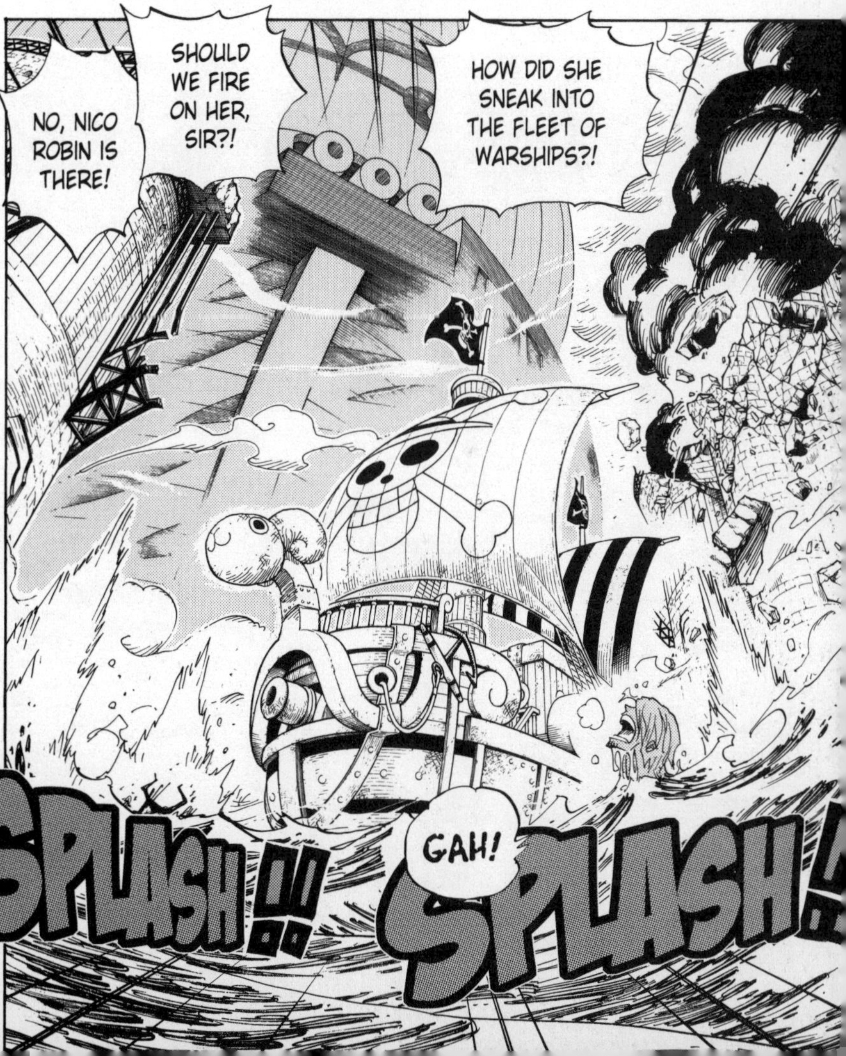
HOW DID SHE SNEAK INTO THE FLEET OF WARSHIPS?!
SHOULD WE FIRE ON HER, SIR?!
NO, NICO ROBIN IS THERE!
SPLASH!!
GAH!
SPLASH!!

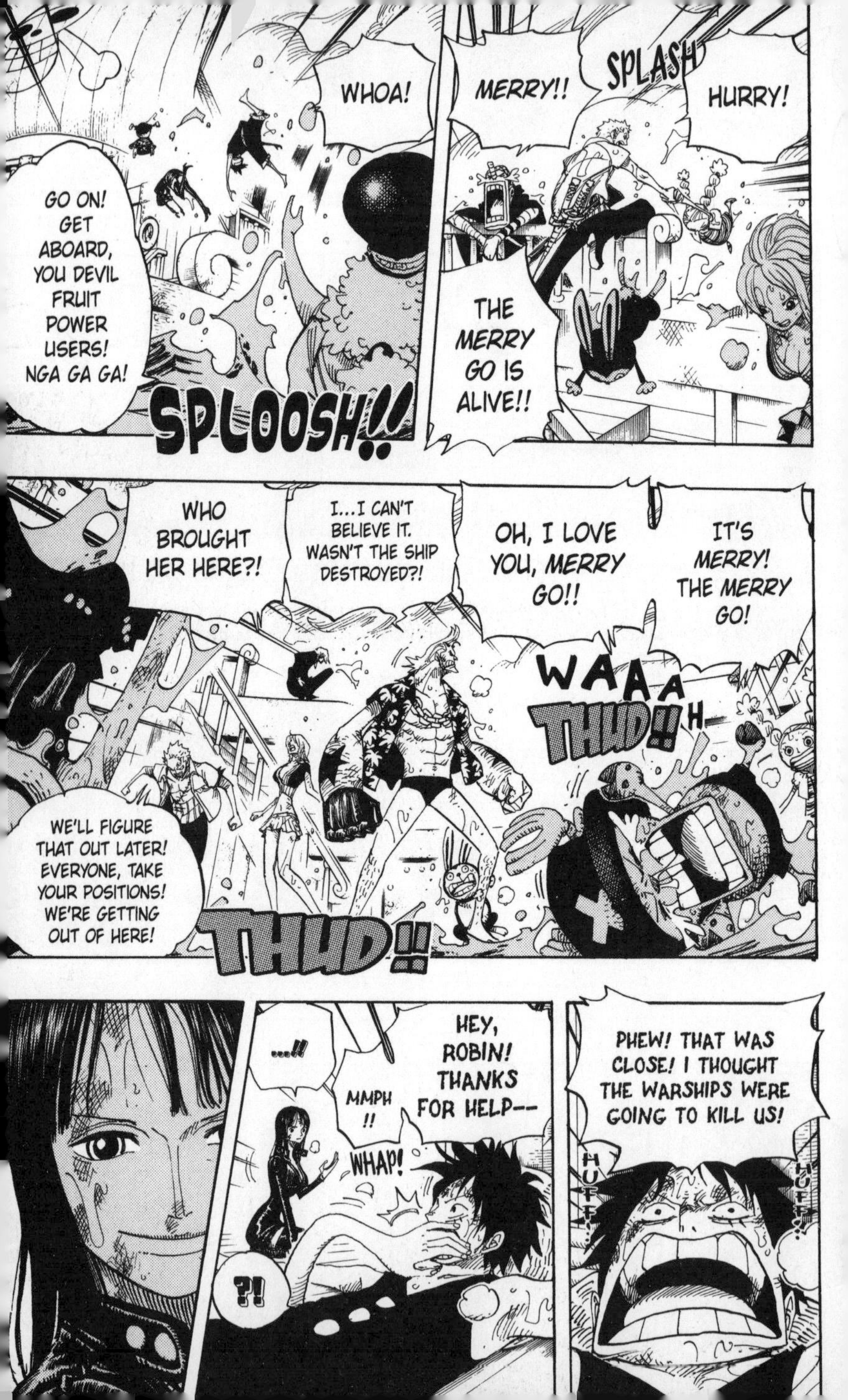
HURRY!
SPLASH
MERRY!!
THE MERRY GO IS ALIVE!!
WHOA!
GO ON! GET ABOARD, YOU DEVIL FRUIT POWER USERS! NGA GA GA!
SPLOOSH!!
IT'S MERRY! THE MERRY GO!
OH, I LOVE YOU, MERRY GO!!
WAAAAH
THUD!!
I...I CAN'T BELIEVE IT. WASN'T THE SHIP DESTROYED?!
WHO BROUGHT HER HERE?!
WE'LL FIGURE THAT OUT LATER! EVERYONE, TAKE YOUR POSITIONS! WE'RE GETTING OUT OF HERE!
THUD!!
PHEW! THAT WAS CLOSE! I THOUGHT THE WARSHIPS WERE GOING TO KILL US!
HUFF...
HUFF...
HEY, ROBIN! THANKS FOR HELP--
MMPH !!
WHAP!
...!!
?!

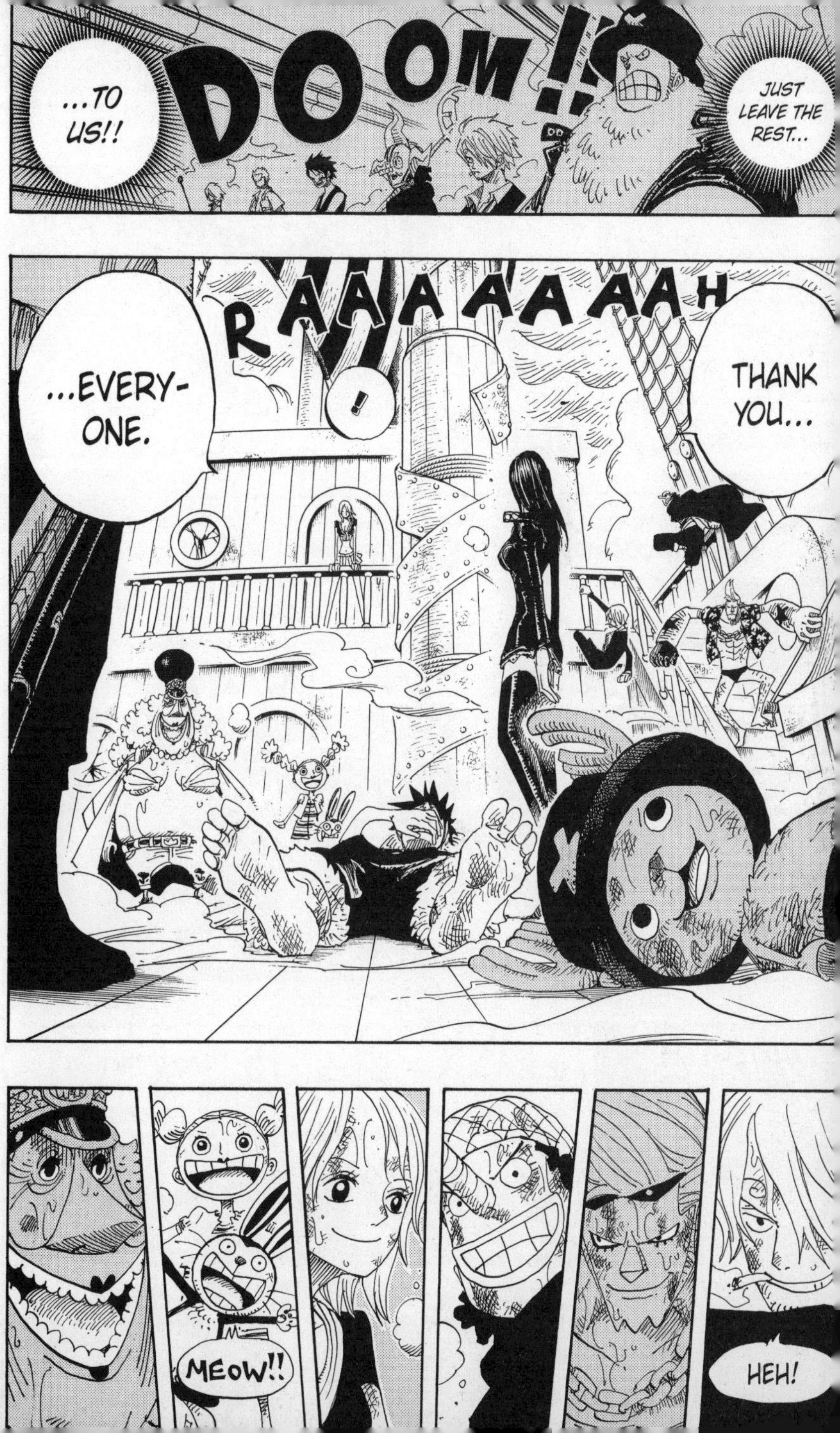
JUST LEAVE THE REST...
DOOM!!
...TO US!!
THANK YOU...
RAAAAAAH
!
...EVERY-ONE.
HEH!
MEOW!!

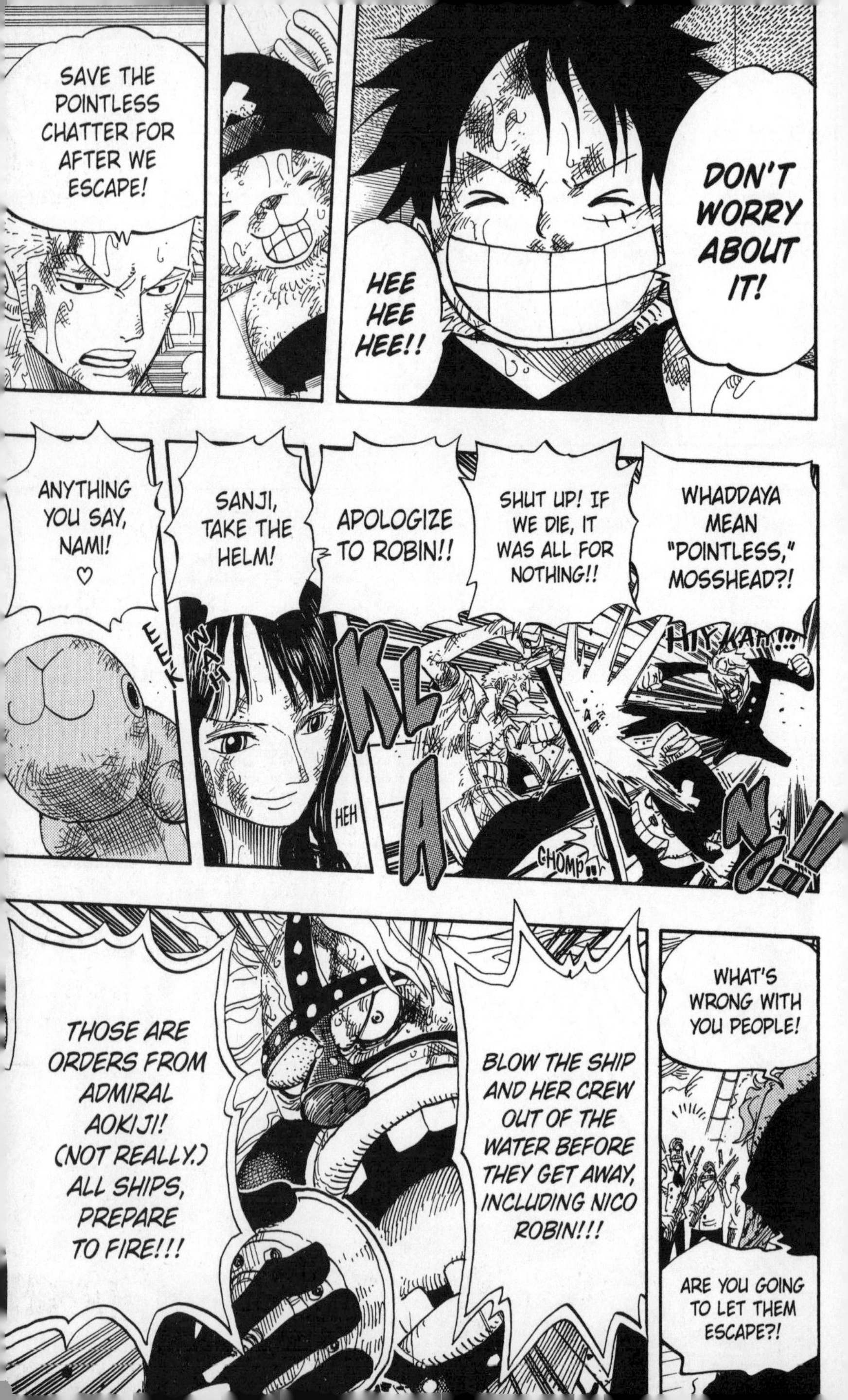
DON'T WORRY ABOUT IT!
HEE HEE HEE!!
SAVE THE POINTLESS CHATTER FOR AFTER WE ESCAPE!
WHADDAYA MEAN "POINTLESS," MOSSHEAD?!
SHUT UP! IF WE DIE, IT WAS ALL FOR NOTHING!!
APOLOGIZE TO ROBIN!!
KLANG!!
CHOMP
SANJI, TAKE THE HELM!
HEH
WAH
KEEE
ANYTHING YOU SAY, NAMI! ♡
WHAT'S WRONG WITH YOU PEOPLE!
ARE YOU GOING TO LET THEM ESCAPE?!
BLOW THE SHIP AND HER CREW OUT OF THE WATER BEFORE THEY GET AWAY, INCLUDING NICO ROBIN!!!
THOSE ARE ORDERS FROM ADMIRAL AOKIJI! (NOT REALLY.) ALL SHIPS, PREPARE TO FIRE!!!

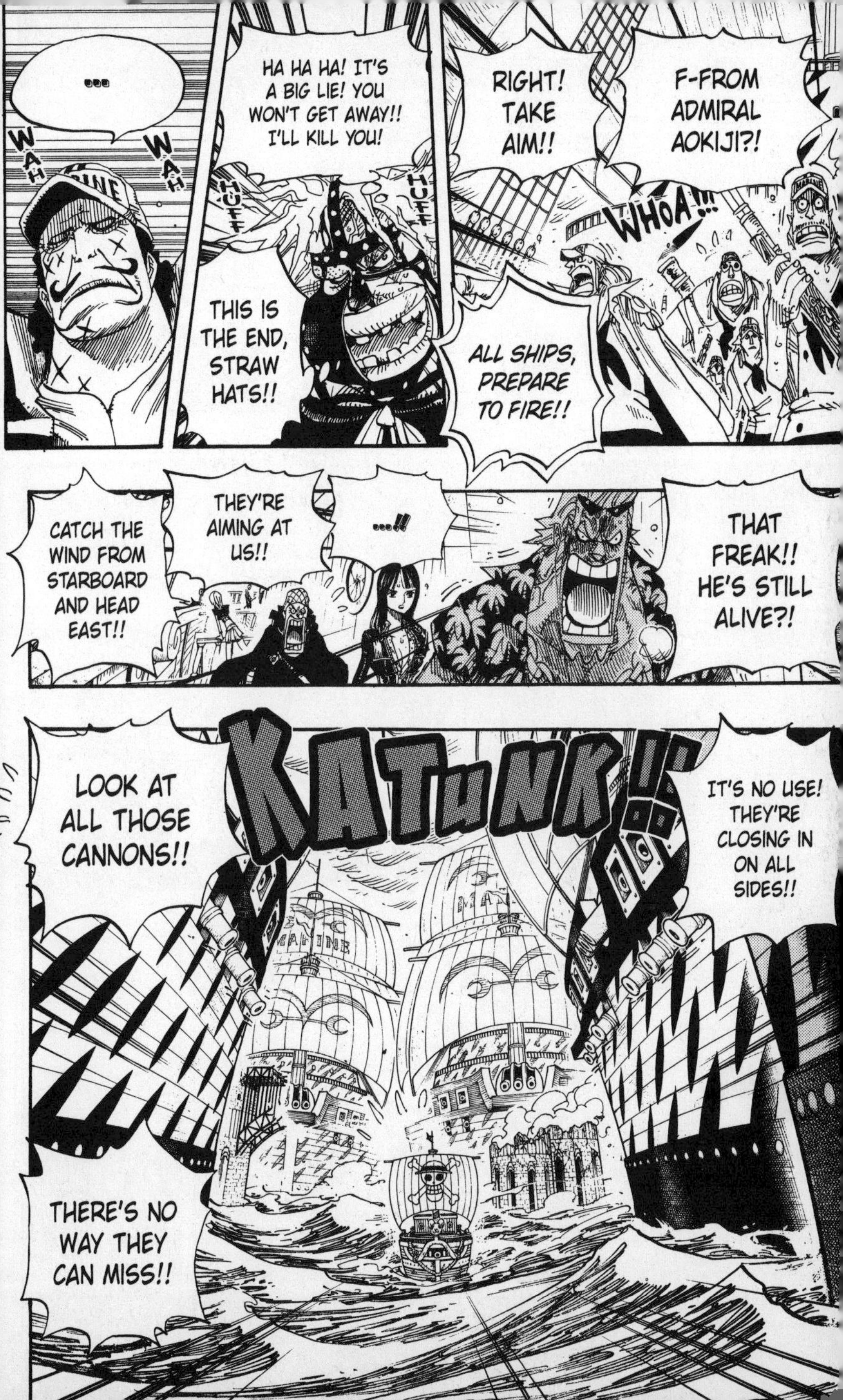
F-FROM ADMIRAL AOKIJI?!
WHOA!!!
RIGHT! TAKE AIM!!
ALL SHIPS, PREPARE TO FIRE!!
HA HA HA! IT'S A BIG LIE! YOU WON'T GET AWAY!! I'LL KILL YOU!
HUFF
HUFF
THIS IS THE END, STRAW HATS!!
...
WAH
WAH
THAT FREAK!! HE'S STILL ALIVE?!
...!!
THEY'RE AIMING AT US!!
CATCH THE WIND FROM STARBOARD AND HEAD EAST!!
KATUNK!!
IT'S NO USE! THEY'RE CLOSING IN ON ALL SIDES!!
LOOK AT ALL THOSE CANNONS!!
THERE'S NO WAY THEY CAN MISS!!

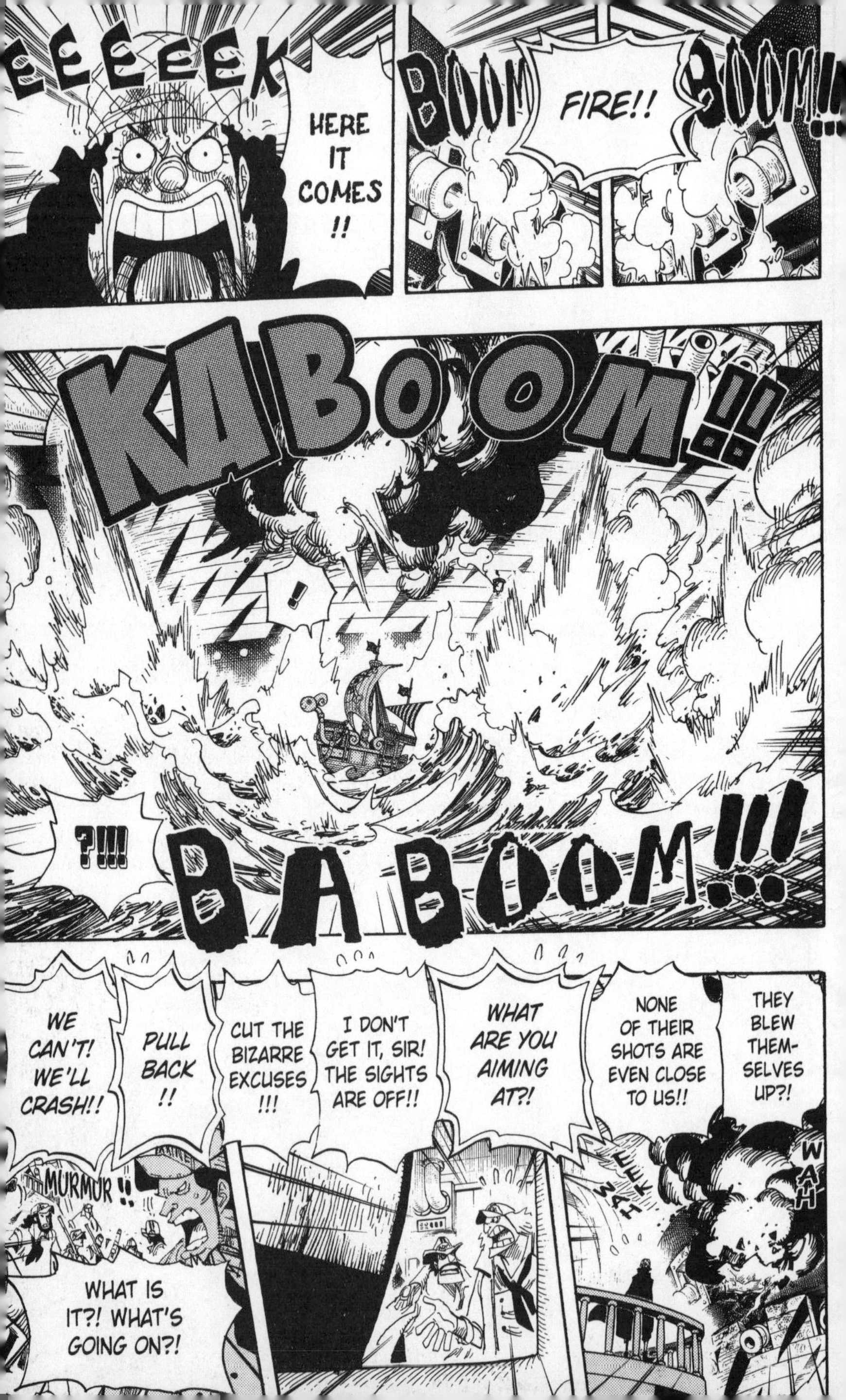
BOOOM!!!
FIRE!!
BOOM
EEEEEK
HERE IT COMES!!
KABOOM!!!
!
?!!!
BABOOM!!!
THEY BLEW THEM-SELVES UP?!
WAAH
EEEK
WAH
NONE OF THEIR SHOTS ARE EVEN CLOSE TO US!!
WHAT ARE YOU AIMING AT?!
I DON'T GET IT, SIR! THE SIGHTS ARE OFF!!
CUT THE BIZARRE EXCUSES!!!
PULL BACK!!
WE CAN'T! WE'LL CRASH!!
MURMUR!!
WHAT IS IT?! WHAT'S GOING ON?!

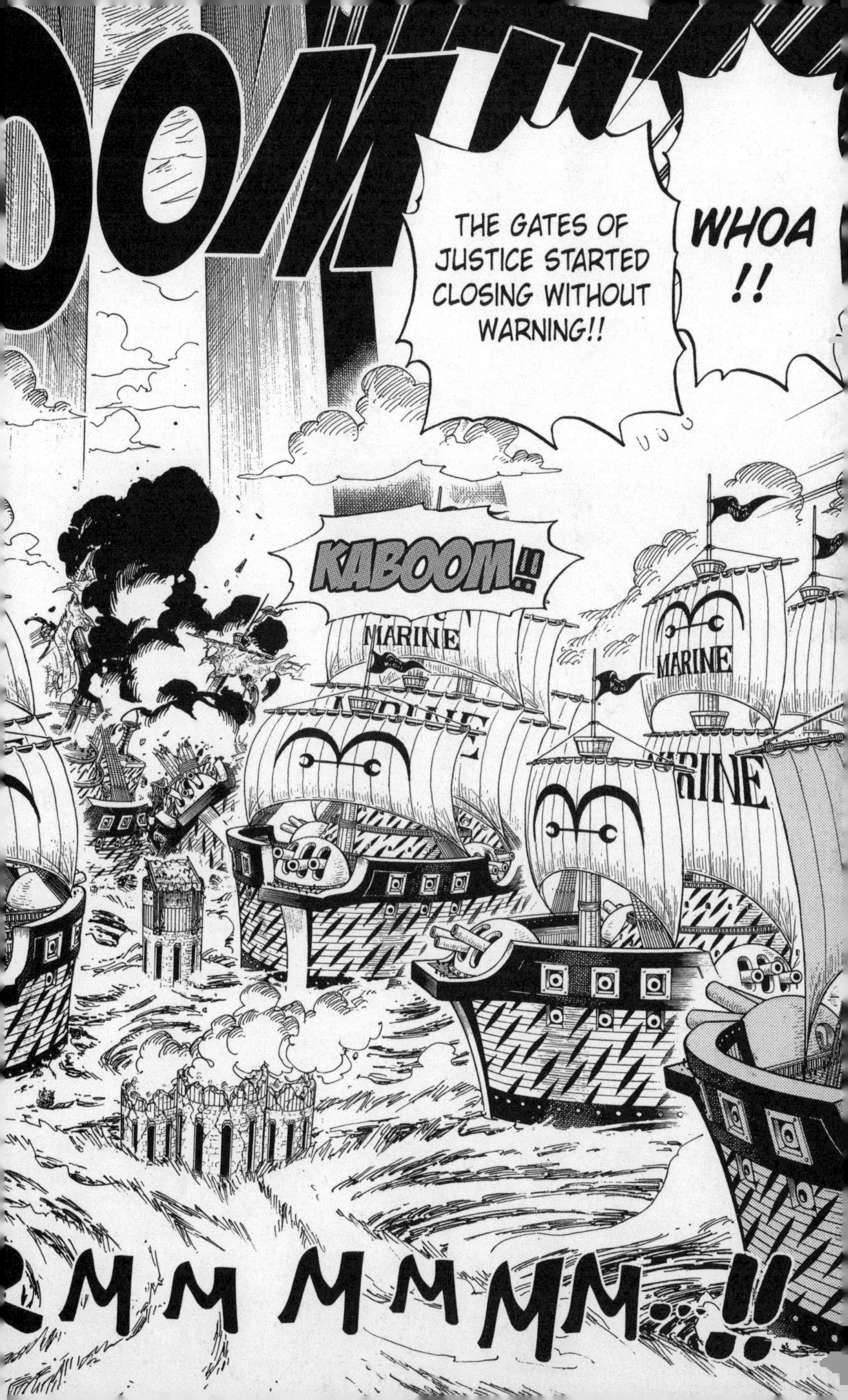

WHOA!!
THE GATES OF JUSTICE STARTED CLOSING WITHOUT WARNING!!
KABOOM!!
RMM MM MM MMM...!!

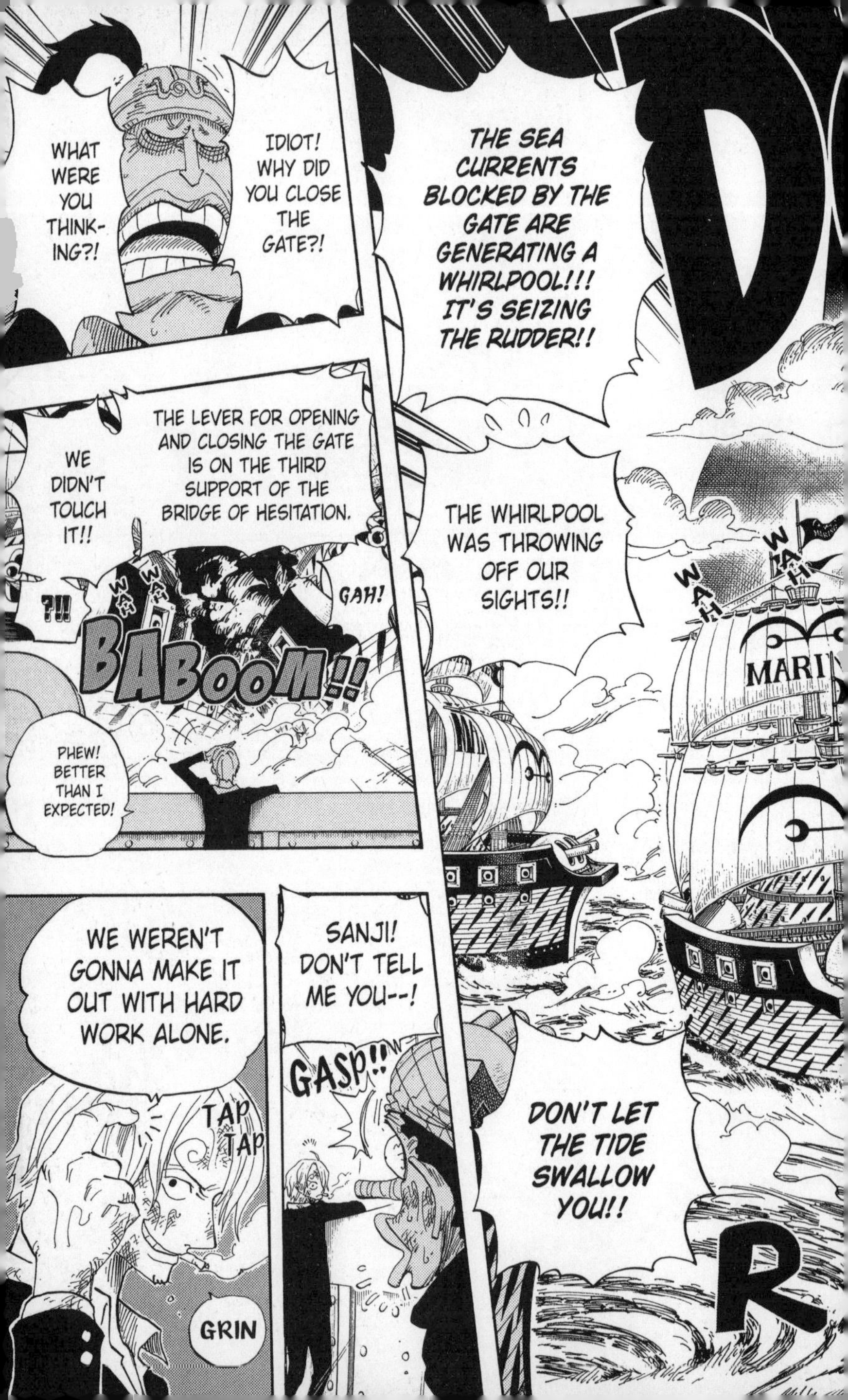
THE SEA CURRENTS BLOCKED BY THE GATE ARE GENERATING A WHIRLPOOL!!! IT'S SEIZING THE RUDDER!!
THE WHIRLPOOL WAS THROWING OFF OUR SIGHTS!!
WAH WAH
DON'T LET THE TIDE SWALLOW YOU!!
IDIOT! WHY DID YOU CLOSE THE GATE?!
WHAT WERE YOU THINKING?!
THE LEVER FOR OPENING AND CLOSING THE GATE IS ON THE THIRD SUPPORT OF THE BRIDGE OF HESITATION.
WE DIDN'T TOUCH IT!!
?!!
WAH WAH
GAH!
BABOOM!!
PHEW! BETTER THAN I EXPECTED!
SANJI! DON'T TELL ME YOU--!
GASP!!
WE WEREN'T GONNA MAKE IT OUT WITH HARD WORK ALONE.
TAP TAP
GRIN

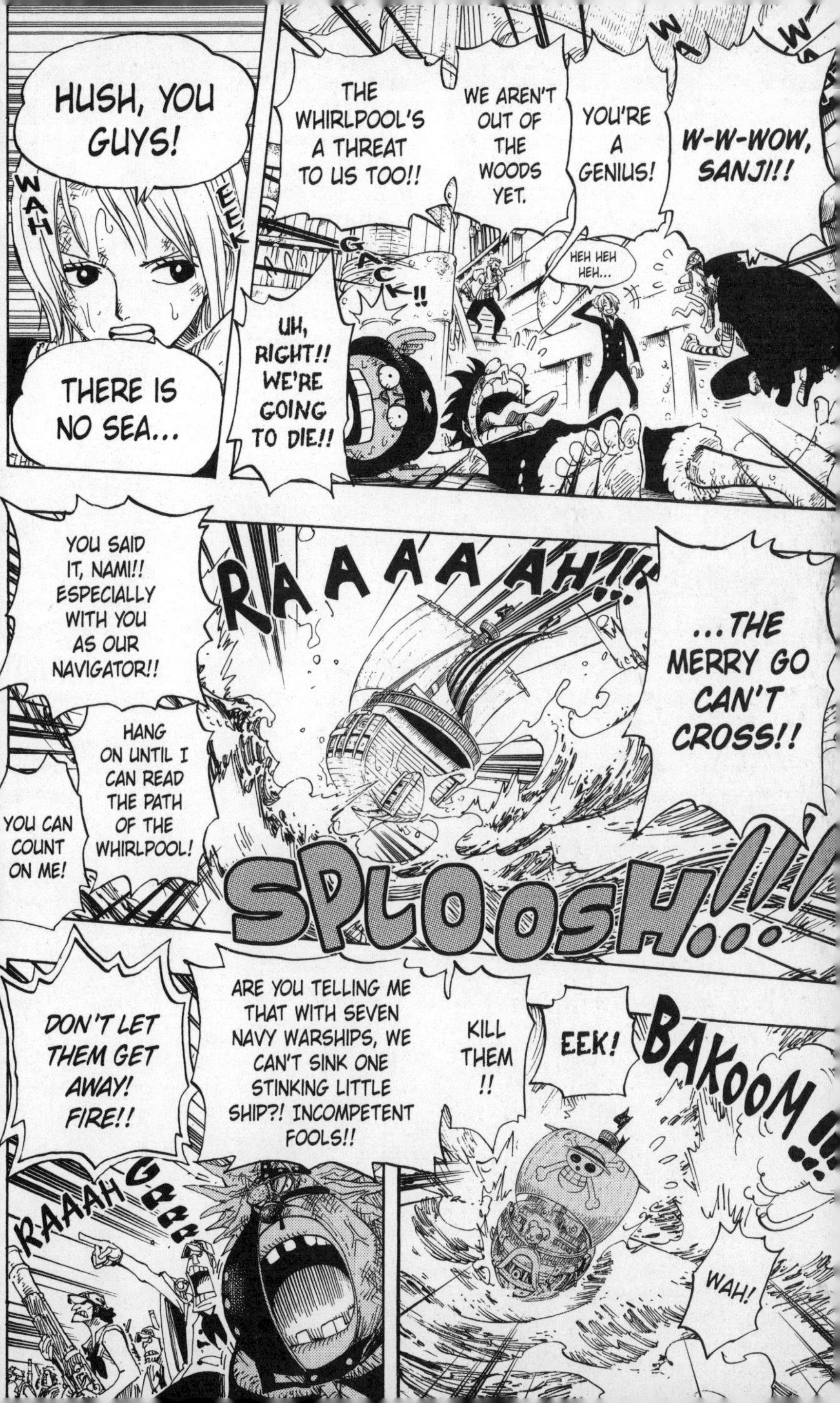
W-W-WOW, SANJI!!
YOU'RE A GENIUS!
WE AREN'T OUT OF THE WOODS YET.
HEH HEH HEH...
THE WHIRLPOOL'S A THREAT TO US TOO!!
GACK!!
UH, RIGHT!! WE'RE GOING TO DIE!!
HUSH, YOU GUYS!
WAH
EEK
THERE IS NO SEA...
...THE MERRY GO CAN'T CROSS!!
RAAAAAH!!!
SPLOOSH!!!
YOU SAID IT, NAMI!! ESPECIALLY WITH YOU AS OUR NAVIGATOR!!
HANG ON UNTIL I CAN READ THE PATH OF THE WHIRLPOOL!
YOU CAN COUNT ON ME!
BAKOOM!!
EEK!
WAH!
KILL THEM!!
ARE YOU TELLING ME THAT WITH SEVEN NAVY WARSHIPS, WE CAN'T SINK ONE STINKING LITTLE SHIP?! INCOMPETENT FOOLS!!
DON'T LET THEM GET AWAY! FIRE!!
GRRR
RAAAH

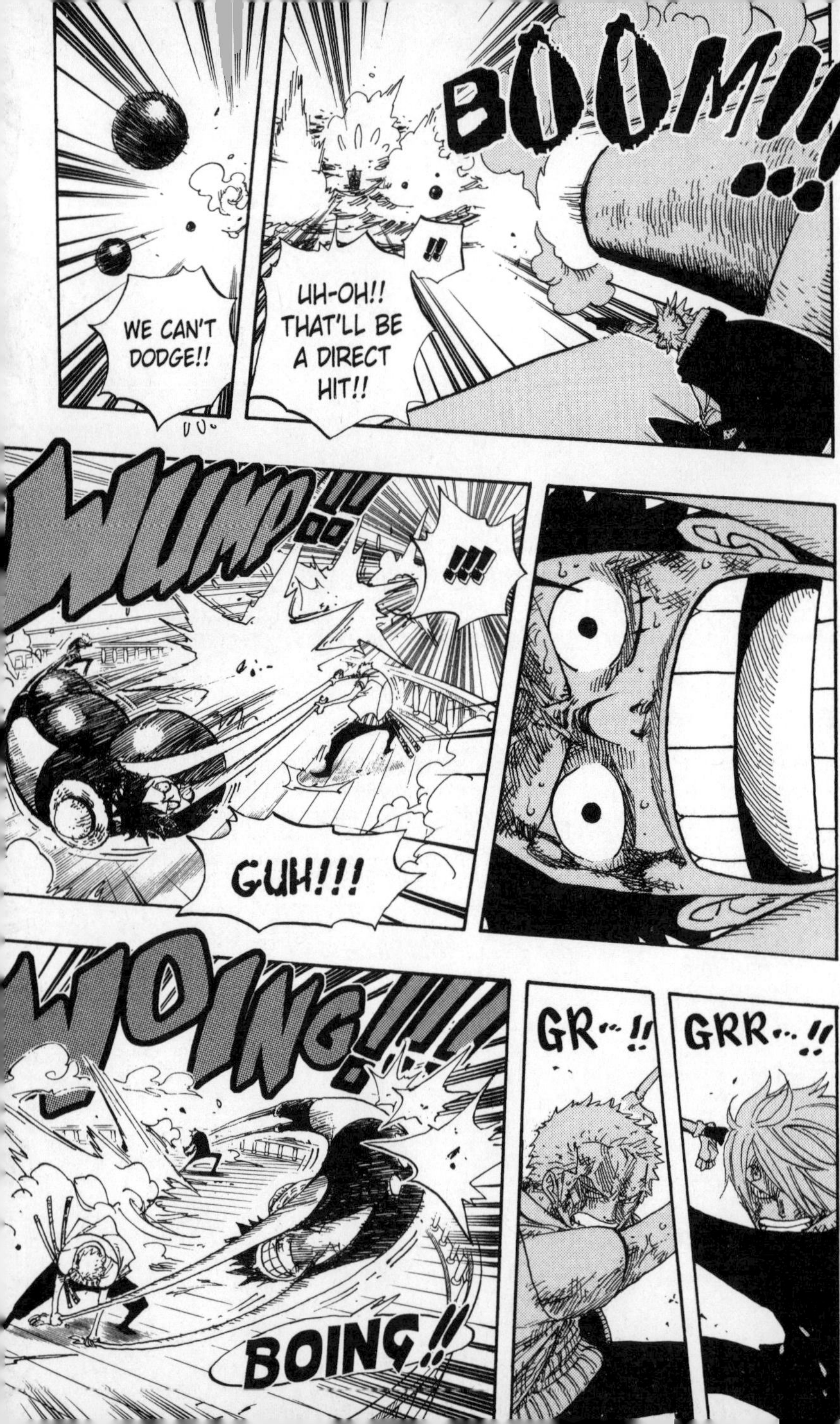
BOOM!!
!!
UH-OH!! THAT'LL BE A DIRECT HIT!!
WE CAN'T DODGE!!
WUMP!!
!!!
GUH!!!
GRR...!!
GR...!!
WOING!!!
BOING!!

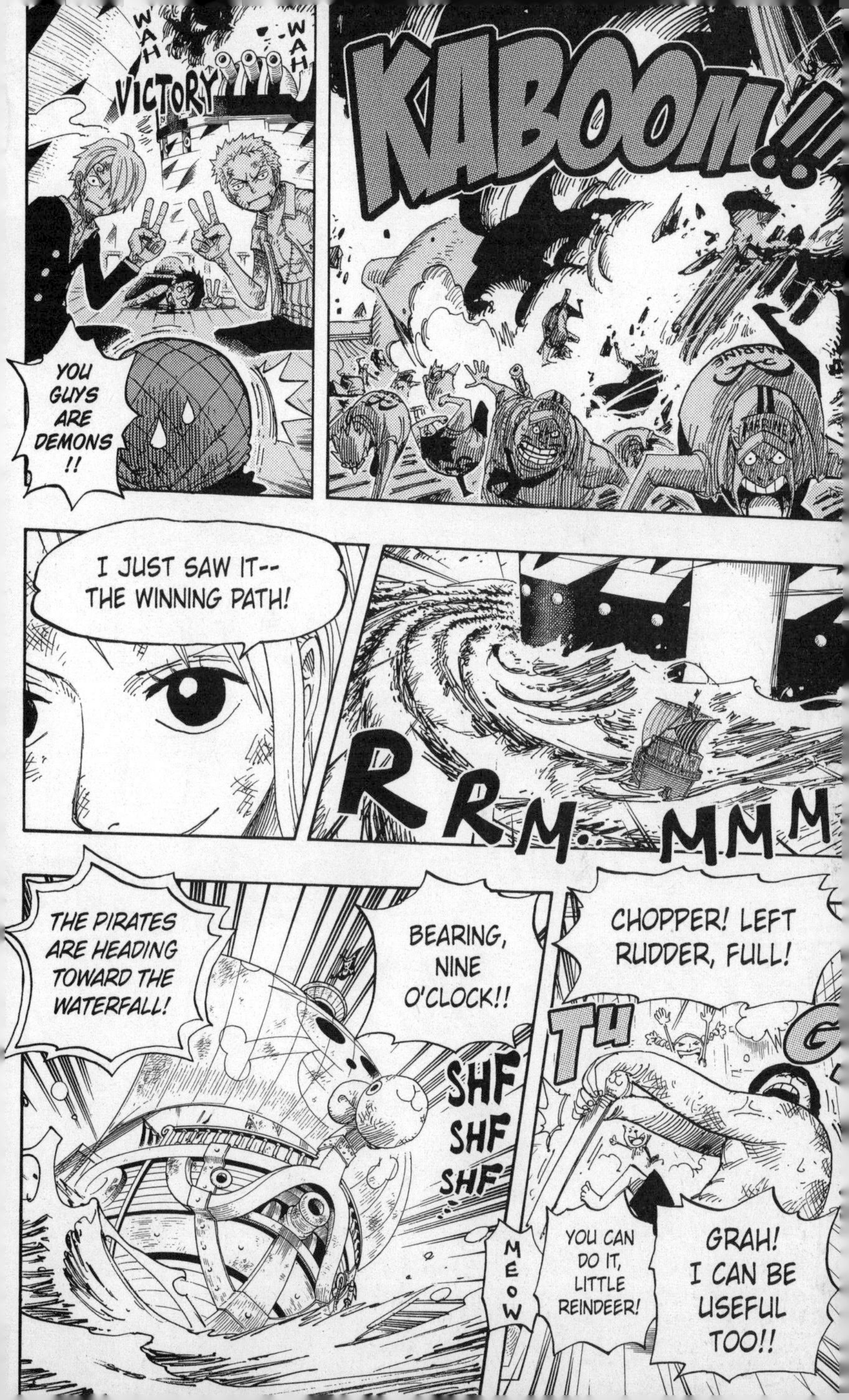
KABOOM!!
WAH
WAH
VICTORY
YOU GUYS ARE DEMONS!!
RRRM... MMM
I JUST SAW IT-- THE WINNING PATH!
CHOPPER! LEFT RUDDER, FULL!
TH
GRAH! I CAN BE USEFUL TOO!!
YOU CAN DO IT, LITTLE REINDEER!
MEOW
BEARING, NINE O'CLOCK!!
THE PIRATES ARE HEADING TOWARD THE WATERFALL!
SHF SHF SHF

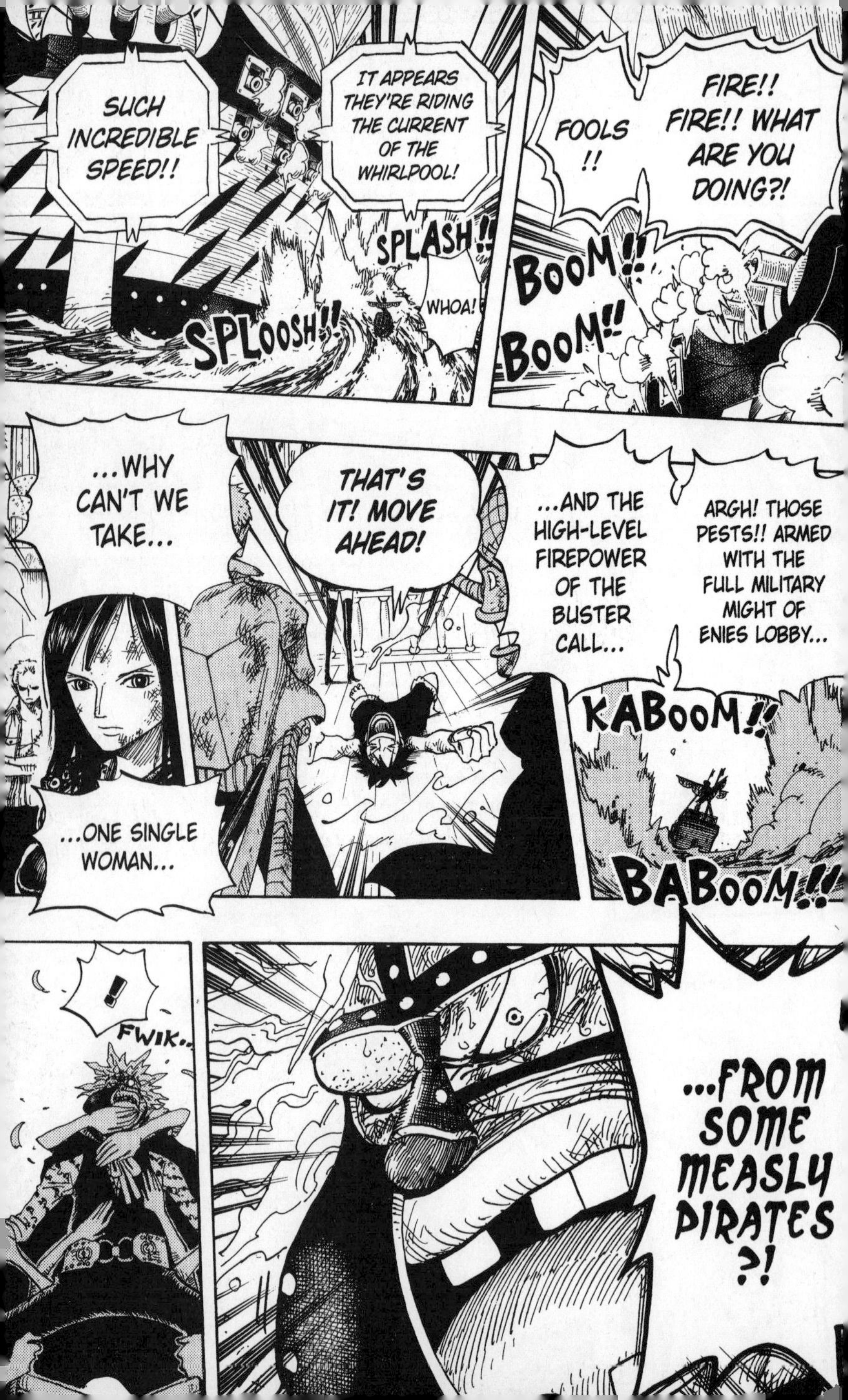
FIRE!! FIRE!! WHAT ARE YOU DOING?!
FOOLS !!
BOOM!!
BOOM!!
IT APPEARS THEY'RE RIDING THE CURRENT OF THE WHIRLPOOL!
SUCH INCREDIBLE SPEED!!
SPLASH!!
WHOA!
SPLOOSH!!
ARGH! THOSE PESTS!! ARMED WITH THE FULL MILITARY MIGHT OF ENIES LOBBY...
...AND THE HIGH-LEVEL FIREPOWER OF THE BUSTER CALL...
KABOOM!!
BABOOM!!
THAT'S IT! MOVE AHEAD!
...WHY CAN'T WE TAKE...
...ONE SINGLE WOMAN...
...FROM SOME MEASLY PIRATES ?!
!
FWIK..

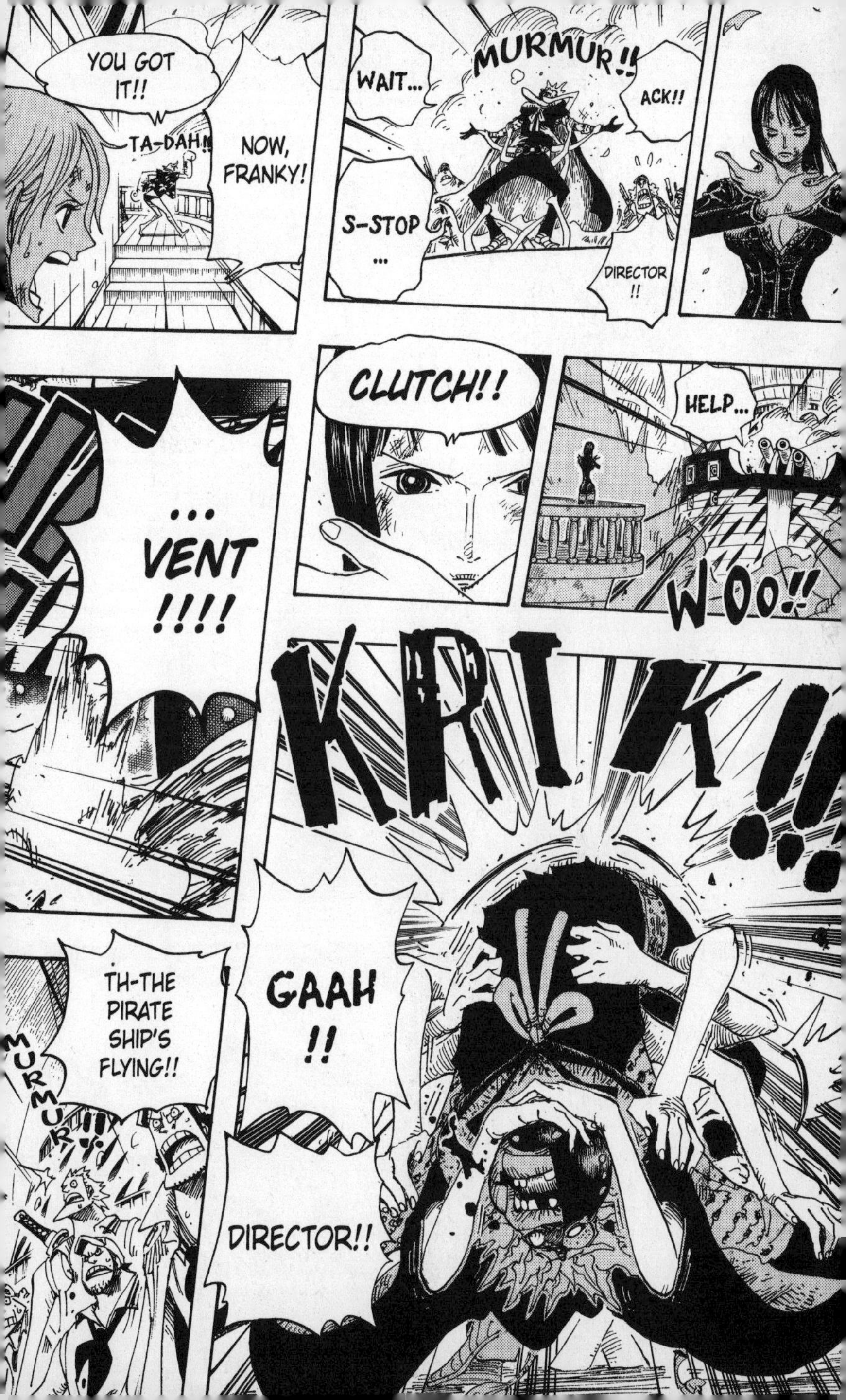
ACK!!
MURMUR!!
WAIT...
DIRECTOR !!
S-STOP ...
NOW, FRANKY!
YOU GOT IT!!
TA-DAH!!
HELP...
WOO!!
CLUTCH!!
... VENT !!!!
KRIK!!
GAAH !!
DIRECTOR!!
TH-THE PIRATE SHIP'S FLYING!!
MURMUR!!

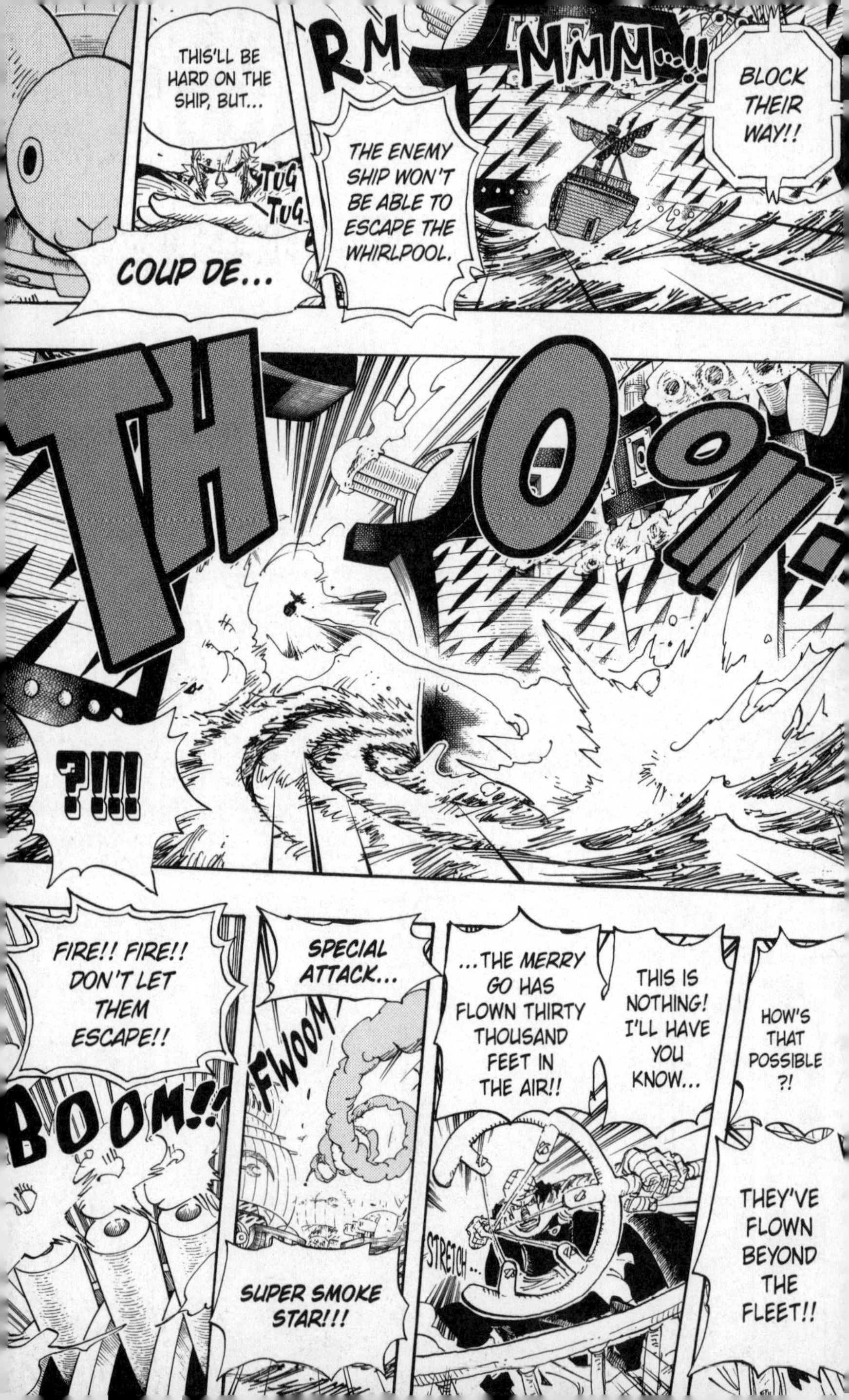
RMMMM...!!
BLOCK THEIR WAY!!
THE ENEMY SHIP WON'T BE ABLE TO ESCAPE THE WHIRLPOOL.
THIS'LL BE HARD ON THE SHIP, BUT...
TUG TUG
COUP DE...
THOOM..
?!!!
HOW'S THAT POSSIBLE ?!
THEY'VE FLOWN BEYOND THE FLEET!!
THIS IS NOTHING! I'LL HAVE YOU KNOW...
...THE MERRY GO HAS FLOWN THIRTY THOUSAND FEET IN THE AIR!!
STRETCH...
SPECIAL ATTACK...
FWOOM
SUPER SMOKE STAR!!!
FIRE!! FIRE!! DON'T LET THEM ESCAPE!!
BOOM!!

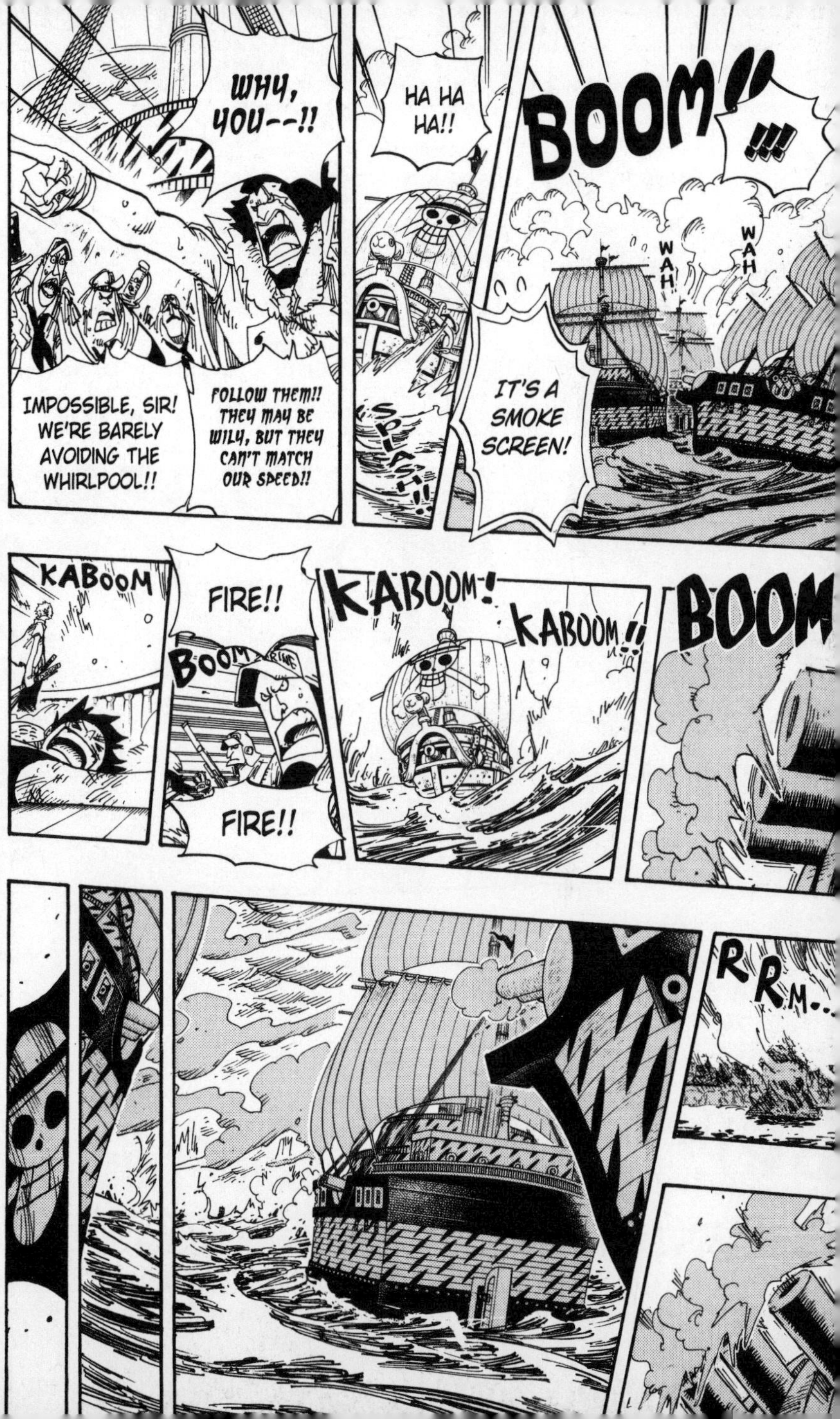
BOOM!!
!!!
WAH
WAH
IT'S A SMOKE SCREEN!
HA HA HA!!
SPLASH!!
WHY, YOU--!!
FOLLOW THEM!! THEY MAY BE WILY, BUT THEY CAN'T MATCH OUR SPEED!!
IMPOSSIBLE, SIR! WE'RE BARELY AVOIDING THE WHIRLPOOL!!
BOOM
KABOOM!
KABOOM!!
FIRE!!
BOOM
FIRE!!
KABOOM
RRM...

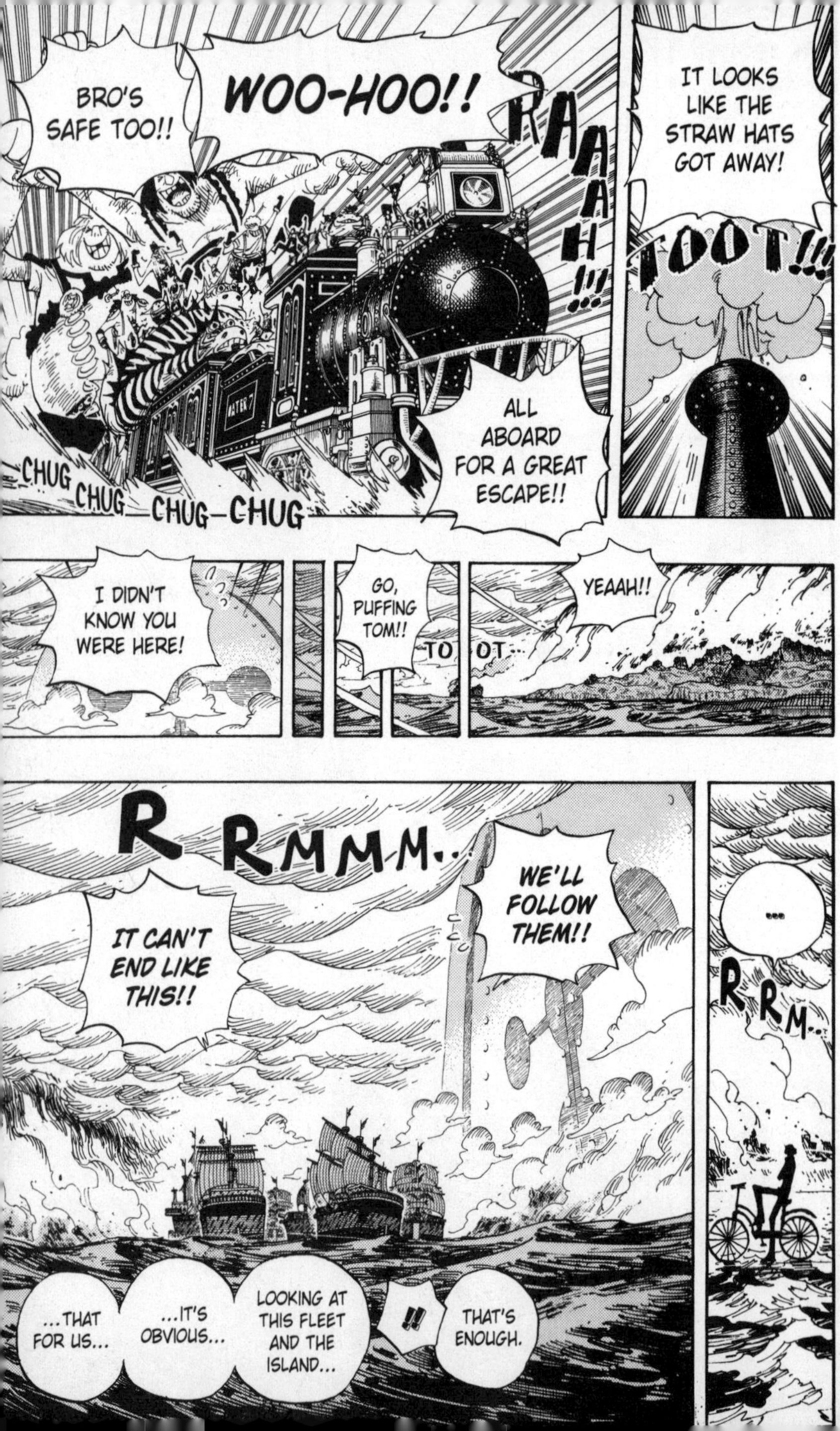
IT LOOKS LIKE THE STRAW HATS GOT AWAY!
TOOT!!!
RAAAAH!!!
WOO-HOO!!
BRO'S SAFE TOO!!
ALL ABOARD FOR A GREAT ESCAPE!!
CHUG CHUG CHUG CHUG
YEAAH!!
GO, PUFFING TOM!!
TOOT...
I DIDN'T KNOW YOU WERE HERE!
...
RRM...
RRMMM...
WE'LL FOLLOW THEM!!
IT CAN'T END LIKE THIS!!
THAT'S ENOUGH.
!!
LOOKING AT THIS FLEET AND THE ISLAND...
...IT'S OBVIOUS...
...THAT FOR US...

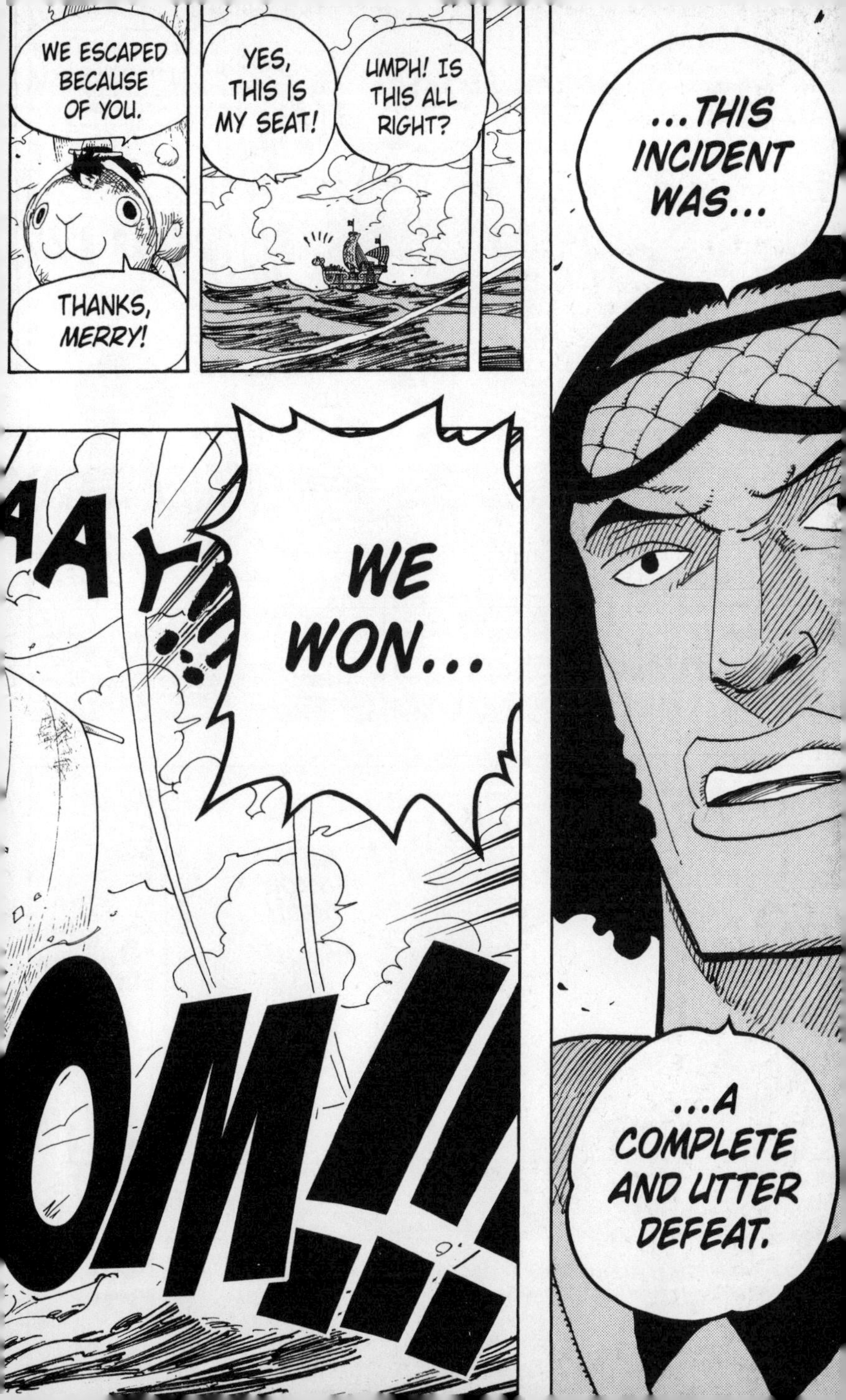
...THIS INCIDENT WAS...
...A COMPLETE AND UTTER DEFEAT.
UMPH! IS THIS ALL RIGHT?
YES, THIS IS MY SEAT!
WE ESCAPED BECAUSE OF YOU.
THANKS, MERRY!
WE WON...

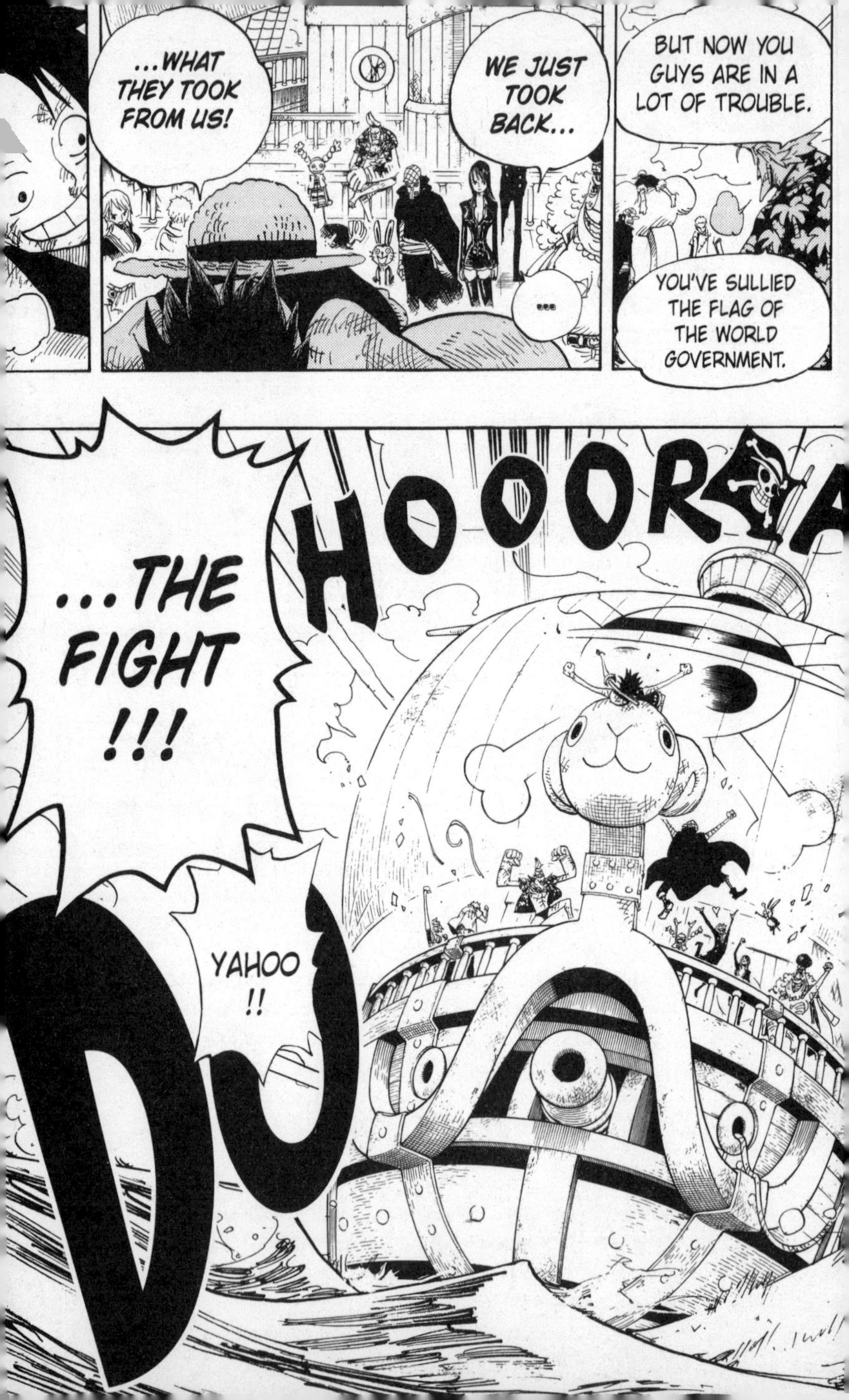
BUT NOW YOU GUYS ARE IN A LOT OF TROUBLE.
YOU'VE SULLIED THE FLAG OF THE WORLD GOVERNMENT.
WE JUST TOOK BACK...
...WHAT THEY TOOK FROM US!
...
HOOORA
...THE FIGHT!!!
YAHOO !!
DO

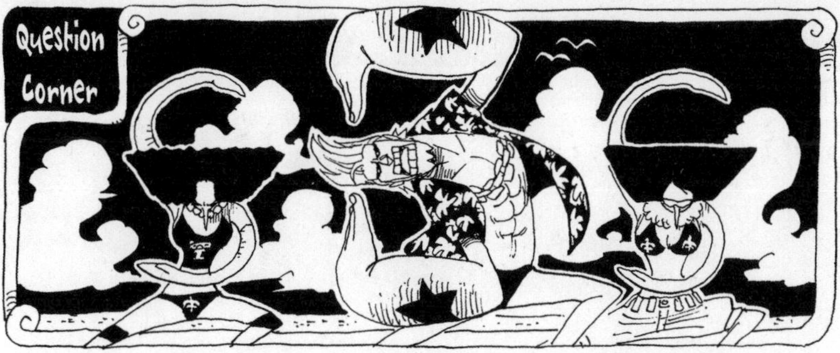
Question Corner

Q: Hello, Oda Sensei. Are you taking care of your health? My name is Kimeunhyang. *One Piece* volume 41 was published recently in South Korea. Now for my question. In the logo, where Luffy's silhouette makes the "I", what is the thing (→) between his hips and his legs? A skirt? Surely not! I want to know so badly I'm having trouble sleeping.

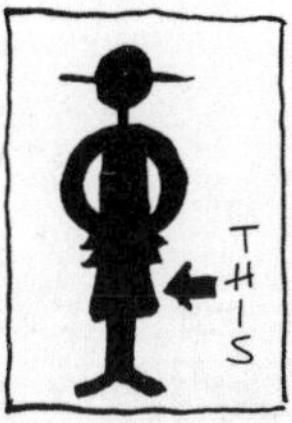
THIS

A: Thanks for writing. Here we've got a question from South Korea. You'll probably understand if I draw a picture. Maybe the area around the hands is a little confusing.

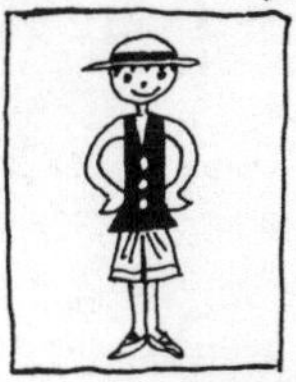

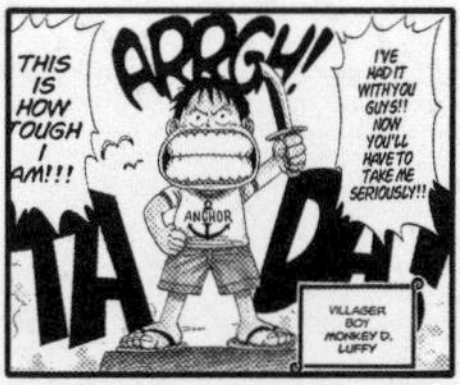
THIS IS HOW TOUGH I AM!!!
ARRGH!
I'VE HAD IT WITH YOU GUYS!! NOW YOU'LL HAVE TO TAKE ME SERIOUSLY!!
TA DAH!
ANCHOR
VILLAGER BOY MONKEY D. LUFFY

Q: Hiya, Odacchi! I made some time during my incredibly busy summer break to research something. You use sound effects like DOOM! and DOOOM!! a lot, don't you? I counted how many times you've used DOOM all the way through *One Piece* volume 42, chapter 409! (Sound effects included: DOOM, DOOOM, DADOOM, DADOOOM, BADOOOM*) I can't vouch for my accuracy, but there were roughly 1,469 DOOMs! (DOOM!!) On average, that's approximately 3.5 DOOM-type sound effects appearing per single chapter. Did you know that? No other manga artist uses DOOM so much. All right, everyone, a round of applause! CLAP CLAP! Wow! All right, now that you're feeling pretty good… The Question Corner is over!!! (DADOOM)

--M of SYAM

A: Waaaaait! Let me say something! Just how much time do you have on your hands?! (laughs) But really, thank you. That's how many scenes I have confidence in! See you next volume!

*Even if the questions from overseas or from small children have grammatical mistakes in them, I have them printed just the way they are, because the effort they put into them makes me happy.

Chapter 430:

A LIGHT SNOW OF REMINSCENCE FALLS

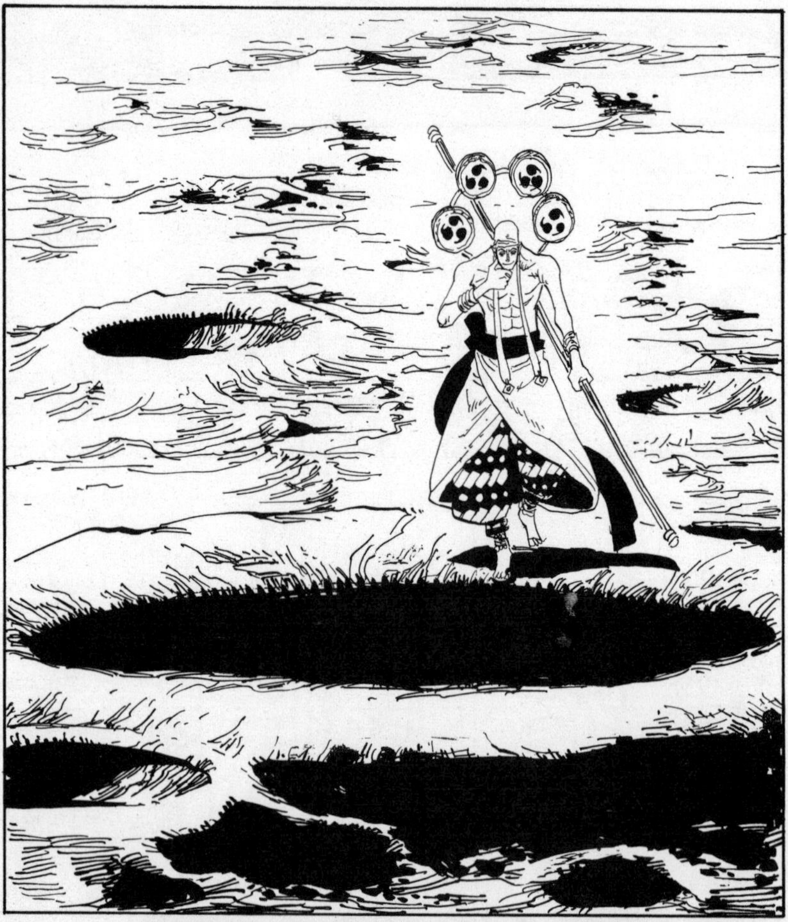

ENERU'S GREAT SPACE MISSION, VOL. 3:
"SENSING SOMETHING IN THE CRATER"

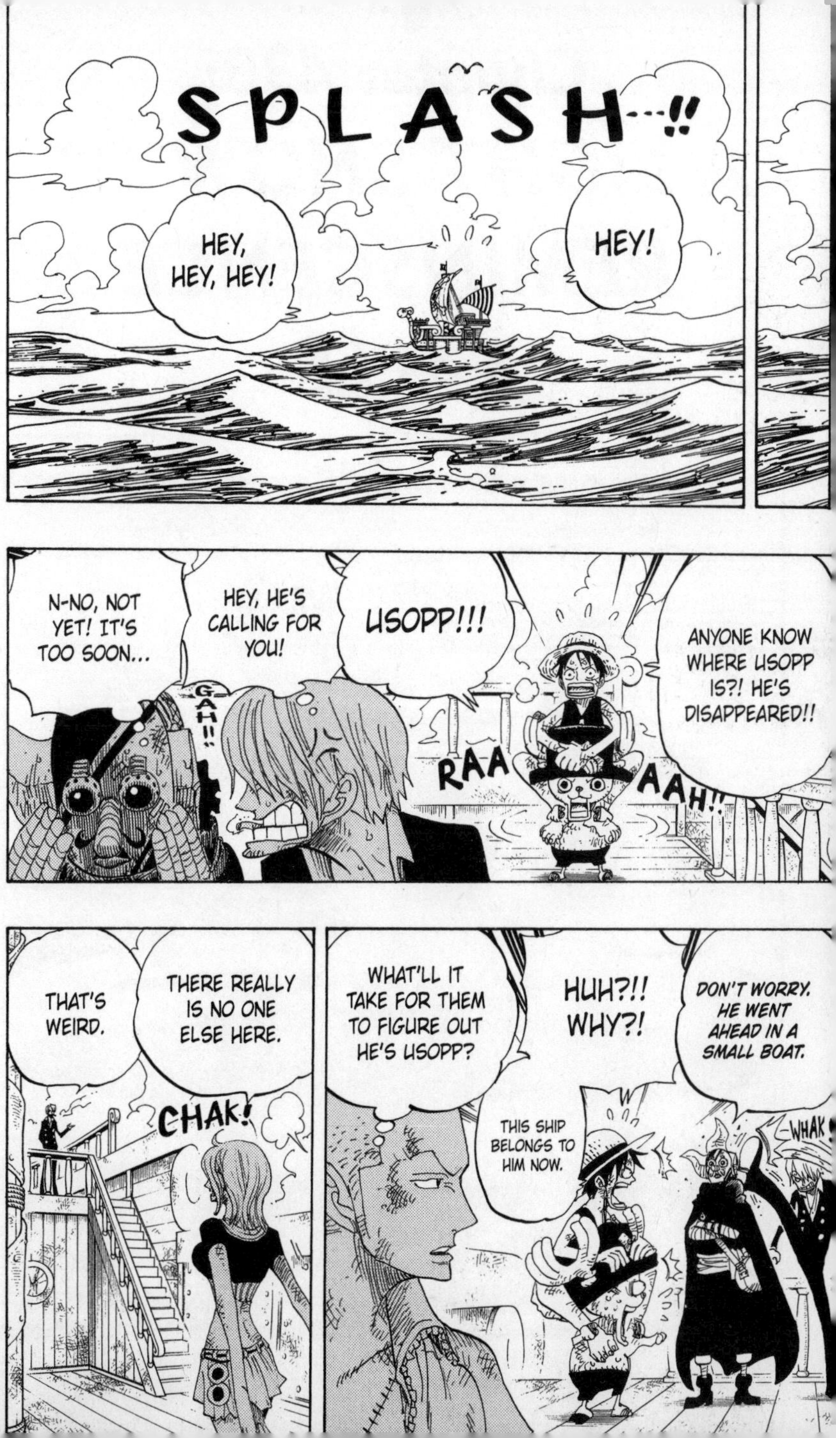
SPLASH---!!
HEY!
HEY, HEY, HEY!
ANYONE KNOW WHERE USOPP IS?! HE'S DISAPPEARED!!
RAAAAH!!
USOPP!!!
HEY, HE'S CALLING FOR YOU!
GAH!!
N-NO, NOT YET! IT'S TOO SOON...
DON'T WORRY. HE WENT AHEAD IN A SMALL BOAT.
WHAK
HUH?!! WHY?!
THIS SHIP BELONGS TO HIM NOW.
WHAT'LL IT TAKE FOR THEM TO FIGURE OUT HE'S USOPP?
THERE REALLY IS NO ONE ELSE HERE.
THAT'S WEIRD.
CHAK!

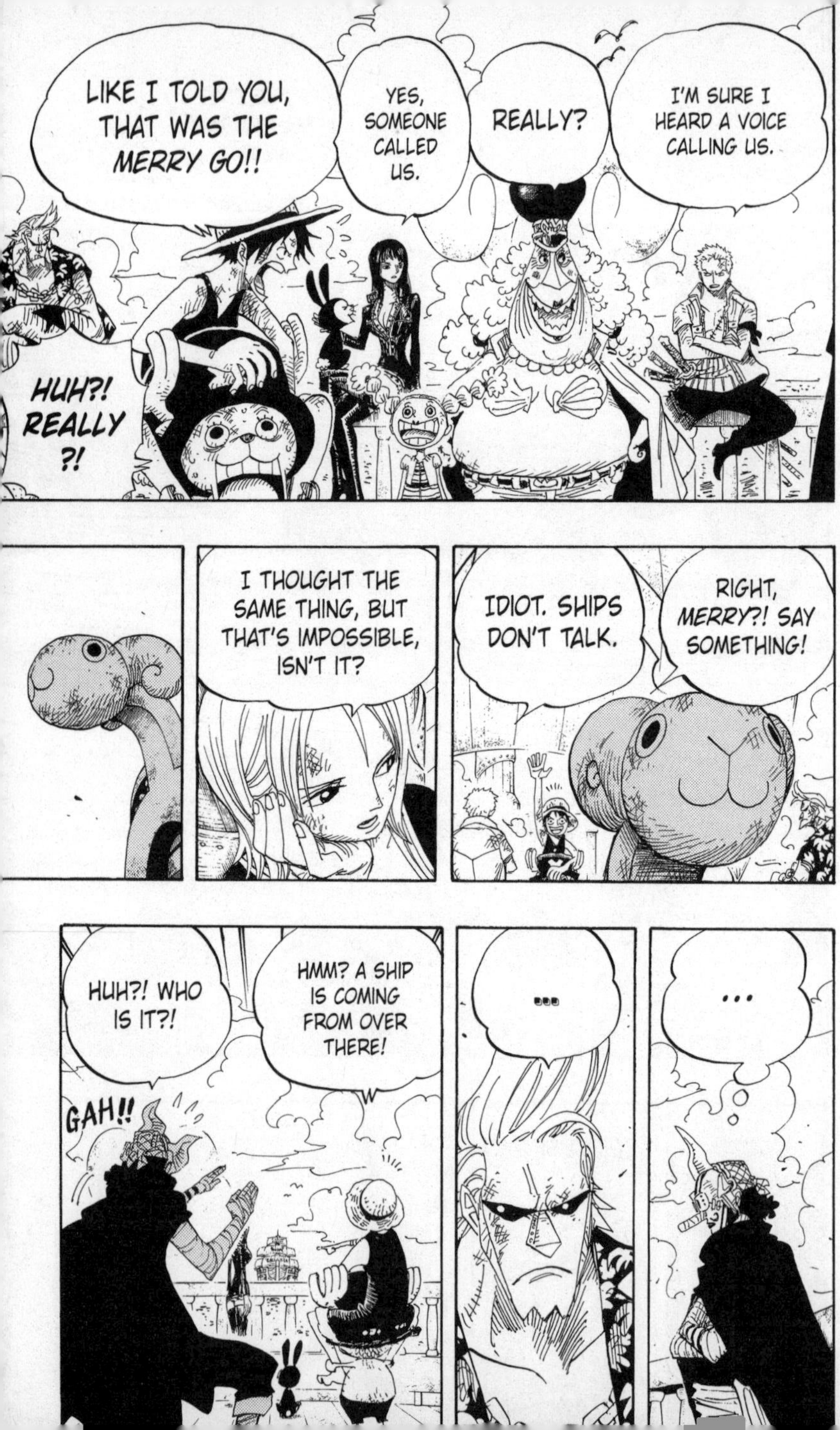
I'M SURE I HEARD A VOICE CALLING US.
REALLY?
YES, SOMEONE CALLED US.
LIKE I TOLD YOU, THAT WAS THE MERRY GO!!
HUH?! REALLY?!
RIGHT, MERRY?! SAY SOMETHING!
IDIOT. SHIPS DON'T TALK.
I THOUGHT THE SAME THING, BUT THAT'S IMPOSSIBLE, ISN'T IT?
...
...
HMM? A SHIP IS COMING FROM OVER THERE!
HUH?! WHO IS IT?!
GAH!!

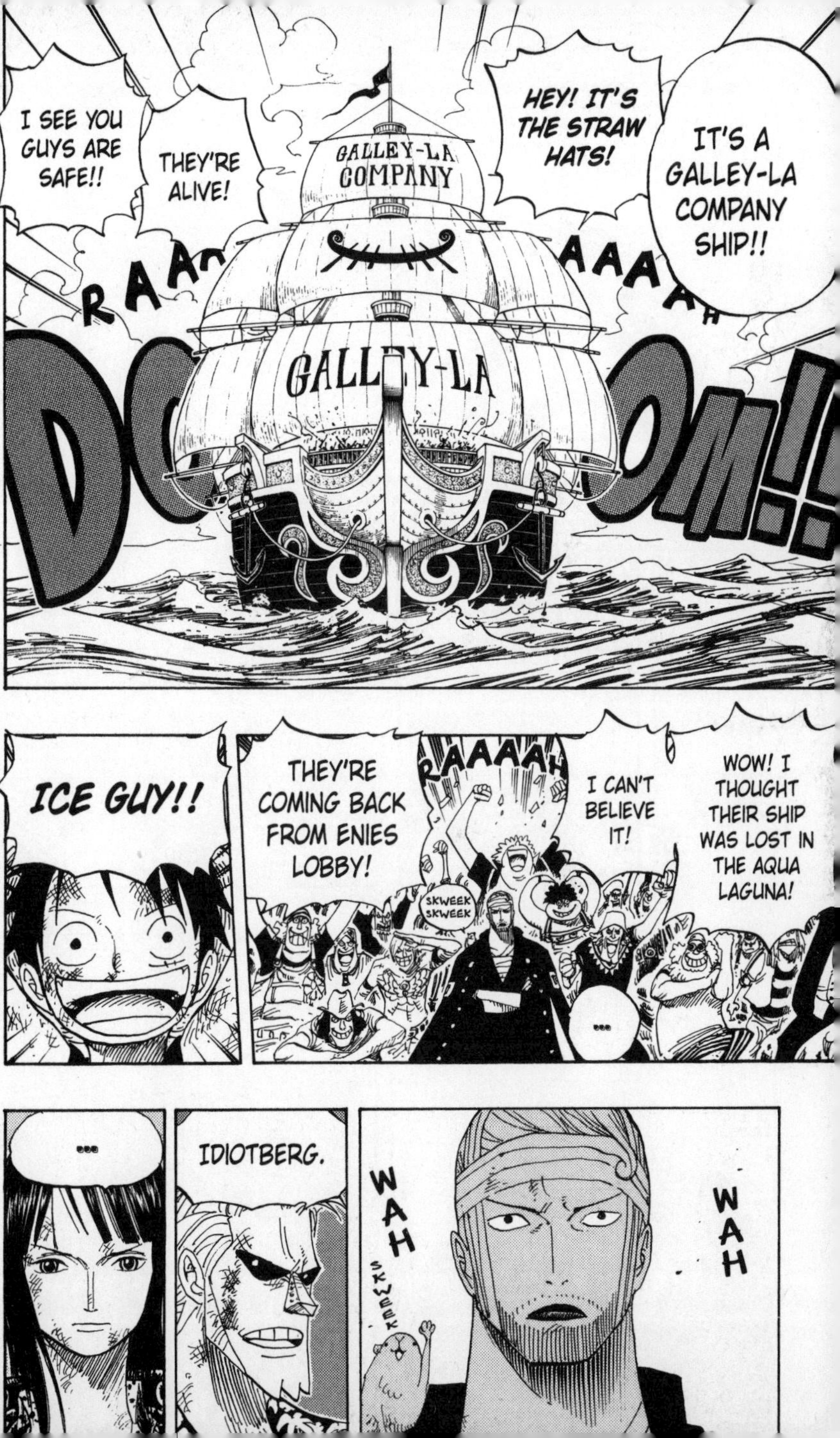
IT'S A GALLEY-LA COMPANY SHIP!!
HEY! IT'S THE STRAW HATS!
GALLEY-LA COMPANY
THEY'RE ALIVE!
I SEE YOU GUYS ARE SAFE!!
RAAAAAAH
GALLEY-LA
DOOM!!
WOW! I THOUGHT THEIR SHIP WAS LOST IN THE AQUA LAGUNA!
I CAN'T BELIEVE IT!
RAAAAH
THEY'RE COMING BACK FROM ENIES LOBBY!
SKWEEK SKWEEK
...
ICE GUY!!
WAH
WAH
SKWEEK
IDIOTBERG.
...

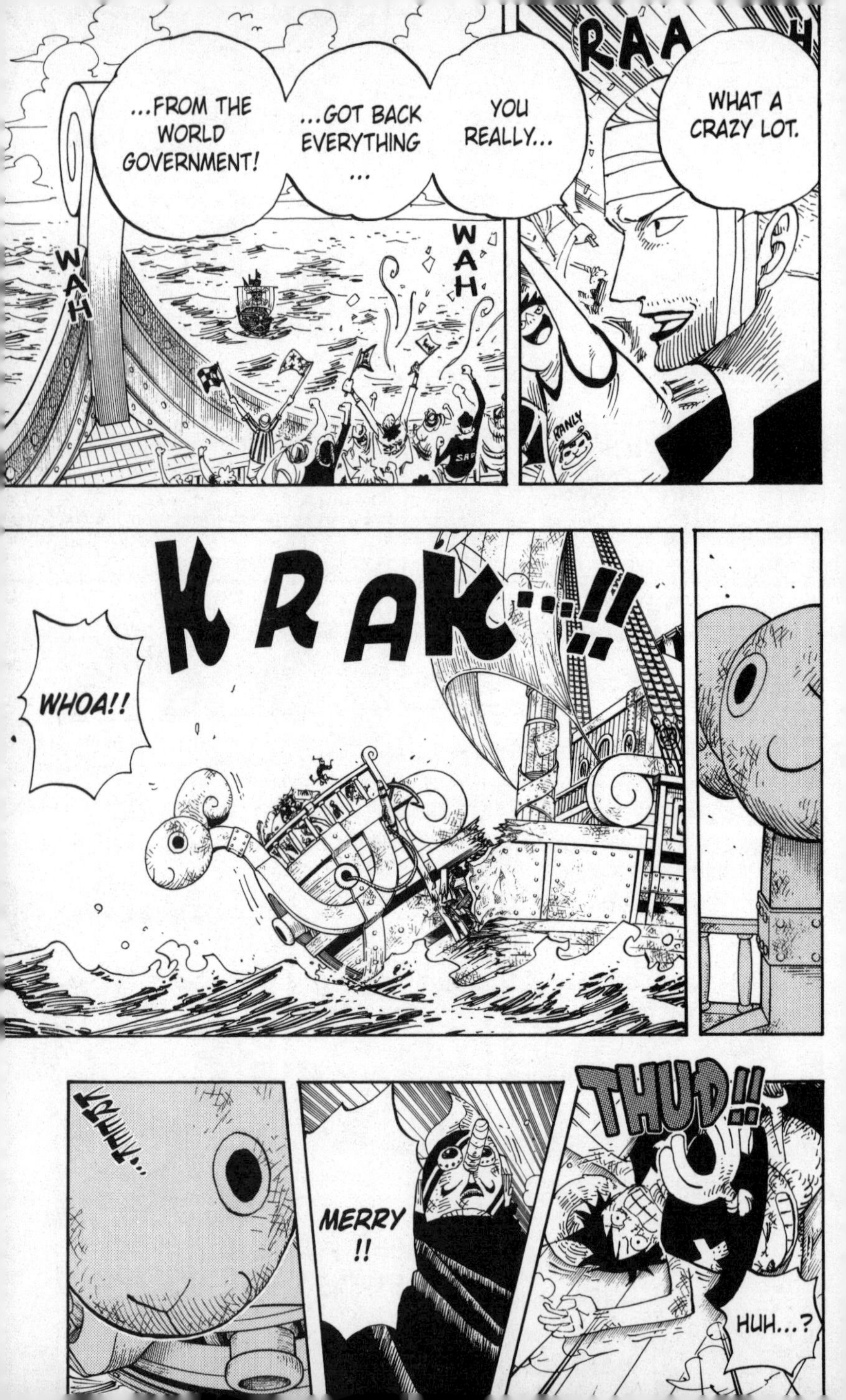
RAA
WHAT A CRAZY LOT.
YOU REALLY...
...GOT BACK EVERYTHING ...
...FROM THE WORLD GOVERNMENT!
WAH
WAH
KRAK...!!
WHOA!!
THUD!!
HUH...?
MERRY !!
KREEK...

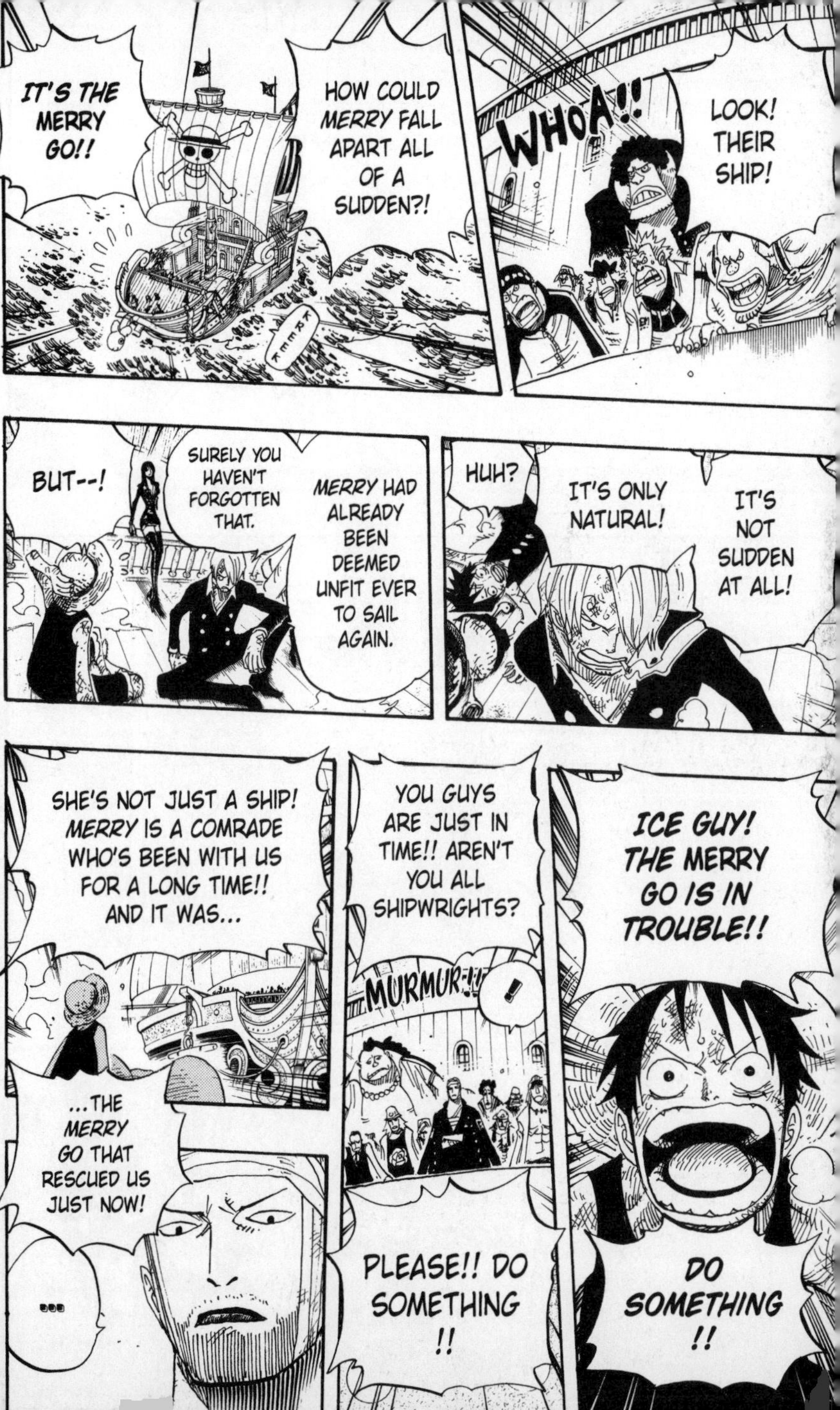
WHOA!!
LOOK! THEIR SHIP!
HOW COULD MERRY FALL APART ALL OF A SUDDEN?!
IT'S THE MERRY GO!!
KREEK
IT'S NOT SUDDEN AT ALL!
IT'S ONLY NATURAL!
HUH?
MERRY HAD ALREADY BEEN DEEMED UNFIT EVER TO SAIL AGAIN.
SURELY YOU HAVEN'T FORGOTTEN THAT.
BUT--!
ICE GUY! THE MERRY GO IS IN TROUBLE!!
DO SOMETHING!!
YOU GUYS ARE JUST IN TIME!! AREN'T YOU ALL SHIPWRIGHTS?
MURMUR!!
!
PLEASE!! DO SOMETHING!!
SHE'S NOT JUST A SHIP! MERRY IS A COMRADE WHO'S BEEN WITH US FOR A LONG TIME!! AND IT WAS...
...THE MERRY GO THAT RESCUED US JUST NOW!
...

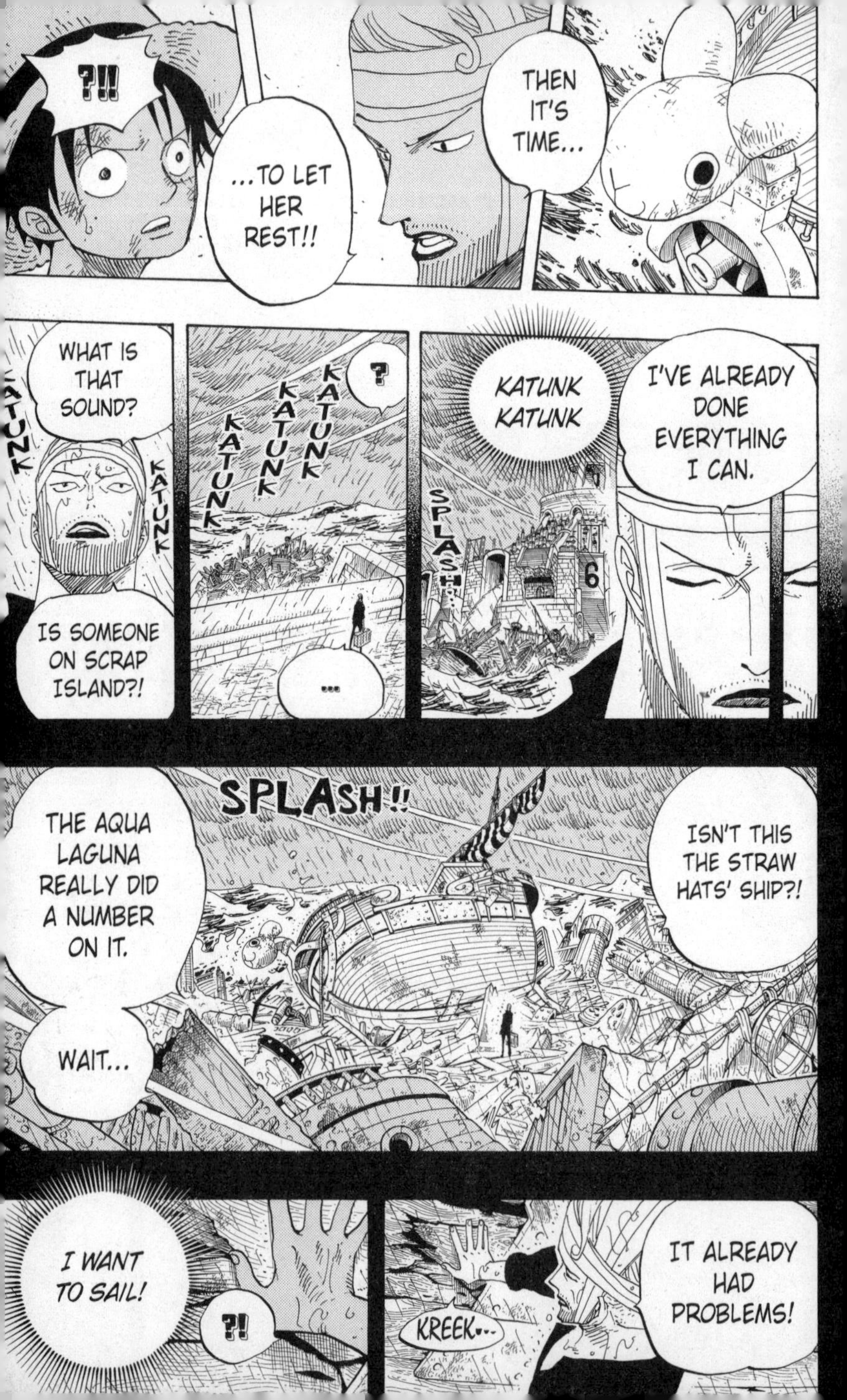
THEN IT'S TIME...
...TO LET HER REST!!
?!!
I'VE ALREADY DONE EVERYTHING I CAN.
KATUNK KATUNK
SPLASH...
6
?
KATUNK KATUNK KATUNK
...
WHAT IS THAT SOUND?
KATUNK
KATUNK
IS SOMEONE ON SCRAP ISLAND?!
SPLASH!!
ISN'T THIS THE STRAW HATS' SHIP?!
THE AQUA LAGUNA REALLY DID A NUMBER ON IT.
WAIT...
IT ALREADY HAD PROBLEMS!
KREEK...
?!
I WANT TO SAIL!

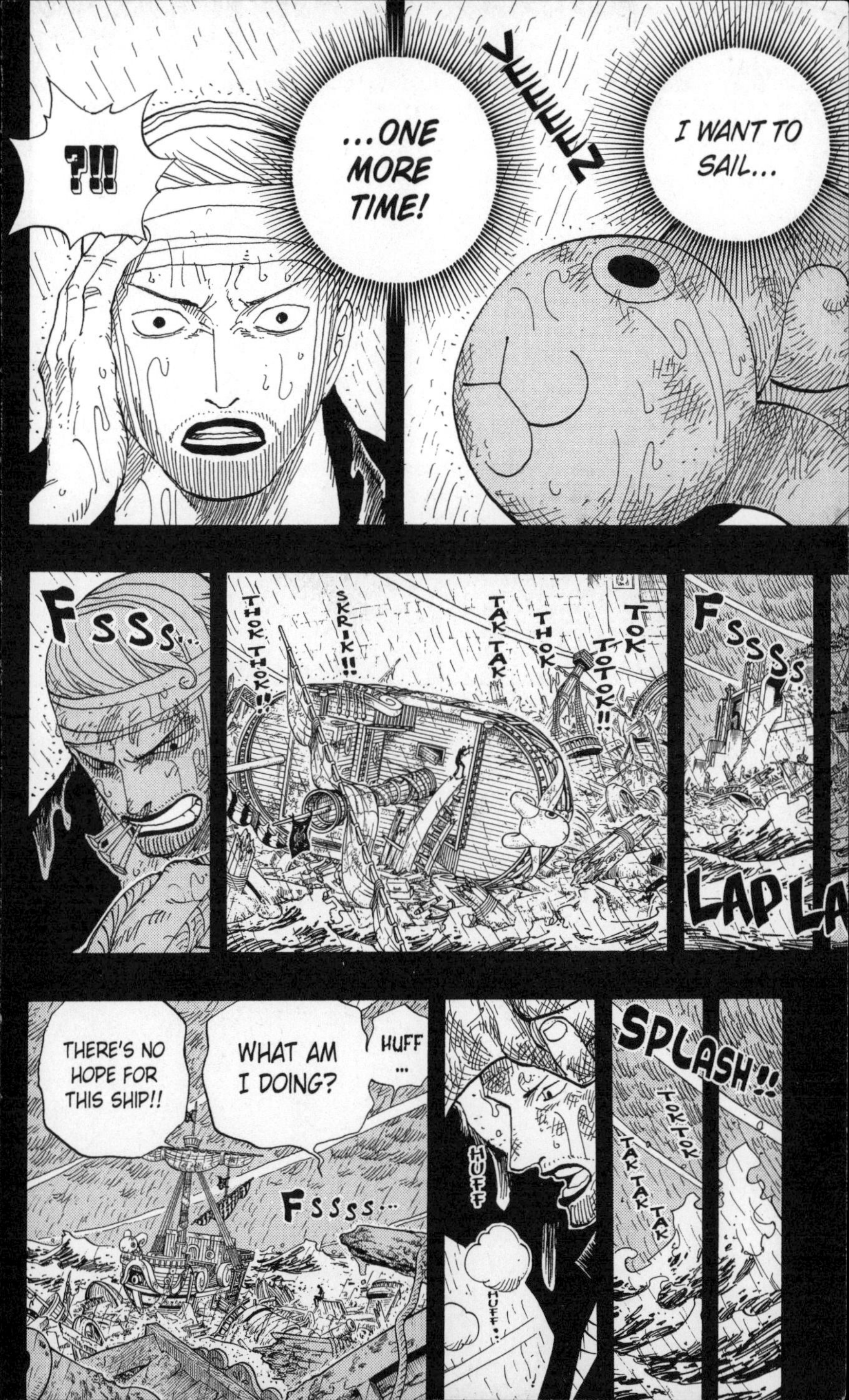
I WANT TO SAIL...
...ONE MORE TIME!
YEEEEENZ
?!!
FSSSSS...
LAP LA
TOK TOTOK!!
THOK
TAK TAK
SKRIK!!
THOK THOK!!
FSSS...
SPLASH!!
TOK TOK
TAK TAK TAK
HUFF
HUFF...
HUFF ...
WHAT AM I DOING?
THERE'S NO HOPE FOR THIS SHIP!!
FSSSS...

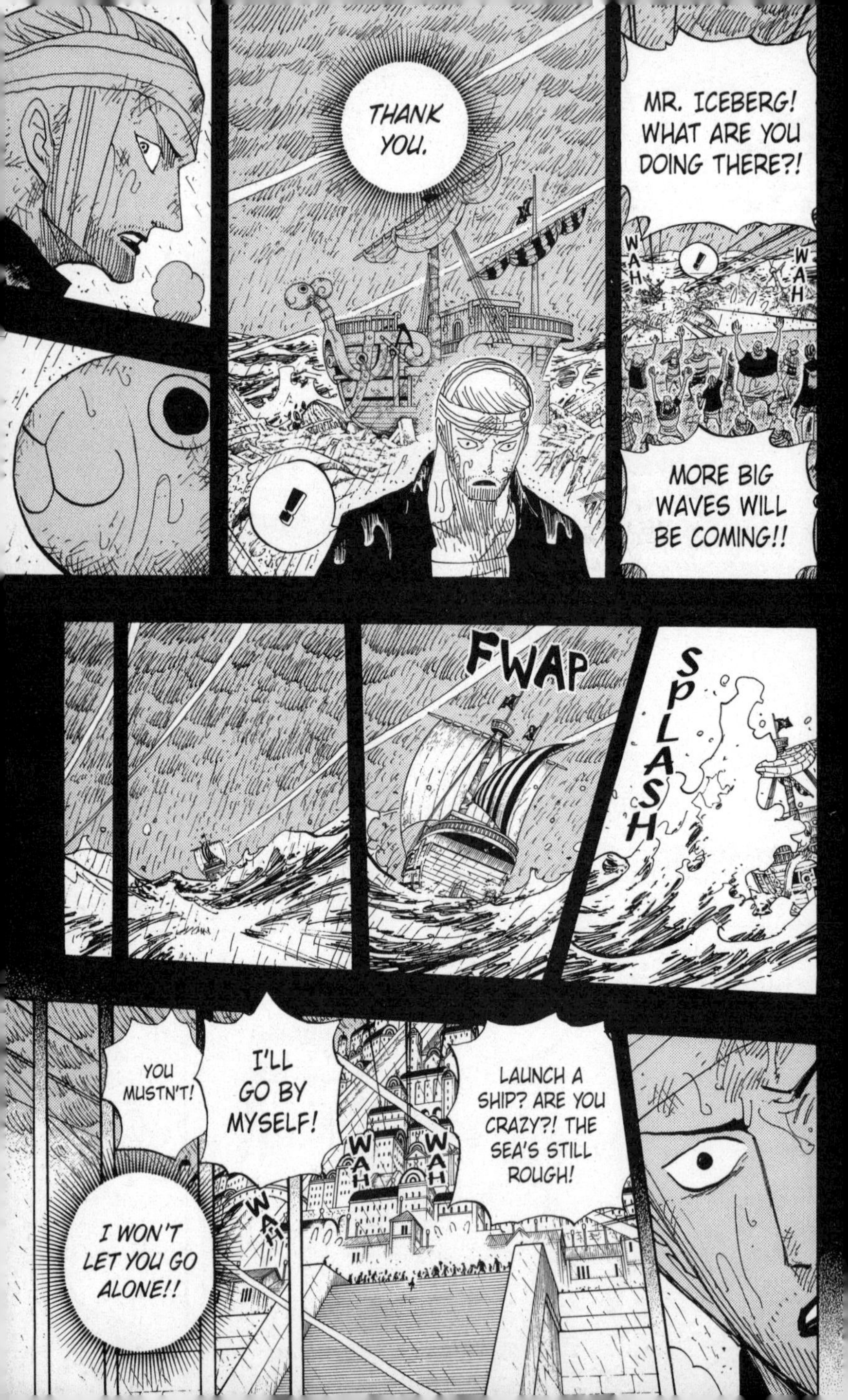
MR. ICEBERG! WHAT ARE YOU DOING THERE?!
WAH
!
WAH
MORE BIG WAVES WILL BE COMING!!
THANK YOU.
!
SPLASH
FWAP
LAUNCH A SHIP? ARE YOU CRAZY?! THE SEA'S STILL ROUGH!
I'LL GO BY MYSELF!
WAH
WAH
WAH
YOU MUSTN'T!
I WON'T LET YOU GO ALONE!!

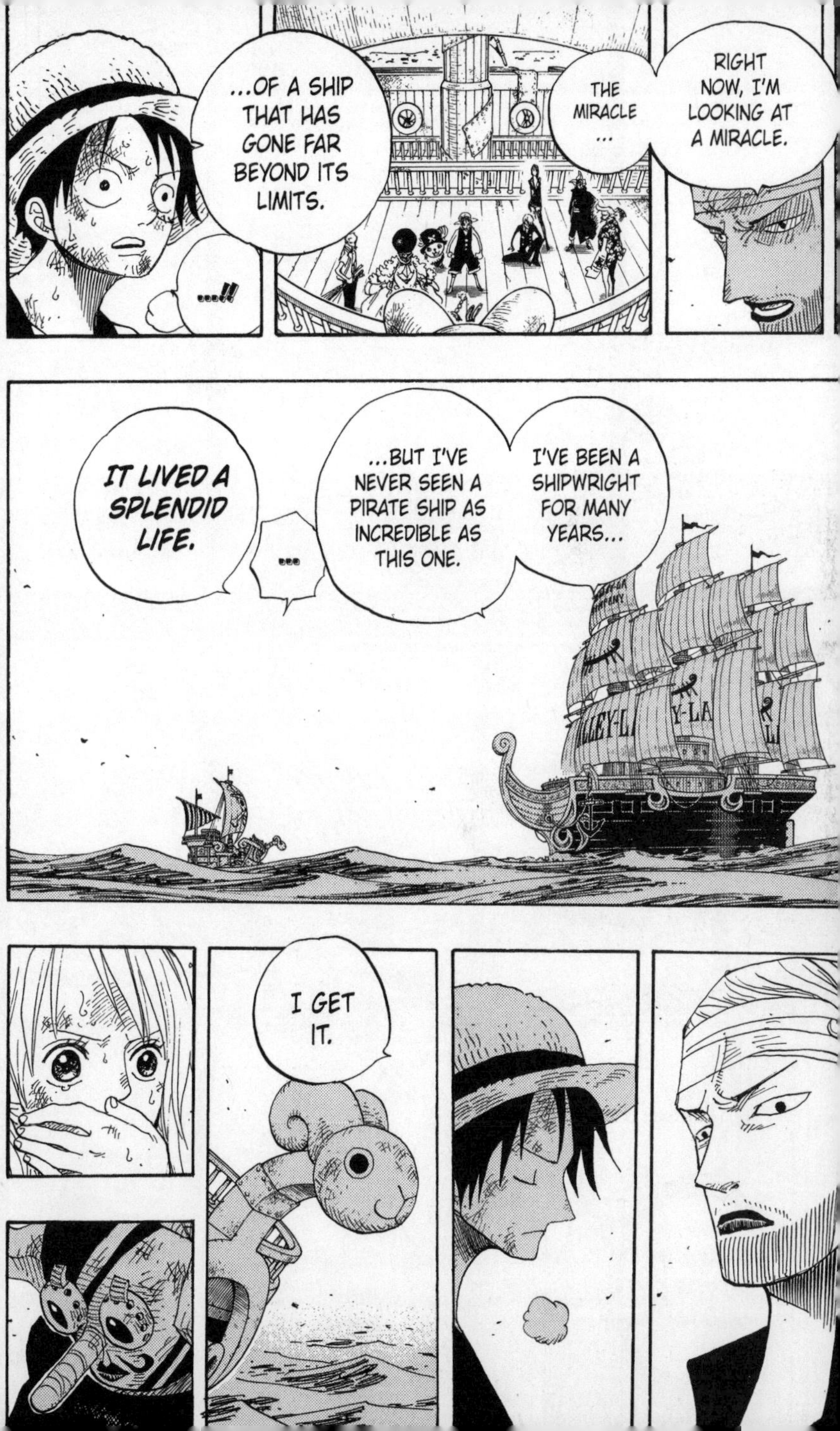
RIGHT NOW, I'M LOOKING AT A MIRACLE.
THE MIRACLE ...
...OF A SHIP THAT HAS GONE FAR BEYOND ITS LIMITS.
...!!
I'VE BEEN A SHIPWRIGHT FOR MANY YEARS...
...BUT I'VE NEVER SEEN A PIRATE SHIP AS INCREDIBLE AS THIS ONE.
...
IT LIVED A SPLENDID LIFE.
I GET IT.

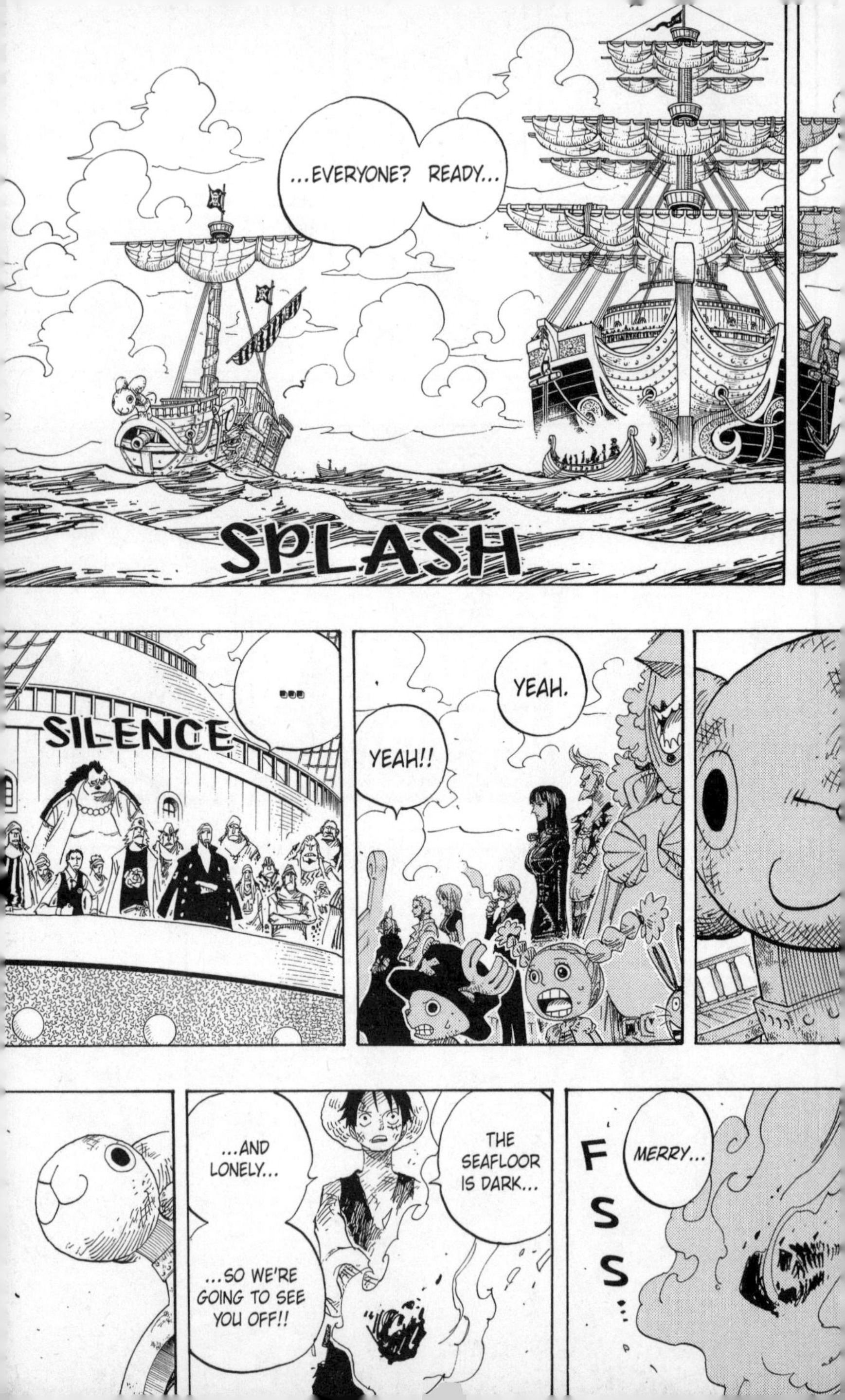
...EVERYONE? READY...
SPLASH
YEAH.
YEAH!!
...
SILENCE
MERRY...
FSS...
THE SEAFLOOR IS DARK...
...AND LONELY...
...SO WE'RE GOING TO SEE YOU OFF!!

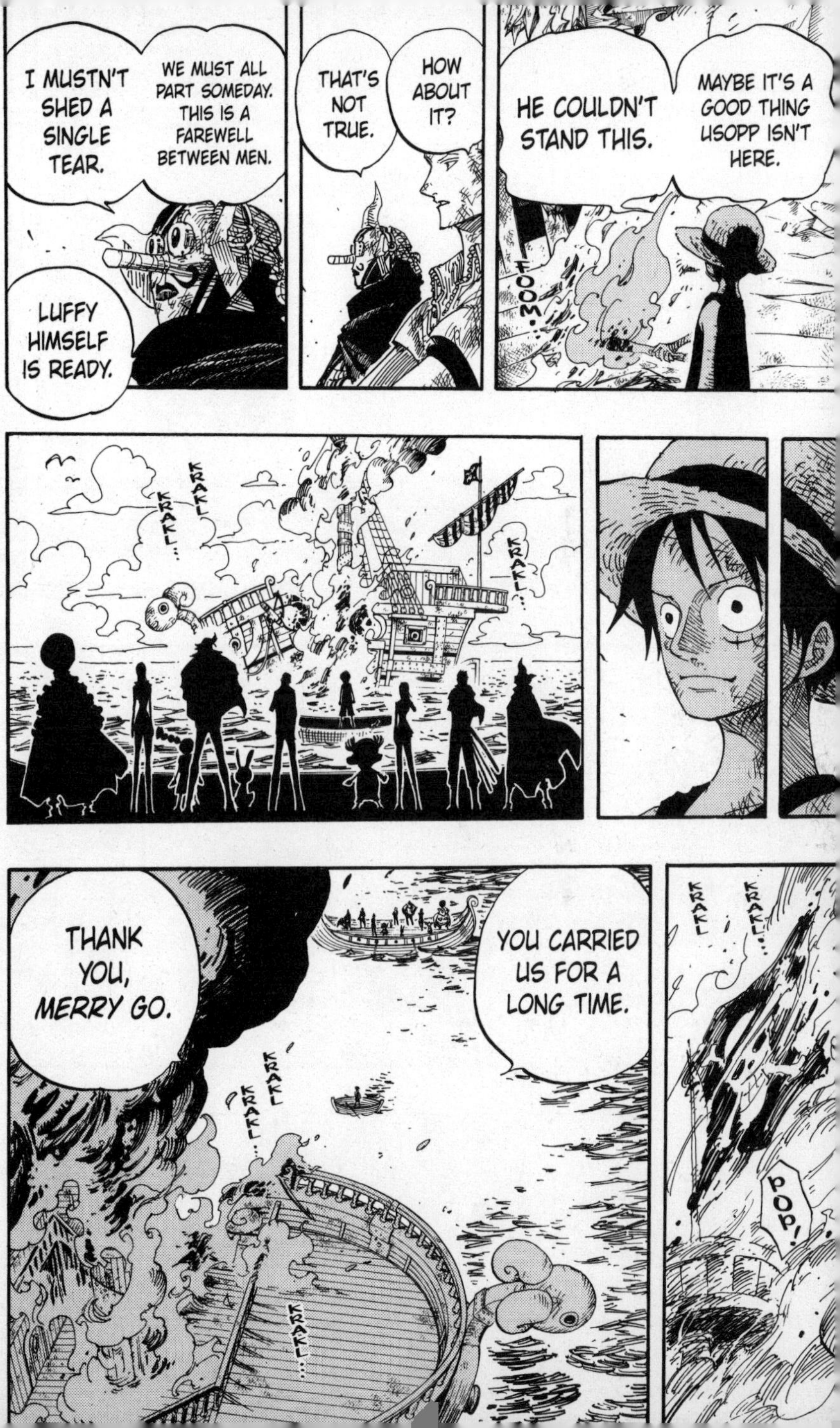
MAYBE IT'S A GOOD THING USOPP ISN'T HERE.
HE COULDN'T STAND THIS.
FOOM...
HOW ABOUT IT?
THAT'S NOT TRUE.
WE MUST ALL PART SOMEDAY. THIS IS A FAREWELL BETWEEN MEN.
I MUSTN'T SHED A SINGLE TEAR.
LUFFY HIMSELF IS READY.
KRAKL...
KRAKL
KRAKL...
KRAKL
KRAKL...
POP!
YOU CARRIED US FOR A LONG TIME.
THANK YOU, MERRY GO.
KRAKL
KRAKL...
KRAKL...

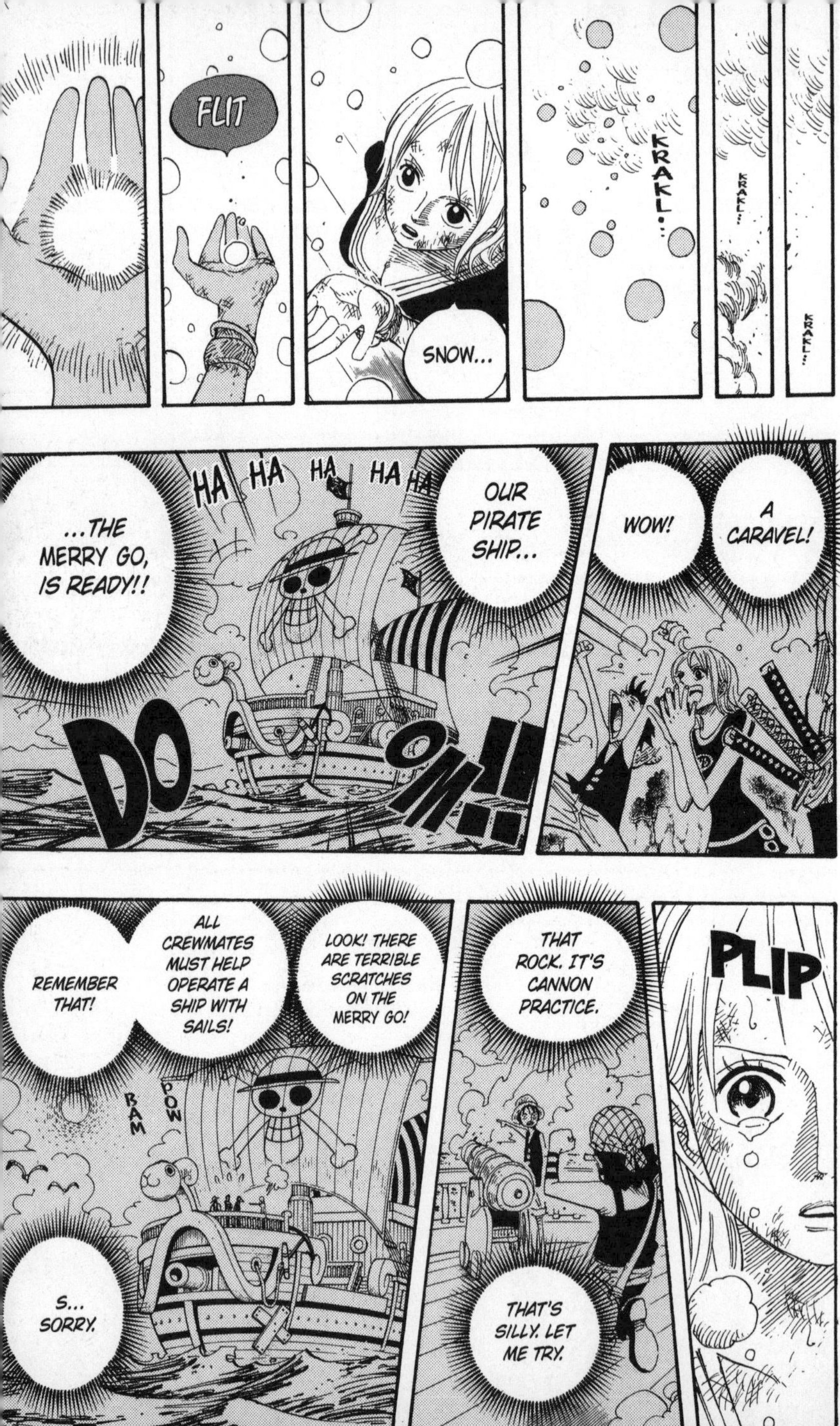
KRAKL...
KRAKL...
KRAKL...
SNOW...
FLIT
A CARAVEL!
WOW!
OUR PIRATE SHIP...
HA HA HA HA HA
...THE MERRY GO, IS READY!!
DO
OM!!
PLIP
THAT ROCK. IT'S CANNON PRACTICE.
THAT'S SILLY. LET ME TRY.
LOOK! THERE ARE TERRIBLE SCRATCHES ON THE MERRY GO!
ALL CREWMATES MUST HELP OPERATE A SHIP WITH SAILS!
REMEMBER THAT!
POW
BAM
S... SORRY.

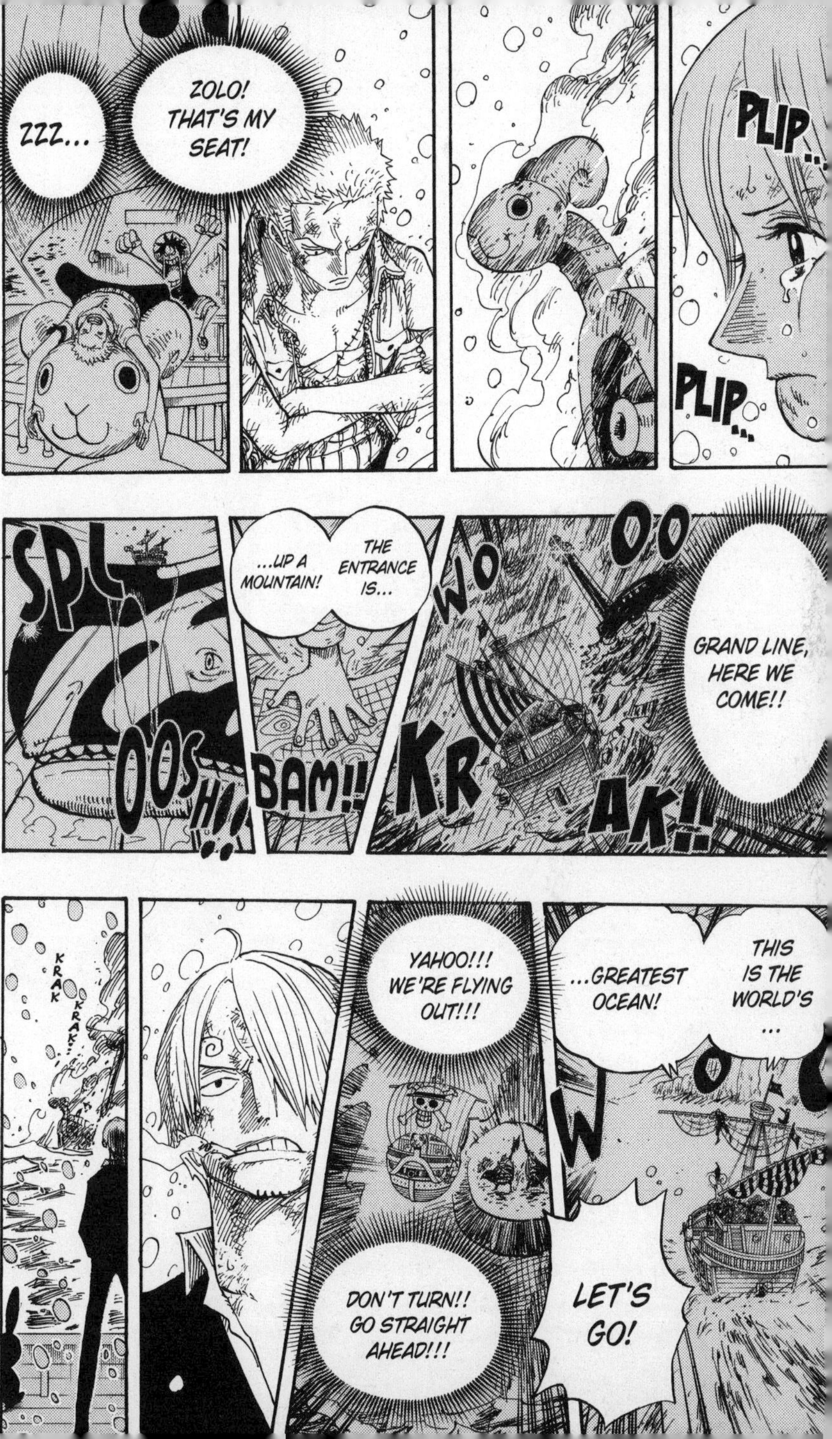
PLIP...
PLIP...
ZOLO! THAT'S MY SEAT!
ZZZ...
GRAND LINE, HERE WE COME!!
WOOO
KRAK!!
THE ENTRANCE IS...
...UP A MOUNTAIN!
BAM!!
SPLOOSH!!
THIS IS THE WORLD'S...
...GREATEST OCEAN!
LET'S GO!
WOOO
YAHOO!!! WE'RE FLYING OUT!!!
DON'T TURN!! GO STRAIGHT AHEAD!!!
KRAK
KRAK

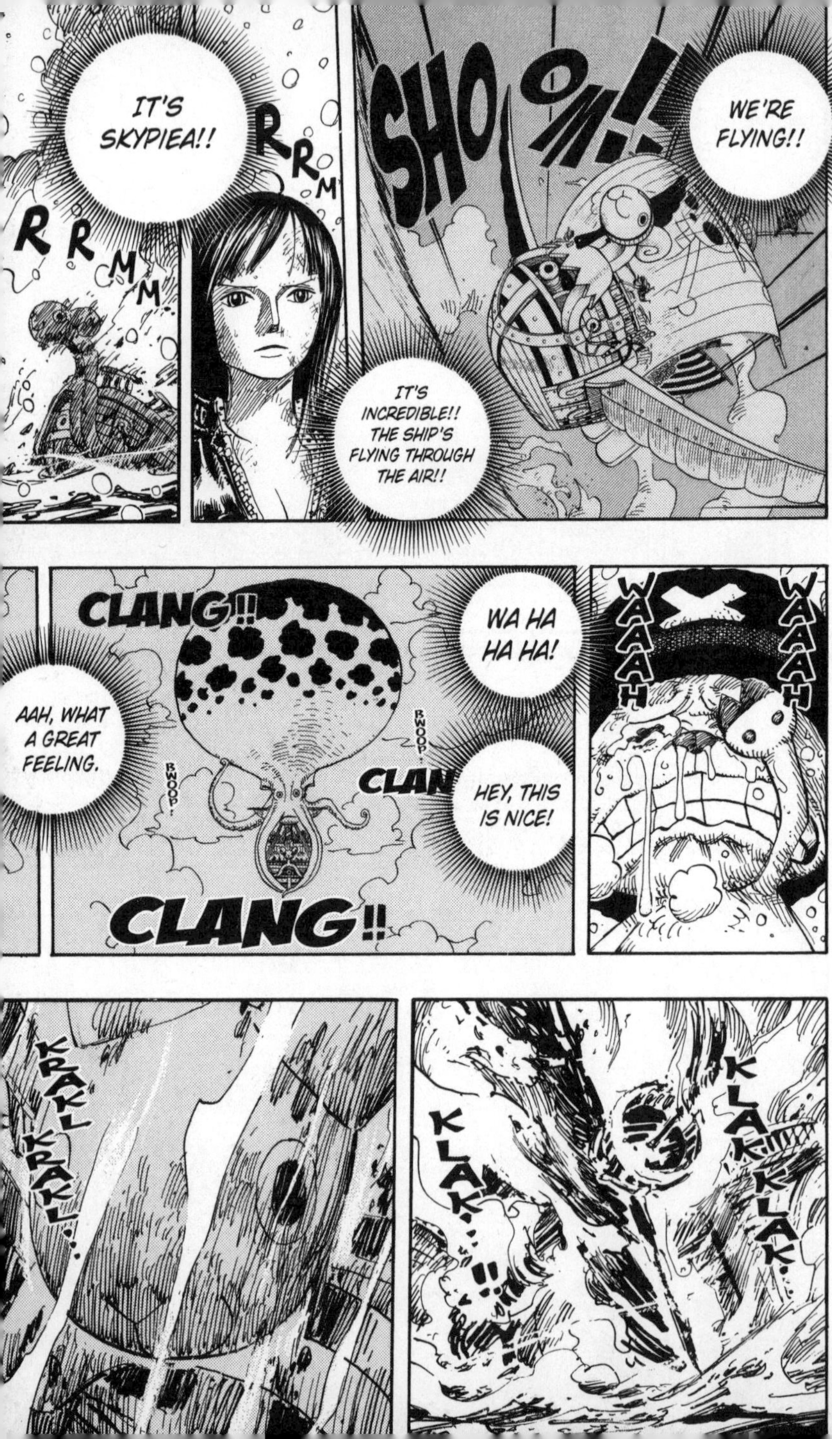
SHOOM!!
WE'RE FLYING!!
IT'S INCREDIBLE!! THE SHIP'S FLYING THROUGH THE AIR!!
RRRM
IT'S SKYPIEA!!
RRRMM
WAAAAH
WAAAAH
WA HA HA HA!
HEY, THIS IS NICE!
CLANG!!
BWOOP!
CLAN
BWOOP!
AAH, WHAT A GREAT FEELING.
CLANG!!
KLAK KLAK KLAK...
KLAK...!!
KRAKL KRAKL...

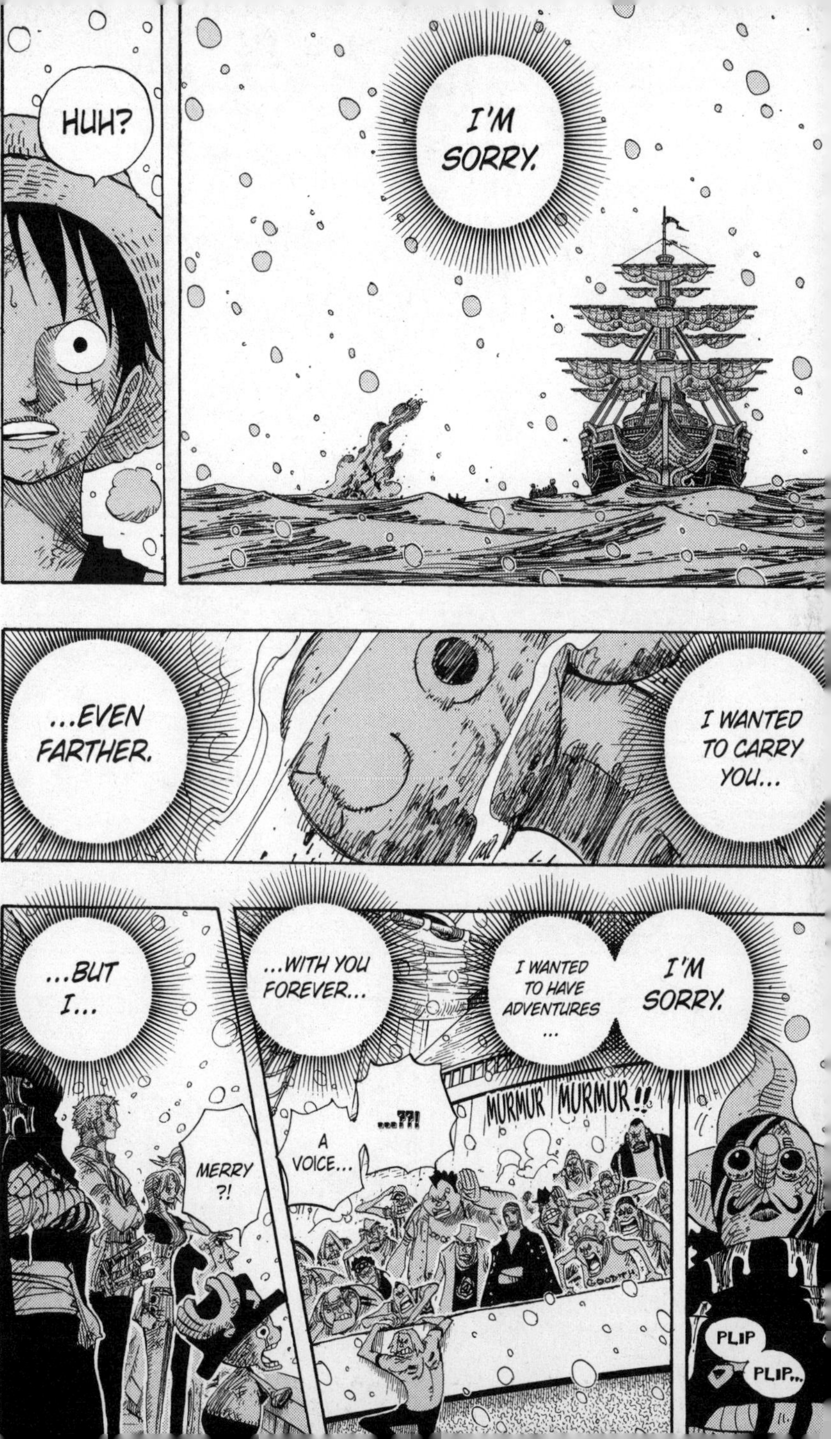
I'M SORRY.
HUH?
I WANTED TO CARRY YOU...
...EVEN FARTHER.
I'M SORRY.
I WANTED TO HAVE ADVENTURES ...
...WITH YOU FOREVER...
...BUT I...
PLIP
PLIP...
MURMUR MURMUR!!
...?!
A VOICE...
MERRY ?!

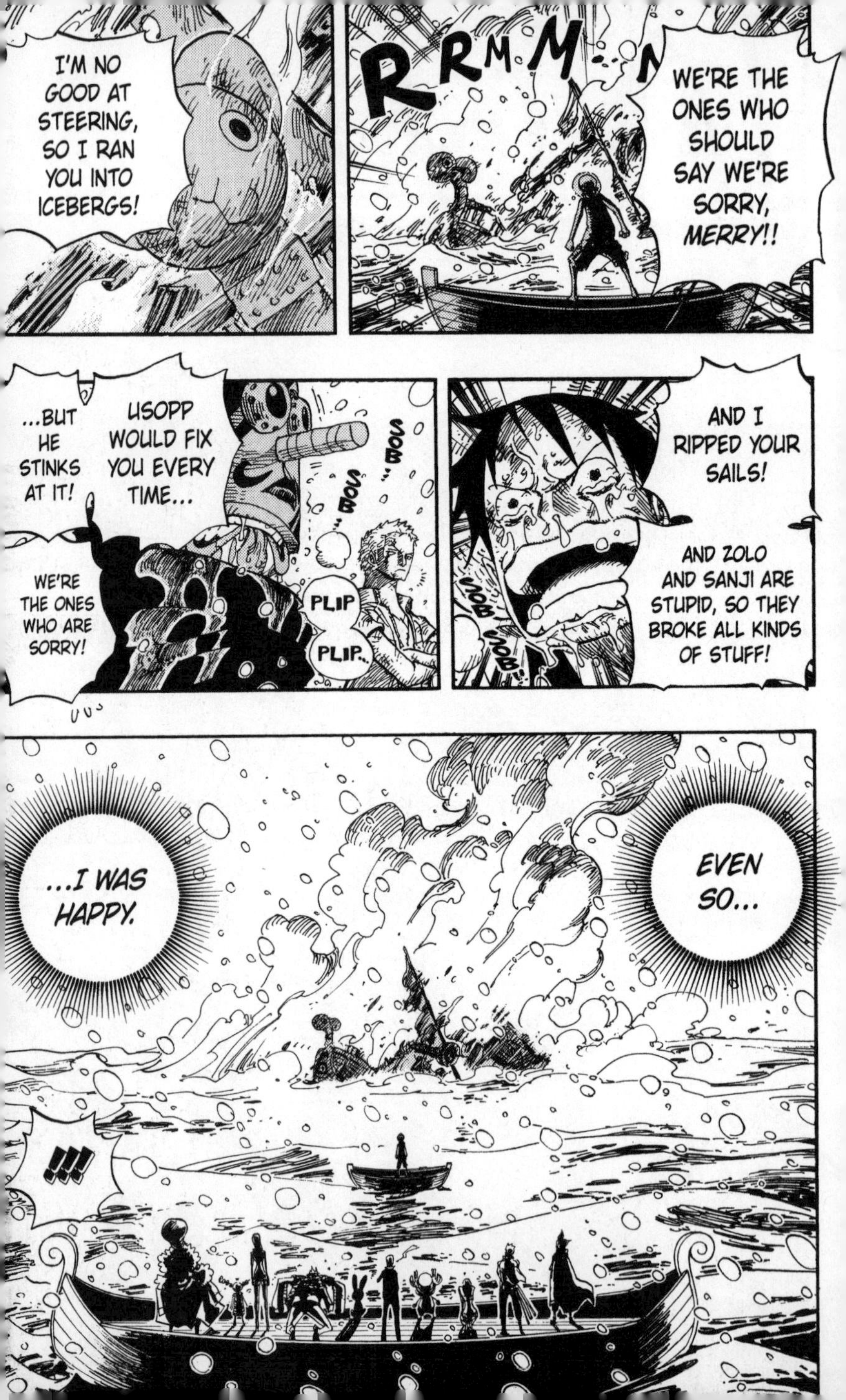
RRMMM
WE'RE THE ONES WHO SHOULD SAY WE'RE SORRY, MERRY!!
I'M NO GOOD AT STEERING, SO I RAN YOU INTO ICEBERGS!
AND I RIPPED YOUR SAILS!
AND ZOLO AND SANJI ARE STUPID, SO THEY BROKE ALL KINDS OF STUFF!
SOB SOB
USOPP WOULD FIX YOU EVERY TIME...
...BUT HE STINKS AT IT!
SOB... SOB...
PLIP
PLIP...
WE'RE THE ONES WHO ARE SORRY!
EVEN SO...
...I WAS HAPPY.
!!!

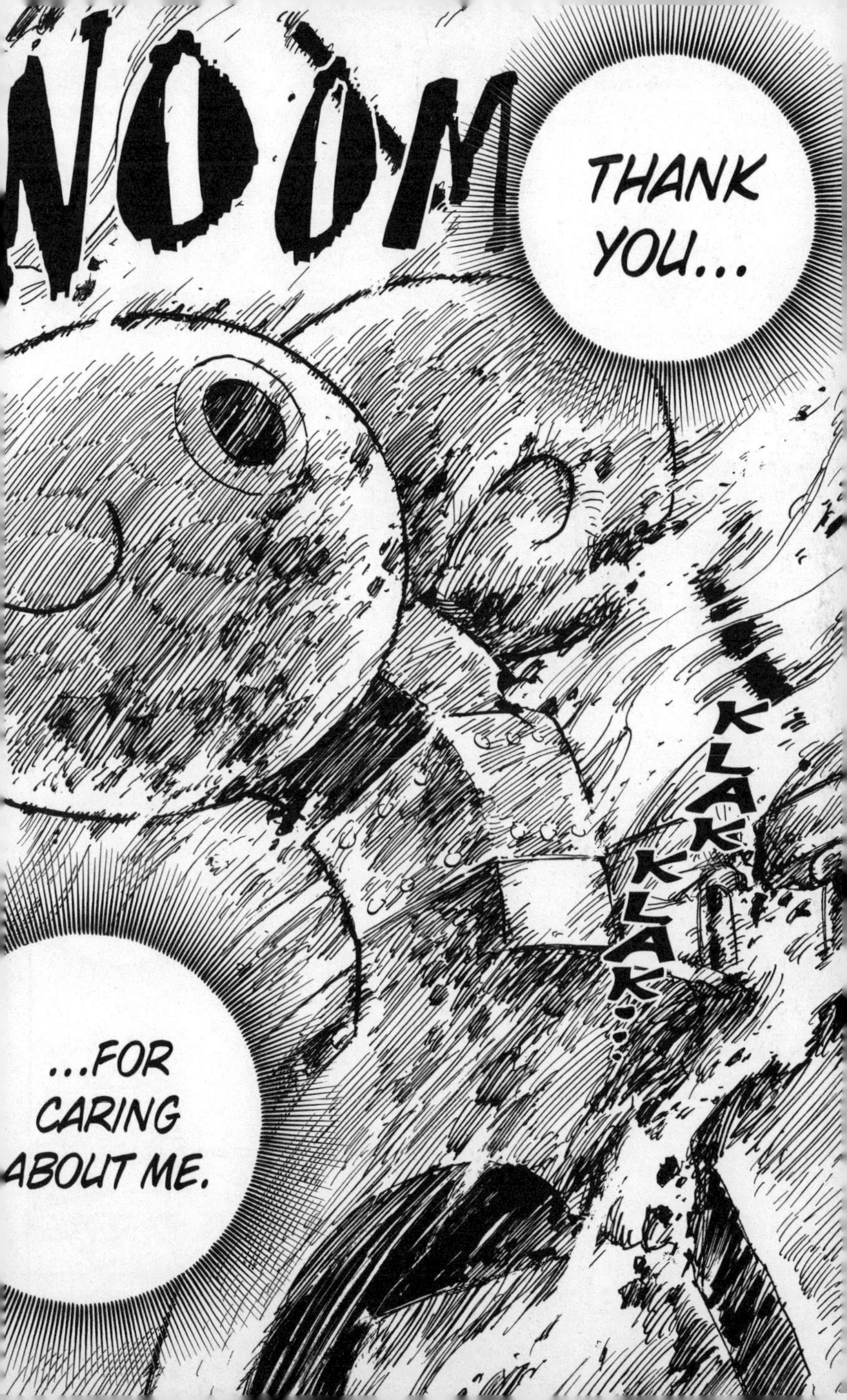
NOOM
THANK YOU...
KLAK KLAK...
...FOR CARING ABOUT ME.

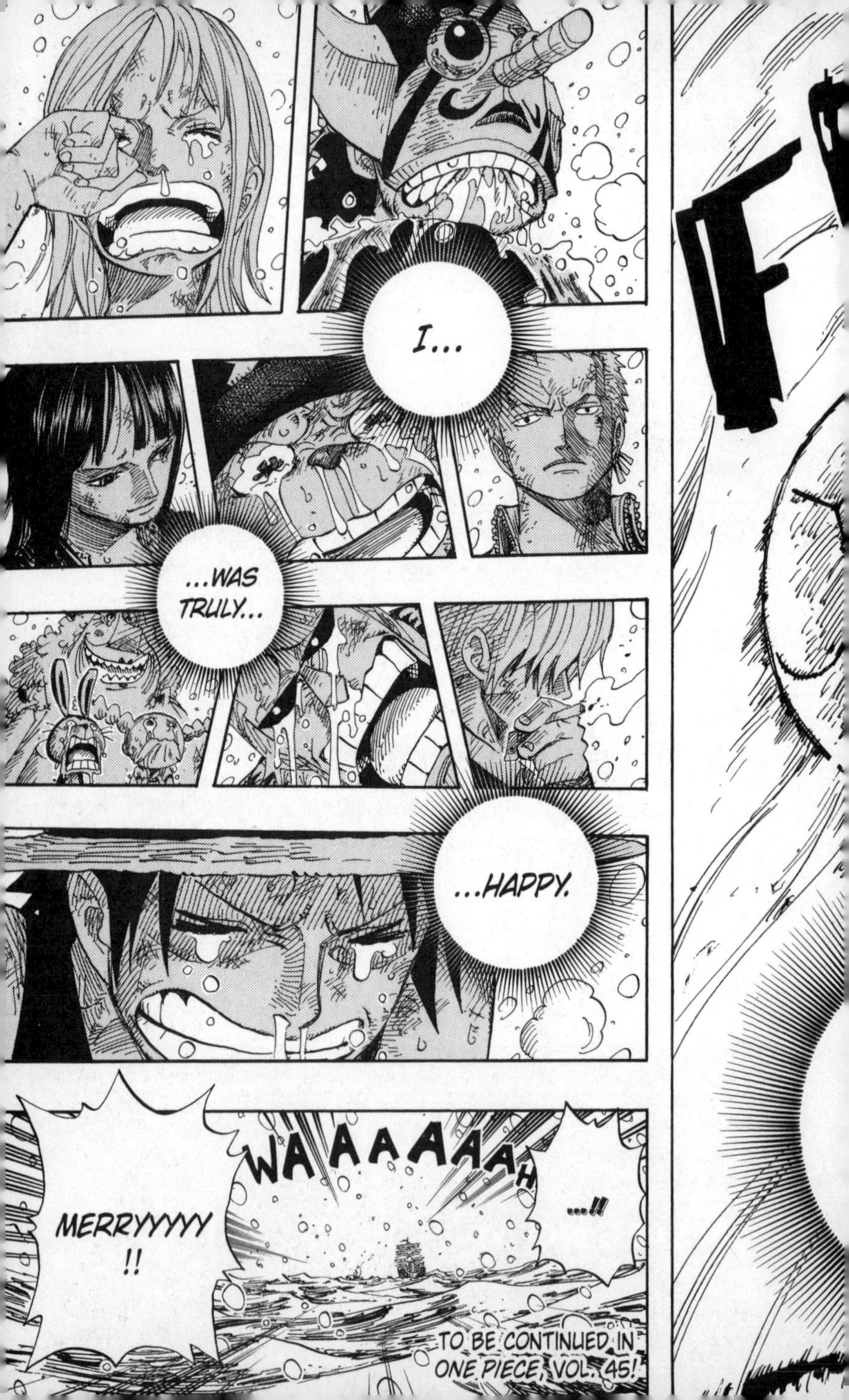
I...
...WAS TRULY...
...HAPPY.
WAAAAAAH ...!!
MERRYYYYY !!
TO BE CONTINUED IN ONE PIECE, VOL. 45!

COMING NEXT VOLUME:

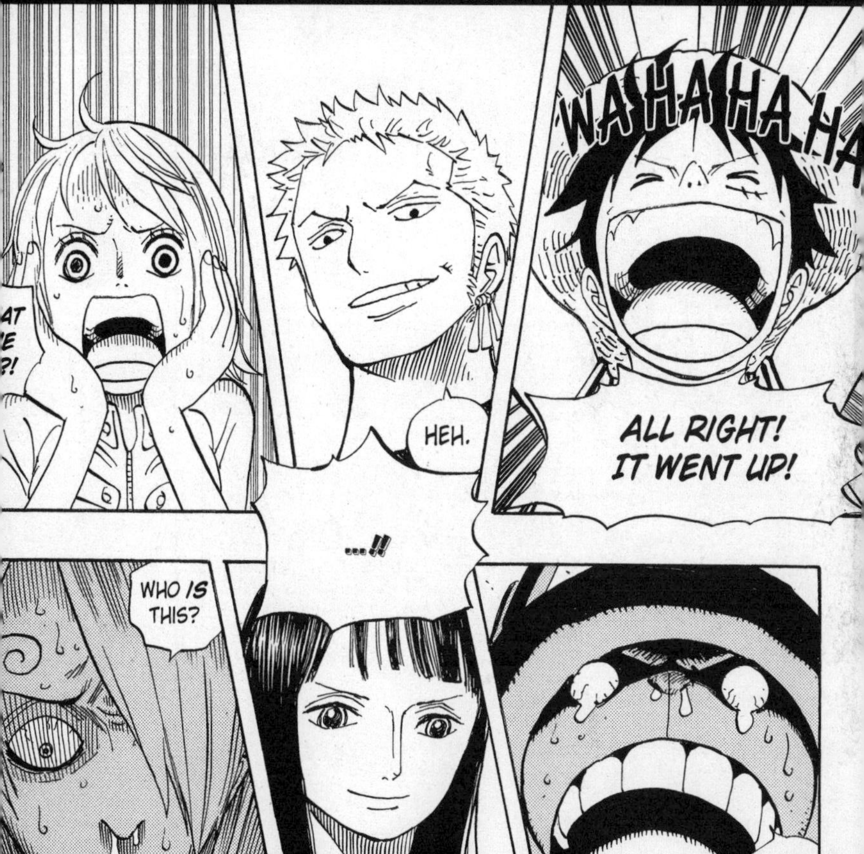
WA HA HA HA
ALL RIGHT! IT WENT UP!
HEH.
FIFTY...
...!!
WHO IS THIS?

Life returns to normal for the Straw Hats. Their friends on Water Seven even help them find a new ship. Things are looking decidedly up for the crew—that is, until they realize that their latest adventure has raised their bounties, making them all the more “wanted”!

ON SALE NOW!

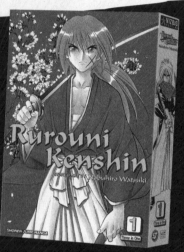
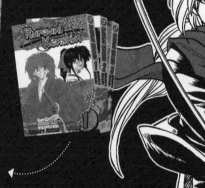

IN A SAVAGE WORLD RULED BY THE PURSUIT OF THE MOST DELICIOUS FOODS, IT'S EITHER EAT OR BE EATEN!

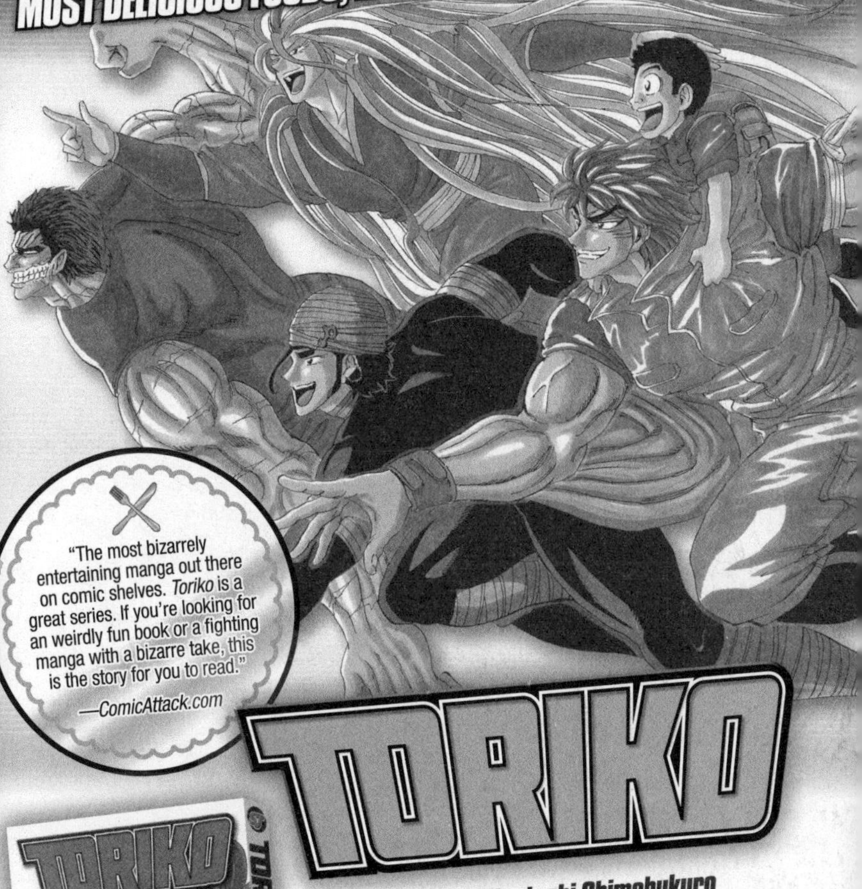

"The most bizarrely entertaining manga out there on comic shelves. *Toriko* is a great series. If you're looking for an weirdly fun book or a fighting manga with a bizarre take, this is the story for you to read."
—ComicAttack.com

TORIKO

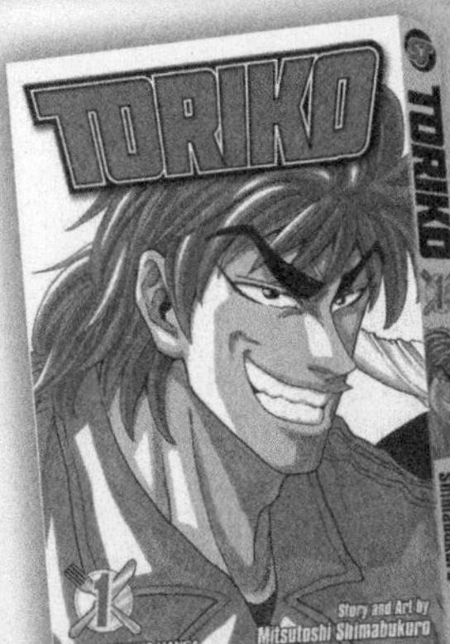

Story and Art by Mitsutoshi Shimabukuro

In an era where the world's gone crazy for increasingly bizarre gourmet foods, only Gourmet Hunter Toriko can hunt down the ferocious ingredients that supply the world's best restaurants. Join Toriko as he tracks and defeats the tastiest and most dangerous animals with his bare hands.

RATED T TEEN ratings.viz.com

www.shonenjump.com   www.viz.com

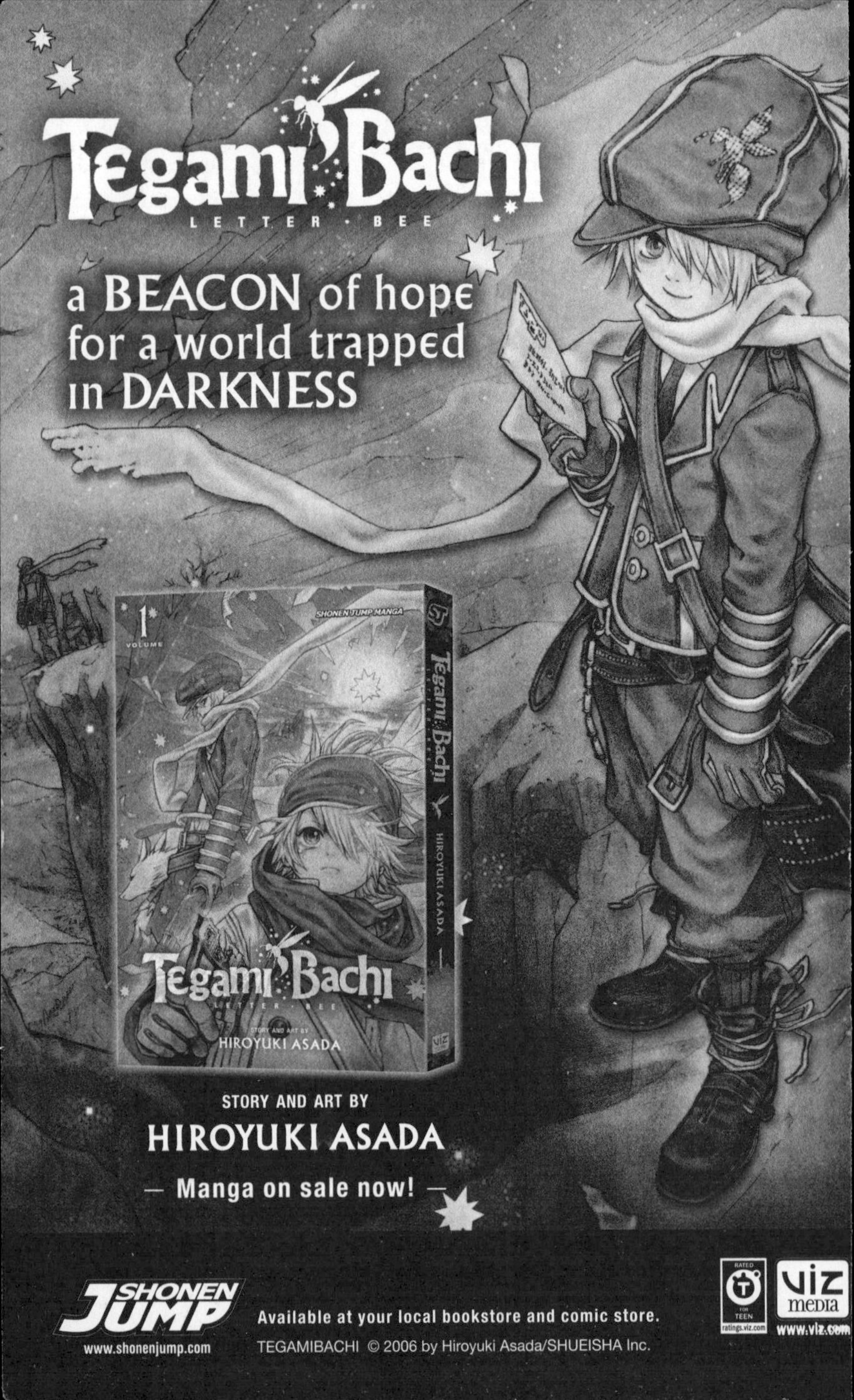
Tegami Bachi
LETTER · BEE
a BEACON of hope for a world trapped in DARKNESS
SHONEN JUMP MANGA
1 VOLUME
Tegami Bachi
LETTER · BEE
STORY AND ART BY
HIROYUKI ASADA
STORY AND ART BY
HIROYUKI ASADA
— Manga on sale now! —
SHONEN JUMP
www.shonenjump.com
Available at your local bookstore and comic store.
TEGAMIBACHI © 2006 by Hiroyuki Asada/SHUEISHA Inc.
RATED T FOR TEEN
ratings.viz.com
viz media
www.viz.com

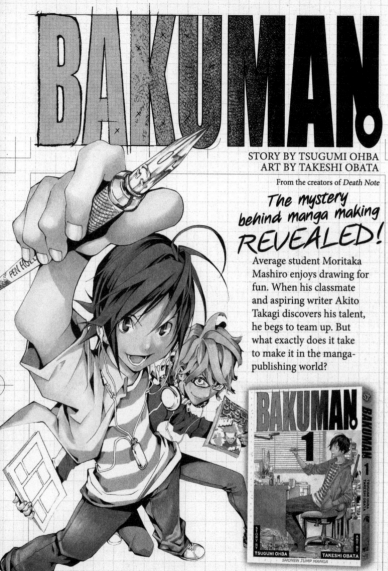

BAKUMAN。

STORY BY TSUGUMI OHBA
ART BY TAKESHI OBATA

From the creators of *Death Note*

The mystery behind manga making REVEALED!

Average student Moritaka Mashiro enjoys drawing for fun. When his classmate and aspiring writer Akito Takagi discovers his talent, he begs to team up. But what exactly does it take to make it in the manga-publishing world?

Bakuman。 Vol. 1
ISBN: 978-1-4215-3513-5
$9.99 US / $12.99 CAN *

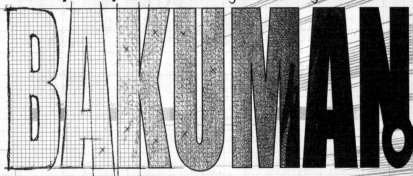
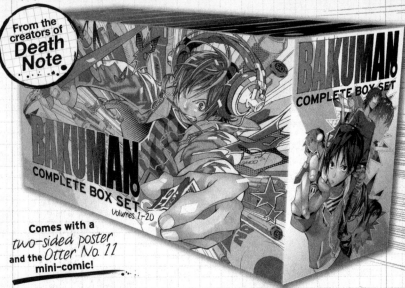

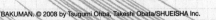

You're Reading in the Wrong Direction!!

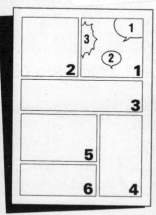

Whoops! Guess what? You're starting at the wrong end of the comic!

...It's true! In keeping with the original Japanese format, **One Piece** is meant to be read from right to left, starting in the upper-right corner.

Unlike English, which is read from left to right, Japanese is read from right to left, meaning that action, sound effects and word-balloon order are completely reversed...something which can make readers unfamiliar with Japanese feel pretty backwards themselves. For this reason, manga or Japanese comics published in the U.S. in English have sometimes been published "flopped"— that is, printed in exact reverse order, as though seen from the other side of a mirror.

By flopping pages, U.S. publishers can avoid confusing readers, but the compromise is not without its downside. For one thing, a character in a flopped manga series who once wore in the original Japanese version a T-shirt emblazoned with "M A Y" (as in "the merry month of") now wears one which reads "Y A M"! Additionally, many manga creators in Japan are themselves unhappy with the process, as some feel the mirror-imaging of their art skews their original intentions.

We are proud to bring you Eiichiro Oda's **One Piece** in the original unflopped format. For now, though, turn to the other side of the book and let the journey begin...!

—Editor

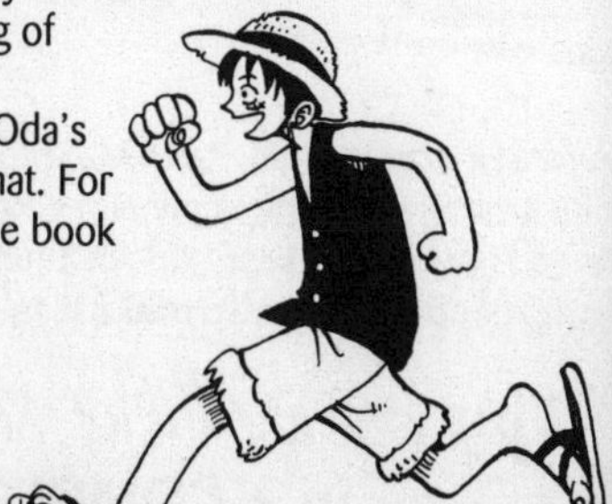